Praise for *Substance Over Style*

Grow Your Confidence, Purpose, and Impact as a Leader

"Theories about academic leadership are fine, but I'd trade them all for the experiential wisdom delivered here by Don DeHayes. Forty-five years working in higher education have given him an understanding that few others possess. He offers dozens of useful tools and other advice about running the modern university, but three broad perspectives anchor this book. One, people matter most—students, staff, and faculty. Two, only authenticity and transparency will build the trust needed to lead. Three, diversity, inclusion, and equity are imperatives for success, regardless of what politicians say. Anyone—no, everyone—who seeks to lead a college or university needs to read this book and then act like Don DeHayes says."

—**Larry A. Nielsen**, author, *Provost: Experiences, Reflections, and Advice From a Former "Number Two" on Campus*, and several other books; former Executive Vice Chancellor and Provost at North Carolina State University

"*Substance Over Style* is a substantive and refreshingly practical guide to leadership applicable in academia and transferable to other non-profits—particularly those working across multiple jurisdictions and audiences. It offers a blend of lessons and strategies, recognizing that context is everything! Masterfully navigating the complexity of "academic ecosystems," it demonstrates how to build trust, nurture teams, plan, budget, create a culture of philanthropy, and much more. Read it!"

—**Ann Pesiri Swanson**, *Executive Director, Chesapeake Bay Commission from 1988 to 2022, Founding Member and Chair of The Rubenstein School Advisory Board, The University of Vermont*

"DeHayes offers a practical and very useful leadership guide to the complexities of the higher education ecosystem. Through the lens of many years of experience in the trenches of academia, he navigates critical internal and external factors elucidating how such systems are interconnected by sharing real case studies, personal reflections, and deep insights across all divisions of the institution."

—**Stephen J. Hegedus**, *Provost and Vice President for Academic Affairs, Western Connecticut State University, Former Ace Fellow*

Bring Out the Leader Within You—Shape Your Career, Values, and Institution

"*Substance Over Style* hits the mark perfectly and at the precise moment when higher education leaders must engage in complex, multidimensional thinking and decision-making. DeHayes emphasizes the need for academic leaders to have a sincere appreciation for the interconnectedness and context of each element within the academic ecosystem."

—**Dr. Nancy Matthews**, *Provost and Executive Vice President, Central Michigan University*

"Outstanding! *Substance Over Style* serves as a keystone informational piece of work that outlines specific areas of professional development necessary for aspiring—and current—higher education leaders who are seriously reflective about their professional practice."

—**Dr. R. Anthony Rolle**, *Dean, College of Education, University of South Florida Fellow, National Education Policy Center, Past-President, National Education Finance Academy*

Gain Practical Strategies for Planning, Budgeting, and Fundraising

"*Substance Over Style* is well-researched, well-written, and discusses many areas important for higher education leaders to know that other books don't cover. . . . The set of chapters on budget, enrollment management, and strategic planning really add value as few leadership books provide in-depth guidance to fiscal management. These chapters alone are certainly worth the price of the book."

—**Dr. Laura Beauvais**, *Professor Emerita of Management and Organizational Behavior, former Vice Provost for Faculty Affairs, University of Rhode Island*

"The perfect combination of practical information and lessons in strategic thinking for our department chairs and other emerging leaders! Information is presented in a way that will help you navigate the complex and ever-evolving world of higher education whether you are a complete novice or well along one of the many different paths to leadership."

—**Dr. Rachael Kipp**, *Associate Provost for Academic Planning and Accreditation, Suffolk University*

Substance

OVER STYLE

Substance
OVER STYLE

A FIELD GUIDE TO
LEADERSHIP
IN HIGHER EDUCATION

LESSONS, STORIES,
AND INSIGHTS

DONALD H. DEHAYES

BRG
SCIENTIFIC

WASHINGTON, DISTRICT OF COLUMBIA

For rights and permissions, please contact: BRG.Scientific@gmail.com or
BRG Scientific
3025 Ontario RD NW #407
Washington, District of Columbia 20009

www.BRGScientific.com

ISBN: 979-8-9862821-7-6 (Hard Cover)
ISBN: 979-8-9862821-6-9 (Paperback)
ISBN: 979-8-9862821-8-3 (eBook)

Library of Congress Control Number: 2023922605

Editor: Melissa Stevens
Indexer: Shelley Quattrocchi
Cover Design and Interior Formatting: Becky's Graphic Design,® LLC

Dedicated to Mom, Dad, Brady, and Betty
for your enduring love, inspiration, and patience

Contents

A FRAMEWORK
for ECOSYSTEM
THINKING

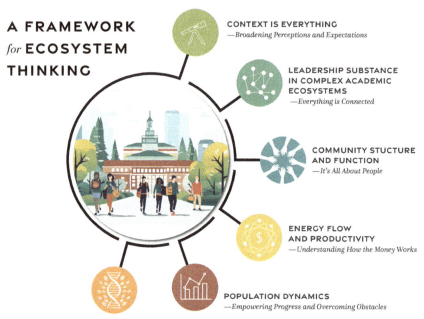

CONTEXT IS EVERYTHING
—Broadening Perceptions and Expectations

**LEADERSHIP SUBSTANCE
IN COMPLEX ACADEMIC
ECOSYSTEMS**
—Everything is Connected

**COMMUNITY STUCTURE
AND FUNCTION**
—It's All About People

**ENERGY FLOW
AND PRODUCTIVITY**
—Understanding How the Money Works

POPULATION DYNAMICS
—Empowering Progress and Overcoming Obstacles

EVOLUTION OR EXTINCTION
—Emerging Unknowns in a Changing Climate

Preface

There are many books about leadership in higher education. Here's why you should read this one! I have spent forty-five years working in academic institutions—twenty-six years in academic leadership positions and the remaining time engaged in teaching, research, and academic and professional service as a faculty member. As I reflect on those experiences, I am convinced that effective leaders understand and care about the culture and working surface of the academy, value the ideas and experiences of others, and possess the leadership qualities, collaborative spirit, and self-awareness to grapple with challenges and create opportunities every day in complex academic ecosystems. After all, that is the purpose of these jobs.

This book offers an informed and distinctive hands-on examination of the nuance, complexity, and peculiarities of leadership substance in higher education rather than a scholarly focus on leadership styles and theories often featured elsewhere. It is a deep dive into the inner workings of universities replete with stories and examples, including distinct challenges from and responses to the COVID-19 crisis and areas where leaders become embroiled in conflicts that lessen their effectiveness. This how-to guide aims to cultivate higher education leadership and inform, inspire, and nurture the next generation of faculty, staff, student, and administrative leaders by sharing experiences, strategies, and lessons learned.

The Genesis of This Field Guide

This field guide emanated from a leadership seminar for faculty and professional staff that I codeveloped and delivered during the 2019-20 academic year. The seminar consisted of six sessions ranging from two to four hours and included readings, interactive discussions, group problem-solving, and informal presentations focused on self-reflection, personnel management, strategic thinking, decision-making, fostering innovation, governance, budgeting, and more. Because it was our first offering, we planned on accommodating approximately twelve individuals; we had thirty-two requests from faculty and professional staff, even though all volunteered their time without being released from other responsibilities. We invited sixteen individuals, and thirteen of them now occupy leadership positions as chairs, associate deans, deans, vice provosts, or vice presidents. There was genuine interest among faculty and staff in professional leadership development and a desire and need for a practical guide to stimulate their interest and address critical topics. *Substance Over Style: A Field Guide to Leadership in Higher Education* was born in that moment to foster leadership development across higher education today.

Leadership at the Working Surface

Most higher education leadership books are written through the lens of corporate leaders, faculty scholars, or former presidents. The latter typically offer a mostly high-level overview of the academy. Such books often address leadership styles, principles, theories, or the importance of strategic or servant leadership. Conspicuously, few, if any, leadership books reflect the experienced-based perspectives of provosts, who as "chief academic officers" work every day across the entire university to navigate the challenges and opportunities in advancing the academic mission and the institution. This practical field guide, in contrast, is informed by my many years as provost, dean, and faculty member as well as a trustee, accreditation commissioner, and president of a national organization, and extensive experience navigating the ups and downs of the working surface of universities. Almost everything within universities interfaces directly or indirectly with the academic mission and the Office of the Provost. The provost has a ground-level view and hands on all the levers that impact the day-to-day operations, activities, and problems of universities whether related to people (e.g., students, staff, faculty, administrators), teaching and learning, research, community outreach, budgets, fundraising, grievances, business operations, capital projects, etc. This comprehensive overview of the working surface of the entire academic ecosystem provides unique hands-on learning about what works and what doesn't in academic leadership as well as an engaging platform to inform aspiring leaders.

An Academic Ecosystem Framework

Just as natural ecosystems are complex, dynamic entities that respond to ever-changing internal and external forces, so too are academic ecosystems. The parallels are real and important. While sunlight is the primary energy source that flows through natural ecosystems, money is the key energy driver in academic institutions along with morale, creativity, and productivity—crucial intangibles that influence learning and discovery at every institution.

All ecosystems, including academic ones, comprise numerous interconnected and interacting components that trigger synergistic or antagonistic responses to changing conditions. That is, changes in any one factor, whether a planned intervention or an unintended perturbation, send repercussions throughout the ecosystem in response to an initial trigger and subsequent secondary responses. For instance, a breakdown in campus maintenance may negatively impact the yield of new students, leading to enrollment declines, budget shortfalls, reduced pay increases, and low morale for faculty and staff. Everything is connected in academic ecosystems, and even subtle changes can have large impacts. Leaders must understand such interconnections.

Natural ecosystems are shaped by the interaction of abiotic and biotic factors. Academic ecosystems comprise myriad disciplines, administrative and business functions, investment strategies, financial aid challenges and opportunities, technological and physical infrastructure, legal matters, and all sorts of internal and external political machinations and outside forces at local, national, and global scales. All of this is superimposed on a diverse array of constituents, including students, parents, faculty, staff, administrators, trustees, alumni, donors, legislators, and many others, each with their own expectations, needs, and desires. Indeed, the world of higher education is a complex web of interconnected relationships and moving parts where every action, policy, or decision shapes the institution for better or worse in predictable and unpredictable ways.

To be clear, academic leaders don't need to be steeped in ecology. *Leadership substance*, however, entails the capacity to "think like an ecosystem." That is the ability to visualize interconnections, extract clarity from complexity, and recognize the short- and long-term implications of proposed actions, decisions, and policies. Good ecosystem thinkers anticipate potential problems, thereby turning challenges into opportunities. Higher education needs authentic leaders who can think and act strategically—true ecosystem thinkers—with the knowledge, skills, and values to lead with their hearts and minds to ensure our institutions are confronting challenges and constantly evolving. This field guide provides a unique academic ecosystem framework and compilation of observations, insights, and lessons learned for aspiring higher education leaders.

Preparing a New Generation of Leaders

Whether you are faculty, staff, a graduate student pondering leadership for the first time, or a trustee or experienced administrator exploring new leadership roles, this field guide will inform and shape your evolution as a leader. The aim is to imbue your experience with a deep understanding of nuanced interconnections across the academic enterprise, highlighting not only the academic mission as the primary purpose but also the major revenue stream for institutions. Filled with reflections from the day-to-day navigation of the perils of budget shortfalls, pandemics, enrollment declines, delicate and often divisive personnel conflicts, student protests, and political battles, *Substance Over Style* serves as a compass for your transformative leadership journey. Read and digest the content of this book and join a new generation of higher education leaders ready and able to address the looming challenges on the horizon.

Acknowledgments

I have been extraordinarily fortunate throughout my career. I have worked with insightful, hard-working, experienced colleagues whose passion for higher education is contagious. Simply being in their presence has been inspirational. My colleagues in the Provost Office at URI and The Rubenstein School at UVM are especially notable. Thank you to my faculty, staff, and administrator colleagues at URI, UVM, NAUFRP, UCAR, and NECHE and to the thousands of students who taught me to listen, learn, overcome struggles, and strive for meaning and purpose in education and life.

Writing a book is a wonderful opportunity for reflection and, for me, has been an engaging and joyful process. Reviewing drafts of a book written by someone else, on the other hand, is a chore—it takes time, attention to detail, and a bold willingness to offer candid reactions and suggestions for improvement. I am enormously grateful to numerous reviewers who read drafts of the entire manuscript or specific chapters aligned with their interests and expertise. Ann Morrissey served as the manuscript's first reader, offered superb advice, commentary, and encouragement, and helped shape the book's organization. Through her lens of academic planning and professional development, she patiently read and reread chapters and helped hone key messages. Laura Beauvais dug deeply into the manuscript and offered insightful critiques and numerous thoughtful suggestions, all of which I incorporated. Her expertise in organizational behavior, management, and faculty affairs provided a necessary and valuable perspective. Cliff Katz plowed through the manuscript while on a ski trip, offering insightful comments while navigating glades and avoiding avalanches. His extensive knowledge and commentary about university budgets and finances were especially helpful. Dave Dooley volunteered to read the manuscript out of interest. His deep insights about higher education and leadership experiences as a president, provost, department head, and faculty member informed

XVI | SUBSTANCE OVER STYLE

wonderful suggestions, which are woven throughout the book. Thank you all for your input, ideas, and efforts.

My wife Betty, an accomplished author and scholar, offered constant encouragement and exquisite commentary on some of the most complex chapters. She consistently reminded me that every word matters and challenged me to keep the reader rather than myself in the forefront. I hope I was able to step up to that challenge. Despite being one of the busiest people on campus, Matt Bodah took the time to review several chapters; his insights and expertise added substance and relevance. As non-academics with close ties to and knowledge about universities and the business world, Kent and Diane Fannon were wonderfully patient and thoughtful sounding boards as I too often shared my ideas about the book. They also reviewed several chapters and provided helpful suggestions. I am also indebted to John Peterson for his creative input, thoughtful advice, photographic contributions, and great promotional ideas.

I am grateful to the team at BRG Scientific, especially Ted Grand and Pete August, who welcomed me and my ideas for this book into the BRG Scientific family. BRG Scientific's mission, commitment to quality, and desire to be "pleasing to the eye and soul" immediately captured my attention and interest. It has been wonderful working with the team. I hope *Substance Over Style* ascends to the standards Ted and Pete have established. I am immensely grateful to my editor, Melissa Stevens of Purple Ninja Editorial, for her patience, persistence, and attention to detail and for improving the manuscript while maintaining my voice and story. Becky Bayne of Becky's Graphic Design somehow took my assemblage of words and phrases and creatively and imaginatively transformed them into a beautiful book. Thank you, Melissa and Becky, for the opportunity to work with and learn from you.

I am indebted to the late Dr. Hugo John, the inaugural Director and Dean of the School of Natural Resources at UVM. When I was a newly minted PhD at the tender age of twenty-five, Hugo hired me as an assistant professor and mentored and inspired me throughout my academic career. He believed in me and guided me forward, which was no small task. Thank you, Hugo, I am forever grateful.

Finally, I graciously acknowledge support from URI Cooperative Extension and resonate with their commitment to provide learning opportunities and apply practical knowledge to improve the lives of people. Hopefully, *Substance Over Style* contributes to that mission.

PART I

CONTEXT IS EVERYTHING

Broadening Perceptions and Expectations

We are shaped by our experiences, including cultural, historical, social, and environmental influences. Such context impacts our behavior, understanding, actions, and decisions. The complexity of the natural world and the landscape of higher education can seem overwhelming as we grapple with the divergent and synergistic forces that shape natural and academic ecosystems. Understanding context, ourselves, and each other helps shape our perceptions and expectations from observations, patterns, and disruptions, and enlightens a sense of purpose for our actions. Indeed, context is everything!

CHAPTER ONE

A Field Guide to What, for Whom, and for What Purpose?

In the context of the world in 2023, there is a need for a new generation of authentic leaders with the understanding, skills, values, and courage to navigate the increasingly complex landscape of expanding higher education challenges and opportunities. The polarization of society, especially the politicization of higher education, has created almost daily attacks by certain segments of society, including some governing boards, legislatures, and governors, on course content and curriculum, pedagogy, academic freedom and tenure, and the value of a college education. Challenges associated with declining enrollment, evolving roles for faculty, rapidly advancing technologies, myriad impacts of COVID-19, rising costs and student debt, growing mental health problems, and greater presence and awareness of racial injustice on our campuses and in society seem daunting. These same issues, however, also represent opportunities and mandates for strategic re-engagement, problem-solving, and institutional evolution. Indeed, this is an important time for impactful and principled higher education leadership grounded in ethics and compassion for the human condition. The next generation of leaders will need to address these and other challenges and, at the same time, inspire an engaging path forward to re-establish the clear and critical value and importance of learning and education to individual quality of life and sustaining an informed society and democracy. There is much to do. It is both an exciting and exasperating time for existing and aspiring leaders of our colleges and universities.

Despite what some may believe, academic leaders are not simply born into these important and complex roles. Experience matters. Leadership must be cultivated, nurtured, and inspired. Those who have navigated the ups and downs of leadership in the trenches can contribute to cultivating the next generation of thoughtful academic leaders by sharing their experiences and lessons learned. My hope is that this book fulfills that niche.

Why a Field Guide?

Although I have spent most of the past twenty-six years in academic leadership positions, I had a very rewarding teaching and research career as a faculty member with expertise, interests, and passion in forest biology and ecosystem ecology. During my years as a graduate student and then as a faculty member, my colleagues and I frequently talked about fieldwork, the importance of knowledge rooted in field experience, gaining credibility in the field, and ground-truthing our laboratory or theoretical research in the real world of natural and disrupted ecosystems. None of us would ever acknowledge an ecologist or natural historian of any kind who had no or only limited field experience. For me, the academy has become my real-world ecosystem, and my various roles as faculty, associate dean, dean, provost, accreditation commissioner, trustee, and president of a national professional organization represent the "fieldwork" that I have always loved to do and that I have been doing in one form or another for my forty-five years on university campuses. My intention is to capture and share much of this hands-on learning, or field experience, about the substance of leadership in this field guide.

To cultivate effective leaders, we must first identify the key distinguishing and necessary attributes, characteristics, and requirements associated with successful leadership in colleges and universities. Field guides are designed to do exactly that—to identify distinguishing characteristics between or among individuals who may otherwise appear to be similar. Field guides not only focus on specific features that are reliable for identification but also highlight the variability and diversity that exists and assist the reader in understanding and appreciating their distinctive features. Finally, field guides assist newcomers in gathering critical information and, hopefully, communicating it clearly so it can be understood and utilized in practice.

There are many elements to leading effectively and navigating the complex world of academic ecosystems, including the myriad interconnected parts. Each college and university is different, and even the disciplines represented may vary from one institution to the next. But, just as with fieldwork, we can reliably identify common features and approaches that consistently exist across multiple ecosystems and at different scales, which is true in relation to leadership in higher education as well. It all begins with the hard work of truly understanding yourself—who you are, what you and your institution care deeply about, and what truly matters in the world. Without clear answers to these questions, aspiring leaders run the risk of espousing directions without support, flailing their arms, and getting in the way of others and real progress. Leaders who don't inspire followership are an obstacle rather than an asset.

Leadership Substance

If there is anything I have learned in my forty-five years in higher education, it is that authentic leadership matters immensely. This is true at the level of departments, schools, colleges, and entire universities and may be more essential today than ever before. Effective leadership is essential for programs and institutions to evolve, remain relevant and viable, and improve their reputation as well as to build community spirit on campus and create and sustain a meaningful experience for students, faculty, alumni, and other constituents. Furthermore, leadership, especially transformative leadership, is hard work and is not meant for those with a casual interest. Most faculty do amazing work teaching students, conducting cutting-edge research and scholarship, and exercising their governance responsibilities to shape the academic core mission. Without effective leadership, however, such efforts are invariably splintered, resulting in waning resources, struggling programs, dwindling morale, and the departure of some of the most talented faculty and staff. Indeed, dedicated faculty are essential, but not sufficient to create and sustain excellent programs and institutions. Simply put, leadership matters!

Many higher education leaders have been asked hundreds of times to describe or discuss their leadership style. Perhaps such inquiries seek to understand effective or characteristic leadership behaviors or the manner or style in which we conduct ourselves and carry out the responsibilities of our positions. It seems rather simplistic, however, to attempt to define and catalog certain styles of leadership. I don't believe there is or should be a preferred *style* of leadership for all situations; effective leaders need to be inherently adaptable and nimble as they respond to challenges. As such, I have typically tried to dodge the question of leadership style because I am convinced that there is something much deeper and more complex to effective and transformative leadership than *style*. Following years of experience and reflection, I am convinced that the critical questions and issues relate to understanding leadership *substance* because it takes much more than style to be an effective leader in complex higher education institutions. This book, I hope, captures the nuance, complexity, and peculiarities of *leadership substance* in higher education ecosystems.

In a nutshell, effective leaders identify and address key institutional challenges and mobilize the community to pursue bold aspirations. As such, dynamic and substantive leadership is critical and inspires a cascade of advances in myriad ways, such as:

- inspiring a new vision and collaborative efforts to chart a strategic path forward;

- exhibiting behavior that is respectful, supportive, and engaging;

- building trust through transparency, inclusiveness, consistency, and honesty;

- encouraging and modeling collaboration by building effective teams;

- challenging the *status quo* and welcoming new ideas and innovation;

- addressing existing problems within the institution;

- creating open lines of communication by both sharing information and carefully listening without judging; and

- advancing a culture of achievement, pride, and community.

Leadership substance forges an institution's vibrancy, engagement, and capacity to instill pride and confidence in the university community. I have observed academic units, and even entire universities, move from a struggling place of low morale, insufficient resources, stagnation, and increasingly irrelevant programs and curricula to thriving programs in high demand under new inspirational leadership. I have also seen the exact opposite happen—programs or institutions quickly spiraling downward after appointing new leaders who seemed paralyzed and who did not have the skills, attributes, or commitment needed to move the institution forward. Why and how can such scenarios happen so often? Effective institutional leadership, or the lack thereof, is the answer; but what is effective institutional leadership? What does it look like? How can we cultivate a new generation of leaders who can and will advance the academy, especially during these times of deep polarization in society? See "Inspirational and Transformational Leadership during a Troubled Time" for an unlikely example.

Inspirational and Transformational Leadership during a Troubled Time

Context: In 2000, the University of Vermont (UVM) community was divided and highly factionalized, and the university was facing difficult financial challenges. An athletic scandal involving hockey—a near religion in Vermont—further exacerbated the difficulties. Faculty were organizing to unionize. The tension between the board of trustees and the university leadership was palpable, and morale was at an all-time low within the community. The board abruptly fired the president—the first and only female president at UVM—who was admired by many on campus, which created further angst and dissension. Various factions immediately began lobbying for their favorite interim candidates, who would be expected to support their agenda, likely only furthering the divide on campus.

Interim President: The board of trustees surprised everyone and appointed Edwin Colodny, an attorney, former CEO and chair of the board of US Airways for sixteen years, and an unlikely and unknown choice for interim president. Given his nonacademic background, many were wary of his appointment. Colodny, a Burlington native, had just returned to Vermont after retiring from his roles at US Airways. He was handed a deeply divided and struggling institution and immediately understood his role was to right the ship, rebuild morale, and position the institution to attract and hire a high-quality permanent president. In one year, he did exactly that.

Colodny was a bright, experienced, humble man with an understated personality and the unique ability to communicate clearly and connect with all people, ranging from the grounds department staff, faculty, deans, vice presidents, donors, and alumni. Despite being new to campus, he immediately understood exactly what was needed and spent his time creating goodwill, sprucing up the campus to improve morale, employing his savvy financial management skills to clean up budgets, and building relationships across the institution. He was consistent, led with his values, and was very comfortable asking questions and acknowledging what he did *not* know or understand about higher education institutions. He exuded trust, placed confidence in others, and quickly earned the respect of the community. Simply put, Ed Colodny was an amazing leader who transformed the mood, appearance, and vitality of a very complex institution in one year.

As a dean trying to close a major gift just prior to Colodny's arrival, I had the unique opportunity to work closely with him, learn from him, and watch with awe as he engaged people and confronted complex problems directly in a quiet, yet effective, manner. Indeed, Ed Colodny personified the substance of leadership and demonstrated that leadership matters. Following his success at UVM, he was immediately appointed interim president of Fletcher Allen Health Care, which was also plagued with challenges at that time.

Learning Leadership in the Trenches

For the most part, academic leaders have had little or no formal training or preparation for the leadership positions and responsibilities that they have either stumbled into or purposely chosen to pursue. Regardless of how they got there, most end up learning or not learning on the job—no doubt stubbing their toes along the way. Certainly, some have had the opportunity to attend something akin to a half-day workshop for new department chairs; a few have had the good fortune to attend an extensive, and typically expensive, weekend or longer leadership seminar or perhaps even a semester or yearlong leadership fellowship sponsored by a higher education organization, such as the American Council on Education. These are likely valuable experiences but require a significant commitment from participants, many of whom are reluctant to transition into the leadership role that they either volunteered for in a weak moment (maybe because no one else would do it) or entered to try something new. So, maybe it is not surprising that many leaders are not able to mobilize the forces to advance programs and institutions as they simply don't have the knowledge, skills, experience, or wherewithal to do so.

Most of the major books and published articles on leadership, including those specific to universities, are written by successful corporate leaders, academic management and leadership scholars, professors of educational leadership, executive educators, and leadership coaches and consultants. While these individuals bring valuable scholarly perspectives or experiences from a different context than higher education, most have not been embedded in the trenches of the academy every day navigating the demands, disputes, and decisions of academic leadership positions. Reflections from addressing the potential perils of budget reductions, pandemics, enrollment declines, delicate and often divisive personnel management and conflicts, protests, politics, grievances, and fundraising—often within the media spotlight—provide hands-on, experience-based information directly beneficial to aspiring leaders.

My intention is to bring my years of hands-on experience across multiple institutions and sectors to the dialogue about leadership in higher education. Reflecting upon and understanding my roles, responsibilities, accomplishments, and even my shortcomings have been key elements of any success I may have had. I acknowledge that these experiences were shaped by the possibilities and privileges of my personal circumstance as a white male navigating faculty and leadership roles within and across mostly public flagship research universities, including my role as president of a national organization. These experiences were broadened through my role as a trustee for the University Corporation for Atmospheric Research, which provides oversight of the National Center for Atmospheric Research for the National Science Foundation. I also benefited from my time as a commissioner on the New England Commission on Higher Education, which is responsible for the accreditation of all public and private, two- and four-year, nonprofit and for-profit higher education institutions in New England. Grounded in these experiences, this field guide offers observations, insights, and lessons about what works and, equally important, what doesn't work in leading a change agenda in higher education institutions. And, yes, it is a change agenda that is needed. Keeping the trains running does not require leadership or instill confidence. It simply maintains the *status quo* in an ever-evolving world of education, research, and opportunity.

Indeed, I have had the good fortune to learn firsthand about the joys and pitfalls of leadership in the trenches working side by side with faculty and staff colleagues and many presidents, provosts, deans, and other academic leaders. In so doing, I have grappled with ever-changing challenges, pursued tangible opportunities, and engaged in the hard, but very rewarding, work of implementing new programs, initiatives, and ideas to advance our colleges and universities. This book captures those moments and struggles and provides a much-needed roadmap for future leaders.

During my many years in academic leadership positions, I worked closely with and had an opportunity to observe numerous presidents, provosts, vice presidents, deans, directors, and chairs. Some were very effective leaders and mentors, and some were not. I learned a ton from individuals in both groups. Although well-intentioned, some were both highly confident and highly ineffective, a particularly dangerous combination, which creates more chaos and confusion than progress. Along the way, I think I learned what works and what doesn't and the critical attributes of effective leadership. So, in many ways, this book is a grassroots compilation of observations, missteps, and insights derived from learning by doing.

For Whom?

This collection of observations, insights, and lessons represents a "how-to" guide aimed largely at faculty, professional staff, and graduate students who aspire to educational leadership positions or simply find themselves in a leadership position whether they sought it out or not. No doubt, the focus relates to aspiring leaders who care about and understand the academic core mission of colleges and universities and, to that end, may be perceived as especially aimed at faculty, department chairs, directors, deans, vice provosts, provosts, and presidents. We certainly need more faculty interested in academic leadership and ways to support their development. The academic ecosystem, however, also includes interconnections with administrative, business, and student support services and relies on informed colleagues who contribute their expertise and understand the academic enterprise.

Higher education institutions need to do a better job of developing students as future leaders. Graduate students, especially those enrolled

in educational leadership, college student personnel, and higher education student affairs programs, will benefit directly and abundantly from
courses and programs emphasizing experienced-based learning focused
on the nuances of higher education leadership, which is the purpose of
this field guide. Furthermore, today's PhD students, postdoctoral fellows,
and new faculty across all disciplines preparing to enter the university as
educators, research scholars, departmental colleagues, future committee
and task force members, or leaders of research teams will benefit from an
understanding of leadership competencies to enhance their career readiness and potential to contribute.

In essence, for those just starting out, this field guide will help demystify the work of academic leaders and provide a better understanding of
the inner workings of the academic ecosystem, which may help them be
more effective in their faculty roles. Graduate schools are increasingly
offering noncredit, micro-credential (e.g., badges) professional development programs on important topics to inform emerging scholars and
better position them in the highly competitive higher education employment sector. In a recent article, Jessica Hutchins makes a compelling case
for formal leadership training programs aimed at graduate students and
postdoctoral fellows to develop self-awareness, leadership approaches,
and leadership skill-building.[1] This book nicely fills that niche and adds
value for graduate student learning and professional development for
new and emerging scholars.

The observations and insights compiled here also connect with professional staff in largely nonacademic roles within universities, such as
those in facilities, finance, enrollment management, human resources,
student affairs, communication and marketing, and other critically
important areas of higher education leadership. Rather than competition among the internal divisions within higher education institutions,
all parties need to recognize the primacy of the academic core mission as
the reason the institutions exist in the first place. I have learned through
the years that this is a hard pill for some to swallow and is often interpreted by some as an indication that their nonacademic work is viewed
as less important. In fact, that work is *very* important. By understanding
and even celebrating the academic mission, with all the nuances and
complications associated with it, all professionals within the university
community will be more effective at designing and delivering services
that support and enhance the academic mission and student experience

and, as such, the institution. We can all take pride in our collective efforts and achievements that elevate the institution.

Members of governing boards, who often come from private and nonacademic sectors, will also benefit from this deep dive into the world of academic leadership and learning about the inner workings of the institutions that they are entrusted to govern. Because of their fiduciary and governance roles and their responsibility for hiring university presidents and chancellors, trustees should value this inside look at distinctive elements of leadership in institutions of higher education. Similarly, members of university and college advisory councils will also find relevant information that can provide important context for their advisory efforts.

While most of the observations, insights, and lessons here are focused on higher education institutions, there is an abundance of transferable knowledge and skills relevant to other sectors, especially nonprofits, government agencies, and policy institutes. As such, students from many majors who are preparing for careers in these sectors will benefit by developing an understanding of leadership with its many implications for success. Whoever might choose to give this a read, whether student, staff, faculty, academic leader, or board member, I hope you find it helpful in informing and inspiring your leadership development and pursuit of a life and career with purpose and meaning.

PART II

LEADERSHIP SUBSTANCE IN COMPLEX ACADEMIC ECOSYSTEMS

Everything Is Connected

Higher education ecosystems are dynamic entities consisting of numerous constantly interacting component parts. Changes in any component have repercussions that flow throughout the system in response to the initial trigger and secondary multi-layered interactive impacts. Leadership in higher education ecosystems is likewise complex and entails understanding its myriad properties, including internal and external factors, a vast array of constituents, and many extant and evolving academic disciplines. Leadership substance involves the ability and willingness to synthesize observations and inputs and adapt so that the unity and dynamic nature of academic ecosystems is evident and sustained. Indeed, the substance of leadership matters!

CHAPTER TWO

Who Are You, What Do You Care About, and What Motivates You?

Honesty, integrity, and humility are wonderful and critically important virtues that are undoubtedly desired, or perhaps even essential, for effective leadership. But as aspiring leaders, how do we wrap our minds around these virtues? Must our leaders be saintly to successfully lead and advance their institution? All of us would like to believe that we exhibit these admirable attributes, but most of us also understand that we are actually flawed human beings. No doubt, we each have strengths, but we also possess weaknesses, biases, and blind spots that we bring to every situation, analysis, and decision with which we engage. Does that suggest we are dishonest or lacking in integrity and not cut out for leadership positions? I don't think so.

As I noted in chapter 1, preparing to become an effective higher education leader begins with each of us doing the hard work of understanding who we are, what we care about, what motivates us, and how those inherent features interface with our abilities to lead, the likelihood others will follow, and the probability of accomplishing something and advancing the institution. In particular, truly understanding why we aspire to a leadership position is critical to one's success or failure in that role. While there may not be a clear right or wrong answer to this question, understanding our interests, passions, motivations, and career drivers relates to how we lead and interact with others.

In my various academic administrative positions, I led or actively participated in searches for presidents, provosts, vice presidents, vice provosts, deans, and directors and, through those processes, interviewed hundreds of individuals seeking higher education leadership positions. Although few would admit it upfront, it has been clear to me that many aspiring academic leaders are attracted to the job advancement, perceived prestige, image, and compensation that comes with such positions more than to the actual work that must be done or to the opportunity to lead an effort to develop solutions to the unique challenges of the institution. In the end, I believe effective leadership entails truly caring about the issues and the institution, digging in to do the work, believing that you have something to give rather than something to gain from the position, and, yes, recognizing that there will be many frustrations along the way. Be prepared for, and even find a way to savor, the many frustrations and challenges that are inherent in such leadership positions. Are you ready to grapple with ambiguity and complexity? I hope so because that is what you signed up for as you navigate the intricate network of interconnected relationships and moving parts inherent in higher education ecosystems.

How does one honestly and effectively discern who they are, what they really care about, and their true motivations for seeking a leadership position? I think the hard work of honest self-reflection is not only important for aspiring leaders but also for continuous assessment and improvement for both individuals in leadership positions and for the institution.

Honest Self-Reflection

I am far from an expert on human behavior, or even truly understanding my own behavior. I do believe, nevertheless, that it is critical for each of us to grapple with our motivations for the positions and advancements that we seek and to identify our best understanding of the attributes we may bring to such positions. I have observed too often situations where the needs of individual leaders get in the way of them effectively doing their job of advancing the department or institution. This may be especially true in higher education where individuals rather than groups are accustomed to and often need or want praise, recognition, or credit, which shapes how they lead and can undermine their credibility or deter others from getting on board. Can we honestly answer the question about whether we truly care about the work and advancing the institution, or are we really interested in pushing our own agenda, promoting ourselves, or generating a track record of administrative experience in preparation for the next position up the administrative ladder? Too often, I fear the latter set of issues may prevail.

Interestingly, in his book entitled *Provost*, Larry Nielsen referred to himself as an "accidental provost," who didn't aspire toward or groom himself for that position.[2] Yet, he found himself willing and able to take on the hard work and responsibilities of that very complex and challenging position. I admit that I am intrigued by that idea. Sometimes, rather than having carefully charted a career path, we find ourselves at a place of leadership through honest self-reflection, humility, a level of confidence and intrigue, and an interest in applying ourselves to something new, complex, and important. Honest self-reflection will not only help us understand the motivation for our leadership aspirations, but also help each of us identify our strengths, weaknesses, and biases and, in so doing, allow us to measure our own fit and effectiveness in our roles and potential areas for growth and further development.

Such thoughtfulness is hard to achieve because it is difficult to be honest with oneself about personal motivations, shortcomings, and biases. Self-reflection is made complicated by self-deception about our true nature or feelings or an inherent need or desire to inflate our virtues or importance. None of us will comfortably conclude that we are self-focused, interested primarily in prestige, power, or money, or motivated by the perception of a position rather than the opportunity to apply our skills to do good. However, failure to dig deep and honestly self-reflect runs the risk of one becoming a disingenuous leader whose actions are incongruent with stated values and priorities. Self-deception invariably prevents us from seeing beyond our own experiences, opinions, and priorities and obstructs our ability to lead effectively. As a faculty member many years ago, I was stunned to observe administrators who were consistently unwilling or unable to invest in exactly the areas that they stated were institutional values and priorities, which undermined their credibility and the confidence of others in their leadership.

Consistent effort is required to conduct honest self-reflection—to ask yourself the tough questions about who you really are, what you truly care about, and what motivates you. You may be able to get some assistance by seeking candid and critical input from close colleagues about your persona or their interpretation of your actions, or by paying careful attention to the feedback you receive through your workplace review process, including annual reviews from your department colleagues and dean if you are a faculty member. Input derived from 360-degree reviews may provide some especially helpful insights. Perhaps one of the many leadership or interpersonal profile tests that are routinely available, such as the

Leadership Strengths Quest Survey Profile or Myers-Briggs test, may be helpful as well. Leadership coaches can also be beneficial in helping individuals gain clarity and insights toward reaching their greatest potential.

Regardless of the approach, each of us should take time periodically to find space for serious internal contemplation about motivations and actions in our work, especially when grappling with wicked problems or reflecting on setbacks. See "Discovering Unplanned Moments of Contemplation and Self-Reflection" for an example of finding moments of contemplation.

Discovering Unplanned Moments of Contemplation and Self-Reflection

Many of us, as part of our work and routine, will frequently pour our full attention into specific problems we are trying to solve or questions we are trying to answer. This can be a very effective approach for conducting an analysis of complex issues. Sometimes, however, we may need to separate ourselves from such directed thinking to free our mind from the existing tracks of our thoughts to create opportunities for new, fresh, and unencumbered ideas and reflections. For me, this frequently occurs in an unplanned and spontaneous manner when I am driving alone for a few hours, on a long bike ride, or rhythmically casting my fishing line into the water (and typically never catching any fish). Somehow, without provocation, my mind is cleared from previous perspectives and biases, and I am freed up to dig a bit deeper into what really is motivating my interests and approaches on some topics I have been grappling with. While perhaps a bit unusual, these unplanned moments of contemplation have provided me with excellent opportunities for honest self-reflection leading to fresh new conclusions and perspectives. Each of us may have very different approaches and settings for gathering our most honest and contemplative thoughts. It is worth searching for those places.

There are pointed questions you can ask yourself about why you are considering the pursuit of a leadership position. Frame tough questions for yourself and jot down your answers so you have a record. Questions such as the following may be helpful:

- What are the challenges the institution (department, college, etc.) is facing, and am I truly ready and inspired to spend my time and energy on those issues rather than my own academic interests or agenda?

- Assuming the institution is constrained by insufficient resources, would I be willing to take on this difficult work even if there is little chance of improving the resource base for my unit (department, college, etc.)?

- How important is the level of compensation to my decision on whether to pursue this leadership opportunity? If there are multiple leadership positions to choose from, would I select the one with the best salary or the one with the most interesting challenges?

- Am I willing and able to honestly acknowledge the problems confronting the institution (department, college, etc.), engage colleagues clearly and openly about the challenges, and seek their ideas to move forward?

- What happens if (*when* is more realistic) things don't go my way? Am I willing to live with ongoing struggles, and how will I respond to setbacks?

Whatever approach you may choose and questions you may pose, remember the purpose is to get an honest picture and assessment of your values, interests, and motivations so that you can become a more informed and consistent leader who will inspire followership by others. Such an honest self-assessment will also assist you in charting your career path forward.

Postulates about Leadership That Are Worthy of Consideration

As you engage in honest self-reflection, you will hopefully come to better recognize your own values, personality, work ethic, needs, and a true sense of commitment. The opportunity then emerges to overlay your values and personality traits with the attitudes, behaviors, expectations, and perspectives that may be important for effective academic leadership. The following postulates about effective leadership in higher education are perhaps more conceptual than factual, but nonetheless worthy of serious consideration as you reflect on your motivation or fit for leadership.

Effective institutional leaders give up the right to think about themselves.

Or, at the very least, they need to place the institution ahead of their own interests, agendas, and need for recognition. This element of leadership is critical to building a great institution. It may not be easy for academics who are acculturated to a reward system that recognizes tangible and personal (e.g., teaching awards, scholarly publications, grants, exhibitions, promotions) rather than collective accomplishments. Effective leaders need to understand the working surface of the university, appreciate the difficult and challenging work of the faculty and staff, and not believe, even for a minute, that the institution, including its successes and failures, is all about them. If you can put your ego on the back burner, you will have the time and inclination to celebrate the innovative contribution and commitment of those in the university who actually do the important work of learning, discovery, and community engagement.

Effective leaders must be willing to be continuous learners.

Most of us perceive that we ended up in leadership positions because of our accomplishments, knowledge, expertise, and/or reputation to date. In reality, effective leaders must be prepared to live a life of continuous learning to the fullest every day. While presumably we each have a good command of our subdiscipline and perhaps overall discipline, most faculty and staff have little experience navigating the interconnected working surface of academic ecosystems that is critical to the mission. There is so much to learn and understand that cuts across academic disciplines, business functions, investment strategies, legal matters, people and personalities, and political machinations of various types and impacts. The effective leader *gets to* rather than **has to** take this all in, and frankly, it is one of the joys of a leadership position. So, if you are not prepared to expand your learning horizon rather than rely on your existing knowledge base or expertise, and even be a bit humbled by all that you need to learn, then you may be on the wrong path. The effective leader **gets to** enjoy the challenges, complexity, and layered texture of the university and observe, and hopefully enhance, the dynamic working surface of the university.

Effective leaders need to expend more effort on understanding than explaining, listening than defending, and encouraging than mandating.

Active listening is not only helpful for information gathering but also conveys to the contributors that you hear their concerns or ideas and respect their input and perspectives. Working toward understanding and believing, not just hearing about, concerns that are expressed allows the leader to get a richer exposure to the experiences of others because understanding encompasses nuance, feelings, and emotions as well as ideas. A true understanding of the perspective of others allows the leader to share in their experience to some degree, which should better inform efforts to address challenges and improve the work of the university. This sort of empathetic element forces the leader to acknowledge and set aside their own biases and to understand the experience of others, and not simply hear what they want to believe or that which reinforces their position on some issue. Attention to true understanding, active listening, and inspirational leadership is critical to building community. And, to put it simply, to build strong institutions, community matters, especially during difficult times—and there will always be difficult times. See "Black Lives Matter: Hearing Voices, Feeling the Pain, and Taking Next Steps" for an example of careful listening that led to an institutional change agenda.

Black Lives Matter: Hearing the Voices, Feeling the Pain, and Taking Next Steps

In the wake of the George Floyd murder in May 2020, there was a strong and passionate resurgence of the Black Lives Matter movement nationally, including on many campuses. In addition, there was a proliferation of statements from institutional leaders that condemned the George Floyd killing and pledged support for the Black community and for anti-Black racism on campuses and in society more broadly. While certainly supportive, such statements alone did not carry much weight or relief to communities that have been marginalized and oppressed.

Triggered by angst in our community, the university president and I met several times with a group of eight to ten Black faculty and staff leaders on our campus to learn about their experiences, especially on our campus, and their concerns and ideas. Mostly, we listened; we could hear the pain in their voices and their concerns about the need for *actionable* strategies and not just statements of outrage and pledges of support. One colleague shared that "instead of saying things, we need to do things," while another offered "we don't need more bold statements, we need more bold actions." They were right.

The dialogue, listening, and understanding conveyed at those meetings led to the development of *Anti-Black Racism: An Academic Affairs Action Agenda for Change*, which included eight concrete and actionable strategies and investments to ensure equal opportunity for all in the university community to learn, thrive, and succeed.[3] The action agenda represented a change in the campus conversation and paradigm from one focused on celebrating diversity to one focused on dismantling systems of oppression. While there remains much to do, active listening led to understanding and the development of strategic actions to move forward. Implementation is underway and ongoing.

Effective leaders understand that ideas, even good ideas, are routine and abundant, but it is the implementation of those good ideas that is hard work and the essence of leadership.

Not uncommonly, faculty become interested in administrative positions because they like new ideas, especially their own ideas. This is a common and natural phenomenon, and there is nothing inherently wrong with it. However, too many leaders begin their work by trying to impose their ideas on others and seeking their buy-in (Figure 2.1). It rarely works. One quickly learns that many others also have good ideas, perhaps even better ones, and creating a competition of idea generation may not be an effective use of anyone's time, energy, or expertise. As a result, some administrators find themselves simply working alone on their idea and promoting their own mantra, which doesn't change or improve anything. In fact, it may alienate the exact colleagues they need to engage.

Leading a change agenda is very nuanced work. Shaping ideas collectively with other very smart people is the first step toward implementation and creating co-ownership of ideas that then morph into new directions, initiatives, programs, and positive change. Some say this may be the only way to bring about change in higher education. Implementation is invariably incremental, requires perseverance, and often involves the allocation or reallocation of resources with a host of challenges that come with that. If you hope to make a difference as a leader, prepare to dig in for the long haul. Don't lose your great ideas, but also don't delude yourself into believing that your ideas alone are the job of leading.

"I haven't read your proposal yet, but I already have some great ideas on how to improve it!"

Figure 2.1. A leader promoting their own ideas rather than engaging others to advance a change agenda.
Copyright Randy Glasbergen; Printed with permission from Glasbergen Cartoon Services

Effective leaders understand that leading a change agenda is both challenging and exhilarating, and you must care deeply about the work and the institution.

While you will no doubt endure frustrations and some bumps and bruises along the way, the work of leading change and advancing an institution is necessary and critically important. It is the substantive foundation of the evolution of learning, discovery, the future of work, and our institutions' very purpose and quest for progress. In exchange for digging in and investing sweat equity with your colleagues in leading and conducting this important work, you get to observe and savor the learning, new forms and areas of scholarship, personal growth of so many students and colleagues, and institutional advancement shared by the community. Frankly, there is no greater level of satisfaction for the hard work and investment than to witness the rise of the university before your eyes and the emergence of a strong sense of pride in the community.

Effective leaders understand that simply adding money is not sufficient to advance or transform a program or university.

It seems that almost everyone believes that simply adding resources is key to advancing a program or institution. It is almost always among the first questions a new chair, dean, or vice president asks. I have heard it a hundred times: our program is underfunded; we simply need more resources to get better. Frankly, I don't buy it. Aspiring leaders who believe their job is simply to get more money allocated for their college, program, or center are misinformed or fooling themselves. No doubt, more money can help. However, unless the programs, curricula, educational delivery, research foci, and the like are contemporary, relevant, respected, and engaging, throwing money at the problem won't help much and will likely just dig a deeper hole. A strategic leader understands that they need to engage the community in rebuilding programs and creating entirely new ones that are attractive, relevant, and essential. This is the important work of leadership. They also need to carefully examine how they are spending the resources they already have. In fact, successful re-invention of programs and reallocation of resources is exactly the right way to garner the additional resources desired and needed to build programs and, at the same time, advance the university.

Effective leaders know that their program and institution can't do everything and they, as the leader, can't do it alone.

Effective leaders understand the need to work with colleagues to develop a thriving vision for the future and a distinctive programmatic niche that highlights strengths and important future directions. Co-development of that vision and niche helps create community buy-in as well as a better plan. Further, building a leadership team of respected peers with contrasting, yet complementary, views and expertise is essential and effectively shares the workload as well as the achievements. The leader must invite the team to be candid and share challenges as well as agreements and then listen to them. Leaders must recognize and manage conflict and demonstrate the capacity to collaborate and build meaningful partnerships to accomplish important work. These may be partnerships across the campus and/or with other institutions, agencies, nonprofits, corporations, and private individuals through philanthropy. Such partnerships are typically built around trust and identifying common ground that benefits all parties.

Effective leaders must have a high tolerance for ambiguity.

The world of higher education leadership is dynamic, which is why it can be simultaneously fascinating and frustrating. Leaders must be comfortable living in a world of ambiguity, especially as it relates to efforts to solve large-scale problems that don't have solutions. For sure, the larger the problem, the greater the complexity and the less likely that the traditional problem-solving tool kit will effectively *fix* such pervasive issues, such as climate change, poverty, racism, income inequality, etc. Just because the problems are large, complex, and long-term doesn't give us a pass in trying to overcome them. It just means we need to take different approaches to address and improve upon the circumstances that contribute to those problems. We must move from the goal of developing solutions to alternative strategies that may be more abstract, such as risk analysis, scenario planning, and adaptive management to ensure continuous progress and improvement.

Improving Self-Awareness

These postulates about effective leadership emerged from my own observations and experiences. The list is not comprehensive, but these are real issues that I have thought about and encountered for many years. At the very least, I hope this list provides each of you the opportunity to discern how your personality, interests, and values gleaned from self-reflection intersect with the leadership work needed in universities and the likelihood of successful outcomes of that work. For example, are you prepared to give up the right to think about yourself or to start from scratch in learning a whole new world well beyond your discipline and the expertise that has defined you to date? Do you care enough about the work to actively listen to and empathize with the experiences of others and live in a world of ambiguity where solutions are sometimes impossible because they don't exist? Are you prepared to put your ideas aside because other ideas may either be better, more likely to be implemented, or have greater buy-in? I hope the answer to these questions is a resounding yes, because we need a new generation of authentic and courageous leaders who bring their creativity, passion, persistence, and integrity to the campus every day, even as we acknowledge our imperfect selves.

Self-reflection, in many ways, is a test of our honesty in assessing who we are and in defining our strengths and weaknesses. It is a core foundational element of effective leadership because it defines our honesty and conveys to others a certain level of confidence about the veracity of our statements and consistency in our beliefs and actions. As such, whether we can and will be trusted ultimately will depend on the outcomes of our introspection and our ability to act sincerely in our efforts to continuously improve our leadership.

Frequent effective exercises in self-reflection will lead to greater self-awareness (i.e., a clearer understanding of who we are—our values, interests, and motivations, including blind spots and biases). As we engage in the hard and important work of leading, our values and motivations will no doubt evolve, further highlighting the need for continuous self-analysis. By better understanding ourselves and certain situations, we are better prepared to thoughtfully choose our path forward and address the often-daunting challenges our institutions face and that our leaders must address.

Understanding People—Balancing Self-Confidence and Self-Management

While universities are often characterized by beautiful ivy-covered towers and elaborate campuses with substantial infrastructure, they are

far and away people-intensive institutions. The work of universities—
learning, discovery, and community engagement—is all about people.
As such, academic leaders need to understand those people—who they
are, what they do, and what they care about—a topic covered in detail
later in this book.

In the context of self-reflection, leaders must exhibit sufficient
self-confidence and self-management to effectively navigate relationships
with a broad and diverse array of constituents from on- and off-campus
in a clear and respectful manner. Suffice it to say, academic leaders
must be sufficiently self-confident to trust their own judgment, garner
trust from others, and delegate responsibility to and acknowledge the
success of others. Self-confident leaders will have the responsibility and
the courage to speak the truth when misinformation is shared, offer
their own perspective, position, and values, and acknowledge when their
analysis led to a wrong decision or unexpected outcome. Self-confidence
must be balanced with self-control to maintain a respectful atmosphere
and to maintain composure when facing challenges.

Managing a major public research university during the COVID-19
pandemic became a living day-to-day exercise of balancing *honest
self-reflection, self-confidence, and self-management.* Our *self-reflection*
constantly included questioning whether we were doing the right things
and making any progress with limited and ever-changing information.
We exhibited *self-confidence* by frequently sharing with the community
what we knew and did not know in both face-to-face settings and written
formats and by being open to responding to questions and reactions of
fear and anxiety. We employed *self-management* by maintaining and
conveying a sense of calm in an effort to serve as a stabilizing influence
within the community. While it was, and still is, a heartbreaking public
health crisis, managing a university through a dynamic and pervasive
pandemic was, and remains, a rich challenge of leadership that touches
on all the issues outlined in these postulates and in every ounce of
strength, perseverance, and resilience in all of us.

CHAPTER THREE

Building Trust Is Essential and Sometimes Not So Easy

Authentic leaders instill trust by consistently exhibiting honesty, integrity, and humility, while at the same time conveying respect, compassion, and self-confidence in their relationships and interactions with others. Trust is essential to successful leadership, especially in people-centric higher education ecosystems dependent upon shared responsibility for problem-solving and the future vitality of the institution. By success, I am referring to the institution advancing and progressing toward achieving its strategic goals rather than personal success for the individual leader. Trust is foundational to the quality of our working relationships, and personal ones as well, and is a tangible asset that creates an interconnection between credibility and productivity. To be trusted, you don't have to be right all the time, and you certainly don't need to be perfect. Indeed, trust is the glue that holds together the community within the ecosystem. However, it is critical that you understand and acknowledge that you are not right at times and that you, like the rest of us, have flaws in your character. Frankly, others become aware of our flaws and imperfections rather quickly, maybe before we do ourselves. So, it's heartening when we are willing and able to acknowledge them as well.

Trust Must Be Earned in the Academy

Universities are packed with very smart people who are busy with their work, ask good questions, are accustomed to critiquing ideas and people, and want or need to observe positive actions and, most importantly, consistency and credibility in their leaders. Whether we like it or not, trust must be earned in university settings. There is limited automatic trust in leadership simply because of title, position, or hierarchy. Frankly, I think that is a fair expectation. In fact, there may be an inherent level of initial unsubstantiated distrust that must be overcome. The community expects its leaders to provide a moral compass for the institution and to take on and address the challenges ahead as well as the extant dysfunctional issues within the institution. They will judge whether they can trust us not by whether we are perfect or always correct (they already know we are not), but rather by our authenticity and character as reflected in our consistency in translating our words, values, and proclamations into actions, deeds, and measurable progress. In part, trusted leaders are expected to invest in that which they say they value. That investment is not so much about the allocation of resources, although that is expected too, as it is about gaining credibility related to consistency in behavior.

In his enlightening 2017 book entitled *Good People,* Anthony Tjan[4] distinguishes between competence and goodness and emphasizes that we often seek *competence* in our leaders, which is certainly necessary but may not be sufficient for effective or transformational leadership. Real *goodness* represents much more than competencies and accomplishments; it's about people's humanity and encompasses their values, the qualities inherent in their character, and their humility and authenticity. Tjan posits that goodness in leadership imprints good values and qualities onto others and models a culture of good people as a competitive advantage for the organization that creates authenticity and real meaning in the workplace. To be sure, experience and accomplishments matter in choosing our leaders, but so do character and authenticity.

Authenticity

In my experience, we too often observe leaders who may offer false or exaggerated congratulatory praise for very minor achievements, feign concern in a sincere tone, and then immediately forget or ignore the issue, or convey contrasting messages to different audiences telling each group what they want to hear. Furthermore, in their zeal to advance their agenda, some individuals may at times share incomplete or inaccurate information that misrepresents reality to promote their perspective or desired outcome. These types of behaviors, even if intended to make everyone feel good at that moment, will undermine trust because they are not authentic. Authenticity requires honesty and consistency in our behaviors, values, and actions. Simply put, those who modify their behaviors, values, or messages from one moment or person to the next or misrepresent reality won't be trusted, nor should they be. Once trustworthiness has been breached, it may be impossible to regain. So, try your best to be authentic always, even when tempted to go with the flow or please the crowd.

The Being Trusted versus Being Liked Paradox

It is important to distinguish between instilling trust and being liked. No doubt, there will be circumstances when individuals within the community disagree with the priorities of the academic leader or the way that leader interacts with others and carries out their responsibilities. In some cases, there may even be disdain for leaders because of strong philosophical differences, but that is different from distrust. In fact, a leader's honesty, consistency, and transparency about certain values and priorities, which are typically key elements that are expected to foster trustworthiness, may trigger long-term disagreements that contribute to one being disliked or criticized by a segment of the community. Those leaders, however, can still be respected and trusted, even while clashing with those with different perspectives on the issues. In fact, this kind of situation is not uncommon, especially for those in upper-level leadership positions with an oversight role that impacts large numbers of faculty, staff, and students. This is a common component of the landscape of leadership in higher education. So, be prepared for it. We are all familiar with the following slogan emerging after an extensive debate where the participants declare in the end that they will simply have to agree to disagree. In many cases that is the best outcome, and it's OK.

There are at least two other serious issues to consider in relation to the being trusted versus being liked paradox relevant to leadership in higher education. Unfortunately, in my experience, these two issues surface often among institutional leaders, especially inexperienced ones, whose desire or need to be liked or accepted may overwhelm their adherence to a set of principles, priorities, and values, thereby undermining their effectiveness. First, I have seen too many leaders make decisions they perceive as popular rather than the best, most strategic, or correct institutional decision. That is, the need to be liked or popular may get in the way of informed strategic decision-making and transformative leadership.

Feeling Good While Doing Harm

Decisions influenced by popularity rather than strategy happen frequently, especially in relation to resource allocation investments when leaders respond to the squeaky wheel rather than to the well-defined priorities outlined in the strategic plan. Such an investment of invariably limited resources not only leads to a drain of scarce funds that are needed for expanding programs but, more importantly, sends the wrong message to members of the community who helped develop and have bought into the strategic plan as the university's path forward and investment priorities.

Over a period of several years across multiple institutions and out of frustration, I coined the phrase "good management penalty." This principle refers to leadership decisions that provide support for declining programs or institutions that have not made serious efforts to improve at the expense of those that are advancing because of their hard work and efforts to transform their programs. In essence, the programs or institutions that have worked hard and made investments to improve are penalized for their commitment. They perceive that if they sat back and did nothing, they too would get bailed out with an influx of resources. This sort of behavior, which may have a short-term "feel good" impact for the decision-maker or quiet the squeaky wheel, is deeply problematic and can be demoralizing. See "Good Management Penalty" for some tangible examples of this principle in action.

The Good Management Penalty— Undermining Trust and Morale

Leadership decisions that seem to reward a lack of effort and creativity, and undermine and even penalize the hard work, productivity, and creativity of units/institutions happen too often. Such decisions are short-sighted and reflect a lack of understanding of incentives, disincentives, good management, and recognition for efforts, and are frequently demoralizing and undermine trust in leadership. Here are a few examples that will illustrate the point:

Example #1: Technology evolves rapidly, and not long-ago academic units did not have base budgets for hardware and software upgrades. As a dean years ago, I knew we had to upgrade hardware and software for our faculty and staff and in our classrooms and laboratories on a regular and predictable schedule to ensure our personnel and programs remained contemporary. Every year we scrimped and saved and allocated scarce vacancy funds to support upgrades on a three-year rotating basis. Other colleges allowed their hardware and software to become horrifically anti-quated and then whined incessantly to the provost office to provide extra funding to pay for their upgrades all at once while they were spending their vacancy dollars on end-of-the-year wish lists. Of course, the provost succumbed to that request and funded technology upgrades for those units that had done nothing to invest in their own upgrades. This entailed a significant investment across several colleges. In so doing, they quieted the squeaky wheels and inspired me to coin the phrase "good manage-ment penalty" to highlight the disincentive for units to take on the respon-sibility of upgrading their own facilities. The decision was demoralizing to our faculty who would have enjoyed annual spending on their wish list items; they wondered aloud why we had to pay, while others got bailed out for their lack of attention and responsibility.

Example #2: Driven by our own commitment to educational attainment, our institution invested resources and focused diligently to enhance enroll-ment, student retention, graduation rates, and the number of degrees awarded annually, which was also a priority of the state. This involved chal-lenging work, including curricular revisions, advising upgrades, faculty development, student aid investments, policy changes, etc. Years later, and with very positive results, the state instituted a performance funding model for allocating financial support to all state institutions based on exactly the metrics that we worked so hard to improve. When it came to the actual allocation of funds, however, the metrics were ignored, and all institutions, regardless of mission, enrollment, and performance, received the same fixed dollar appropriation increase. Once again, this was done to ensure sufficient funding for the underperforming institutions at the expense of the flagship, which had invested its own resources in making tangible improvements. You can imagine the reaction of our faculty and staff who felt penalized for stepping up and doing the right thing.

Example #3: The good management penalty can also emerge with leaders who attempt difficult reallocation of internal resources to meet strategic goals, enhance financial solvency, and develop programs with social relevance and high student demand. A dean of a college with eleven different health programs, including an associate degree program (the only one in the flagship public research university), proposed moving the program to the state college system, which was a better fit with the mission. Freed-up resources would be reinvested to develop a new high-demand graduate program. The move was supported by the central administration and a powerful member of congress, but students protested to the board of trustees and the dean received many vicious communications. There was also pushback from some faculty with concerns that their programs would be next. The dean, supported by an internal team and the provost, nevertheless persisted. When the transfer was complete, the provost recaptured all the newly released resources for other purposes outside the college, reneging on the initial plan to reallocate to a new high-demand program. Such a bait-and-switch is demoralizing, feeds a narrative of distrust, and heightens the reluctance of deans to take on important, but politically charged, innovations.

Courage to Resist External Pressures

In the climate on campuses today, I have observed, and we all have read about, many situations where pressure from lobbying groups (perhaps students, faculty, alumni, board members, donors, legislators, etc.) leads to bad decisions that compromise academic integrity and freedom on campuses. While issues can be complex, leaders should be careful not to cave to advocacy pressures simply to please some group of constituents. In my mind, our leaders have a moral responsibility to maintain academic standards and the courage to uphold academic policies developed through shared governance, unless significant extenuating circumstances must prevail. I urge aspiring leaders at all levels to resist the temptation to fold into decision-making driven largely by one's need to please or to respond to external pressures that undermine institutional standards, policies, or protocols. To be clear, it is not the deviation from a policy that is the primary concern, as that may be appropriate or necessary at times, but rather choosing to do so for the wrong reasons (i.e., to please or react to external pressure). Succumbing to such influences undermines trust and the confidence of the community in your leadership.

Discernment versus Flip-Flopping

This leads to my second issue relevant to the consistency–credibility expectations necessary to build trust. That is, effective leaders sometimes should and do change their positions, priorities, and values on issues, even priorities memorialized in strategic plans. Such changes, what politicians often disparagingly refer to as flip-flopping, shouldn't occur primarily in response to lobbying or to temporarily promote the popularity of leaders, but rather because new data or results of new and different analyses shed fresh light leading to discernment that changes one's perspective and understanding of facts or impacts. In my view, it is bold and courageous for leaders to modify their position on an issue in recognition that the landscape of knowledge and understanding has changed as illuminated by new information—what I often refer to as *new data*.

Extrapolating from ideas expounded by Stephen Carter in his book *Integrity*, possessing the courage to change one's position when provided new information reflects integrity.[5] A trustworthy leader is recognized as being open to the possibility of being persuaded by another's compelling perspective. In fact, this measure of integrity should reinforce trust and confidence rather than be interpreted as a breach of trust or the abandoning of values or priorities. I'd rather follow an enlightened and authentic leader willing to reconsider their viewpoint when given new information than be stuck behind a stubborn individual locked into their positions and unwilling to learn from and adapt to a changing landscape.

A Special Time for Trust and Compassion

It is common to toss around the terms trust, courage, and integrity as we discuss and define their importance to authentic leadership, but the meaning of actions associated with these qualities can be rather nuanced. Despite the subtle variations that may exist around these terms, I am more convinced than ever that *trust,* including consistency in *honesty, integrity,* and *humility,* is essential if leaders are going to effectively lead, inspire followership, and implement a meaningful and transformational agenda for change in institutions of higher education. Truly caring about the well-being of others (i.e., *compassion*) and creating a culture of support, empathy, and opportunity is also critical. Indeed, these qualities may reflect the *goodness* Tjan suggests is necessary for authentic leadership that adds value throughout an organization.

The need for such trust in leadership may be more pronounced at this moment than ever before. The persistent personal and professional disruptions, frustrations, and sacrifices associated with COVID-19 along with politically motivated dissemination of misinformation and disinformation have drained the energy and taxed the soul of many faculty, staff, and students on our campuses. The politicization of COVID-19 in many places has further exacerbated demoralization on some campuses. This highlights the importance of leaders actively exhibiting honesty, integrity, humility, and compassion and taking extra steps to sustain meaning as well as function in the workplace, all while trying to make the best decisions to mitigate health, safety, and financial impacts.

Evidence derived from numerous recent reports conveys the perception that many leaders have not been visibly sensitive to and overtly grateful for the extra efforts and sacrifices faculty and staff have endured over the past few years. Many faculty have shared that they have not felt supported, valued, or acknowledged by their leaders, whom they assert only care about enrollment and the bottom line and have folded to legislative leaders and demands, even if it placed the health of the community at risk. Many faculty, staff, and students bemoan the deterioration of a sense of belonging and the lack of recognition and appreciation for their efforts from the administration, and they long for leaders who care about sustaining a sense of community.

In academic ecosystems, it is the biotic community—the people— who do the teaching and research, offer support services, and generate most of the revenue that drives the institution forward. Their morale, creativity, and productivity shape the purpose, relevance, and accomplishments of the institution and are worthy of attention. It has been a challenging landscape for everyone to navigate over the past few years. My intention is not to ascribe blame, but rather to actively listen to and hear the voices in the community. Leaders must understand, however, that they don't have a choice of either managing the details of a crisis *or* exhibiting honest compassion for the people in the trenches doing the work. They must do both. All of us in leadership positions, including myself, can and must do better.

CHAPTER FOUR

Effective Leadership Practices: Transparency, Ecosystem Thinking, Communication, Culture, and Community

Colleges and universities have an abundance of very smart people with expertise in a broad array of subjects and skill sets. Leading a change agenda in complex organizations and responding to an accelerating pace of challenges emerging from within and outside the academy, however, is typically not part of the skill set of most faculty and senior staff. Even for those who may have taken leadership or management courses in graduate school, most have not grappled with the hands-on leading of organizations in the face of messy, multifaceted challenges. Furthermore, leadership strategies gleaned from corporate and other nonprofit sectors may not be applicable in the distinctive world of higher education where institutional challenges typically require institutional engagement and solutions. The good news is leadership development can be learned, and university personnel are very good learners. In fact, cultivating a new generation of leaders needs to become a priority for colleges and universities. While there may be specific skills necessary in certain situations, there is a common set of fundamental elements of effective leadership that aspiring leaders should understand and put into practice.

Transparency

Transparency, or the open sharing of information used to make informed decisions, is a visible manifestation of honesty, integrity, and trust and is integral to authentic leadership. Creating transparency also typically involves inviting and accepting input from others, especially those who may be impacted by the decision or policy under consideration. In addition to creating openness and building trust, transparency in many institutional transactions informs about the rationale for decisions, can stimulate buy-in, and may also help the community become more aware of the constraints under which the institution is operating. In this case, the building of trust extends in both directions. The community trusts the leader because of their openness, and the leader trusts the community with what may be viewed as sensitive information.

Given what are almost always mysteries, myths, and suspicions about budget matters on university campuses, transparency is particularly impactful when it informs university-wide financial issues. A year after I became provost at The University of Rhode Island (URI), at the request of our president, we made a bold move to increase transparency about the allocation of new resources at the university and to ensure there was comprehensive input to guide investments. We formed the URI Strategic Budget and Planning Council (SBPC) comprised of faculty, staff, students, deans, vice presidents, and a community member. As provost, I chaired the council. The SBPC vetted all funding proposals and made recommendations to the president about strategic areas for investment. The president accepted almost all those recommendations. The SBPC is an excellent example of transparency that dramatically improved the working surface of the university, led to impactful strategic investments, and better informed the university community broadly about university financial issues. See "SBPC: Combining Strategy and Transparency for Financial Investments" for an elaboration of the work of the council at URI.

Conducting university business in a transparent manner may require extra time to share information and solicit input, but it is invariably time well spent that leads to better policies and greater support for the intent of those policies. Too often in the interest of moving forward quickly or the perceived need to get a new policy or decision in place as soon as possible, a small group of administrators will meet to craft a policy or discuss a critical issue without stakeholder input. This is a mistake, has the potential to undermine trust, and leads to bad policies and decisions.

SBPC: Combining Strategy and Transparency for Financial Investments

The SBPC's primary function was to ensure the university's strategic plan guided resource allocations and investments, and that reallocation served as the preferred approach to funding new initiatives, when possible. To that end, the council developed a set of budget principles and processes for reviewing all proposals for new institutional investments and to advise about strategic reductions during difficult times. The SBPC also developed recommendations and processes for budget reinvestments, capital expenditures, allocation of contingency funds, and a fund balance carryforward process. To ensure transparency, all SBPC meetings were open to the community, and all minutes, proposals, and recommendations were posted on a website for anyone to review. Individuals on the SBPC were trusted with sensitive financial information, came to understand the university's budget, and functioned as university citizens rather than partisans.

Over the course of a decade, the SBPC recommended, and the president endorsed, many millions of dollars of strategic investments across all divisions of the institution, including adding more than sixty new faculty lines in strategically important areas; bringing on a chief diversity officer and support staff positions; hiring professional advisors; adding fifty new graduate teaching assistantships; expanding counseling services; opening a veteran affairs office and a business engagement center; advancing global education; elevating men's and women's athletics; hiring experiential learning coordinators; and performing a complete overhaul and upgrade of IT services and security. By openly sharing financial information and involving faculty, staff, and students in strategically vetting all proposals for new funding, the SBPC not only ensured informed recommendations about investments but also built a bridge of trust and confidence in the community, which squelched previously existing myths about financial resources on campus.

Frankly, because of the likely need for rework to correct deficiencies, it frequently isn't even time efficient. It's just not that hard to do this right. As I have often stated to my colleagues on campus, our university has managed to operate for 130 years without this policy or decision; we can certainly invest another week or two to ensure critical stakeholder input helps us get it right.

While transparency is essential, there is also a need for selective limitations, especially regarding personnel matters and potential litigation. In the interest of fairness, many personnel decisions or issues may benefit from candid and constructive one-on-one transparency, but they should not be broadcasted or discussed widely. There are other difficult and sensitive areas of university business that could easily be misinterpreted, misconstrued, or taken out of context that must be addressed in a confidential manner. The university's Office of the General Counsel can provide guidance to university leaders on specific matters that should be carefully and privately considered.

Ecosystem Thinking

Perhaps stemming from my academic training in ecosystem ecology, I am intrigued with, actively engaged in, and a believer in the importance of "ecosystem thinking," a value-added planning and implementation strategy that recognizes organizations as a web of interconnected and interacting networks and relationships. Perhaps I am over-glamorizing the idea. It may simply be an alternative descriptor for systems or strategic thinking, an important executive skill for leadership development in the business world. In my view, ecosystem thinking involves understanding and appreciating complexity, interconnectedness, and interaction of component parts and resilience in our institutions. The ideas and nomenclature align closely with the field of ecosystem ecology—hence the ecosystem reference. In this context, *complexity* refers to the many predictable and unpredictable moving parts and relationships in higher education ecosystems; *interconnectedness* and *interaction* refer to potential synergistic and antagonistic influences among component parts; and *resilience* refers to the potential reaction or response to a certain action, policy, or disruption and the ability to move forward, even when faced with hardship.

These ideas align with those of Margaret Wheatley who, in her award-winning 2006 classic entitled *Leadership and the New Science,* eloquently describes interdisciplinary applications of natural sciences, including quantum physics and ecology, to organizational development and business management.[6] Regardless of the exact descriptors used to characterize it, ecosystem thinking involves looking forward in multiple dimensions to discover unique opportunities through innovative and interconnected ideas. Good ecosystem thinkers are always searching for something new and different, a distinctive *niche* to use another ecological term, and challenge conventional thinking. They have the uncanny ability to extract clarity from complexity by visualizing and verbalizing interconnections. Simply put, they can connect the dots in a coherent manner.

Ecosystem thinkers have the foresight to recognize and anticipate the short- and long-term implications of their actions, initiatives, and policies. This involves the capacity to predict unintended consequences of policies and investments and being prepared to *adaptively manage* (yet another term derived from ecology and conservation) the vagaries and risks associated with those projections. For example, most university policies are well-intentioned, believe it or not, and designed to improve or safeguard the institution when they are proposed. However, when viewing a policy in retrospect, its value is not always evident. This occurs because a new policy encourages behavior changes that may trigger workarounds of what was intended initially. The policy may have solved the problem of the day, only to create a new set of unanticipated challenges that then must be adaptively managed. Good ecosystem thinkers can anticipate unforeseen consequences of a newly developed policy and create opportunities to adapt it rather than manage the consequences. By anticipating the potential problems associated with a proposed action before they happen, good ecosystem thinkers can turn challenges into opportunities.

While this may all seem rather abstract, it is a valuable and practical skill or mindset in leaders. Most everything within academic ecosystems is connected to and will influence something else. Leaders must understand those connections. As a simple example, the university base operating budget is managed separately from the auxiliary and enterprise budgets (housing, dining, parking, etc.) and by different players. Even though they are totally separate, those budgets do interact and connect through the cost to students and families. A simultaneous increase in housing, dining, parking, or recreational fees to students limits the possibility of increasing tuition and effectively devalues the partial tuition scholarship provided through the financial aid office because students are impacted by the total cost. In turn, this may lead to a reduction in yield of incoming students or retention of existing students with an accompanying loss of tuition revenue necessary to cover the base salaries and operations for the institution. A small reduction in yield resulting in say only fifty fewer students in an entering class of 3,250 would result in a $2 million loss in year one to be compounded over four years. It's all connected, and subtle changes have large impacts. An ecosystem thinker understands those connections and their importance and prevents such an occurrence from happening.

A good ecosystem thinker understands, for example, that unspent funds in a college budget flow into a central reserve fund for institutional investment, but it also incentivizes nonstrategic end-of-year spending by colleges and limits the possibilities for college investments. To better align incentives and encourage college-based investments in new revenue-generating or reputation-enhancing activities and/or new research opportunities, we would be better off allowing colleges to carry forward a portion of their unspent funds for their own strategic investments, which would incentivize careful annual budget management to maximize that strategic investment pool. Again, the opportunities and interconnections are abundant and palpable, but the details matter. Ecosystem thinkers understand those details and adapt to maximize benefits and strategic positions.

Ecosystem thinking is a critical skill set for leaders and can have positive implications in at least three different areas:

1. **Identifying new opportunities.** By understanding the drivers of the institution's value proposition, good ecosystem thinkers can uncover new and distinct opportunities that add further value and identify potentially important investments that may not yet be fully shaped. To maximize this sort of strategic exploration, leaders benefit from engaging with institutional colleagues who bring differing perspectives to the table. In contrast, pulling together a homogenous group or always the same set of players is likely to squelch new ideas and drive consensus in the direction of conformity, which is counter to good ecosystem thinking.

2. **Problem anticipation and projection.** Good ecosystem thinkers can project, at least to some degree, both intended and unintended consequences that may occur in response to implementing something new, and they are prepared to respond to problems in advance or during the implementation phase. Ecosystem thinkers

are good problem solvers because they can anticipate the types of issues that will arise.

3. **Adaptive management.** Ecosystem thinkers understand that they will likely need to adjust their goals or steps along the way because there are always uncertainties about outcomes from new actions. They are prepared to learn by doing and to expect the unexpected, and they recognize the value of iterative approaches. Even if one cannot project in advance the type of adjustments that will be necessary, simply recognizing that decisions are often the first step in a multi-step process to be followed by adaptive management strategies is a profound leadership strength and institutional advantage.

As the challenges that institutions face become more complex and the pace of change accelerates, higher education will need leaders who can think, act, and implement strategically—*true* ecosystem thinkers. This is a skill set that can be nurtured and honed over time if one has the mindset for self-improvement, the curiosity to understand interconnections and interactive forces, the imagination to pursue novel and innovative thinking, and the courage to set aside the ideas, structures, and behaviors of the past. Ecosystem thinking as a form of strategic thinking is increasingly an essential element of effective leadership in higher education. It also represents a potential learning tool for the community. A community engaged in transparency, ecosystem thinking, shared and informed decision-making, and adaptive management also learns how to think in systemic ways.

Informed Decision-Making

Effective leaders get things done, which means after gathering information and weighing risks and alternatives, a decision must be made and shared with the larger community. Some decisions, such as new courses and curricular decisions, are usually made by vote of the faculty, and the majority carries the day. Majority decisions are not always the right or best decisions and may tend to favor the *status quo*, but they generally work. The stakes are usually not too high, and these decisions can easily be changed if they don't work out well.

Major personnel, budget, space, and policy decisions are likely to be more complex with higher stakes, significant trade-offs, and often some politicking and maneuvering behind the scenes. Invariably, the leader gets to make these decisions, but everyone lives with the consequences. It's not as scary as it may sound, although the trepidation is proportional to the stakes or scale of trade-offs that might be impacted by the decision. There are never guarantees about outcomes, and no one gets it exactly right all the time.

Also, it is relatively rare that decisions about complex matters are either right or wrong. That is, once a decision is made it is likely that additional steps may need to be taken to mitigate any implications that may or may not have been predicted. So, be prepared for adaptive management of emerging outcomes following major decisions. Think for a moment about the decision to shift 3,200 classes to fully online delivery in the span of a week in March 2020 because of the COVID-19 pandemic. The decision to make the transition was inevitable, but the adaptive management steps to mitigate the ensuing chaos, such as providing support for faculty, staff, and students to help with the transition and responding to the onslaught of parental fears and concerns, were much more nuanced. We did the best we could to prepare, respond, and adapt, and were mostly successful in doing so, although there were certainly some unhappy individuals.

Decisions often need to be made quickly and sometimes with less information than is ideal. Yet, effective leaders have no choice but to make decisions based on the information available. How can we increase the probability that we make the "right" decision or choose the "best" option before us? To be as prepared as possible, you can often do your homework in advance. Assuming some understanding of the nature of the issues impacting the decision and time to prepare, there are at least three dimensions to this homework:

1. **Asking the right questions**, including the tough questions, will steer you in the right direction. Thoughtful leaders can quickly drill down to the key issues that need to be carefully considered. Sometimes taking a devil's advocate approach to defining the questions is helpful and certainly better than posing softball questions that will likely lead to the answer you want. The latter isn't helpful and will appear insincere.

2. **Gathering data to inform decisions and understand risks and implications.** Asking the right questions will lead you to the data needed to inform the issue and decision-making process. I

emphasize the importance of decisions being *data-informed* rather than *data-driven* because there are many important nonquantitative factors, such as morale, logistics, maintenance, etc., that may also influence decisions. To be clear, good data is essential, but it is not the only information that needs to be considered. While it should go without saying, accurate data is essential. Frequently, departments or divisions attempt to generate their own data to study a problem. I urge you to resist the temptation to do this unless there is no other option. Self-generated data is often problematic because it invariably involves different definitions of terms, assumptions, or fiscal years than are being used at the institutional level and may even be publicly available, which is a concern. Frankly, this happens too often. By using institutional data, for example, from the Institutional Research Office or the University Budget Office regarding financial information, your analysis of the issues should align with other university studies and lend credibility to your conclusions. It is counterproductive when someone produces a different data set that undermines your conclusions because you or someone else used the wrong data or a false set of assumptions. Once gathered and carefully analyzed, it is important to share the data with other stakeholders who may help make interpretations and, at the very least, understand the basis for the decision to be made. As illustrated in Figure 4.1, there is rarely a shortage of strong opinions and debate within academic ecosystems, which reinforces the importance of careful consideration of pertinent data in the decision-making process. Finally, by gathering and carefully considering pertinent quantitative and qualitative data, you are also well on your way to monitoring that same data to measure the impact of your decision.

3. **Collaborating with colleagues and those impacted by the decision**, including those who will bring a different opinion or experience than your own. All of us are collectively smarter than any one of us. It is helpful and important to pull in a team of colleagues that can help in framing the right questions, gathering the best information and data, and thoroughly analyzing and interpreting that data, including qualitative information. For deans and senior administrators, it is almost always beneficial to include faculty and others who will be impacted by the decision in the conversation.

This will not only produce a more informed review and a better result, but it will also build trust that the process included a thoughtful, thorough, and fair assessment of the risks and alternatives. No doubt, there will be differences of opinion, but most will understand that a decision must be made and the basis for the decision that ultimately emerges. See "Leading during Crisis" for an example of scenario planning and risk management to inform decision-making in the absence of good data, such as during the COVID-19 pandemic.

"When you two have finished arguing your opinions, I actually have data!"

Figure 4.1. Divergent opinions may be worth considering, but data more effectively informs good decision-making.
Copyright Timo Elliott; Printed with permission

Leading during Crises: Scenario Planning and Risk Management during the COVID-19 Pandemic

Following the abrupt transition of all classes to virtual delivery in spring 2020, ensuring teaching with technology support for faculty, and committing to virtual delivery of summer sessions, we had to make numerous difficult decisions about the 2020 fall semester in the face of the rapidly exploding COVID-19 pandemic. Students, parents, staff, and faculty were anxiously asking for information every day and tensions were high. Issues of in-person instruction, residential life, maintaining enrollment, COVID testing, and financial concerns, including the potential for lay-offs, were among the many issues of concern. Little was understood about COVID, and both state and CDC guidance was evolving rapidly. Given the lack of specific information and clear data to inform decisions, we embarked on a scenario planning and risk management effort. A twelve-person team chaired by the provost was assembled; it included faculty senate and union leaders, key vice provosts, a dean, health service and risk management expertise, chief diversity officer, director of campus communication, and our academic planning facilitator.

- **Overriding University-Wide Goal:** To protect the health and safety of the community, sustain the financial viability of the institution, and ensure academic progress for our students while maintaining the university workforce at or near full capacity, if possible, under all scenarios.

- **Approach:** Initially developed four scenarios for the fall 2020 re-opening of the campus with multiple learning constructs within each scenario to accommodate varying learning outcomes, class sizes, and strategies to de-densify the campus resulting in nine scenario-construct combinations. All scenarios were vetted by the faculty senate, faculty union, the *ad hoc* remote teaching and learning task force, and the Council of Deans.

- **Risk Assessment:** Each of the scenarios was subjectively assessed by the scenario planning team against fifteen risk factors in five categories: financial; equity; schedule/facility impacts; safety and health; and course complexity/training. An interactive summary matrix and associated heat map allowed visualization that led to a new flexible-mixed model that was recommended, approved by the president and board, and successfully implemented in fall 2020 (Figure 4.2).

Applied Model	Financial Impacts			Equity	Schedule/Facility Impacts			Safety & Health Impacts				Course Complexity/Training			
	Negative Retention/Enrollment impact	Tuition/fee discounting	Additional course sections negative budget implications	Equity	Requiring expanded weekly schedule days and hours	Complexity of scheduling	Quarantine and absenteeism related adjustments	Potential health/safety risks	Covid testing usage	Increased cleaning	Density IRC impact	Faculty training needs	Multiple modalities per course	Proportion online courses	Level of course planning restructuring required
Scenario 1	0.0	0.0	0.5	0.0	1.0	1.0	1.0	1.0	1.0	1.0	1.0	0.0	0.5	0.5	0.5
New Flex Mixed	0.5	0.5	0.8	0.5	0.3	0.3	0.5	0.5	0.5	0.5	0.5	0.8	0.3	0.8	0.8
Scenario 3	0.5	0.8	0.0	0.5	0.0	0.5	0.3	0.3	0.5	0.8	0.3	1.0	0.3	0.8	1.0
Scenario 4	1.0	1.0	0.3	1.0	0.3	0.0	0.0	0.0	0.0	0.0	0.0	1.0	0.0	1.0	1.0

Figure 4.2. Summary risk matrix assessing four teaching and learning scenarios against fifteen risk factors and an associated "heat map" allowing visualization of the overall level of risk (green = low, yellow = medium, red = high) with each of the four scenarios.

The heat map visualization on the previous page was helpful in sharing the proposed model with the board and faculty. Scenario planning/risk analysis, although certainly not perfect, is an alternative collaborative approach for informed decision-making in the absence of data, reliable projections, and consistent information.

Clear and Abundant Communication

Communication is always critical and often complicated. The complexity relates to the timing of communications, the need to craft messages that inform very different audiences who may need and want different information, and the sharing of information in a clear and understandable manner. This became especially evident in the early phase of the pandemic. While we were communicating regularly with students and their parents about details related to classes, residence halls, social distancing, etc., faculty were asking very good and appropriate detailed questions about issues they were grappling with, such as virtual teaching support, access to laboratories, testing availability, ventilation systems, etc. In response, we created numerous virtual face-to-face forums for faculty and FAQs to get pertinent information out to the community as efficiently as possible. Faculty appreciated the opportunity to voice their concerns, share their observations, and request certain information that was important to them.

The bottom line is people want and need to know what is going on, and failure to communicate in a clear and timely fashion is often interpreted as the leaders either not caring or not knowing what is going on. Both are terrible messages to convey. Communication is very much a component of transparency and building trust and can inform the community of details so that they can understand the rationale for decisions, especially ones that may be complex or counterintuitive. Clear, open, and timely communication is ultimately about showing respect by understanding the need for individuals to have information so they know and understand their options and can make good decisions for themselves (Figure 4.3).

The mode of communication is also important. Information needs to be presented in a clear and concise form. I have seen too many long and rambling university communications where the most important information is in the last of too many paragraphs. Bad idea! Lead with the punchline and, if possible, keep it brief and informative. For complex and challenging issues, leadership must develop and implement a communications plan that reinforces crystal clear messages that the university needs to convey to various constituent groups. That plan will no doubt involve multiple, consistent, and coordinated messages coming from several university leaders.

Written communications can be shared broadly and provide a status record for a point in time. When issues are challenging, also meeting with faculty, staff, and student groups provides an opportunity to share information, respond to questions, and genuinely convey what you know and, equally as important, what you don't. During or after challenging institutional situations, it is also important to convey thanks to the community for stepping up and contributing to address the challenges and keep the university moving forward. Clear communications should reinforce that you don't take the extra efforts of the community for granted. Social media communications and text messages can be an effective way to keep people updated but are invariably rather impersonal.

While institutional communication from leaders is very important, so is personal communication. Great leaders find ways to reach out and connect with people in the community. I'm not referring so much to great orators or charismatic individuals who can command an audience, but rather to genuine, humble, and empathetic leaders who understand the importance of speaking with and listening to individuals in the trenches. Charismatic public speaking is also an asset if the messages conveyed represent real values and are backed by actions. Leaders who understand the importance of genuine communication and human interaction can build community, convey understanding, build trust, and express sincere appreciation to those who work hard every day to keep the university operating. To be sure, this form of personal communication must be genuine and reflect the "goodness" of special leaders who care about members of the community.

Finally, in my experience, erring on the side of too much communication with the community is far better than too little. One of the biggest challenges to university leaders is keeping people informed and engaged. Without open and strategic communication, your leadership will flounder.

"What if, and I know this sounds kooky, we communicated with the employees?"

Figure 4.3. Communication is essential to building trust and community. Maintaining open lines of communication with employees should be a proactive strategy rather than an afterthought. *Copyright Andrew Grossman; Printed with permission from Cartoon Resource*

Understanding Institutional Culture

Every university has an institutional culture that reflects prevailing patterns of behaviors, beliefs, myths, and characteristics that become subliminally woven into the life of the community. Within that institutional culture, there may be departmental or disciplinary cultures as well. My sense is that most of us are not thinking about or even noticing the institutional culture in which we are embedded. That was certainly my experience as a faculty member and administrator at the same institution. However, when I changed institutions, the culture difference was immediately evident, and I realized that I needed to understand the culture to effectively lead.

Many aspects of institutional culture can be viewed as positive, such as a culture of excellence, a culture of pride, a culture of achievement, or a culture of respect. Other aspects may represent limitations and need to be overcome or changed to move an institution forward. For example, a culture of constrained resources, a culture of entitlement, or a culture of distrust. While I recognize that this may be an abstract concept, and I am not suggesting that a leader attempt to articulate all or most elements of the institutional culture, I do think it is critical to acknowledge and understand at least some dimensions of the institutional culture.

Culture will influence approaches, processes, and policies that shape the institution and the ability to carry out its day-to-day mission. As such, leaders need to walk the fine line between recognizing aspects of culture or tradition that need to be respected and maintained and those aspects that need to be changed for the institution to evolve and mature. Cultural change is likely to occur slowly if at all. The critical element is to recognize constraining cultural features and then develop implementation strategies that recognize such limitations and allow steady progress and pride in accomplishment to overcome some negative dimensions of culture. Unfortunately, there is no standard practice or recipe for recognizing or changing culture. Yet, understanding aspects of culture is critically important to understanding the institution, its people, and strategies for moving forward. Ignoring cultural constraints is equivalent to ignoring the context for the very institutional problems that you are trying to solve.

Building Community

Building community is another somewhat abstract, yet critically important, concept that lacks a simple formula for implementation. While we can usually sense when the community is strained, the exact steps necessary to strengthen or build community are not always clear. Nevertheless, building community requires the attention of the leader. *An effective leader facilitates community spirit through action and attention.* Throughout my many years as dean and provost, I woke up every morning thinking about building the community of my college or the university more broadly. Invariably, I would ask myself what I could do to demonstrate to the community that I care about who they are, their concerns and frustrations, and the work that they do every day to advance the university. By the way, caring must be genuine. Leaders should care about the people they are leading and the institution they are serving. Simply put, community matters, especially during difficult times—and there will always be difficult times.

There are some important steps that leaders can take to convey that they care and to promote community spirit. Good leaders give their time and attention to the community and show up at events that are important to those who sponsor them. When the chair, dean, provost, or president show up, people notice and appreciate their presence. Folks know that individuals in such positions are busy and have a full calendar. So when you show up, you convey that you care and that matters. In my view, showing up and perhaps giving welcoming remarks comes with the positions we occupy and is a responsibility of leadership. It's about role fidelity. That is, it is not about *me* as an individual showing up, rather it is about the leader making the time to participate in community events and activities.

As dean and as provost, I tried to be everywhere—for example, attending the Honors Colloquium every Tuesday evening during the fall semester, introducing the speaker at the annual Alexander Cruickshank Endowed Lecture in the sciences each year, welcoming the attendees and acknowledging the organizers at the Center for the Humanities Annual Festival, providing remarks at the opening of a new exhibition at the university art gallery, and serving as emcee at the annual University Academic Excellence Award ceremony, to name just a few of the thousands of events. I know the community appreciated the presence of the provost at their event, and it did help build trust and support over time. Frankly, I also enjoyed these events and learned a ton about the amazing work being done by our faculty and students. What could be better than that?

Inclusion also helps build community. Whether it relates to strategic planning, efforts to promote diversity and social justice, organizing campus events, or analyzing critical issues, inviting others to participate is welcoming, produces better outcomes, and sends a clear message that the community perspective is valued. Reaching out to pull the community together sends a message about caring, cohesion, and the importance of us getting to know each other and recognizing our similarities and differences. At URI, we created annual academic summits during my time as provost. These summits designated a full day during the January break each year when faculty were invited to participate, present, discuss, or debate a series of topics related to a particular academic theme. While these summits were primarily about the exploration of important academic topics, we were careful to build time, sessions, and meals to encourage quality community time for faculty to get acquainted with their colleagues from other disciplines. See "Annual Academic Summits to Engage Faculty and Build Community" for a description of the events.

Annual Academic Summits to Engage Faculty and Build Community

Beginning in 2009, annual summits were held to engage the academic community in discussion of significant academic topics and to gather input relevant to the university's future. Summits were hosted by the provost's office and planned in collaboration with a faculty steering group. Typically, 175 to 640 faculty participated in all-day events, including discussions, workshops, and ignite sessions that featured the work of our own faculty as well as keynote presentations. Detailed notes were gathered and shared along with follow-up steps or initiatives. Academic summits became community-building and small-scale planning events; faculty participants spoke positively about the opportunity to engage with and get to know their colleagues and think about the future at the summits.

Some of the annual summit themes were:

- Academic Planning: Implementing a New Vision for the University
- Engaging Students in Learning with Technology
- Interdisciplinary Learning and Discovery: Advancing Cluster Hire Themes
- Rethinking Education in the Age of Technology
- Transformative Scholarship in the Twenty-First Century and Beyond
- Higher Education in the Twenty-First Century: Designing Our Future
- Big Innovative Ideas for the University's Future
- Academic Challenges for Higher Education
- URI 2035: The World of the Future and Our Place in It
- Research, Scholarship, and Creative Work: Inspiring Convergence
- Who Are Our Students? How Do They Learn?
- Anti-Racism at URI: Academic Curriculum and Pedagogy

Other Elements Worthy of Your Attention

Challenging the Status Quo

An important role for university leaders is to challenge the **status quo** and push the institution toward strategic change and continuous improvement. Universities and colleges are known for their programmatic stability and glacial pace of change, especially regarding the curriculum and the development of new learning outcomes relevant to a rapidly changing world and the future of work. That is why I refer repeatedly to leading a change agenda. We really don't need leaders to simply carry out perfunctory duties. Critiquing aspects of our current programs is necessary with an eye toward improving, updating, and modifying both content and delivery. One of the key roles of academic leaders is to create a state of **productive restlessness**. Restfulness, or complacency, undermines academic enterprises that depend on unleashing their intellectual capacity, innovative potential, and entrepreneurial spirit for their success and, frankly, for their resources. As a biologist, I know that universities must be evolving organizations—always changing, adapting, reinventing, fine-tuning, and growing toward a state of greater fitness within their defined niche. Our institutional leaders must lead those efforts by asking tough questions, pushing expectations, and challenging all of us toward continuous improvement.

Don't Believe Everything You Hear

Often leaders, especially individuals new to their role, will reach out to many members of the community to listen and learn. This is certainly a good thing to do. However, you should be careful and consider at least some of what you hear with a grain of salt. Some input you receive may be misinformed or reflect incomplete information or long-term beliefs that are cultural myths. Such myths exist almost everywhere. In particular, you will frequently hear from nearly everyone that they are underresourced, down some number of faculty lines, or that their dean, provost, or president doesn't understand or value whatever it is that they do. Often individuals will declare if they only had more money, they would be a great department, or if they just had more faculty lines, they would be able to recruit more and better students. While these perceptions may be real for the individuals sharing the information, they are not typically grounded in reality.

Remember, there are at least two sides to every issue. Hearing such concerns might prompt you to investigate the details to dig out some real data to either confirm what you are hearing or correct the misperceptions. I'll give one quick example to punctuate the point. A new leader on campus met with some faculty and an associate dean and heard that the college was substantially underresourced and then shared that information with me. We investigated the details and found that college had been allocated numerous positions that the dean had requested and had a $500,000 surplus in their budget. The individuals sharing the information were either out of touch, there was a communication breakdown within the college, or the exchange was an effort to lobby the new leader on campus for resources.

Stay in Your Lane and Respect Reporting Relationships

Remember as a leader that it is important to understand and respect reporting relationships as you venture out into the community to meet everyone. Let me be clear, it is wonderful and important to meet individuals in the community, and they will appreciate your outreach. However, there is a pecking order of reporting relationships that should be understood and respected. As a new provost years ago, every time I walked across the quadrangle, I was approached by faculty and department chairs who wanted to meet with me. I learned very quickly that these individuals wanted not only to welcome me as the new provost, but, more importantly from their perspective, it was an attempt on their part to work around their chair and/or dean to lobby for their priorities, usually for more resources, or share complaints or concerns about the chair, dean, or previous provost. Obviously, none of that is productive or helpful. I responded by making a commitment to the deans that I would not take such meetings without inviting the dean to join the meetings. Interestingly, when I agreed to meet with the inquiring faculty members with their dean present, many of them never followed up.

In addition, vice presidents, provosts, and presidents need to remember that we hire deans as the leaders of their colleges and hold them responsible to advance the college. As a former dean, I am very sensitive to and respectful of the roles and responsibilities of deans. We as senior leaders need to resist the temptation of planning new initiatives with faculty without the dean or chair's knowledge, participation, and support. Even though well-intentioned, such initiatives on the part of institutional leaders can undermine the authority, expertise, and effectiveness of deans and chairs. A member of the senior administration may be unaware of other initiatives in the department or college; and pushing an exciting new agenda can distract faculty and staff from the work they are supposed to be doing and create tension among the leaders. Frankly, this happens too often, can be very disruptive, gets in the way of institutional advancement, and undermines the authority and responsibilities of dedicated chairs and deans.

Exhibiting Stamina and Perseverance

If immediate gratification is a major driver for your work, then you will likely experience some frustration with academic leadership. Because of the complexity of many of the issues and the slow pace of change, especially cultural change, in higher education institutions, stamina and perseverance are essential characteristics of effective leaders. Institutions rarely change overnight. So, academic leaders need to be prepared to stick with the agenda or decision and allow time for the community to respond, adapt, and measure or observe progress. Pushback is inevitable. So, be prepared for critiques and try not to be defensive or dissuaded from doing what is necessary. Also, be prepared to fine-tune details as time passes because any initial analysis or decision, even if largely correct or moving in the right direction, will no doubt benefit from tweaks and modifications along the way. In fact, it is advantageous to state upfront with new strategic initiatives that adjustments should be expected as you move forward to adapt to unanticipated factors and natural evolution over time.

As we initiated numerous new initiatives to enhance student retention and graduation rates, I had to repeatedly remind myself, the campus community, and especially our governing board that it will take four to six years to observe improvement in the four- and six-year graduation rate of an entering class of first-year students following the introduction of new initiatives, although there certainly are indicators that can be measured along the way. Nevertheless, tangible evidence of progress, which is sometimes necessary to convince the community that the effort is worth the work and the changes are making a difference, often lags behind the implementation. Both the academic leader and the community more broadly must be steadfast and exhibit sustained commitment to allow the evolution of the impact of their efforts. Now, some thirteen years later,

we have observed extraordinary improvements in retention and graduation rates, and a culture of student success now proudly exists among
many on campus. Indeed, stamina and perseverance pay dividends.

Find a Way to Maintain a Sense of Humor

Effective leaders find the space to take their work very seriously, but not
take themselves too seriously. It's a delicate balance. A sense of humor
is an important way to express joy in this work, even during the most
challenging times, and to defuse tense situations that will undoubtedly
emerge, often on a daily basis. Maintaining a sense of humor is essential
to staying focused and preserving your own well-being while effectively
leading a vital change agenda on your campus.

Trust Your Instincts

This list of attributes and characteristics is rather lengthy. Don't be
intimidated by it all. Your own instincts will no doubt kick in and guide
you as you build trust and exhibit authentic leadership. Pay attention to
the details, but also trust your instincts and understand your role. Also,
know that all of us make mistakes and you will too. Responding to our
own errors in judgment with transparency, thoughtful communication,
and resilience will go a long way. Demonstrating care and interest in the
community will build trust and create some human capital for investment in the next issue that emerges from the change agenda. Embracing
collaboration is a way to create collective leadership to advance and transform your university.

Inclusive Leadership: Advancing Diversity, Equity, Inclusion, and Social Justice

Fulfilling the Nation's Promise of Equal Opportunity for Higher Education

Almost every institution of higher education in America has expressed a deep institutional commitment to advancing diversity, equity, inclusion, and social justice (DEIJ) as part of its mission, vision, and/or strategic plan. As such, DEIJ is viewed as mission-critical—an essential core value of those institutions—and should be fully woven into the fabric of all institutional operations, learning experiences, and individual responsibilities.

Despite eloquent statements about the importance of DEIJ and often significant efforts and investments, creating and sustaining truly inclusive learning environments continues to be a challenge on many campuses. Students of color on predominantly white campuses often feel marginalized, equity gaps in retention and graduation persist, campus climate can be unwelcoming for historically underrepresented populations of students, staff, and faculty, and experiences of implicit bias and microaggression are not uncommon concerns. Faculty diversity often lags behind student diversity, creating a paucity of role models for students of color and other marginalized groups. Historical reminders of oppression on some campuses may undermine a sense of belonging for some and contribute to creating a divided community. Reflecting on such issues, US Department of Education Secretary Miguel Cardona noted that too many institutions spend "enormous resources to climb college rankings and compete for the most affluent, highest scoring students."[7] In a recent article in *The Chronicle of Higher Education*, he proposed a new compelling vision for college excellence—"one defined not by privilege, legacy, and selectivity, but by equity, inclusivity, and real upward mobility for students of color, immigrants, working parents, adult learners, and rural and first-generation college students."[8] These are complex issues requiring an intersectional approach to address inequities relating to all groups and individuals whose liberties and safety may be at risk. There is much to do to create inclusive campus communities where all have an equal opportunity to learn, thrive, and succeed.

For the DEIJ mission to be realized, leaders at all levels of the institution must embrace this commitment; exhibit the understanding, skill, and mindset to adopt inclusive approaches to their leadership; identify patterns of inequity and injustice within their campuses; and establish and sustain actionable strategies to shape a diverse, equitable, and inclusive campus community. Indeed, following the thoughtful perspectives of Dr. Ibram X. Kendi in his 2019 book *How to Be an Antiracist*, such strategies must not only recognize and eliminate racist policies and behaviors, but also develop, support, and advance antiracist policies and behaviors through actions and ideas that eliminate educational inequities.[9]

The intense partisan politics and polarization in society today are a threat to efforts to advance diversity, equity, inclusion, and social justice on our campuses that undermines a key purpose of higher education in America—to fulfill the nation's promise of equal opportunity for all to higher education and full participation in the economic, cultural, and civic life of our democracy. University leaders must constantly be mindful of educational equity and inclusiveness and be diligent about ensuring these purposes are not compromised. It is not only in the best interests of communities facing educational inequities and fulfilling the nation's promise but also in the best interests of society more broadly and our institutions specifically.

Getting the Language Right

The language of diversity and equity matters so that the quality and impact of discourse and community efforts can be understood and enhanced. While the terminology is ever-evolving, the "Racial Equity

Tools Glossary" provided by MP Associates, Center for Assessment and Policy Development, and World Trust Educational Services[10] is contemporary and helpful for productive dialogue on university campuses. In the context of higher education today, it is important to consider an inclusive view of *diversity* that encompasses the many ways that people differ, including race and ethnicity, gender, sexual orientation and gender identity, age, religion, national origin, socioeconomic status, and physical ability, and to recognize that individuals may connect with multiple identities. Diversity also recognizes and respects different ideas, perspectives, and values, which are core to learning and critical to the mission of educational institutions.

Equity represents the fair treatment, access, opportunity, and advancement for all students, staff, and faculty as well as efforts to identify, recognize, and eliminate barriers to the full participation of underrepresented groups. Improving equity requires that we must first identify patterns of inequity that may exist and implement practices that enhance fairness and justice in institutional processes, procedures, and resource distribution, including student educational outcomes and success.

Inclusion implies intentionality in creating welcoming environments where individuals and groups are respected, supported, valued, and encouraged to fully participate in the community. For colleges and universities, inclusion relates not only to people but also to the integration of diversity and equity into the academic core mission, including curriculum content and inclusive pedagogy. An inclusive campus climate embraces differences, conveys respect in words and actions for all people, and creates value from the diversity in the community. Inclusion means empowering a sense of belonging for all and ensuring equal learning opportunities and outcomes on our campuses.

Social justice expands upon equity concepts to promote a fair distribution of opportunities and resources across society, including equality in learning environments and educational systems, and involves overt efforts to dismantle systems of oppression. Injustice occurs when race, gender, poverty, or disability limit educational opportunity. Social justice also represents an educational framework designed to encourage analytical thinking, broaden worldviews, challenge conventional opinions, and inspire empathy and understanding.

Anti-racism, according to Kendi, involves the work of actively opposing racism and any policies that produce or sustain racial inequities between groups.[11] In using the term *policies*, Kendi refers to "written and

unwritten laws, rules, procedures, processes, regulations, and guidelines that govern people."[12] An *antiracist* is someone who supports antiracist policy through their actions or ideas. In contrast to racist ideas
that suggest one group is inferior or superior to another in some way,
antiracist ideas suggest that "racial groups are equal in all their apparent
differences and there is nothing right or wrong with any racial group."[13]
Antiracists' ideas, according to Kendi, assert that "racist policies are the
cause of racial inequities."[14]

Inclusive Leadership

Our nation is facing a renewed reckoning of inequality and racism that
implicates almost every aspect of society and our institutions. On an
almost daily basis, we witness a barrage of incidents that disrespects
and endangers lives and livelihoods. The 2020 resurgence of Black Lives
Matter, triggered in part by the murders of George Floyd, Breonna Taylor,
and Ahmaud Arbery, highlights the persistent and pervasive racial
injustice within our society. Violence against Asian and Asian Americans is occurring with increased frequency, and there is a long history
of oppression of Black, Latinx, and Indigenous people and communities.
Gender inequities persist. Discrimination and harassment of women
and members of the LGBTQ+ community are continuing problems. The
recent Supreme Court decision to overturn Roe v. Wade further targets
women, including students, staff, and faculty at our colleges and universities, by limiting their reproductive rights and potentially compromising
their health and well-being. The COVID-19 pandemic has exacerbated
such inequities with disproportional impacts on people of color and
economically impoverished communities and has further surfaced
educational inequities and opportunity gaps in higher education and
K-12 schools. This is indeed a complex time in our nation. By committing
to advancing diversity, ensuring equitable practices and processes, and
facilitating inclusion that empowers a sense of belonging for all on our
campuses, higher education leaders can unite their university communities toward a common goal of equality and justice for all.

Placing DEIJ efforts at the center of the institution's mission, values,
and strategic goals is necessary and important, but it is not sufficient
to ensure progress in overcoming educational and opportunity inequities that exist in society. While it may be popular and relatively easy to
espouse DEIJ as an essential institutional core value, it is much more

difficult to institute and sustain a set of actionable strategies to shape and support a diverse, equitable, and inclusive campus community. As some faculty of color have passionately shared with me, "instead of saying things, we need to do things"—a clarion call for meaningful actions over eloquent words. Leaders at all levels must develop and embrace inclusive leadership; exhibit a visible commitment to diversity; make diversity, equity, and inclusion an institutional priority; and hold themselves and others accountable for progress. While there are many elements of inclusive leadership described in the business world,[15] the following set of core characteristics is relevant to inclusive leadership in higher education.

Inclusive leaders:

- recognize their own blind spots and biases and seek diverse perspectives to shape their opinions and inform their decision-making;

- are collaborators with the capacity and inclination to change perspective when given new information or a new understanding based on the experiences of others;

- view diverse talent as a competitive advantage and understand they must invest time and resources to make progress in creating an inclusive environment;

- recognize that their own privilege or position may prevent them from truly understanding the living experiences of others, but nevertheless benefit from listening to, learning from, and acknowledging those experiences;

- are culturally competent, attentive, and adaptable to the cultures of others; and

- ensure that antiracist policies and practices are institutionalized in the operations of all offices and that each unit understands its responsibilities in shaping an inclusive and equity-minded campus community.

Why Advancing DEIJ in Higher Education Matters

Removing barriers to equal educational opportunity and student success and nurturing a sense of belonging for all students, staff, and faculty is necessary for higher education to fulfill its societal promises and purposes. As such, university leaders have an ethical obligation to strive for racially equitable educational outcomes as well as an educational responsibility to advance diversity, equity, inclusion, and social justice in higher education. Simply put, advancing DEIJ in higher education is the just and responsible path to pursue. Equally as compelling, there are economic development, demographic, student success, and learning and cultural enrichment imperatives as well.

Economic Development Imperatives

Education can serve as a great equalizer to economic disparity by improving opportunities for social and economic mobility. To fulfill this role, higher education institutions must recruit, retain, and educate diverse populations of students to address the current and future national and global workforce needs, including developing in students the cultural competency to participate and actively contribute to an increasingly pluralistic society. Higher education institutions must leverage the talents of diverse populations of students to create a next-generation workforce steeped in innovation and respect for difference.

Demographic Imperatives

Demographic shifts combined with the already declining number of high school graduates across much of the nation highlight the importance of incorporating DEIJ as a core strategy for higher education institutions. Future students will come from increasingly diverse racial, ethnic, and socioeconomic backgrounds and first-generation college families, while the traditional population of White non-Hispanic high school graduates is projected to decline. To meet enrollment and revenue targets, higher education institutions must incorporate actionable strategies to attract, support, and graduate diverse populations of students, including increasing the diversity of faculty and staff. Failure to create a diverse, equitable, and inclusive community will have significant financial consequences for many institutions.

Student Success Imperatives

Increasing student diversity must be accompanied by greater accountability on the part of institutions for positive outcomes and success for all students. Retention, credit completion, and graduation often lag for students from historically underserved populations, which may be the result of previous academic preparation, insufficient or misaligned support services, lack of role models, or students experiencing a disconnect from the campus community and implicit bias. Institutions must track student progress by population, ensure that interventions and opportunities are in place to support struggling students, and examine practices and pedagogies that may impede progress for certain student populations. Such actions not only enhance student success but also institutional reputation and financial sustainability. Increasingly, measures of student success are reflected in accreditation standards, state performance funding models for public institutions, and revenue generated from tuition, fees, housing, and gifts. Ensuring that student success strategies are aimed at *all* students is necessary to sustain institutional vitality.

Learning and Cultural Enrichment Imperatives

There is increasing evidence that diversity and inclusion add intrinsic value to the learning environment and foster enhanced academic and cognitive outcomes and improved intergroup relations for all students.[16] Diversity encourages alternatives to conventional thinking, greater levels of empathy, and cross-cultural and critical thinking skills, and empowers individuals and organizations to adapt to changes in society.[17] These are key elements of education and learning for all students that contribute directly to institutions meeting their academic core mission and reason for being. Furthermore, institutions that strategically embrace diversity, equity, and inclusion promote a culture that counters stereotypes, minimizes bias, and creates an environment that respects and values difference.

Creating Resilient Communities

To many, it is intuitive that biodiversity creates strong and resilient natural communities and ecosystems that are better able to adapt and respond to disturbance. This concept is rarely controversial or challenged by students, colleagues, or politicians. Yet, extending the principles of biodiversity to racial and ethnic diversity creating stronger and more resilient human communities seems to frequently be confronted with challenges and discomfort. As educators, we need to grapple with why that is. Recognizing that humans are one species, racial/ethnic diversity in human communities encompasses the different histories, struggles, experiences, and stories that shape who we are and what we care about and stand for. Those human experiences matter. They offer different ideas and ways of understanding and addressing challenges and create the potential for resilience in human communities. Biodiversity also celebrates the uniqueness of individuals, which similarly interconnects with individual identities and stories and the intersectionality of multiple identities within each individual. I draw this parallel between *biodiversity* in natural communities and *racial/ethnic diversity* in human communities to highlight the discordant nature of beliefs and to promote the importance of creating and sustaining diversity, equity, and inclusion in our institutions.

Political Attacks on DEI

Despite powerful imperatives and the higher purpose of education to provide equal opportunity for all in America to learn, thrive, and succeed, DEI programs, curricula, and spending are under attack in many states across the country. As of June 2023, twenty-two states have proposed anti-DEI legislation, including bills to eliminate DEI offices, staff, and training programs or bans on teaching critical race theory or "divisive concepts" in public colleges and universities.[18] These proposed actions are a form of censorship that undermines academic freedom, informed civil discourse, and the very essence of our democracy, and they ignore history, racism, and bias aimed at minoritized communities. They also undermine student learning, exacerbate economic and health disparities, accentuate racial discord, and limit economic development and employment potential at a time when there is already a talent shortage in the workforce. Such politically motivated attacks on DEI are directly counter to ecosystem thinking and to understanding the interconnections of actions and consequences critical to effective leadership. Advancing DEI is not only the right and just thing to do, but it is also in the best interests of states to encourage opportunities that lift the prospects of their citizens through education at public institutions. Driven by political polarization, the attacks appear to be grounded in power dynamics, disdain for difference, fear, and a desire to suppress opportunities for others, although couched as pushback against political correctness run amok. As a nation, we must do better.

Advancing diversity, equity, inclusion, and social justice should not be depicted as a political position on the right or the left, but rather as an essential mission-critical component of the learning enterprise woven into the fabric and core functions of our educational institutions. To do so, institutional leaders must place racial and gender equity at the center of the institution and ensure it is incorporated into operations, investment strategies, and decision-making. This is in the best interests of our students, *all of our students*, and society as a whole.

What Can Inclusive Leaders Do?

Active Participation and Engagement

While chief diversity officers (CDOs) can be critical point persons for DEIJ initiatives on our campuses, inclusive institutional leaders should also be visible voices and active participants in DEIJ efforts. CDOs alone cannot be held responsible for the elimination of racial and gender inequities across the institution. Leaders need to carry the mantle and demonstrate their commitment through action. Participation doesn't mean all leaders need to be DEIJ experts, but rather willing and able to expend time, energy, and resources to learn and engage in efforts to advance the mission-critical DEIJ cause. This might include attending diversity-focused seminars, organizing and participating in retreats or other programs designed to improve DEIJ, and speaking publicly about the centrality of DEIJ initiatives to the institution's mission and well-being. Furthermore, while inclusive leaders may not be able to prevent discriminatory or racist behaviors or actions among some individuals, they can and must publicly condemn such acts of injustice, including following relevant campus policies and procedures for addressing such incidents.

Leaders might find particular benefit in creating and participating in diversity task forces or advisory councils to engage with DEIJ issues on campus or in a college or department and to explore ideas and initiatives for improvement. In addition to engaging campus leaders about important issues and generating input about potential solutions, active participation in such task forces demonstrates leadership commitment, highlights the importance of DEIJ efforts, and sends a clear signal about the leader's willingness to learn, identify, and improve upon their own shortcomings. This can be a powerful message to the community about the centrality of DEIJ work across the university.

Shortly after I became provost, I noted that most of the discussion and concerns about diversity issues on campus came from staff in student affairs and other parts of campus. At that time, those discussions mostly focused on increasing diversity among students, which is an important, but limited, component of the larger DEIJ issues in higher education. I recalled a similar situation from my previous institution as well. Faculty- and academic-related issues were rarely part of the conversation. To broaden the dialogue and focus DEIJ's attention on issues pertinent to the academic core mission, student success, and faculty diversity concerns, I formed an Academic Affairs Diversity Task Force (AADTF) in 2009 that was co-led by the provost and vice provost for academic and faculty initia- tives. The AADTF continues in full force today. The direct involvement of the provost and vice provost in the task force signaled the importance of the work and our collective commitment to make progress and ensure new ideas and initiatives recommended by the task force were imple- mented and tracked. Gradually over time, deans of many of the colleges within the university developed similar diversity councils aimed at recog- nizing and addressing DEIJ issues and supporting students, staff, and faculty of color at the college level. See "The Academic Affairs Diversity Task Force: A Shared Governance Approach to Diversity and Anti-Racism Related to the Academic Core Mission" for a description and some of its accomplishments.

The Academic Affairs Diversity Task Force: A Shared Governance Approach to Diversity and Anti-Racism Related to the Academic Core Mission

The AADTF comprises faculty from every college chosen by the colleges and key staff members working on diversity issues within academic affairs as well as the CDO. College faculty representatives rotated periodically so faculty engagement broadened over time. The task force met monthly for ninety minutes, although meetings frequently ran longer because of the vigor and depth of the discussions. The AADTF focused exclusively on academic issues pertinent to DEIJ, such as strategies to incorporate diversity in courses and curricula, inspire inclusive pedagogy, increase diversity among faculty, and address equity gaps among students in certain courses and programs. Perhaps the greatest value was the opportunity to learn from each other and develop a ground-level sense of the DEIJ concerns within the community. The AADTF also developed and sponsored initiatives designed to encourage a more inclusive community. The work represented faculty perspectives on mission-critical issues and provided a direct conduit to faculty governance processes as needed.

Some specific AADTF accomplishments included:

- developing a framework for multicultural competency and successfully advocating for a new diversity/inclusion learning outcome requirement in the university's reinvigorated general education program;
- sponsoring mini-grant programs to stimulate new course development and speaker programs focused on DEIJ issues in the context of disciplinary curricula;
- sponsoring faculty workshops on inclusive pedagogy and equitable learning that engaged hundreds of faculty;
- inspiring and supporting the development of a Diversity and Inclusion Badge offered by the Graduate School as a transcripted micro-credential for graduate students;
- supporting the development and expansion of the Distinguished Multicultural Post-Doctoral/Faculty Fellows Program aimed at recruiting and retaining outstanding scholars from historically underrepresented groups interested in tenure-track faculty positions;
- spawning the development of college-based diversity committees in several colleges;
- shaping the content of *Anti-Black Racism: An Academic Affairs Action Agenda for Change*, an eight-point action and investment plan to advance DEIJ across the academic mission; and
- developing templates for requesting language and an assessment guide for use in seeking and equitably evaluating diversity statements from candidates in searches for faculty and administrative positions.

I have participated in and chaired numerous committees, councils, and task forces at multiple universities and organizations. The AADTF is by far the most engaging, productive, and meaningful committee in which I have engaged. I attribute this to the importance of the work, the dedication and hard work of the members, a consistent focus on improvements, candid and constructive conversations about difficult issues, and the willingness of the members to learn about themselves and listen to each other.

Implement Equity-Minded Examination of Policies, Practices, and Outcomes

Inclusive leaders understand that increasing diversity in the community is important but insufficient without systemic efforts to advance equity and inclusion. The USC Center for Urban Education (CUE) calls for leaders to exhibit *equity-mindedness*—recognizing "the contradiction between the ideals of inclusive and democratic education . . . and policies and practices that contribute to disparities in educational outcomes for racially minoritized students."[19] Equity-mindedness includes awareness that racial identity, inequities, and power asymmetries influence opportunities and outcomes, as well as responsibility for eliminating such inequities. While presumably unintentional, some institutional practices, policies, and systems in higher education may favor or impact some groups more than others. Equity-minded practitioners exercise agency by analyzing institutional policies and practices that contribute to educational inequities and disparate outcomes among racial and ethnic groups and by developing solutions and support services to address equity gaps. Institutions, for example, must not only recruit and enroll a diverse class of students but also eliminate equity gaps in retention, graduation rates, access to majors, honors programs, and internships. As suggested by USC CUE and depicted in Figure 5.1, the proportional racial representation of the entering class should be mirrored in the graduating class to achieve equity, even if the total number of graduating students has decreased.

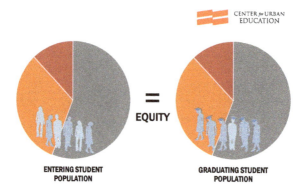

Figure 5.1. An illustration of racial equity in proportional graduation outcomes.[20]
Reprinted with permission from the Center for Urban Education (CUE), Rossier School of Education, University of Southern California

The COVID-19 pandemic surfaced and exacerbated many such educational inequities. The differential impact of the pandemic on low-income and communities of color, first-generation college students, and some, mostly female, faculty with primary childcare responsibilities became starkly apparent. The abrupt transition to entirely virtual teaching and learning during spring 2020 made clear pre-existing equity gaps in access to electronic devices, high-speed internet, and varying complexities of students' home living circumstances during the pandemic as well as economic and health stresses for some families. Childcare and school closures created unpredictable challenges for faculty navigating their careers and trying to maintain productivity in their teaching and research while providing full-time care for children and/or family members. While many institutions attempted to provide flexibility or relief by loaning devices and providing internet hotspots for students or extending the tenure clock for pretenure faculty, potential inequities were certainly evident, and no doubt persisted for some in the community.

Inclusive leaders ensure that every campus office brings a lens of equity-mindedness to the practices and outcomes of our programs and policies. In so doing, leaders recognize that identifying and addressing equity gaps is an institutional responsibility. This pertains to equity in administrative functions as well as academic outcomes. For example, the vice president for administration and the leadership of the human resources department should be held accountable for the establishment of and adherence to workplace, personnel, and compensation policies and professional development of staff that reflect a culture and commitment to DEI. Are our hiring practices and opportunities for the advancement of faculty and staff contemporary, and do they reflect the stated institutional commitment to inclusion and equity regarding race and gender?

Similarly, the athletic department shares the responsibility to ensure equity and leverage culture shifts and difficult conversations among student-athletes, coaches, and staff. Student affairs leaders should engage student organizations and leaders in this mission-critical work as well. This work might further include carefully studying possible racial or gender inequities in the admission process and financial aid allocations, and monitoring disaggregated student outcomes in retention, graduation, participation in honors programs, undergraduate research, internships, etc. With focused efforts and objective exploration, these analyses may surface inequities that can drive improvements. The targeted questions must first be posed by inclusive leaders who recognize diversity, equity, and inclusion as institutional imperatives and who are prepared to exert their influence to establish DEIJ as priorities deeply embedded in the mission, values, and strategic plan.

Bring Visibility to Inclusion

Inclusive leaders not only pledge their support for diversity, equity, and inclusion on campus but also ensure that the institution publicly recognizes the outstanding accomplishments of individuals from historically underrepresented groups as well as those from the majority. Whether it relates to selecting or advocating for individuals to serve as members of the board of trustees, receive honorary doctorate degrees at commencement, be recognized as outstanding alumni, be an invited speaker at college or university events, etc., it is important that the faces and voices of the institution reflect the diversity and inclusion espoused in the mission, values, and strategic plan. These individuals serve as role models to students, staff, faculty, and alumni and represent excellence and accomplishment in their life's work. For too long in too many places, the accomplishments of many from minoritized populations have been invisible and overlooked.

Bringing visibility to inclusion is not about political correctness, tokenism, or diminished standards, but about living up to the inclusion commitment espoused in our mission. It is about honoring the broad array of individuals whose outstanding contributions are awe-inspiring and worthy of attention, and about creating equity-minded teachable moments for the community. This is not an effort to exclude or slight individuals from the majority, but rather to ensure equity in who and how we select individuals to emulate as role models, especially for students.

Higher education institutions, and land grant institutions in particular, have recently begun to better understand their own histories and the Indigenous nations whose homelands their campuses occupy by formally adopting and broadcasting Indigenous Land Acknowledgements. While some may take for granted that they reside on land taken from Indigenous people, official Indigenous Land Acknowledgements honor the resilience of the Indigenous nations and First Peoples as the original stewards of the land. Furthermore, they raise awareness about land-based and environmental injustice, recognize the exploitation and genocide that took place, and awaken the campus community to its marginalized history and the active Indigenous communities in the area.

To be genuine and meaningful, a land acknowledgement must be more than a branding statement. Acknowledging the land is an indigenous protocol, and such statements should be accompanied by institutional policies, practices, and programs that offer support, especially educational support through scholarships, and recognition of the local Indigenous communities. Such statements and policies recognize the contributions and continuation of the First Peoples, represent the voice and empowerment of Indigenous people, and serve as a visible catalyst for DEIJ in the university community. See "The University of Rhode Island Indigenous Land Acknowledgement Statement" for an example statement and associated programs at URI.

The University of Rhode Island Indigenous Land Acknowledgement Statement

In close partnership with the Narragansett Indian Tribe, the University of Rhode Island developed and adopted the following Indigenous Land Acknowledgement Statement:

> The University of Rhode Island occupies the traditional stomping ground of the Narragansett Nation and the Niantic People. We honor and respect the enduring and continuing relationship between the Indigenous people and this land by teaching and learning more about their history and present-day communities, and by becoming stewards of the land we, now too, inhabit.

The statement recognizes the Indigenous people, both past and present, who have lived on and stewarded the land on which URI now resides and shows gratitude and respect to Indigenous people and cultures. The university has further established the Narragansett Undergraduate Scholarship for students who are citizens of the federally recognized Narragansett Indian Tribe based on that citizenship. In its first year, the university awarded $175,000 to fifteen students; an additional fifteen to twenty students will benefit in year two.

Furthermore, the Tomaquag Museum and the university have agreed to partner to establish a new Tomaquag Museum on eighteen acres of URI land adjacent to the main campus in Kingston, Rhode Island. The Tomaquag Museum, which originally opened in 1958, is home to an extensive collection of artifacts of Indigenous history and culture. These efforts acknowledge and respect the original inhabitants of the land the university occupies today, honor and support members of the Narragansett Indian Tribe, and reinforce an important part of the university's land grant history, mission, and values.

Make Time and Space for Difficult Dialogues

Conversations about potential racial and gender inequities are difficult and uncomfortable for many, including individuals sharing their experience of bias and those who may possess or exhibit some form of bias. Former Attorney General Eric Holder captured the discomfort and tension when he stated "people feel uncomfortable talking about racial issues out of fear that if they express things, they will be characterized in a way that's not fair. I think there is still a need for dialogue about things racial that we have not engaged in."[21] Further, he shared that "though there remain many unresolved racial issues in this nation, we, average Americans, simply do not talk enough with each other about race. It is an issue we have never been at ease with and given our nation's history this is in some ways understandable."[22]

As learning organizations, universities must be places where difficult conversations can happen in a respectful manner so individuals can extend their capacity for expanded patterns of thinking. Forward-thinking leaders must find ways to engage the community in dialogue about inequities that exist and explore ways to enhance diversity, equity, inclusion, and social justice throughout the institution. Creating time and space for dialogue that includes listening and learning as well as sharing and validating the experiences of others is important. Dialogue entails a two-way exchange of information rather than one party talking at others and can be focused on resolving problems or uncovering solutions. While university-wide conversations are important, they often involve mostly the "choir"—those who are already deeply engaged and who may benefit less from the listening and learning.

My sense is there is likely to be better engagement, impact, and meaning in difficult dialogues at the unit level, such as department, college, division, or institute meetings or retreats. For example, the president should hold DEIJ retreats for the senior executive team, the provost for the Council of Deans, deans for department chairs, and chairs for the departmental faculty and staff. In such situations, the players know each other, have a common bond and interest related to their work, and are more likely to follow up on ideas. With difficult topics, sometimes a facilitator or guest speaker may be able to prompt the dialogue and help build a bridge to stimulate more meaningful conversations. Some individuals may choose not to participate, but creating a forum for difficult dialogues highlights the importance and relevance of the work and the centrality of DEIJ work to the mission and identity of the institution.

Ensure Responsibility and Accountability

If DEIJ efforts are truly mission-critical and espoused as central core functions that define the institution, then campus leaders must be responsible and held accountable for advancing DEIJ in their units and across the university. As such, monitoring progress, including areas where progress has been limited, is important and must not only reflect annual head counts of diverse students, staff, and faculty but also include reports of qualitative efforts toward implementing process changes and potential interventions to address the identified issues. This might include disaggregating data to better understand and address equity gaps in retention, unproductive grades in select gateway courses, and graduation rates.

While leaders themselves cannot singlehandedly change the culture of institutions, they can establish a set of expectations of others, especially of their direct reports, to ensure advancing the DEIJ agenda is holistic and sustainable. Such expectations will have little meaning without appropriate measures of accountability on a regular basis. We certainly are accustomed to holding academic units accountable for other mission-critical productivity measures, such as enrollment, retention, credit hours generated, research awards and expenditures, patents, etc. It is responsible to do the same for DEIJ measures that are deeply embedded in the institution's mission and critical to the institution's financial viability, reputation, and position in the national and global higher education marketplace.

Annual unit DEIJ accountability reports are meant to be helpful guides that highlight the institution's steadfast pursuit of continuous improvement while also identifying areas of continuing concern where alternative approaches may need to be implemented. Annual accountability also drives units to focus on DEIJ issues pertinent to their unit and to ensure that conversations are ongoing throughout the institution, leading to a better understanding of racial and gender equality and educational inequities that may exist on our campuses.

As provost, I worked closely with the deans of the colleges to develop a standard template for an Annual College DEIJ Accountability Report that includes a brief college self-assessment, reflections, and plans for the coming year as well as specific information related to students, staff, and faculty, curriculum, and community-building. The reports highlight areas that we all agreed were important areas of focus for each college and the institution at the time. Given the priority of DEIJ in the university's strategic plan and mission, the reports are submitted each year as part of the college's annual budget request process and discussed at each college's budget hearing. As with other strategic goals, including those reports as part of the annual budget process is consistent with the strategic importance of DEIJ efforts and the expectation of focus and progress in this area. It also provides an opportunity for colleges to make and justify budget requests to pursue new innovative initiatives in support of their DEIJ efforts. While this template for reporting may not be right for every institution, the expectation of annual reporting allows you to mark progress and ensure accountability. See "Sample Template for Annual College DEIJ Accountability Report" for a template.

Sample Template for Annual College DEIJ Accountability Report

College Diversity Statement and Self-Assessment

- Share the vision statement for DEI from the college diversity plan.
- Provide college's self-assessment, including areas of progress and need.

Faculty and Staff

- Report on practices undertaken to ensure search committees are inclusive and have engaged in implicit bias training.
- Report on the effectiveness of strategies to enhance retention of faculty and staff of color.
- Report on the success of initiatives to ensure diversity in the faculty search process (e.g., selected "grow your own" programs, partner programs, distinct outreach efforts, and strategies for increasing applicant pools, such as utilization of the NSF Survey of Earned Doctorates).
- Report on the status and trajectory of diversity in faculty and staff in your college/unit over the past ten years.

Students

- Report progress on retention and completion of undergraduate and graduate students of color and recruitment of graduate students of color.
- Report on progress in reducing equity gaps in academic performance and retention of students from underrepresented populations.

Diversity and Inclusion in the Curriculum

- Report of the number of courses offered and credit hours completed within the College with explicit DEI/anti-racism learning outcomes and courses that incorporate inclusive pedagogical practices.

Professional Development and Community-Building

- Report on the extent and nature of faculty and staff professional development aimed at awareness of implicit bias, cultural sensitivity and competency, power and privilege differentials, and progress toward social justice.
- Working with the campus climate survey results, evaluate the climate, practices, and protocols of the college toward alleviating inequities in expectations, contributions, and responsibilities.

Reflection and Opportunities

- Reflect on progress and obstacles.
- Plan for next year's efforts.

Developing an Action Agenda to Advance DEIJ

Many institutions strive to increase the *diversity* of students, staff, and faculty, but such efforts must also be attentive to *equity* and *inclusion* to be successful in attracting and retaining individuals from underrepresented groups and supporting an environment where all can thrive. Most certainly, institutions need to provide a welcoming and collegial atmosphere that allows students, staff, and faculty from underrepresented populations to feel that they are equal, connected, and valued members of the university community. If we are serious about fostering a sense of belonging for all, it will require community effort and attention to make changes in some fundamental aspects of how we organize and deliver the teaching, research, and service responsibilities of our institutions and hold each other accountable for progress. That is, the *status quo* simply won't get it done. Students, staff, and faculty of color are seeking *actionable* strategies to advance DEIJ in addition to the spoken and written pledges of commitment and concern. Indeed, it is necessary to change the conversation and paradigm from one focused on supporting and celebrating diversity to one focused on advancing an anti-racism agenda and dismantling systems of inequity that may exist on our campuses.

While there has been intense political pushback in some states and school systems about diversity initiatives in education, it is difficult for me to understand arguments against advancing an anti-racism agenda. Simply put, it is both responsible and beneficial. Each institution needs to understand its distinct challenges and opportunities to advance DEIJ on its campuses, although there are no doubt common issues of concern at many institutions. As a strategic priority, resource investments will likely be necessary to advance an action agenda. Leaders must be prepared to make such strategic investments. Some potential action items worthy of the attention of inclusive leaders are discussed below.

Infusing Diversity in the Curriculum

We live and work in a multicultural society, and students must understand and navigate a world of diversity of thought, experience, and meaning. The curriculum needs to reflect that diversity. The curriculum represents currency in universities. Faculty have primary responsibility over the content and delivery. Administrators, however, can recommend and incentivize curriculum upgrades and have a responsibility to do so in mission-critical areas. There are abundant opportunities to infuse diversity, anti-racism, and social justice learning opportunities and outcomes into the curricula across disciplines.

In fact, one can argue that failure to do so may misrepresent full coverage in some disciplines as they exist in the world today, such as sociology, anthropology, history, economics, philosophy, political science, art, music, literature, and much more. There is room to weave diverse perspectives and inclusive pedagogy in the sciences as well. For professional fields, such as business, nursing, pharmacy, physical therapy, engineering, and education, one can provide compelling reasons for students to understand diversity and equity in their preparation for the workforce and their responsibility to provide service to diverse communities. General education programs should ensure meaningful learning about race, equity, and social justice for all students; graduate students too must learn and reflect on DEIJ perspectives, especially those aspiring to join the professoriate as future teachers and scholars.

There are also opportunities to develop and offer minors, certificates, or micro-credentials focused on social justice, DEI, or anti-racism that might be attractive to some students and their future employers. Creating more flexibility within curricula can encourage cross-disciplinary opportunities through streamlined double majors, such as business or sociology and Africana Studies, leading to enhanced learning opportunities. This is not about some form of "indoctrination," as the highly politicized attacks on critical race theory assert, but rather a responsibility to educate and prepare students for the world in front of all of us. In *Teaching for Diversity and Social Justice* and *Readings for Diversity and Social Justice*, Maurianne Adams and colleagues provide comprehensive perspectives on curriculum design, social justice education, all forms of oppression, and strategies for change.[23]

Unmasking the Hidden Curriculum

Higher education administrators and faculty need to acknowledge that there is a *hidden* curriculum that includes unwritten rules, expectations, norms, and behaviors that are not formally communicated to all prospective students yet are foundational to success in college today. This may include understanding college application and financial aid processes (including completing the FAFSA for students and families), SAT/ACT preparation programs, the helpful role of academic and career advisors, identifying academic interests and choosing a major, etc. Students from college-educated families and well-resourced high schools with college counseling and readiness programs possess "cultural capital" and often understand basic parameters that help them navigate the transition to college.

In contrast, first-generation or at-risk students from underresourced high schools and often historically underrepresented or immigrant populations have typically not had the benefit of such implicit messages, support networks, or experiences and may be disadvantaged simply because of their background or neighborhood. Thus, all students are not equally familiar with the norms, practices, and expectations of our institutions. Higher education leaders need to bring the hidden curriculum out of the shadows to ensure that strategies for navigating the college experience, career readiness, and higher education opportunities are equally known and available to all students. This is not a request to lower expectations or standards, but rather to provide extra support for students who by virtue of their background may be inherently less prepared to navigate the transition into college and, as such, to be

CHAPTER FIVE | 81

successful academically. Such support will not only benefit very capable students who may be less prepared through no fault of their own, but also benefit the institution by enhancing retention, time to degree, and institutional reputation.

Professional Development and Support

Advances in DEIJ will depend in part on administrators, faculty, and staff educating themselves about ways to better support a culture of inclusion throughout the university community. This might include providing anti-racism or implicit bias professional development programs for administrators, faculty, and staff as well as inclusive pedagogy support for faculty and graduate teaching assistants across all disciplines. In my experience, attempting to mandate all faculty to attend inclusive pedagogy or implicit bias workshops, while well-intentioned, may be counterproductive and suggestive of token efforts designed to look good rather than really encourage and guide improvement. Such mandates may also be perceived by some as a form of viewpoint discrimination or a violation of academic freedom.

At my university, we found workshops aimed at entire departments that might include disciplinary examples or challenges along with offerings from our Office for the Advancement of Teaching and Learning resonated with many faculty. The disgruntled individuals that pushed back at all costs were outliers and were not likely to benefit from programs forced upon them anyway. Formally recognizing faculty and staff excellence in contributions to DEIJ on campus will further highlight the importance and value of such efforts. Given the integration of DEIJ in each college's strategic plan, it may be necessary to create diversity coordinator positions, such as assistant dean for diversity, in each college to work with faculty, staff, and students on the implementation of college plans and to coordinate efforts and ensure cross-campus collaboration in advancing the university strategic DEIJ agenda.

Diversifying the Faculty

Given the demographic changes nationwide and intentional efforts on the part of some institutions to increase student diversity, many institutions have observed an increase in the diversity of their students. In fact, between 1997 and 2017 the proportion of nonwhite undergraduates increased from 28 percent to 45 percent across all types of colleges.[24]

Although many colleges have expressed commitment to increasing faculty diversity, comparatively little progress has been realized in recent years, and faculty diversity has lagged student diversity. In the fall of 2020 about 75 percent of full-time faculty were white compared with 55 percent of the entire undergraduate student population.[25] The mismatch between student and faculty diversity has potentially negative implications both for students and faculty of color, including a paucity of role models for students of color and a disproportionate effort on diversity initiatives and mentoring for faculty of color.

Faculty play a prominent role in the search and hiring of their colleagues, but most have relatively little experience with search processes. Leaders must ensure that search chairs and committees are informed of best practices and that extra efforts are made to build diverse applicant pools and fully recognize the qualifications and contributions of candidates of color. The stakes are high, and it may require formal training for search committees to ensure equitable review of all applicants. It is important to emphasize that conducting aggressively affirmative searches is not about lowering standards for important faculty or administrative positions, as some anti-diversity zealots might claim. Rather it is about ensuring a thorough understanding of the true needs of each position and the potential for each candidate to fulfill those needs.

Issues such as the academic pedigree of candidates or preferences for candidates with relationships with former advisors or current colleagues are factors that may create implicit bias against candidates from historically underrepresented groups. Search committee members, chairs, and deans need to hold each other accountable to eliminate such considerations in the candidate review process. Furthermore, leaders should create clear expectations that departments take overt steps to ensure a welcoming and supportive atmosphere for new colleagues, especially faculty of color. While faculty often control the search processes for their colleagues, academic leaders control the resources that allow the hiring of those positions. Given the demographic changes in the nation and the growing disparity between student and faculty diversity, it is time to transform search and hiring processes and prioritize recruitment, hiring, and retention of faculty and staff of color.

Building Pipeline Programs

Often challenges in diversifying the faculty are attributed to the lack of doctorate degree holders in certain fields, especially in some STEM disciplines. Departments and colleges at research universities can create partnerships with their graduate schools to create pipeline and mentoring programs designed to produce and support PhDs in underrepresented disciplines, including providing funding to support emerging scholars of color. Overt efforts to demystify graduate education and openly recruit promising students of color into PhD programs have the potential to create new pipelines with promising career paths to fill a void in the higher education faculty hiring marketplace. Recruiting high-achieving students who have had undergraduate research exposure, which is abundant at many minority-serving institutions (e.g., HBCUs), or who are graduates of nationally prominent STEM-focused programs, such as the Meyerhoff Scholars Program at University of Maryland, Baltimore County have a high potential for success.

At URI, we established a Distinguished Multicultural Postdoctoral Fellows Program to support emerging outstanding scholars from historically underrepresented groups interested in pursuing tenure-track faculty positions at URI or other institutions. Cohorts of three fellows are awarded each year in different thematic areas of institutional need with the potential for the post-doc fellowships to transition directly into tenure-track faculty positions. The fellows, who are recruited and mentored by departments, are given the opportunity to develop as a teacher-scholar, advance their existing or new scholarly work, and participate in personalized professional development opportunities, including travel support. Efforts such as these demonstrate commitment and hold promise to address faculty diversity gaps in selected disciplines and to increase the diversity of faculty overall.

Recognize DEIJ Contributions in Promotion and Tenure Reviews

If diversity, equity, inclusion, and justice are truly central to the academic core mission and strategic plans of our institutions, then evidenced-based teaching, research, and service contributions of faculty that advance DEIJ should be encouraged, valued, and recognized in faculty evaluations and promotion and tenure review processes, along with standard measures of productivity in teaching, research, and service. Faculty contributions to advancing DEIJ may come in many different forms and may be either a central or peripheral component of the professional work of each faculty member. The magnitude of contributions may differ substantially, but the message should be that there are ways each of us can have a positive impact on advancing the DEIJ agenda. Formally acknowledging DEIJ contributions in faculty teaching, research, and service sends a clear message that the responsibility for advancing the mission-critical goal of a more diverse, equitable, and inclusive institution rests on the shoulders of all of us.

Considering DEIJ teaching, research, and service contributions in faculty reviews is not without controversy. Some faculty view including evaluation of DEIJ efforts as a political litmus test or a violation of academic freedom and First Amendment rights. My sense is that there is room to recognize and reward the mission-critical DEIJ contributions of faculty without undermining otherwise productive faculty who are only minimally engaged in such work. Administrators and faculty should work collaboratively to develop mutual agreement on a framework for evaluating DEIJ expectations and contributions as well as establishing an equitable set of guidelines and examples relevant across disciplines. The University of Illinois at Urbana-Champaign (UIUC) has approved a requirement for all faculty to submit a diversity contribution statement for tenure and promotion.[26]

Expect Resistance and Pushback

I believe advancing DEIJ and an anti-racist agenda in colleges and universities is the right, just, and necessary path for higher education leaders to pursue. Despite this moral imperative, your efforts as a leader to bring about such change will be met with resistance from within and outside the campus community. This may be especially true at some public institutions that are governed by state laws, legislatures, governors, and policies that may reflect political partisanship rather than best practices, despite the tangible benefits to local communities and economic development of a diverse and educated workforce. There are many factions that will push back against any efforts to advance diversity, even though it is a prominent goal in the mission or strategic plan. One only needs to glance at the political attacks focused on critical race theory (CRT), even in states without CRT curricula, and attempts to disrupt diversity-related coursework and DEIJ training among faculty and staff. Even within campuses, you may be accused by some students, staff, faculty, or alumni of political correctness, "wokeness," viewpoint discrimination, or violating constitutionally and contractually protected academic freedom by advancing a DEIJ agenda. Such resistance may be exacerbated when resources are allocated in support of diversity initiatives and hiring, as some will claim that their favorite department, program, or project is a better investment.

Some individuals within historically underrepresented communities on campus may also express their frustration at efforts seen as too little, too late, insincere, an administrative facade, or moving at a glacial pace to bring about improvement. I understand those perspectives and the frustration. There has been too little change, too little progress at too slow a pace, and too much of the burden has fallen disproportionately on the shoulders of a small subset of minoritized faculty, staff, and students on our campuses. Inclusive leaders must stick with it, ensure that there is an action agenda for change that reflects input from the community, and make the investments necessary to move the agenda forward.

Leaders can counter the resistance by being honest, transparent, visibly engaged, and persistent. Call out those who are disruptive and self-serving. You will no doubt encounter obstacles; adapt, monitor, and share progress, communicate openly, and keep driving the agenda forward. The only real change that ever takes place in universities is incremental change—one step at a time. You can't let the naysayers, or your own sensitivity to criticism, derail the necessary work. Don't forget to remind yourself and the community that the future of the university depends on the efforts each of us is willing to undertake to ensure justice and equity for all. The important work to be done belongs to each one of us.

PART III

COMMUNITY STRUCTURE AND FUNCTION

It's All about People

In an ecological sense, a community is an assemblage of populations that exist and interact within an ecosystem. Each has a profound presence, function, and an array of needs, wants, and expectations. It is the interaction, however, within and among the populations that defines the unique and ever-changing characteristics of the ecosystem. Similarly, higher education communities comprise an assemblage of populations, including students, staff, faculty, alumni, and many external constituents. Communities have an inherent structure shaped by the roles and array of functions displayed by each population; yet, at the same time, dynamic interactions among populations change continuously, creating unique challenges and opportunities and distinctive niches for each institution. Indeed, our institutions are all about people!

CHAPTER SIX

Who Are These People and What Is Their Niche?

Sustaining a Spirit of Innovation

As university administrators, many of us may spend much of our time working with data and information, such as budgets, student credit hours, research awards and expenditures, enrollment patterns, retention, graduation rates, rankings, etc. Despite the importance of this preoccupation, I am convinced that universities are really all about people, their morale, commitment, and sense of pride and accomplishment. Indeed, our people are our greatest asset. Effective leaders must always be cognizant of, engaged in, and sensitive to human resource management because the human resource is the foundation of higher education institutions. *Successful leaders engage the faculty and staff by inspiring forward rather than imposing downward.* The innovative spirit of the community needs to be cultivated and encouraged to continuously bubble upward. If the spirit of innovation and creativity of the faculty and staff is hampered or frustrated, the institution's accomplishments and potential will also be diminished, including the students' academic experience. So, as administrators, ensure you are spending your time and efforts on real and continuous improvement, or get out of the way.

Effective university leaders understand the work in the trenches and truly recognize and appreciate the difficult and challenging work of the faculty and staff—the individuals that deliver the institution's mission to students, scholars, and external constituents. Too many administrators, however, lose track of who is actually doing the primary work of the university. To truly lead, effective academic leaders must find a way to connect with people—to nudge, cajole, create incentives, and, most certainly, remove disincentives to stretch the community to explore, discover, and address the most compelling questions facing humanity. Good leaders inspire community commitment to learning, scholarship, and societal engagement that matters deeply in the world and defines the academic core mission of our universities.

Leaders must also reach out and build partnerships with people at other universities, agencies, nonprofits, and corporations, and with alumni, donors, and legislators to complement and leverage the capacity, expertise, resources, and potential of the institution. Leadership is very much about managing and inspiring people, listening to their ideas and concerns, and charting a collectively informed path forward.

To inspire forward, leaders must also be sensitive to the work they are requesting of others as part of the change agenda and careful to not overburden the community with too many new initiatives at once. This should be part of the careful and active listening agenda for leaders. I was guilty of violating this principle in my first few years as provost. While the campus was engaged in an array of new initiatives, I proposed adding yet another one to the list—exploring the potential of implementing a four-credit curriculum. With both students and faculty overwhelmed with too much work, I thought the efficiency of a four-credit curriculum would provide a reprieve for everyone while allowing greater depth to student learning. It was too much at once and turned people off, rightly so. I was insensitive to the workload I was creating for others, which resulted in a missed opportunity for the university. See "Administrative Insensitivity and Mistiming Created a Missed Opportunity" for a brief explanation of my administrative misstep and its implications.

Administrative Insensitivity and Mistiming Created a Missed Opportunity

The campus was fully engaged in developing an academic strategic plan; the faculty were reinventing general education; and efforts to increase retention, graduation, and student success were underway. Then I did the unthinkable: I urged the college and faculty senate curriculum committees to explore the implementation of a four-credit curriculum for all or most courses and majors. After all, there is nothing sacred or strategic about the standard three-credit curriculum model, except that most of us are accustomed to it.

The concept was that a four-credit curriculum would enhance student success because students would manage four, four-credit courses rather than five, three-credit courses each semester; faculty teaching loads and course preps would be reduced, freeing up time for research, scholarship, or other activities. I had done some homework, and there was good evidence that the four-credit curriculum is both efficient and effective for students, faculty, and programs, but the transition is a lot of work.

Frankly, I was convinced it was the right idea for lots of reasons, but I quickly learned it was horrible timing on top of everything else already in motion. I blew it. While a few programs did successfully pursue this path, the pushback was immediate and lasting, and the initiative went nowhere. In retrospect, I should have waited until other work was completed, allocated funds to explore it thoughtfully with the faculty senate or an *ad hoc* faculty task force, and more realistically understood and articulated the transitional challenges. It was a mistake that created a missed opportunity.

Understanding the People

The complexity of academic ecosystems is a function, in part, of the plethora of constituents—including students (and increasingly their parents), faculty and staff, deans, alumni, donors, board members, legislatures, governors, and many more—and each has their favorite agenda items. While they all matter, it is neither possible nor prudent to attempt to satisfy the competing agendas and wishes of so many constituents and still move the institution forward. University priorities and investments need to be deliberate and aligned with the university's strategic plan. University leaders get to engage the broad array of constituents, build commitment to priorities, fend off the resistance that will no doubt emerge, find the necessary resources, and ensure that the university continues to make progress. At times it can be an unenviable task, but you just have to love the opportunity to be in the middle of it all. There are many internal and external constituents, but the key constantly interacting players that shape the academic ecosystem are students, staff, faculty, deans, senior administrators, the provost, the president, and members of the governing board. Who are they and why do they matter?

Students

Let's face it, students are the bread and butter of every higher education institution. Tuition and fees as well as housing and dining are major revenue streams for almost all institutions, whether public or private or with substantial or minimal endowments. At many public institutions today, funding from state appropriations pales in comparison to revenue from tuition and fees. Indeed, almost all institutions are enrollment dependent, although elite private institutions and some major public flagships may be less enrollment sensitive. The demographic decline in the number of high school graduates, the increase in high school dropouts across the nation, and the recent decline in high school graduates choosing to attend college have led to financial crises and numerous college closures and mergers. No doubt, that trend will continue.

More importantly, however, our institutions exist primarily for learning and discovery—the academic core mission—and students are the centerpiece as prominent learners who also contribute to discovery by participating in research, scholarship, and creative work led by the faculty. As such, the student experience is critical and includes student engagement in learning through their classes, internships, research and entrepreneurship projects, academic advising, career guidance, study abroad, and cocurricular experiences, such as clubs, sports, theater performances, concerts, and residential living experiences with peers. For traditional-aged students, going to college is partly about learning and preparation for a career, but it is also about emotional maturity, learning to make good decisions, making new friends, and, hopefully, becoming responsible and contributing adults and citizens. Leaders need to understand and communicate the full array of student needs and interests to ensure the institution remains relevant to its bread-and-butter constituents.

Student access and student success are critical to the lifeblood of the institution and require the attention and investment of leaders at all levels. To ensure equitable access, institutions need to provide viable pathways for students from challenged socioeconomic or academic backgrounds who may be the first in their families to attend college, and who need financial assistance to pursue a college education. Institutions must have a strategic and adaptable financial aid model in place to meet the needs of their students, whether they are recent high school graduates, adults exploring college opportunities, veterans, or active members of the military. To be clear, strategic allocation of financial aid is not only a critical institutional investment to support students and their families but also the most powerful enrollment management tool available. Without a robust and strategic financial aid model and careful attention to net revenue generated via enrollment, higher education institutions will struggle, and increasingly state funding may not be available as a bailout.

Institutions need to remove barriers, hidden or otherwise, that impede progress to students earning their degree in a timely manner. Leaders must play a critical role in ensuring an efficient, relevant, and engaging curriculum and instructional delivery while providing support to retain students and guide them to the completion of their degrees. This means focused dialogue with faculty and advisors about their responsibility to ensure contemporary learning opportunities. Careful monitoring of student credit completion by semester and year, retention, graduation rate, degrees awarded per year, and time to degree along with efficient transfer pathways and quality academic advising are helpful tools to measure progress.

Students too need to step up and take advantage of the extensive services available, seek assistance when needed, and do the work asked of them in their classes. There is increasing evidence of a drift away from academic learning as a focus for many students and growing questioning of the value of a college education. In my experience, most faculty are willing and able to help, but students need to reach out and seek faculty support. Although anecdotal, many faculty have shared that few students, especially those struggling in their classes, come to either in-person or virtual office hours. Some students, such as first-generation college students, may not be aware they should seek assistance. This is where inclusiveness and belonging efforts can make a difference. University leaders must ensure such programming exists, is effective, and reinforce to students the primary focus on learning and discovery. Perhaps some university leaders are complicit in supporting this drift from the academic core mission to one of attracting students with amenities and by over-catering to their desires.

The concept of students as customers and the adage the "customer is always right" is one that is deeply problematic and undermines student learning, maturity, and growth, and contributes to increasing fragility and discomfort with "struggling" that is evident in society today. Paradoxically, this increasing fragility, or lack of "grit" to use the language of Duckworth,[27] undermines a major component of workforce preparation that students appear to be seeking and that is necessary for their success in life, college, and work. In her book entitled *Grit*, Duckworth emphasizes that outstanding achievement is dependent on developing a special blend of passion and persistence, attributes that appear to be wanting in many students today.

As academic leaders, we need to recognize and address these issues to best serve our students' needs. We must acknowledge that learning is a two-way enterprise that requires a compact between teacher and student that each will do their part to ensure that meaningful learning happens. That is, students must understand that they are collaborators in creating their education. An education is not something faculty *give* to students, it is an outcome of students and faculty working together. I recognize that this may be easier said than done, and it will take time, commitment, and creativity—indeed, passion and persistence.

Unfortunately, during this time of deep polarization and economic disparity in our country, there is evidence of growing tension between student and parent expectations and demands related to curriculum and course content, grades, and pedagogical approaches, which are the purview of faculty experts teaching the classes. This emerging clash is unfortunate and needs to be managed carefully and thoughtfully. No doubt, the accelerating cost of higher education, the associated student debt crisis along with growing angst related to public health threats and changes in learning modalities resulting from the ongoing pandemic has only served to exacerbate this tension. (Note: In mid-2021, student debt in the United States was $1.7 trillion—double that of a decade ago.)

Finally, we are also observing increased anxiety, depression, and mental health challenges in many of our students today, which has prompted greater attention and investment in counseling services on our campuses as well as faculty and staff training to observe signs of danger or difficulty, such as the Mental Health First Aid program. Psychologist Dr. Jean Twenge, in her groundbreaking 2017 book *iGen* (referring to Generation Z), makes a compelling case connecting the wholesale generational transition to a world of smartphones, social media, and excessive screen time to unprecedented levels of anxiety, depression, and loneliness.[28] Also noting increasing mental health issues on campuses, Lukianoff and Haidt, in their 2018 book *The Coddling of the American Mind*, describe a rapidly expanding "culture of safetyism" among students, who may associate certain kinds of speech, book, and course content as making them feel unsafe and jeopardizing their mental health.[29]

This increase in fragility has led to students seeking protection from words and ideas that they don't like or that make them uncomfortable, which potentially interferes with their social, emotional, and intellectual development and ability to navigate the everyday challenges of life. This is anathema to a major purpose of higher education, which is to expose students to different perspectives so they can rationally and independently find their way to a set of personal beliefs. To some degree, our task as educators is to make students "uncomfortable"—to challenge their worldview and assumptions—while simultaneously keeping them safe. Whether you agree or not with the explanations provided by these authors, the issue of accelerating mental health challenges is well-documented and serious and does not appear to be going away soon. These books are an important read for all higher education leaders so that we might better understand this generation, more effectively educate and guide our students and our faculty, and better prepare emerging future leaders.

University leaders need to listen to students and understand their needs and interests. As both dean and provost, I created student advisory boards comprising a cross-section of students from the college and university, respectively. All interested students were welcomed. Often different students would show up on different days depending on the issues of interest, which was fine. The purpose of these advisory boards was simply to seek student input on emerging initiatives and hear from them about areas of concern and pride. I would provide pizza and soft drinks, and we would eat and chat for about ninety minutes or so about once per month. Frankly, it was always enjoyable and informative. To engage and involve students during the process of creating collegewide or university strategic plans, I also organized and facilitated student summits to solicit their ideas and reactions. The input was always insightful and helpful and was incorporated into the plans. Finally, students at most institutions are organized into student governments, which are typically run by students for students. As provost, I frequently met with the student government leadership and the academic affairs student representative in particular. I have consistently been impressed with the organization and work ethic of student government associations.

Staff

Staff may be the unsung heroes of university campuses. Their work is essential to the well-being and operations of the university but goes unnoticed too often, including by many university leaders. When things are running well, no one notices. When systems break down or are inefficient, everyone points fingers at someone else, usually the staff. We need to do better. Leaders need to address such issues, not by also pointing fingers, but by addressing fundamental systemic problems that exist. Everyone gets frustrated by ongoing inefficiencies or dysfunctional services. Administrators need to own those problems, devise solutions, and not simply look the other way or blame their staff.

In interconnected academic ecosystems, the work of the staff empowers the teaching, research, and outreach efforts integral to the academic core mission. Executive and administrative assistants are the first to greet an angry student, parent, faculty member, or legislator; maintenance and custodial staff keep our facilities open, clean, and operational; IT staff keep our complex networks up-to-date, secure, and accessible to the community; admissions professionals deliver enrolled students; health service providers and counselors keep our students healthy and safe; budget analysts stay on top of the complex and ever-changing financial circumstances and only get attention when financial matters take a turn for the worse; and, research staff members keep our laboratories and field stations running, calibrated, and producing quality data every day. These staff, and many others, keep our universities operating. Indeed, facilities exist to *facilitate* the important work of the university, but they don't function without the dedicated staff who keep them running.

It is especially important that university leaders understand their role in promoting and modeling a culture of service and building a sense of pride among staff for their critically important support roles in empowering the academic core mission. Building a culture of adaptive, agile, and responsive support processes and opportunities for professional development and advancement enhance progress in many aspects of the core mission, and will also improve morale, collegiality, and pride throughout the institution. Finding joy and satisfaction in facilitating a safe and productive learning and scholarly environment or streamlining an administrative process that allows for more efficient and effective operations is important and should be an expectation of our staff colleagues. Such a culture of service won't just happen on its own and needs to be consistently cultivated, reinforced, and celebrated by the leadership.

Faculty

Simply put, universities are defined by their faculty. Yes, many of us are fortunate enough to work on beautiful campuses with wonderful new buildings (until they become old buildings) or historical ivy-covered buildings of distinctive architecture. But don't be fooled for a minute, the faculty is the university. The expertise, commitment, creativity, impact, and reputation of faculty are the foundation of the university. So, we must select and tenure our faculty carefully and thoughtfully because the university's success depends on them. Students are critically important, but they pass through our world on the way to becoming productive citizens and alumni. The staff fuels the faculty engine of curiosity, innovation, learning, and discovery by facilitating important work. But without the critical work of the faculty, these beautiful places sit dormant, and there would be little need or motivation for the work of the staff.

Most faculty have dedicated their lives to studying, expanding their expertise, and creating and disseminating new knowledge, information, and interpretations. For the most part, faculty are driven by their curiosity—an innate desire or need to understand, solve problems, delve into complexity, and create learning in themselves and others. At successful universities, faculty are among the leaders in their fields, and it is through them and their work that universities become known for their academic expertise and contributions throughout the world. Indeed, faculty generate, analyze, and disseminate knowledge and discoveries. Most faculty are extremely hard-working and committed to their work almost all the time. It irks me enormously when I hear some outside the academy suggest that faculty spend just a few hours each week teaching a class or two. That is bunk. As dean and provost, I was constantly engaged in dialogue with faculty members about work matters at all hours of the day and night seven days a week.

As in most organizations, there is also a small subset of faculty who are not productive, which is disappointing, frustrating, and damaging to the department and college. Faculty are expected to carry their weight in teaching, research, and service; and the failure of some to do so invariably shifts their workload onto colleagues and reduces both morale and department productivity and reputation. Although this can be difficult to address at times, academic leaders, including chairs and deans, should not give them a pass. To the extent possible, an individual's work effort should be modified to take full advantage of the areas where they can contribute to the needs and goals of the department. If someone's research productivity is consistently diminished, for example, it is appropriate for them to be assigned heavier teaching or service responsibilities to ensure all the needs of the department are met and that all faculty are fully engaged in their university work.

In most cases, if someone's teaching and research productivity is consistently ineffective, that likely signals a bad tenure decision was made sometime in the past. Departments and colleges must live with bad tenure decisions for many years, which highlights the importance of careful and constructive evaluation of faculty and clear expectations of what is necessary for their success. Finally, faculty must remain up-to-date in their field and with contemporary pedagogy to effectively engage new generations of students, including understanding DEI issues and applying modern technologies to ensure engaged and impactful learning. The vast majority of faculty, including tenured faculty, step up to this challenge and, as a matter of pride and commitment, strive to remain current, impactful, and engaged.

While we often refer to "the faculty of the university" as if it is a distinct, single-minded body, it is far from that. There are many faculties within each institution, and the needs, interests, and personalities in each vary greatly. They are by no means a homogenous body. Faculty have different expertise and cultures that vary to some extent by disciplines, such as the arts, humanities, social sciences, science and engineering, health professions, and business, etc. Earnest Boyer, in his classic 1990 book entitled *Scholarship Reconsidered: Priorities of the Professoriate* refers to the richness of the faculty as a "mosaic of talent" to be celebrated.[30] Indeed, that mosaic defines the strengths and serves as the foundation of our universities.

There are also categories of faculty based on the primary focus of their positions. Tenured and tenure-track faculty engage in teaching, research, and university governance and professional service. There are also full-time faculty whose work is more narrowly defined, such as teaching faculty, clinical faculty, and research faculty. Faculty of practice bring real-world experiences to students and academic departments. Part-time faculty, often referred to as adjunct faculty, are hired on a per-course basis and may work at multiple institutions simultaneously. These positions are all critically important to the mission of the institution. In fall 2021, 56 percent of faculty were full-time across all types of institutions—a slight shift toward full-time faculty from 50 percent in 2011, but down from 70 percent in 1975.[31] Thirty-two percent of faculty occupied full-time tenured or tenure-track positions in 2021. At Research 1 (R1) doctoral universities, 73 percent of faculty are full-time compared to 61 percent at Research 2 (R2) universities; and 50 percent (at R1s) and 41 percent (at R2s) are tenured or tenure-track compared to 35 percent full-time and 18 percent tenured or tenure-track at community colleges.[32]

The amazing breadth and depth of faculty expertise along with the independence of thought are both awe-inspiring and challenging.The faculty is the university's strongest asset and biggest management challenge. One can pretty much count on there being multiple views and reactions from faculty to almost any emerging university policy, procedure, or initiative. As a leader, discussing, debating, and working with the faculty early and often is essential if you hope to get things done, and your job is to get things done.

I want to bring special attention to department chairs—the faculty leading each academic department. Chairs too are unsung heroes. They ensure classes are carefully scheduled, curriculum is up-to-date, annual reviews are conducted thoroughly and objectively, and they get to listen to the gripes from their faculty colleagues as well as potentially from their dean and provost. In addition, chairs teach their own classes, remain engaged in their scholarly work, and advocate for their department with the dean, provost, and president whenever possible. For the most part, they do all this important work in exchange for an additional chair stipend and a workload adjustment, usually a partial teaching release, so they have time to engage in administrative duties. While typically selected by their colleagues, some chairs reluctantly take on that role because it's their turn within the department or because no one else is willing to take it on. I want to acknowledge and thank all who have served as chairs. A strong chair makes an enormous difference in terms of departmental engagement and progress toward implementing a departmental-level change agenda. Also, these individuals often become future leaders of the academy.

I would be remiss if I did not highlight the built-in tension that exists between "the faculty" and "the administration" at most universities. Leaders want to lead, and scholars want to analyze, question, and offer alternative perspectives and explanations. Often this creates a clash. Shared governance gone awry can also contribute to conflict or tension in some situations. Faculty and staff and, at times, students will draw attention to administrative processes that are broken or inefficient and cause grief and frustration within the community. They then expect administrators to address those problems, which is not an unreasonable expectation. If those problems don't get fixed, then the faculty will roll their eyes at the administrator who didn't get it done. Chairs especially may think out loud about the administrative resource (i.e., the salaries) being translated into a couple of faculty or staff lines that would make a big difference for their department.

Many faculty also have long memories, while administrators are likely new to the institution or their leadership role within it and often don't understand the history of conflicts, initiatives that didn't work, or perceived broken promises by previous administrators. Such tension is not a bad thing or a good thing, but it is a real thing. In the best cases, there is productive healthy tension; in the worst cases where collabo-ration and cooperation are antithetical, there can be total dysfunction. Leaders must consider and understand that tension and make extra efforts to build trust and transparency. In fact, it provides an even more compelling reason for collaborative leadership, careful listening, and working in partnership to advance the university.

Deans

Deans are the leaders of each of the colleges, schools, and university libraries. They serve more or less as CEOs, except at the college level rather than for the entire institution. They get to manage people, space, and facilities, allocate and manage resources, establish priorities, raise money, make personnel decisions and recommendations, and listen to and act upon concerns, complaints, and ideas, both good ones and bad ones, from almost everyone—students, parents, staff, and faculty as well as the provost and president. Deans of some colleges will also be responsible for the management of unique enterprises, such as research vessels, field stations, performance venues, external partnerships, international offices, etc., along with all the potential legal and liability complexities that may come with those responsibilities. Most importantly, deans will lead efforts to develop college-based strategic plans, make decisions about resource requests and allocations, and ensure the implementation of plans and the advancement of the college.

Recognizing that resources are limited at most institutions, deans have specific responsibilities to be thoughtful in managing the financial resources of their colleges to ensure that investments are aligned with priorities. This means deans have to say no to some requests from chairs or other faculty and need to be prepared to provide an honest and respectful rationale for their decisions, especially when it relates to resource allocation. In fact, for a dean to do this part of their job well, they will likely say no many more times than yes each year. I emphasize the importance of being *honest* as well as respectful because it will be tempting to provide an excuse for a no decision that is not entirely true or transparent, such as the provost or president made that decision, or we don't have funds to meet your request.

In reality, deans must choose to prioritize and allocate resources to requests that are deemed most important and in alignment with the strategic plan of the college, such as investments in programs with enrollment growth, new academic programs, graduate student assistantships, or important areas of research and scholarly excellence in the college. Providing a clear and transparent explanation is important to reinforce the process and priorities of the college, even if some individuals might be disappointed or concerned that their favorite item is not a strategic priority. It is also critically important that the rationale associated with the decisions is consistent over time. Faculty will very quickly learn about other funding decisions that did not follow protocol and side deals made with certain favored colleagues or departments. Such deals create irreparable distrust and contribute to the tension between the faculty and the administration discussed previously.

Deans get to advocate for their college while at the same time looking out for the best interests of the university. When I first became provost,

I had a candid but respectful, I think, conversation with the sitting deans about the importance of walking that fine line and offered that the moment a dean's college advocacy undermined the university, they would be gone as dean. Deans must serve as dedicated university citizens and at times seize the opportunity to partner with their colleagues to build new cross-college interdisciplinary programs and/or research centers. While I didn't always agree with the opinion or perspective of all my dean colleagues, in my roles as both dean and provost, I always felt the deans and vice provosts were among my most important and informed colleagues. Their thoughts and opinions always mattered, even if I disagreed with them. In my view, the dean's position is among the most important in the university. Strong, innovative, and entrepreneurial deans are critical to building a great university. For that reason, experience as a dean is essential background for anyone interested in becoming a provost, and possibly a president as well.

Being a dean is a big and complex job, but it is also one of the best administrative roles in the university. Most deans, except for the dean of arts and sciences, get to continue to work as a dean in their academic discipline or field of interest and experience while simultaneously leading a major academic enterprise. The dean of the liberal arts college may come from a humanities, social science, art, or science background and has responsibilities to oversee programs that cut across all domains of knowledge from physics to economics to philosophy to music with all the unique disciplinary cultures that come with them. Yet, despite some extra challenges, it is still a wonderful and impactful role.

Deans are critical players in the university and are stewards of the academic core mission. They interact regularly with students, staff, and faculty as well as with the president and provost. As such, they need to navigate managing in both directions (i.e., both up and down) while keeping their hands on the pulse of the working surface of the university. Great deans are essential in creating great universities.

Vice Presidents and Vice Provosts

The vice presidents, vice provosts, and director of athletics each bring expertise in a specific area of university operation and are responsible for ensuring efficient and effective management of those areas, including careful investment and management of institutional resources. They are collectively responsible for creating and sustaining smooth and efficient administrative processes at the university and should be held accountable to do so. The vice presidents typically serve in an advisory capacity to the president as a leadership council. Vice presidents often oversee divisions within the university, such as Administration, Student Affairs, Research, Academic Affairs, Advancement, etc.

I struggle with the divisional construct because it implies *dividing* the university into components, which otherwise must function in the context of a *whole* or *unified* institution. In so doing, it creates the perception or reality of a win-lose proposition and competition among divisions for resources and attention, which, at times, spurs tension among their leaders. In an academic ecosystem framework, the work of the divisions must be highly interconnected and interdependent. Each vice president needs to understand and celebrate the many ways that their responsibilities and operations, such as housing, dining, recreation, facilities, finances, capital projects, etc., interface with and provide service to the academic core mission of the university. To punctuate this important point, the academic strategic plan of some institutions serves as the university's strategic plan with each of the divisional plans articulating support for both the work of the division and the broader academic mission. Senior leaders must embrace that dual role and responsibility.

Vice provosts not only manage a specific portfolio of work and programs, such as faculty and academic affairs, enrollment management and student success, global strategies and programs, and academic personnel and budget, but they also interface regularly and directly with deans and faculty, which adds another layer of complexity. When organized thoughtfully and effectively, the vice provosts work closely as a team with each other along with the provost and deans in overseeing and ensuring quality, innovation, and vibrancy in the academic core mission. These are complex senior-level positions designed to serve the central university mission in very different ways and are critical to the smooth operation of the entire institution.

President and Provost

The president is the chief executive officer (CEO) of the university and reports to and serves at the pleasure of the board of trustees. The president is ultimately responsible for all aspects of the university, including its most impressive accomplishments and its most persistent challenges. As such, the president must hold the vice presidents and provost accountable to ensure the operations within their purview are efficient, effective, and support the institutional mission and community. While the board of trustees evaluates the president, the president must also carefully manage the relationship between the board and the institution, which is a delicate arrangement. The president, in collaboration with the community, establishes a vision and broad agenda for the university and is responsible for ensuring the strategic plan and investments associated with it advance the institution and position it for a vibrant future. The provost gets to identify and manage most of the details necessary to make that vision and agenda meaningful. The president is the face and voice of the university to both internal and external constituents, including governors, legislators, alumni, parents, and donors, and is the university's most important and effective cheerleader and fundraiser. He/she is also the one who is under fire when things don't go well.

The provost is the chief academic officer and serves in two positions and capacities simultaneously—the position of provost and the position of vice president for academic affairs (VPAA). As VPAA, the provost oversees the academic enterprise, including the deans, colleges, schools, libraries, honors programs, career centers, etc., and ensures the strategic allocation of resources to those units. The other facet of the provost position is to serve as the right-hand partner to the president and oversee admissions, enrollment services, financial aid strategies and investments, information technology, and the entire academic budget that typically accounts for 70 percent to 80 percent of the revenue and expenses in the university's annual general fund operating budget. The provost typically serves as the senior officer of the institution in the president's absence. In many research universities, the provost also functions as the chief budget officer. With an increasing dependency on enrollment (tuition) as the primary revenue stream of most institutions, and responsibility for enrollment management in the portfolio of the provost, it makes good sense for the provost to serve as the chief budget officer. With such a model, the provost is largely responsible for managing revenues and most expenses, while the CFO is responsible for all accounting and other financial matters, such as controller functions, payroll, audit, and all matters related to bonding and managing debt.

Furthermore, the provost interfaces regularly with the leadership of the faculty senate and oversees the Council of Deans. Because of the vast interconnection of all university operations with the institutional mission, this dual position must interface regularly with almost all aspects of university operations. As such, the provost should be fluent and engaged in matters related to DEI; buildings, grounds, and facilities; capital projects; all aspects of research, scholarship, and creative work; curricular and cocurricular experiences of students; and the finances of the institution.

Universities are complex enterprises with a kaleidoscope of moving parts; the provost functionally serves as the COO for all internal matters of the institution. The provost position is steeped in complexity, ambiguity, and ever-challenging financial and personnel matters. Some say it is the toughest job in the academy. According to a survey conducted by CUPA-HR, the median tenure for provosts is approximately three years compared to approximately five years for presidents.[33] As provost for nearly fourteen years at a major public research university, I must admit I loved every moment and aspect of the work, including the myriad challenges. The provost gets to work every day with some of the smartest and most committed people in the world to steward shared governance, advance learning and discovery, and protect the heart and soul of the university. When the provost does well, the university does too.

Relationship between the President and Provost

The president is the number one officer of the university; the provost is the number two officer; and the relationship between the individuals in those positions is critically important. In addition to deep experience, impressive resumes, and a thick skin, the personalities and mindsets of the individuals occupying these positions should mesh so that the president and provost work in partnership. While the nature of that partnership will vary with the players, they often benefit from having complementary expertise, skills, and interests, and may struggle if their interests are competitive or overlapping. The president most often takes sole responsibility for all matters external to the university, while the provost is often responsible for internal matters, although there may be exceptions as necessary or appropriate.

The provost must keep the president informed of major activities and always understand that the president is in charge and has the final word on key issues. The provost must also understand it is their responsibility to protect the president, both the position and the person, to the extent possible, even if that means sacrificing their own position or best interests. The president, in turn, must *let the provost be provost* and resist the temptation to tinker with or micromanage the work underway by the provost office team or meet with deans or faculty leaders without the provost's knowledge or involvement. The CEO of a highly regarded higher education search firm shared that when a former provost is hired as president, the first piece of advice they often give is for the new president to unlearn their former role as provost.

The personality and professional relationship between the individuals occupying these two positions is so important that it is critical that the president plays an active role in the search for a new provost, such as meeting individually with the long list (often about six to nine) of semifinalist candidates before a final slate of candidates is invited to campus for interviews. There is no point in publicly exposing a very qualified provost candidate if there is an inherent incompatibility with the goals, needs, or personality of the president, which are very good reasons not to select them for the position.

The Governing Board

Board Roles and Responsibilities

University governing boards, usually referred to as the board of trustees, board of regents, board of governors, or board of visitors, are ultimately responsible for ensuring the fulfillment of the mission of the institution. As such, governing boards need to understand the academic core mission, institutional history, and higher education shared governance structures. It is helpful if the board is knowledgeable about trends and pressures in higher education as well, although often board members don't have that background. As emphasized by Scott in *How University Boards Work*, the activities of the board are determined by the powers, duties, and responsibilities delegated to it.[34] At the same time, however, the board must exhibit sufficient independence from government, political, and private sector influences to ensure that it is acting in the best interests of the institution, not its own self-interest or that of individual members.

The board is legally entrusted with the institution's care and protects it for the benefit of others.[35] As such, board members serve as responsible stewards of the university's mission, reputation, and resources, and act in good faith to protect it and to identify and manage risks. They have the responsibility for protecting the integrity of the institution's mission and reason for being, which is essential to all nonprofit boards. The board also has fiduciary responsibility for the institution, which requires it to focus on strategic and long-term issues and the intersection of internal and public interests. In most institutions, the board sets the tuition and fee schedule with input from the president and approves the annual institutional budget. In my experience, boards take their fiduciary, tuition-setting, and budgetary approval responsibilities very seriously, as they should. The board's role is to ask thoughtful questions and to ensure the institution is productive, affordable, living up to all aspects of its mission, and carefully and effectively managing risks.

Scott captures the overall role of the board to focus on strategic and long-term issues and "to protect the institution's future from the actions of the present."[36] For effective governance, it is critical that higher education boards discern the distinction between their fiduciary responsibility and role in university governance from the leadership and management responsibilities of the CEO, administration, and faculty. In addition, it is critical for higher education boards to function in a transparent manner and to understand and respect shared governance as shared responsibility for the health and vitality of the institution.

The Association of Governing Boards of Colleges and Universities (AGB)[37] has identified the following basic duties of higher education governing boards:

- ensuring the integrity of the mission

- guarding academic quality, institutional autonomy, and academic freedom

- guarding fiscal integrity (i.e., they have a fiduciary responsibility)

- engaging effectively with students, faculty, staff, alumni, and the community

- selecting, supporting, assessing, and compensating the president

- overseeing strategic planning

- assessing board performance, policies, and practices

Board membership is determined in several different ways. For private institutions, it is typically self-perpetuating, which means extant board members select new members to fill vacancies. Even in such situations, it is not uncommon for the president to suggest or recommend some individuals for the board to consider for vacant positions. For public institutions, board members may be appointed by the governor or legislature, or, in some cases, some or all board members may even be elected by the citizenry. For flagship public research institutions, there is an increasing trend for the board to include a mixture of self-perpetuating positions and others appointed by government officials. In such cases, those appointed by government officials will often outnumber the self-perpetuating members so that the governor or legislature can maintain some influence over the board's actions.

While there are likely philanthropic expectations for board members, board membership is a serious responsibility, and members should have interest, expertise, and commitment for the board to effectively carry out its responsibilities. For example, it is beneficial to both the board and the institution for its membership to include individuals with financial, legal, compliance, risk analysis, or management expertise as well as higher education understanding, divergent political perspectives, and representation of racial and ethnic diversity. Boards of many institutions may include a faculty and student representative, who may be voting or nonvoting members.

Board Effectiveness

Highly effective boards carry out their duties in collaboration with the president and senior leadership as well as with the faculty senate and student government organizations, as appropriate. Trust and transparency are critically important for all parties, and everyone needs to understand that the board has the ultimate legal authority over most matters, especially all things fiduciary. It is particularly important that the board leadership (chair and vice chair) and the president have a strong and respectful working relationship such that either party is comfortable raising questions, pursuing needed information, squelching misinformation, and ensuring the best interests of the institution are paramount. At the same time, as part of their oversight role, the board must hold the president accountable.

In recent years, it has become increasingly apparent that there are areas of potential conflict between the board as a body, or individual board members, and the institution that should be avoided at all costs. At times, overzealous or even well-intentioned board members may cross the line between their fiduciary and governance responsibilities and the management responsibilities of the president and leadership team. Such bureaucratic meddling and micromanagement are inappropriate, a breach of trust, and can be damaging to the institution (Figure 6.1). This kind of interference might entail trustees dabbling in curricular content, pedagogical approaches, personnel matters, or encouraging or even dictating certain types of research. Such behavior extends beyond the scope of the board's knowledge, expertise, and responsibilities and is disrespectful and dysfunctional, even if well-intentioned. Certainly, the board through the chair may wish to inquire privately with the president about matters of concern, and a determination should then be made if the inquiry or concern falls within the scope of board responsibility as defined in their bylaws.

"You know, I REAL-L-L-L-Y hate it when he micromanages."

Figure 6.1. An illustration of board governance gone awry.
Copyright Chris Wildt; Printed with permission from CartoonStock.com

Equally concerning are political manifestations that may emerge and influence board behavior or actions, which is why it is beneficial to avoid singularity of political viewpoints among members. This may be especially relevant when the board has been fully or partially appointed by a political entity, such as the governor or legislative committee. The board is expected to carry out its duties in the best interest of the institution and to be independent of political influence or persuasion. For instance, whether the board chooses to increase tuition and fees and by how much should be based on thoughtful and thorough consideration of institutional financial needs and affordability for students rather than the political desires of candidates running for election to political office. The latter, however, can happen, especially when board members were appointed or confirmed through a political process. On an individual level, every board member as a citizen is entitled to their own political position on contemporary issues in society, but when they vote as a member of the board on university actions, they are not voting as a democrat, a republican, or an independent, or as a conservative or a liberal, but rather as a responsible steward of the institution's mission and best interests. Violations of that trust are not only potentially damaging with respect to specific issues but can inflict long-term damage to institutional governance and even lead to the resignation of the president or other institutional leaders. In the same way that faculty should not impose their personal political views on students, board members should not impose their political viewpoints on institutional decisions, operations, or priorities.

Effective governing boards understand the mission, purpose, strategic priorities, and heritage of the institution, help steer the institution in appropriate directions, and position the university for a vibrant future. As an external body that guides the university through regular interaction with senior leaders, the board helps the institution align incentives to facilitate the effective execution of strategies to achieve the transformational goals outlined by the president. Among the trustee's most important duties are ensuring adherence to the institutional mission and vision, assuring academic quality, and supporting strong presidential leadership. For these reasons, an effective, focused, and engaged board is essential to the success of higher education in America today.

It's All about People

People are the university's strongest asset. Yet, often, leaders pay too little attention to understanding the interconnected roles, needs, and responsibilities associated with the many populations of people comprising the community of the academic ecosystem. As such, morale, creativity, and productivity, crucial intangibles that shape learning and discovery, can be compromised, which can undermine the soul of the institution. If leaders are charged with advancing the university and improving performance, then we all need to find ways to engage, develop, applaud, and care about the *people* of our institutions. Some institutions do this very well, but many do not. This became increasingly evident during the COVID-19 pandemic when many staff and faculty expressed angst when their hard work, sacrifices, and commitment were not acknowledged. I view this largely as a leadership problem rather than a personnel problem. When our leaders don't have the time, inclination, or skill set to attend to the people or don't understand or respect the importance and interactions of the various positions so critical to the university, then it signals we may have the wrong leaders in place. In a sense, this is about building a culture of caring and continuous improvement that we all can embrace, which will profoundly contribute to a culture of pride and achievement throughout the institution.

Collaborative Leadership Is Worth the Effort but Finger-Pointing Isn't

The Faculty Are Not the Problem

So, why is there almost always a layer of combative tension between the faculty and the administration, and what can be done about it? No doubt, trust or the lack thereof sits at the core of that tension, and a perceived lack of transparency feeds distrust. What else contributes to this tension, and is there a way to improve this situation? Lack of follow-through, inclusion, and communication are certainly contributors as is an inherent conviction on the part of some individuals that the other side is misinformed or lacking the knowledge to engage in dialogue or inform decisions. Certainly, misunderstanding about the meaning and power of effective shared governance and, in recent years, the ongoing challenges and universal fatigue from COVID-19 are also major contributors. As administrators and faculty, we need to find our way past this kind of thinking and action. After all, the university belongs to and is dependent upon *us*—all of us; we all benefit when the institution is on a path toward success and continuous improvement rather than mired in internal dissension.

In my many years of experience as a faculty member and as a dean and provost, I have observed unproductive, and often unsubstantiated, finger-pointing, ascribing blame, and criticism by both faculty and administrators. That is, I have worked with administrators who believe, based on both their words and actions, that the faculty are a problem and represent an obstacle to be overcome or avoided in the decision-making process. And, I have worked with and observed some faculty who seem to believe that administrators are bureaucrats who grapple with administrivia of little real consequence all day long. Some might even say that because the academic core mission—teaching, research, and service—is the reason that universities exist, those in the administration are uninformed, irrelevant, and naive about the real work of the university. Frankly, this sort of thinking and speaking on both sides is totally counterproductive, damaging to the institution, and perpetuates the tension.

Academic ecosystems are complex entities in their academic pursuits, financial position, operations, need and desire to be responsive and always improving, and interfacing with numerous external constituents. In reality, together we are smarter than any one of us, and we each bring different and needed expertise to the table. So, if you are an aspiring university leader, whether chair, president, or trustee, and you believe the "faculty are the problem," your perspective is short-sighted and counterproductive. Also, if you believe administrators know best about most things, you will likely find yourself pursuing some unproductive pathways and dealing with conflict. It may take extra time and effort, but engaging the faculty about critical issues and policies that may directly or indirectly influence their work is both essential and respectful. Similarly, if you are a faculty member and believe most administrators are uninformed and not capable of good ideas and that shared governance means you should get what you want or don't need to participate, you will be an obstacle to institutional advancement and undermine the community spirit necessary for progress.

What is needed are board, administrative, and faculty leaders who truly understand shared governance and who are committed to collaborative leadership—working cooperatively to create vibrant, supportive, and engaged institutions committed to learning, discovery, and engagement at the highest level. Indeed, we need a community of administrative leaders and faculty scholars who *understand that shared governance means shared responsibility for the vitality and welfare of the institution*, including the collective pursuit of an aligned set of strategic directions and priorities. This does *not* mean that everyone gets their way, gets to impose their priorities on the institution, or gets to make decisions for the institution. While this may seem obvious, getting shared governance right is a major struggle and limitation at many, perhaps most, institutions of higher education. Failure to do so can transform that layer of combative tension between administration and faculty into an impenetrable chasm that is damaging to institutional progress, morale, and the goals of the community within and beyond the campus. University leaders must consistently reinforce and align through their actions a model of *shared governance as shared responsibility* and set the stage for collaborative engagement and accountability with both the faculty and the institution's governing board.

Understanding Shared Governance

Shared governance is a hallmark feature of higher education in the United States and has been since the beginning of colleges and universities in our country. Despite its defining nature and long-term history, it remains a largely misunderstood and ill-defined concept to many trustees, administrators, and faculty. Shared governance refers to structures and processes through which governing boards, presidents and the senior administration, the faculty, and in some institutions staff councils and student government associations as well, participate in the development of policies and inform decision-making on matters that affect the institution. The concept as described is rather general, which invites different individuals, entities, and institutions to ascribe different meanings often in their own short-term self-interest (Figure 7.1). This lack of clarity certainly contributes to the tension between the faculty and administration, but it also provides an opportunity to pull people together in the interest of creating clarity and effective collaborative processes that emphasize shared responsibility for the vitality and welfare of the institution.

"We want to include you in this decision without letting you affect it."

Figure 7.1. Shared governance as an afterthought contributes to
the tension between the faculty and administration.
Copyright William Haefeli; Printed with permission from CartoonStock.com

In 1966, the American Association of University Professors (AAUP), the American Council on Education (ACE), and the Association of Governing Boards of Universities and Colleges (AGB) jointly formulated a "Statement on Government of Colleges and Universities." The statement affirmed the importance of shared governance and was intended "to foster joint thought and action, both within the institutional structure and in protection of its integrity against improper intrusions."[38] In addition to stating some common principles, the joint statement and endorsement by these three specific organizations, each representing the interests of faculty, higher education administrators, and best practices of governing boards, is especially telling and exemplifies the collaborative nature of university governance. The intention to ensure "protection of its integrity against improper intrusions" is particularly relevant today given recent emerging cases of some governors, legislatures, and governing boards overreach on issues, such as course and curriculum content, pedagogy, academic freedom, tenure, and interference with university leaders' management responsibilities.

While shared governance should be a collegial process that taps the knowledge, expertise, and experience of various groups to advance the institution, the full and ultimate legal authority and obligation over the institution, whether public or private, is vested in the governing board. The president is ultimately responsible and held accountable by the board for institutional successes and shortcomings. Despite this implied hierarchy regarding decisions and outcomes, boards and presidents should operate in a transparent manner and confer with the faculty, especially on academic matters or any issues that may have academic implications. Effective shared governance depends on full transparency, which leads to better decisions and builds trust and collegiality across the institution.

The reference to *shared* in shared governance means that the faculty, president and senior administration, and the board each have some responsibility and role in the analysis of university issues and ultimate decision-making, but the primary role, responsibility, decision-making, and accountability will vary. There are not equal governance responsibilities or roles for all matters under consideration. For example, faculty have primary responsibility for academic matters, such as curriculum, new course approvals, academic calendar, academic policies, and recommending student candidates for the awarding of degrees. However, even on such academic matters, there is usually an approval process that involves a senior administrator (e.g., provost or president), and new programs, departments, and colleges typically require board approval as well.

Similarly, the president is the primary hiring authority and evaluator for senior leaders, and the provost is the same for deans; but they benefit from engaging faculty in such reviews, outlining the responsibilities of those positions, and carrying out the search process. The board, as fiduciary, has primary responsibility for the financial health of the institution, hiring the president, and for all matters related to the academic mission, but its members depend on informed input from the administration, faculty, and broader community to ensure the institution is on a responsible and sustainable path forward. The framing of the institution's strategic plan is a truly shared responsibility of the academic community and benefits from the broadest exchange of information but ultimately will require the approval of the board. To be sure, boards have the ultimate veto power over most matters, but if the process works effectively and collegially, boards should only rarely exercise their veto power, especially about academic decisions.

The Faculty Senate

Most colleges and universities have a defined faculty body that serves as the formal representative governance voice of the faculty. This body is frequently referred to as the faculty senate, and it functions as a legislative body of the faculty. Its members and leadership are typically elected by the faculty, although in some cases the whole faculty may serve in this governance role. While at times faculty senates may get bogged down in details, debates, and internal disagreements, I have been a strong supporter and ally of faculty senates and have had productive relationships and enlightening experiences working closely with the leadership through the years. While all faculty may participate in shared governance, the faculty senate, as the elected representative body, is the formal voice of the faculty in shared governance. Academic leaders, including the president and board chair, should confer with the faculty senate leadership on a regular basis and respect their processes and recommendations. Likewise, leaders should be careful not to circumvent the elected faculty representatives and senate processes by catering to individual faculty members with their own individual agendas or concerns. Such actions only serve to undermine faculty governance.

Faculty Unions

While the faculty senate is the formal representative voice in faculty governance consistent with its established charter of responsibilities, elected leadership and membership, and structured proportional representation across colleges, faculty unions and their members also have a vested interest in shared governance processes and outcomes. Clearly, the national AAUP was a key player in formulating the joint statement on governance referred to earlier. Unions, in contrast, are primarily concerned with the terms and conditions of employment of the faculty but also may negotiate other permissive subjects, such as participation in the search process for the selection of deans. Union leaders negotiate legally binding labor contracts or collective bargaining agreements (CBA) on behalf of the faculty with their employers. These contracts typically include provisions regarding salaries, benefits, working conditions, hiring guidelines, review processes related to reappointment, tenure, and promotion, grievance protocols, etc. The provisions of the CBA provide the framework for faculty working conditions and can only be amended through negotiation and legal agreement between management (usually the institution's board as the employer of record) and the union leadership and membership.

Shared governance relates to many important issues relevant to shared responsibility and accountability for the vitality and welfare of the institution, including the quality and delivery of the academic core mission, that extend well beyond employment conditions, which are the purview of the union. The issues, however, can be complex and nuanced because shared governance may have legitimate interconnections with academic implications of provisions in collective bargaining agreements and union leaders may have concerns with employment implications that emerge because of decisions made through shared governance. Maintaining open lines of communication with both the faculty senate and faculty union leadership about critical or emerging issues will help clarify their respective roles and provide broader insight into potential implications and interests related to pending decisions. As provost, I frequently pulled together senate and union leaders to discuss matters of potential mutual interest and to ensure all faculty entities were aware of and informed about institutional challenges on the horizon. See "Informal Lunches Help Maintain Open Communication and Effective Shared Governance" for an example of an informal approach to building relationships with faculty leadership to promote shared governance.

Informal Lunches Help Maintain Open Communication and Effective Shared Governance

Prior to COVID-19, the vice provost for academic and faculty initiatives and I hosted an informal lunch once per semester with the president and vice president of the faculty senate, executive director, and president of the full-time faculty union (AAUP). The six of us had lunch together in an unstructured setting each semester without a formal agenda. The purposes of these meetings were for any of us to ask questions, learn about issues and concerns, share ideas informally and seek input, and, perhaps most importantly, get to know each other in a collaborative and noncontroversial setting. While none of us knew what issues might be raised, there was always goodwill, never an attempt at a gotcha moment, and frequently a request for clarification about myths or rumors that were bubbling up in the community. The vice provost and I became informed about rumors and were usually able to address them directly before they became widespread. While initially intended to encourage open communication between the provost's office and the faculty leadership, these meetings also created opportunities for communication between the faculty senate and union leadership, who otherwise were not always in regular contact with each other. This small investment of time and resources laid the groundwork for shared governance as we all learned to understand and communicate in an informal setting, which was helpful when we needed to converse about areas of disagreement or during crises.

Student Government and Staff Council

While students and staff may not have a formally recognized role in shared governance at many institutions, they too have an interest in university policies and decisions on certain issues. Beyond the tripartite model of shared governance involving the board, the president and senior administration and faculty, institutional leaders should seek input on relevant issues from students and staff. In most institutions, students are formally organized through bodies referred to as the student government, the student government association, or the student senate. Separate governance structures often exist for undergraduate and graduate students. While they vary widely in their configuration and influence on policy, student governments typically elect their own leaders, form committees to carry out their business, and represent the interests and concerns of the student body about issues of importance to students. In

addition to sponsoring campus events and programs, the student government also recommends or appoints students to serve on institution-wide
committees, including student, faculty, and administrative committees
and, in some cases, student representatives on the board of trustees.
Similarly, on some campuses, staff organizations, often called the staff
council, facilitate communication between the staff and institutional
leaders and represent the voice of the staff on key issues.

At many institutions, staff members are also unionized. In situations
where unions represent academic staff, such as research assistants
and scientists, these unions may also have some formal or informal say
regarding the academic enterprise. Furthermore, graduate assistants,
postdoctoral fellows, medical residents, and even undergraduate student
workers are increasingly unionizing and may represent the largest cohort
of newly unionized workers in the country.

Breaches of Shared Governance Can Lead to Votes of No Confidence

Votes of no confidence are important symbolic statements, usually from
the faculty through the faculty senate, expressing dissatisfaction and
lack of trust in university leaders, usually the president or chancellor,
but they could also be aimed at the provost, a dean, or the board of
trustees. At times, students through the student government may join
in expressing their dissatisfaction with the university leadership. Such
votes often trigger local debate about whether the formal expression of
no confidence is an overreaction of an overzealous faculty or a reflection
of leaders that have lost trust. While each situation relates to specific
institutional details, no-confidence votes mostly reflect a breach of shared
governance, at times including perceived mismanagement of financial
issues. Citing data gathered by McKinniss, a recent article in *The Chronicle of Higher Education* emphasized that no-confidence votes are usually
not a response to a single bad action by leaders, but rather the culmina-
tion of extended dissatisfaction that has festered over time.[39] Unfortunately, votes of no confidence are on the rise with seven of the past eight
years recording the highest number of such votes, including the highest
number ever in 2021.

Votes of no confidence are not only damaging to the leaders targeted
but to the institution as well. Such public expressions of dissent represent a public relations challenge and signal internal dissatisfaction to

prospective and extant students, staff, and faculty with the institution's leadership and potentially an uninviting culture and climate. Such votes can result in public scrutiny of the institution by parents, alumni, donors, and legislatures as well. While votes of no confidence do not have any binding power or automatic consequences for individual leaders, an analysis of more than 235 no-confidence votes since 1989 reveals that approximately half of the presidents receiving votes of no confidence leave office for some reason within a year of the vote.[40]

The rise in the number of no-confidence votes in recent years, which may be exacerbated by pandemic-related decision-making or anxiety, should be a wake-up call to universities. It signals the need for even greater attention to effective shared governance, transparency, clear communication, and collaborative approaches to leadership. Presidents should be committed to collaborative leadership and in close communication and agreement with the provost on the importance of communication and consultation with faculty bodies. As many presidents become more actively engaged externally with political leaders, legislatures, alumni, and donors, some have become less attentive to the voice and concerns of the faculty and staff, including faculty senates and unions. Given the potential institutional and reputational damage from no-confidence votes, efforts should be made by both the administration and faculty to conduct university business through transparent shared governance approaches so that votes of no confidence represent a rare last resort expression of dissent when all other efforts have failed.

Working with the Faculty Senate to Improve Shared Governance

Shared governance is a distinctive and important component of colleges and universities. It is not going to go away nor should it. So, we all need to work harder to make it work better. In fact, it may be even more important today than in the past given the enrollment, financial, and political challenges institutions are facing and the polarization in society about the value, meaning, and cost of a college education. Responding to such challenges will benefit from the collective input and collaboration among faculty, administrators, and the governing board. In response to external political pressures challenging shared governance and academic freedom, there is value in establishing collaborative coalitions of faculty, staff, students, and administrators to reinforce institutional values.

It is in the best interests of the institution, including the faculty, the president and senior leaders, and the board to have a strong, efficient, and collegial faculty senate. Doing so will require institutional investment of time and resources as well as respect for the senate and its processes. A unified faculty senate capable of thoughtful and bold collective action is critical to governance built on shared responsibility. Because some actively engaged and highly productive faculty refrain from active participation in faculty senates and unions, one of the biggest challenges is getting broad-based faculty participation at the highest level of shared governance. At some institutions, faculty senates and union leaders can be dominated by a relatively small subset of "career faculty politicians" who repeatedly cycle through these leadership positions. This subset may not represent the contemporary views or interests of the emerging generation of faculty scholars and sometimes takes on these duties for the wrong reasons, such as campus politics interests or for the workload adjustments that they may provide. While administrators do not and should not play a formal role in the selection of faculty senators and leaders, they can highlight the importance of the faculty voice expressed through the senate, bring attention to impactful senate contributions, and encourage active participation of faculty scholars across the spectrum of seniority and academic disciplines.

I recommend that university leaders consider the following steps to reinforce shared governance through the faculty senate:

- Communicate openly and frequently about the importance of shared governance as a joint responsibility and the important and primary role of the senate in faculty governance.

- Attend senate meetings and participate as appropriate and when invited to do so.

- Publicly recognize the elected leadership of the faculty senate— the president, vice president, and executive committee—as the leadership of the faculty and seek their perspective on important institutional matters.

- While everyone is busy, meet regularly with senate leaders. When I was provost, the vice provost for academic and faculty initiatives and I met each month with the senate president and vice president, with the entire executive committee, and we also attended each monthly faculty senate meeting and fully participated.

- Strategically deploy resources to areas that will strengthen the efficiency and effectiveness of the work of the faculty senate. This might include, for example, some partial summer salary for executive committee members to meet over the summer about time-sensitive matters or selected software purchases to enhance the efficiency of course review processes.

- Ensure senate representation on critical standing administrative committees and *ad hoc* task forces. We were careful to include four of the six executive committee members on the university joint committee on academic planning (JCAP), the president of the faculty senate and other faculty on the strategic budget and planning council, and a faculty representative on the board of trustees.

- Involve senate leadership and/or committees in the review process for proposed new policies and initiatives and ensure that such involvement is not simply *pro forma* after decisions have been made or policies are implemented.

- Collectively establish ground rules as to how the administration will interface with the senate leadership during emergencies or times of crisis when decisions must be made quickly and inform the senate leadership in advance of emerging issues and proposed decisions. We did this frequently during COVID and our partnerships with both the faculty senate and AAUP leadership were helpful, productive, and appreciated by all.

- Ensure that senate leaders or committee chairs are invited to participate, as appropriate, and are welcome to attend meetings of the board or board committees. This provides recognition of their work and collaborative role in governance.

- Regularly engage the leadership of the board, the administration, and the faculty senate to reinforce the differential roles and responsibilities of each entity regarding governance, management, and academic decision-making.

With the increased polarization in society and politicization of higher education evident today, it is increasingly important for boards to understand their governance roles and responsibilities and differentiate them from the administration's management responsibilities and the faculty's

CHAPTER SEVEN | 125

academic and curriculum roles. Whether well-intentioned or deliberate attempts to exercise power, there is increased evidence in recent years of trustees drifting or, at times, jumping headfirst into matters that are the predominant purview of the senior administration and/or faculty. Universities are not corporate entities. Such top-down authority defies the core principle of shared responsibility and triggers distrust that can have long-term negative consequences—exactly the opposite of the board's primary responsibility for protecting the integrity of the institution's mission. The board must trust the president to run the university and the faculty to have predominant authority over the curriculum and academic matters, knowing fully that they have veto power as a last resort if these parties act irresponsibly. Board micromanagement, especially when politically motivated, creates dysfunction and undermines shared governance and the very essence of collaborative leadership.

While the practices outlined above take time and attention, they are mostly straightforward and not hard to do. Yet, such practices profoundly acknowledge and reinforce the partnership, collective action, and shared responsibility among the faculty, administration, and board for the vitality and welfare of the institution. In addition, such practices build trust and mutual respect needed during difficult times, and there will always be difficult times. It takes time and effort to create a culture of shared governance and collaborative leadership at our colleges and universities; it is an investment worth making.

CHAPTER EIGHT

Acquiring and Investing in Talent

Cultivating Talent—The Details Matter

If universities are all about people, then acquiring and investing in talented people is essential and may be the most important thing we do. This is true for students, staff, faculty, and administrators. We recruit talented undergraduate and graduate students through various outreach mechanisms, such as advertising, marketing, social media platforms, videos, campus tours and events, and interactions with individual faculty and staff. Students apply for admission and are accepted if their application and potential for success at the institution meet or exceed expectations or admission standards. Most other personnel are acquired, or hired, through search processes involving a hiring officer, who might be the chair, dean, vice president, provost, or president depending on the nature of the position, and a search committee.

As people-centric organizations, the reputation, productivity, and financial viability of universities depend on attracting and retaining the most talented faculty, staff, and administrators, and there is intense competition with other institutions for the most talented individuals. Talent is the core resource that resides in the center of the community within academic ecosystems. Hence, the search process and search committee members that uncover that talent are critically important and worthy of careful attention. Despite this, know right from the start that searching for talent is an imperfect process that does not always lead to the best candidate. Nevertheless, using search committees, sometimes with assistance from search consulting firms, is how we identify and hopefully hire talented faculty and staff colleagues who will serve the institution for many years.

In my experience, administrators are often rather cavalier about the importance of the role and composition of search committees and offering thoughtful guidance to the committee throughout the search process to increase the likelihood that a talented and diverse pool of excellent finalists emerges. Failure to pay careful attention to details can easily compromise the quality of the final pool and the search process itself. Think about it for a moment. Based on their collective review and evaluation, the search committee will eliminate most applicants, organize the campus interview process, design a process for and compile evaluative input from the community, and submit a summary evaluation report of the finalists to the hiring officer. Their role is enormous, and leaders interested in hiring talent and promoting diversity must provide clear guidelines to the search committee and pay attention to the details. Too often, they don't.

The Search Process and Search Committee

Search committees may not realize it at the outset, but they wield tremendous power and have significant responsibilities in the hiring process. Some may initially think that they have simply been appointed to yet another committee or given an additional service responsibility. If any members express that concern, you appointed the wrong people to the committee. Search committee members will review several dozen or perhaps hundreds of applications and narrow the pool down to three or four finalists to be interviewed on campus. This will not only take serious time, organization, and effort, but it is also a major responsibility for discerning talent and the potential of candidates who will become their colleagues. Invariably, the hiring officer, the unit leader, will appoint the search committee chair and most members and will produce a fine-tuned penultimate draft of the position description that outlines the essential responsibilities of the position and the required and preferred credentials of applicants.

The committee chair should have a good understanding of search processes, the position essentials, and the skill and wherewithal to lead the committee through a fair process of reviewing applications and identifying talent. The chair must also be willing and able to halt any political maneuvering that might take place, such as senior members or administrators attempting to assert undue position influence on a committee with more junior members. This might be especially important in searches that attract internal candidates with whom some members may have either positive or negative biases.

The search committee should include a diverse array of dedicated individuals, often including undergraduate and/or graduate students, willing and able to put time and effort into what may be the single most important task in the university—hiring talented people who may be contributing members of the university community for thirty to forty years. In some institutions, collective bargaining agreements or faculty bylaws may also stipulate processes for selecting some search committee members for faculty or administrative searches. Diversity among members asked to serve should reflect ethnicity and gender, a wide representation of disciplines or subdisciplines, and individuals who will bring a diversity of perspectives. Ensuring ethnic and gender diversity in the candidate pool, however, must be the responsibility of the entire committee and not rest on the shoulders of a few diverse individuals.

Charging Search Committees

As dean charging search committees for faculty positions and as provost charging search committees for dean, vice provost, or vice president positions, I have always presented a written charge to the committee. It is important to provide a written charge so that the chair, committee members, and the hiring officer can refer to the charge later if, or more realistically when, process questions, concerns, or disagreements arise during the review and elimination of applicants or preparation of the committee's final report. Such questions almost certainly arise. In my view, the charge should state clearly that the committee is to submit an unranked list of acceptable candidates with a summary of attributes and potential shortcomings or questions about each finalist as well as laying out details of the search planning process. Typically, it is expected that the search committee submits to the hiring officer no fewer than two and more likely three or four finalists deemed acceptable based on the review process. The charge should also make clear that the committee should organize the campus visits for finalists and seek evaluative input from faculty, staff, students, and others, as appropriate, and that input should be summarized and included in their final report.

As the hiring officer, I also meet with each search committee to discuss the charge, answer questions, remind them of the importance of the work they are about to undertake, and highlight potential "traps" in their review of candidates, such as institutional pedigree, sub-disciplinary biases, possible attraction to candidates that look like them, and the importance of maintaining the confidentiality of candidate information. With respect to confidentiality, I specifically highlight that search committee members must refrain from reaching out to colleagues about the attributes of candidates and reassure them that my office will perform due diligence off-list reference checking with the candidate's permission before any offer is made. The committee needs to understand that they are both evaluating the viability of candidates and recruiting them to the university. So, they simultaneously serve as rigorous reviewers and institutional cheerleaders.

Promoting Diversity, Equity, and Inclusion

It is essential to consistently reinforce the importance of generating diverse applicant pools and carefully considering diverse candidates in alignment with the primary institutional strategic goal of enhancing the diversity of the university workforce. Search committees should form an explicit plan for developing a diverse applicant pool, including an active recruitment strategy and outreach to professional organizations and institutions that especially serve underrepresented populations, such as HBCUs and HSIs. For faculty searches, I ask that search committees review the *Survey of Earned Doctorates*[41] report sponsored by the National Center for Science and Engineering Statistics (NCSES) within the National Science Foundation and by three other federal agencies (NIH, DOE, and NEH). This survey monitors the number of doctoral degrees awarded by discipline and subfield and the number of underrepresented minorities and women receiving doctorates in each subfield. As such, it provides pertinent information as to the potential availability of diverse candidates, which can provide an approximate target for diversity in the applicant pool relevant to each faculty search. This database is a valuable tool to guide the work of search committees.

Given the prominence of promoting diversity in many institutional mission statements, core values, and strategic plans, it has become increasingly common to ask applicants for faculty or administrative positions to describe their contributions to DEI as part of the application process. Such so-called *diversity statements* are in addition to teaching and research statements commonly requested of applicants in faculty searches and reinforce DEI as institutional core values and the shared responsibility of all in the university community. As institutions express commitments to inclusive excellence in teaching, research, and reducing equity gaps in student learning and success, it is helpful to ask applicants to think intentionally about diversity and describe their experiences, record, and potential future efforts toward advancing DEI at the university. Alternatively, or in addition, search committees may ask candidates during interviews to discuss their strategies and experiences in supporting students of color or DEI initiatives more broadly.

Requesting diversity statements is not without controversy. Some faculty view such statements as a violation of their academic freedom, a political litmus test, or an attempt to shape or minimize individual viewpoints, especially in the current polarized political climate. In fact, some states have recently banned the use of diversity statements. If requesting a diversity statement, the search committee should provide clear guidance on their expectations so that all candidates can develop meaningful statements in support of their application and be clear that there is not a specific viewpoint or correct response expected. In addition, the committee should develop an objective and consistent framework for reviewing such statements to ensure an equitable assessment of candidate statements. Recently, the University of California system developed and approved a set of guidelines for requesting DEI statements to be implemented across the ten campuses in the system.[42]

The charge should also include the expectation of a meeting of the search committee with the director of affirmative action to gain further insights on conducting an affirmative search and developing a search outreach plan that is inclusive and equitable, including networks with a high probability of connecting with women and candidates of color. Finally, I typically share the draft position description that was developed and vetted in advance and invite them to review it and offer suggestions and edits. In this way, they share some investment in and ownership of the position.

Committee Final Report

After receiving the search committee report, I meet with the committee to thank them but also to ask questions and to get more information, impressions, and questions from them. Committee members work hard, and toward the end of the search process, they fully understand the magnitude of their responsibility and the qualities of the final candidates. In fact, the search committee members probably have the most comprehensive impression of the attributes of the candidates. They appreciate meeting with the hiring officer to discuss their report. During that meeting, I inform them that I will be certain to notify the search committee first when an offer is made and accepted out of respect for their hard work. I don't want them to learn about the outcome second-hand from others.

Making a Competitive Offer

Negotiations with candidates typically include a host of variables, such as salary, benefits, moving costs, and start-up funds to ensure the candidate can be successful. Because of dramatic market differences, salaries will vary substantially by discipline, geographic location, and level or rank of the position. For academic positions, such as faculty, deans, and vice provosts, it is important to rely on external market-based comparative salary information when gaging a competitive offer rather than relying solely on internal human resources comparisons, which tend to focus primarily on internal unit salary structures. Extensive databases that outline comparative salaries based on subject matter, seniority, and region, such as the Oklahoma State Study and College and University Professional Association-Human Resources (CUPA-HR), can be very helpful to ensure fair and market competitive offers are made. It is critical to continuously build the talent pool, so you should not make lowball offers to save a few thousand dollars in salary. Make market-sensitive offers that are fair and competitive, but still align as close as possible with your budget and existing salary structure in that department. Depending on the economy and changing markets over time, it is possible salaries of new hires will contribute to compression in the compensation of existing talent. Given that universities are heavily people-dependent organizations, my philosophy is that we need to stretch if necessary to get the talent in the door. Periodic compression adjustments may have to be made later if that occurs. You don't want to lose your top candidate because of a few thousand dollars.

Start-up investments can be substantial, especially in science and engineering disciplines. While major start-up investments in equipment, graduate student support, and summer salary have become expectations of candidates, it is also important for candidates to understand the return on investment expectations that accompany such significant start-up costs. Start-up investments are not meant to be a gift, but rather an investment to help new scholars launch their careers at your institution. Candidates should understand that they will be expected to generate external funding from grants to support their research, fund graduate research assistants, and return overhead from grants (formally referred to as *facilities and administration* or *indirect costs*) to the university, college, or department.

Dual Career Assistance

One issue that increasingly emerges at the eleventh hour in searches is the possibility of finalist candidate spousal/partner employment assistance or opportunities. Because dual career partners are common in higher education settings, the need and desire for placement assistance or opportunities for existing partners also surfaces as a retention issue for individuals who were hired recently. It can be a complex human resource issue of tremendous importance to candidates and to the institution, and it is worth some special mention.

It is not uncommon for university faculty candidates or extant faculty to have partners who may also be academics seeking college or university employment. In some cases, top candidates are unable to accept an offer unless there is a position available for their partner or, at least, a strong possibility of a position in the near term. As such, to remain competitive in attracting and retaining talent, it is important to offer help or opportunities, where possible, for partners of faculty or senior administrators. While we have been committed to helping and working creatively to find meaningful employment opportunities for partners on or near the campus, such efforts do not typically represent a promise or guarantee of employment and should not be construed as a replacement for other career search efforts. Most institutions have a dual career policy that should be referenced in the position description and advertisement right from the beginning of the search, so candidates are aware of the criteria and guidelines.

In my experience, most dual career partners of faculty finalists are also faculty and are seeking positions as well, sometimes in the same discipline or department, which adds further complexity. While the goal and desire are to accommodate such situations as best as possible, partner hiring often represents an institutional challenge at multiple levels. "Some Issues to Consider When Providing Dual Career Assistance" outlines an array of concerns to be contemplated and overcome in providing dual career assistance.

Some Issues to Consider When Providing Dual Career Assistance

- Financial: Does the institution, college, or department have the resources to support an additional unanticipated position, including salary, benefits, start-up needs, space, and administrative support?

- Departmental Position Needs: Is the partner's expertise in an area of institutional or departmental need based on enrollment patterns and research foci?

- Departmental Faculty Criteria for Selecting Colleagues: If the partner's expertise matches needs, do the partner's credentials match department expectations, standards, and criteria for new hires, and are they supportive?

- Departmental Concerns: Is there a perception that the partner appointment may preclude approval for the department to search for a future position in a higher area of need?

- Spousal/Partner Appointments in Same Department: Will the appointment raise questions about departmental governance, collegiality, and objectivity?

- Consistency with Affirmative Action Policies, Search Procedures, and Goals: Policies typically require a national search for faculty and senior staff positions, which may conflict with potential partner hires that require rapid action.

When dual career hiring opportunities emerge in the latter stages of faculty searches, the dean, provost, and director of affirmative action should be informed of the situation so possibilities, including exploring funding and the potential for a search waiver, can be examined. Exploration must also involve the chairs and ultimately the faculty of the department that might consider the partner candidate. While these situations are almost always complex, leaders should work creatively and diligently to try to accommodate the partner as best as they can. Sometimes that involves making commitments to the receiving department or creating temporary, part-time, or visiting faculty positions. You should not, however, force departments to make a hire, and in each case, the partner under consideration should be invited to campus to meet the faculty of the department and present a seminar to ensure their interests and expertise align with or complement areas of departmental emphasis. The partner should also be vetted through external references as would be the case with any candidate for a position. The goal is to treat the candidate, the partner, and the department with respect and to work closely with the affirmative action office to ensure equity and inclusion principles are met.

Despite challenges, extra effort is important and often leads to collaborative successes. In many respects, partner hiring can be encouraged as an opportunity for a department and the university, if there is a good departmental fit and need. Being sensitive to and providing dual career assistance enhances effectiveness in recruitment, retention, and diversity, and helps project and sustain a family-friendly campus environment and reputation. Everyone must realize, however, that sometimes it is just not possible to accommodate the partner because of resource limitations, expertise fit, skill set, or institutional needs. This could lead to the primary candidate turning down the offer, or a failed search if there are no other viable finalists in the pool.

A Troubling Trend Toward Closed or "Secret" Searches for Leadership Positions

Over the past decade or two, there has been a growing trend toward closed searches to fill vacancies in leadership positions, especially for presidential and chancellor searches overseen by the governing board. In the purest sense, closed presidential searches do not reveal the identity of any candidates until a single finalist is announced and the board votes, often publicly, to endorse the appointment of that candidate. Such closed searches may include a few faculty, staff, or students on the search committee, but all members commit to secrecy regarding candidate information. The perception among some board members and search firms is that the only way to attract the strongest candidates and hire the best individual is to conduct a totally confidential and, therefore, "secret" search.

In typical open searches, two to four finalists are invited to the campus, meet with various constituent groups, make a public presentation, and respond to questions from the community, which is consistent with shared governance and allows both the community and candidate to gauge fit with the campus culture and values. The upside of an open presidential search, of course, is transparency and shared governance (i.e., the campus community gets to meet and offer input about each of the finalists, even though the board makes the final decision as to who gets selected). Such community participation in the search process sets the new president up for success. Public vetting by the community and the media should not be just token input, but rather insightful evaluation helpful in preventing or minimizing a mismatched hire. There has been a flurry of problematic presidential hires in recent years, as evidenced by presidents who have resigned from their position for one reason or another during the first year or two of their initial contract. The downside of an open search process is that some candidates, especially sitting presidents and provosts at other institutions, may be reluctant to become public candidates.

A secret search process protects the privacy of presidential candidates who might otherwise feel they may be labeled as disloyal to their home campus by their board or community, or perhaps even face reprisals if it becomes known that they are exploring new opportunities. If the campus community believes their sitting president or provost is looking to leave or has one foot out the door, they may no longer be willing to follow their agenda or leadership. These are legitimate concerns. Furthermore, while multiple finalists become public in an open search, only one will be selected. Some candidates worry that being publicly not chosen could damage their reputation and pursuit of other opportunities in the future. I suppose no one wishes to be labeled the alternate candidate in multiple presidential searches.

While I appreciate the importance of candidate confidentiality and understand the predicament for sitting presidents and provosts, closed searches do, in fact, compromise shared governance and often provoke an inherent level of distrust for both the governing board and, at times, for the newly hired president. This is especially true when presidential selections are perceived to reflect the partisan wishes of politicians or powerful board members or donors rather than the needs of the institution. As such, the new president may have an added obstacle to overcome if the community has an inherent distrust for the search process that led to their appointment. Some institutions have moved to a quasi-closed search process in which one or two finalists are quietly invited to campus to meet with a few stakeholder groups. As a strong believer in the power of shared governance and collaborative leadership, it is important that the president and provost work effectively and transparently with the faculty as well as the board. If the search process used in selecting leaders compromises that working relationship, the institution will struggle, and the board will have failed in its primary duty to protect the institution and ensure the fulfillment of its mission.

The tendency toward closed presidential searches has opened the door to similar approaches for provost, vice president, and dean searches at some institutions. This is problematic on multiple fronts and may create the perception that the administration wishes to handpick leaders with minimal faculty, staff, or student input. Given the political climate at present, such a perception is neither collegial nor productive, may be highly divisive, and could unnecessarily create challenges for the new hire. Finalists for these positions have far less risk of exposure than, say, sitting presidents exploring a new presidential position. Most candidates for provost positions will be sitting deans or vice provosts, while most dean candidates are likely to be chairs, associate deans, or deans of smaller colleges.

Emerging as a public finalist for either a provost or dean position is less likely to be viewed as a sign of disloyalty, but rather a positive comment on talent. Most institutions recognize that good leaders will want to advance their careers and often need to go elsewhere to do so. Indeed, emerging as a finalist for a prestigious position demonstrates that you are accomplished and prepared to take on new challenges and responsibilities, which is a positive reflection on your home institution. The lack of transparency in closed searches not only compromises shared governance but also deprives the candidate, as well as the community, the opportunity to scope out the values, culture, and personality of the players on campus and to learn firsthand about the challenges and opportunities associated with the position. This is especially true for deans, who need to work closely with and understand the faculty, staff, and students in the college they aspire to lead.

Retaining Talented Faculty and Staff

Institutions go to great lengths to recruit and hire a talented and diverse workforce who contribute to the vibrancy of the academic ecosystem. Retaining individuals with the best skills and experiences that reflect the diversity of the community and add value to the institution requires careful attention to the needs and interests of those individuals. Losing critical and talented faculty and staff to other institutions, early retirement, or alternative career paths is a lost investment and can be devastating to institutions that depend on their most talented contributors for their vitality.

National and international searches typically take six to eight months or longer to complete and cost thousands of dollars in search committee and community time and effort, advertising, campus visits, and moving expenses. Start-up investments for faculty, especially in science and engineering disciplines, can easily approach or exceed $500,000 to $1 million per position. While most faculty and staff stay at the institution that initially hired them, some institutions have relatively few mechanisms to retain their most talented faculty, staff, and administrators. It is disheartening and frustrating when successful faculty are poached by other institutions, but it happens not infrequently.

Faculty and staff establish their careers and potential through their accomplishments at their initial institution and may begin to explore other opportunities, which is certainly well within their rights. Sometimes the desire to move is stimulated by geographic preferences, opportunities to reunite with family, a more prestigious university, or an endowed position, but greater compensation is almost always part of the opportunity. Wealthy institutions have the salary resources and structures that can be attractive to successful faculty, who will also attract a new start-up package to ensure their success at their new institution. It can be challenging to retain excellent faculty and staff, despite the significant investment made to launch their career. The market is becoming more competitive each year, especially for accomplished faculty, staff, and administrators of color and individuals in high-demand fields. The strain of the pandemic and local partisan politics are also driving some to look elsewhere, including outside of academia.

From a compensation standpoint, the initial hiring institution often has an opportunity to make a counteroffer in hopes of retaining talented individuals. For example, at URI, our faculty collective bargaining agreement includes a clause for Exceptional Salary Increases for Retention (ESI), which typically requires evidence that the faculty member is being recruited by another employer. While this is helpful and has allowed us to retain some excellent faculty, it is at times too little, too late, and such opportunities may not be available to retain talented staff through their collective bargaining agreements or institutional policies. When individuals are aggressively recruited to apply elsewhere, invest their time and effort in applying, and receive an attractive offer, it may be too late to retain them. That is, they have mentally moved on and may seem more connected to the institution recruiting them, even though they have limited experience in that new community.

Recognizing the importance of maintaining the talent at our institutions, leaders must identify in advance the talented individuals within our community that may be a flight risk and make extra efforts to retain them before they are recruited elsewhere. This may include offering a pre-emptive ESI, but making it clear to our most talented faculty and staff that we recognize and value their contributions is equally important. Sometimes offering some summer support, graduate student funding, seed funds to initiate a new research project, or funds to purchase a critical piece of equipment or to assist in completing a book project or art exhibit can be as important as an ESI while also signaling their value to our institution. There are almost always personal and professional risks and potentially unpleasant and unpredictable dimensions (e.g., moving, buying and selling homes, forcing children to transfer schools, leaving friends, etc.) associated with changing jobs. Institutional leaders demonstrating to talented individuals that we value them and their work and wish to incentivize their retention in our community can go a long way to retaining our most talented community members. There is no question that money matters to most people, but acknowledging an individual's value to the university and community is important as well.

Institutional leaders must be diligent and creative about investing in our most talented community members. Many, perhaps most, very talented faculty and staff will begin at some point to ponder what's next in their professional life. If they have earned a promotion to full professor, the highest rank in the academy, or are at the top of their field in a staff role, they should be beginning to think about other opportunities. As a close colleague shared with me, higher education is one of the only sectors in which promotion means you continue to do more or less the exact same job, but with a slightly different title and improved compensation. Some of our most innovative and talented faculty and staff have shared that they can't imagine a future of teaching the same classes, working on the same or similar projects, or continuing to do the same support staff work. They ask: What, if any, growth opportunities might exist? How can I best apply my talent and experience? These individuals represent proven talent with a good understanding of the institutional culture and challenges, and the ability to contribute to advancing the institution. Compensation and goodwill are certainly helpful, but there are other tangible actions that may be worth considering as well.

Succession Planning

Careful grooming of individuals for possible leadership positions is an investment worth making. This might involve offering professional development opportunities for select faculty and staff to attend leadership workshops or offer one on your own campus. As I mentioned earlier, a colleague and I co-developed and offered a leadership seminar for individuals with leadership aspirations. All sixteen of the participants remain at the university and thirteen of them have since moved into leadership positions. Efforts such as this are an investment in professional leadership development and contribute to succession planning for the institution and higher education more broadly.

Succession planning implies not only identifying individuals with leadership interests and capacity but also supporting their professional development through tangible and accessible opportunities. In addition to training and development offered on campus, this might include the possibility of administrative sabbaticals or sponsorship for individuals to participate in higher education leadership development programs, such as those offered by the American Council on Education (ACE) Fellows Program, the Higher Education Resource Services (HERS) Leadership Institute, or one of the several programs offered by Academic Impressions.

Finally, there may be advantages to conducting internal searches for certain positions or hiring internal candidates who understand the culture, challenges, and players on the campus and who can contribute immediately. Positions such as associate deans, vice provosts, directors and associate directors of administrative units, and perhaps even some dean and vice president positions can directly tap into the talent pool on campus, provide advancement opportunities for in-house talent, minimize the learning in place gear up of external candidates, and serve the best interests of the institution and its personnel. Talented individuals should be informed of these opportunities and encouraged to apply.

No Time for Complacency

As a result of a combination of many factors, some emerging as well as well-established scholars and leaders are considering alternative career paths. Our most talented, productive, and engaged citizens have the greatest opportunities to pursue alternative and lucrative career paths. Most institutions cannot afford to lose critical talent that exemplifies the best we have to offer or not be able to attract the next generation of scholars or professionals necessary to advance learning and discovery because they are attracted to other sectors or institutions. Yet, this is happening before our very eyes. A recent national survey of provosts revealed that only 22 percent of respondents believed their institutions are very effective at recruiting and retaining faculty, and 59 percent had concerns that faculty do not feel supported by or connected to the administration.[43] Similarly, in a recent survey, 60 percent of higher education staff indicated they are likely to look for alternative employment.[44]

As people-centric organizations, urgent attention and substantial work is necessary to ensure our institutions attract and retain talent. Our futures depend on it. Leaders cannot be complacent about accepting their critical responsibility and making overt efforts to recognize, acknowledge, and reward the most talented and indispensable members of our community and find ways to retain them. It is often postulated that in most organizations, including colleges and universities, approximately 20 percent of the people generate about 80 percent of the value and productivity. While these are somewhat arbitrary percentages, we must acknowledge that there is a subset of our workforce that holds the organization together through their creativity, productivity, and dedication. We must actively reach out and identify those individuals in our communities who will shape the future of our institutions and make our very best efforts to let them know we care about them and want to ensure they remain in our community.

CHAPTER NINE

Great Expectations: Setting Standards and Rewarding Excellence

Performance Reviews and Personnel Decisions

If hiring talented people is the most important thing we do, and people are our greatest asset, then establishing a clear set of expectations and evaluating, guiding, and informing individuals of their progress, shortcomings, and path to improvement may be the next most important thing we do. Thus, a constructive and respectful performance review process is critically important for all so that individuals know where they stand and can invest their efforts in areas where improvement is necessary or beneficial. Equally as important, such reviews are beneficial for the institution as well because the success of our people, including staff, faculty, and administrators, defines success for the institution.

At most institutions, faculty are reviewed frequently, often annually. If done well, such reviews should guide their performance, inform their status, acknowledge successes, and identify opportunities for improvement. In contrast, despite its importance, the review of staff and administrators is often overlooked by leaders or approached in a cavalier manner inconsistent with the value and importance of personnel performance to the operations of the institution. The human resources department will typically develop and share an instrument and process for conducting staff performance reviews. In situations where staff are unionized, review procedures are negotiated and incorporated into collective bargaining agreements. In my experience, most significant personnel problems arise because of a lack of documented evidence of an ongoing problem from a previous review or insufficient documentation of the issues and steps proposed to address the situation. In a sense, we as leaders are often complicit in perpetuating personnel problems by either not conducting meaningful reviews or sugarcoating weak performance in the review process, creating an illusion that things are going well. This is in no one's best interest and often ends up in a lawsuit if and when drastic personnel actions become inevitable.

Best practice would suggest a constructive annual performance review for each staff member and administrator, including a one-on-one meeting with their supervisor to discuss and capture in writing employee goals, accomplishments, and specific areas for improvement. Such reviews should examine progress in meeting previously established goals and, to the extent possible, also reinforce and align with the strategic priorities of the institution. If specific improvements, efficiencies, or organizational restructuring have been identified as important institutional needs, then progress toward achieving these improvements should be measured and discussed. Especially for administrators, there should be consistent accountability associated with institutional plans and progress.

Although it can be expensive, providing strategic and selective opportunities for professional development for staff may be beneficial to encourage and support their continuous improvement. By *strategic*, I mean professional development opportunities designed specifically to address an area needing improvement, and by *selective*, I suggest a process for individuals to apply for professional development funds with only potentially impactful proposals receiving support. This way, it is not automatic, the staff member is investing their time and effort from the beginning, and there is a high probability of making good use of limited professional development funds.

Reappointment, Promotion, and Tenure Decisions for Faculty

The process, expectations, and timeframes for faculty review are generally described in collective bargaining agreements, faculty handbooks, or university manuals, and they no doubt vary from one institution to the next. Descriptions of expectations and standards in such documents are necessarily rather general and often include lists of examples of what might be expected of faculty. This is because disciplines, departments, colleges, and institutional missions are very different regarding scholarly outputs, cultures, and expectations, and it is not possible or appropriate to apply the standards or culture of one discipline, say chemistry or engineering, to another, such as business, sociology, or art. No doubt, the stakes are high for faculty reviews, not only for the individuals under review who may be seeking tenure or a promotion, but also for the productivity, reputation, and future viability of the department, college, and university. Remember, the university is defined by its faculty.

As dean and provost, I have reviewed and made reappointment, tenure, or promotion decisions on about 550 faculty dossiers cutting across all academic disciplines and professions and multiple universities. Most of those dossiers document dedicated and inspirational teaching, awe-inspiring and impactful research, scholarship, and creative work, and meaningful university and professional service. Frankly, I am frequently amazed at the breadth and depth of accomplishments and important work being carried out by my faculty colleagues, and I learn a ton by reading their dossiers. On the other hand, there are some that just don't measure up—not because of the discipline or field of study, but because there is little or no evidence of sustained productivity in teaching, research, and service. Frankly, after reviewing so many cases across multiple fields, it is not that hard to recognize weak cases. It is our obligation as leaders responsible for the best interests of the department, college, and university in the future to both celebrate faculty accomplishments and identify those that are not measuring up. If earning tenure and promotion are to have real meaning to successful and productive faculty, then it must reflect high standards of performance for which both the individuals and the institution can be proud. The institution collectively needs to adopt, promulgate, and reinforce those standards, which should reflect the institution's mission and values.

The challenge in denying reappointment, tenure, or promotion is typically not in recognizing the weak cases, but rather in ensuring that review processes are understood, followed, and consistent. As provost, I went to great lengths to ensure that each candidate received a fair, thorough, and objective review from my office and worked with chairs and deans to encourage the same at the department and college levels. The vice provosts and I frequently and openly promoted our commitment to and the importance of fair, thorough, and objective review procedures, which helped create some level of confidence in the process. Each year we partnered with the AAUP leadership and ran a promotion and tenure workshop open to all faculty, which described responsibilities, processes, and expectations. The goal was to ensure that everyone understood how the process worked, outline expectations, and dispel common myths. There are almost always myths or folklore on campuses about processes and expectations that are passed on from one generation of faculty to the next, although they may vary from campus to campus. By speaking with and listening to faculty members and others, aspiring leaders can begin to identify those myths and make efforts to dispel them. Dispelling what are presumably (and hopefully) false beliefs helps bring clarity to the process and may reduce some of the angst for those undergoing review. See "Common Myths about Promotion and Tenure Reviews" for examples of some myths I have uncovered through the years.

Common Myths about Promotion and Tenure Reviews

- **Myth #1: There are unspoken secrets to success.** As provost, I was frequently introduced at promotion and tenure workshops as the person who will share the secrets to success. My response was always that the only secret is that there are no secrets. It was important to remind all that as faculty they should know what is expected of them and how the process is carried out. There are neither secrets nor favors.

- **Myth #2: The process is mysterious.** I suppose this is a corollary to the secrets myth. Remind faculty that the process is described in detail in the CBA, university manual, and well-established written departmental and college protocols. Given previous reviews, there should be no mysteries and few surprises.

- **Myth #3: The administration's goal is not to support faculty.** This is clearly not the case. The institution and its reputation are defined by the work of the faculty. The administration and faculty are embedded in the process together. Faculty success is the institution's success. Discussing this openly can quickly and effectively dispel this rumor.

- **Myth #4: Research is the only thing that matters.** This perception is prevalent in some disciplines and suggests that the chair, dean, provost, and president don't care about teaching and service. Explaining that a balanced effort of excellence in teaching, research, and service is essential to the institution's mission, especially for tuition-dependent institutions, is critical. Also, emphasizing the institution embraces a teacher-scholar model of faculty work and depends on true faculty scholars teaching our students can help dispel this myth. Finally, robust shared governance depends upon impactful service.

- **Myth #5: Faculty with a high teaching workload are penalized.** The myth is that scholarly expectations are similar for all, regardless of teaching load. In contrast, responsible administrators must understand the weight of the review is proportional to faculty effort distribution. That is, in the interests of logic and fairness, faculty teaching one course per semester would have higher expectations and standards for research productivity than faculty teaching three courses per semester. Explaining and reinforcing this in faculty reviews can calm nerves and support transparency.

- **Myth #6: Research is defined solely based on grant success and dollar amount.** This belief is often deeply embedded and may even be true for leaders in some disciplines and institutions. If so, it is shortsighted. Leaders must demonstrate that they celebrate all forms of meaningful academic scholarship, including grants, scholarly journal articles, books, exhibitions, performances, etc., which should be peer-reviewed and impactful. The administration acknowledges that grant opportunities are not equally available and expected across all disciplines.

While these myths may not be common to all campuses, every campus has a set of myths hovering around faculty review processes and expectations. Searching them out, addressing them honestly and directly, and making sure they are truly myths will be beneficial to individuals and review processes.

The faculty evaluation process relies heavily on peer review, which is both a strength and a potential challenge. Peer review is understood and valued at universities. Faculty are accustomed to objective external peer review through publication submissions and grant proposal review

processes. Most faculty don't shy away from their work being construc-
tively, even critically, judged by colleagues with expertise in their field.
Departmental peer review in the promotion and tenure review process,
however, has the potential to be influenced, positively or negatively, by
personal feelings and relationships among departmental colleagues. That
is, colleagues may go to great lengths to support or protect a popular
colleague, independent of their performance. This may especially be
true with well-liked junior faculty colleagues with young families. No one
wants to see a colleague with a couple of children lose their job. Alternatively, negative personal experiences toward a junior colleague may
also cloud the objective review of teaching, scholarship, and service.
Such personal connections can compromise the impact of departmental
reviews. Although it is not easy to remove this noise from the process,
evaluations by the chair, dean, faculty standards committee, and provost
must rise above any form of bias driven by departmental relationships
that may compromise a fair, thorough, and objective review at the department level. Academic leaders should be cognizant of the potential for this
type of noise in the system.

Promotion and tenure decisions are inherently anxiety-producing and
can become volatile; extra efforts and sustained open dialogue are necessary to ensure the process is transparent, expectations are clear, and
outcomes are defensible. Several key process and responsibility issues
related to promotion and tenure reviews that leaders should consistently
emphasize are briefly discussed below.

Establish clear expectations in writing at the time of appointment.

Expectations for excellence in teaching, research, and service should
be established in the faculty member's letter of appointment from the
dean, which they sign when they accept the position. Often that letter also
describes workload, such as teaching and graduate student mentoring
responsibilities as well as a general description of scholarly expectations
and service contributions.

Establish departmental expectations and procedures.

Each department should have a written description of its internal review
process so that it is clear to candidates. That process must, of course,
align with the institutional procedures and expectations. Because

expectations, especially in research and scholarship, will vary by discipline, it is important for departments to describe as clearly as possible their expectations for faculty success for promotion and tenure in terms of scholarly products and the quality and impact of faculty work and how that is measured. These documents should describe the nature of scholarly products that are expected, such as journal articles, single-authored books, grant funding, performances, exhibitions, etc., which will no doubt vary by discipline. Setting quantitative expectations, such as threshold scores on course evaluations, number of publications per year, amount of grant funding secured, etc., are almost always problematic and become a source of dispute and confusion. There are effective ways of subjectively describing performance expectations without establishing arbitrary quantitative threshold levels that don't consider the quality or impact of the faculty work.

Provide constructive annual reviews.

This is critically important. Too often deans, chairs, and departmental colleagues provide glowing or overly positive reviews to be supportive of junior faculty, even if the faculty member is underperforming in certain areas. This is not helpful and can be misleading to ascending faculty who are then blindsided later when deficiencies hold them back. This was an issue of concern when I began as provost. So, we ran workshops for chairs on approaches to writing constructive and respectful reviews of faculty teaching, research, and service, including at times recommending that candidates being reviewed participate in workshops offered by the office for the advancement of teaching and learning to improve their teaching. Pretenure and prepromotion faculty are much better served by a constructive review that outlines positive areas of performance and areas needing improvement, including specific things they can do to bolster the performance. Most faculty welcome and benefit from such constructive feedback.

Emphasize the importance of sustained productivity.

Faculty performance shouldn't be about whether they have done enough to earn tenure or promotion, but rather whether their productivity is likely to be sustained. In my view, promotion and tenure should not be thought of as a reward for a job well done, but rather a judgment about the potential for sustained productivity into the future. While no one has a crystal ball that can predict the future, there are important indicators that can help one judge the potential for sustained productivity or lack thereof, such as a growing program of scholarly work and quality products over time, steady improvement in teaching effectiveness, and mentoring graduate students to completion. Those with limited productivity for several years or a desperate flurry of activity at the eleventh hour raise legitimate questions about whether they will be productive in the future. One of the reasons that "time in rank" matters is so sustained productivity can be judged, which is why early tenure or promotion reviews can be challenging.

Ensure faculty understand they need to make their own best case.

Each faculty member will be judged on their own merits. Also, they are responsible for making their own case, and that case must be evidence-based, clear, and concise. Faculty need to understand that overwhelming reviewers with uncurated dossiers is not in their best interest. The dossier should clearly document productivity and positive impact in teaching, scholarship, and service, including describing one's role in team-taught classes, multi-authored publications, and multiple investigator grants. Comparisons with other faculty are not typically a component of a review or part of the promotion criteria because colleagues, even some in the same department or college, often have different roles, expectations, and workloads and focus on different sub-disciplinary areas. Faculty reviews must be consistent with their workload expectations. That is, faculty with a light teaching load (e.g., a 30 percent teaching, 60 percent research, and 10 percent service effort distribution) are expected to document greater research productivity; faculty with a heavier teaching load (e.g., 60 percent teaching, 30 percent research, and 10 percent service effort distribution) should have more weight placed on their teaching than their research productivity.

Ensure best practice in seeking external peer reviews.

Most institutions seek external peer evaluation of candidates under consideration for promotion or tenure. Such peer reviews often focus on the scholarly impact and recognition of the candidate's work and perhaps their service contributions to the profession, if appropriate. A critical issue relates to the selection of those reviewers and their relationship to the candidate under evaluation. External peer reviews should be at arm's length to be useful in the process. That is, every effort should be made to ensure that external reviewers are not friends or collaborators of the candidate. External reviewers should be selected from accomplished scholars in the discipline of the candidate from institutions of similar type (e.g., research institutions, liberal arts colleges, state comprehensives, etc.) as the candidate's institution and should be from individuals of the same academic rank or higher than the promotion under consideration. It is not appropriate to seek external peer evaluation from an assistant professor for an individual seeking promotion to full professor. Too often these practices are not followed or are limited by policy or contract, which renders the reviews ineffective. Best practice indicates that while some reviewers might be suggested by the candidate, others should be added by the chair or dean to ensure an appropriate and objective mix. The request for the evaluation should come from the chair or dean, not the candidate, and each reviewer should be asked to address their relationship with the candidate.

Personnel decisions, especially tenure and promotion decisions, are critically important and must be approached carefully and thoughtfully. Awarding tenure affords job security that is unprecedented in other sectors. Full professor is the highest rank in the academy on a global scale and should connote the highest level of achievement in teaching, research, and service. There are significant consequences to the individuals under review and to the reputation and productivity of the department, college, and institution if we don't get these decisions right. Our leaders must ensure that our processes and expectations are clear, our reviews are fair, thorough, and objective, and that all personnel are respected throughout the process, regardless of the outcome.

Role of Faculty Unions

If the faculty at your institution are unionized, you can expect that the union will advise, support, and represent the interests of the faculty member undergoing review or evaluation for reappointment, promotion, or tenure. In fact, the union has a legal responsibility to do so if requested by the faculty member. The union owes a duty of fair representation to its members, which requires the union to act fairly, impartially, and without ill will or discrimination when pursuing a member's grievance. If a faculty member is denied promotion or tenure, there is a strong probability the faculty member will ask the union to file a grievance, whether you believe it is warranted or not. Threat of a grievance should not influence the decision on promotion and tenure cases, which should be based on a fair, thorough, and objective review of the case presented by the faculty member in their dossier along with annual reviews. Leaders have a responsibility to maintain standards and expectations and to uphold the reputation of the institution. Too often, administrators seem intimidated by the possibility of a grievance and may allow that to shape their thinking about a case. One should not be intimidated. Grievances are simply part of the process, and the burden of proof resides with the faculty member.

If a grievance is filed, it must stipulate the articles and sections of the collective bargaining agreement that were purported to be violated in the evaluation leading to the denial decision. In particular, the candidate and their union representative will likely look initially for procedural violations in the review, which heightens the importance of a fair, thorough, and objective review process that aligns with procedures described in the collective bargaining agreement. No doubt, they will also look for any evidence that the decision was arbitrary and capricious. Simply disagreeing with the promotion or tenure decision or the judgment of the decision-maker is not strong grounds for grievance or reversal of a decision. The exact process for grievances will no doubt vary from one campus or union chapter to the next, but it is likely that there will be a narrow time limit following the decision for filing a grievance and a statute of limitation thereafter. Typically, the union will investigate the complaint and determine the strength of the case and how far it is willing to go in pursuing the grievance process. Grievances will likely include a hearing where the union and the administration present their perspective of the case. It is not uncommon for the union to initially pursue the grievance hearing step because the level of investment is relatively low, and it offers an opportunity to learn more about the case in the back-and-forth of the hearing. If the complainant loses the grievance hearing, then the union may or may not decide to bring the case forward for arbitration.

The stakes are higher for both parties in arbitration, including the cost of arbitrator fees, the need for legal representation by both parties and the binding nature of the arbitrator's decision, which may also serve as precedents for either side in future cases. There are also potential morale concerns for the faculty member and perhaps the department associated with these cases. The arbitrator's decision is accompanied by their rationale for the decision, which will likely include citations of previous cases that influenced the arbitrator's consideration and decision. The power of the precedent is certainly worthy of consideration as to whether to pursue arbitration. If the union determines that the case is not strong, they will likely advise their member to not pursue arbitration or decide to cease representing that individual, which is within their legal purview. If cases go to arbitration, both sides must be prepared for an extended and expensive process leading to the arbitrator's final decision.

While the union may serve as an adversary of the administration throughout this process, it is important to understand that they are fulfilling their obligation to their members. It is the administration's responsibility to ensure the review process leading to the promotion or tenure decision is consistent with the terms in the collective bargaining agreement, fair, thorough, and objective, and based on the evidence provided by the faculty member in their dossier. Establishing clear expectations and ensuring fair and consistent review processes, which should be the responsibility of the administration in any case, will reduce the probability of grievances and/or the likelihood of a successful grievance.

Tenure and Academic Freedom

Academic freedom is sacred to the honest pursuit and sharing of knowledge and to meaningful academic inquiry, learning, and discovery. It is reinforced and preserved through a system of granting tenure to faculty based on their achievements and potential for continued productivity. In so doing, these accomplished teacher-scholars can engage in intellectual inquiry and debate without restraint and free from censorship or retaliation. Unlike free speech, which is the right of each individual to express their opinion however good, bad, or false it might be, academic freedom is grounded in the professional competency of faculty as judged by disciplinary communities of scholars.

Tenure and academic freedom provide faculty scholars an extraordinary opportunity to pursue truth and explore a range of subjects consistent with their scholarly interests and expertise, including subjects that may be embroiled in public controversy and that would benefit from informed analysis, scholarly review, and understanding. With the polarization and politicization of public discourse today, academic freedom and tenure are threatened by some politicians, legislatures, boards, and segments of society *writ large*. This further highlights the extraordinary responsibility afforded with tenure. Academic responsibility implies the continued performance of professional duties and achievements and the advancement of the depth and breadth of one's scholarly pursuits and impact. Tenured faculty not only have the freedom to explore controversial topics, but they also have the freedom and responsibility to be creative and courageous teachers and scholars—to be innovators; to experiment with new approaches to teaching and learning; to update, expand, and advance their scholarly skills and knowledge; and to lend their wisdom and expertise to the betterment of their institution and society. Indeed, the responsibility ascribed to tenure is for each of us to apply our knowledge and expertise toward addressing and solving the most compelling and complex challenges facing humanity now and into the future.

CHAPTER TEN

Building Effective Teams to Advance a Change Agenda

No leader can do the work of implementing a change agenda on their own or in a vacuum. And, even if you could, you shouldn't. As provost, I was very fortunate to work closely with a stellar team of vice provosts, special assistants, and executive assistants who were smart, informed, hardworking, and committed to advancing the institution. They were never shy about offering a different opinion, and we all challenged each other's ideas and learned from each other, which usually led to informed decisions. We got a lot done and moved the institution forward, despite some very challenging times.

At times, self-deception or arrogance may result in disjointed team-building approaches (Figure 10.1). Leaders must recognize the importance of and be thoughtful about building effective teams, seeking their candid input, and supporting them as they move forward and invariably face obstacles along the way. Publicly acknowledging their good work and accomplishments is important as well. Building teams not only shares the enormous workload but also builds buy-in and has the potential to contribute to leadership succession planning.

"If we want to succeed as a team, we need to put aside our own
selfish, individual interests and start doing things my way."

Figure 10.1. Building teams that bring a diversity of expertise, experience,
and viewpoints leads to informed decisions and better outcomes.
Copyright Randy Glasbergen; Printed with permission from Glasbergen Cartoon Service

Creating and Nurturing Leadership Teams

Team building happens at several levels within an institution. It might
be the president or chancellor hiring vice presidents who will both
lead a division and serve as cabinet members or the provost selecting
vice provosts who oversee components of the academic core mission
and hiring deans who will lead colleges and also serve as members of
a council of deans. So, individuals are usually selected to lead, provide
specific expertise, and offer input or advice. For each of these important
functions, there may be a natural tendency for leaders to reach out to or
favor individuals who either think like you, have similar experiences to
you, or agree with you on important issues. Instead, resist the temptation
to choose team members who are like you. It may be easier to reach a
consensus but toward a direction not worth pursuing. Consider individuals who will bring to the table a diversity of expertise, experiences, and
viewpoints and who will have the courage to respectfully offer alternative
views, play devil's advocate, and also see the wisdom in others' opinions
and perspectives.

It is critical to establish clear expectations of the teams you build and
listen carefully to the perspectives they offer. Also, whether you realize it

or not, you will be modeling behavior and work ethic through your own actions. You chose the individuals to bring to the table, so follow your own best judgment and make sure you listen to and learn from what they have to say. *Listening* doesn't mean they are correct, but it is no doubt a perspective worth considering. There is a difference between listening and obeying, however. In the end, when the team discusses or even debates the items on the table, the conversation becomes informed by the details and implications, which leads to better decisions and a greater likelihood of understanding what will happen after the decisions are made. It also offers an opportunity to have candid conversations about progress or lack thereof. In addition, team members become informed and are thus better able to assist in transmitting accurate information throughout the community and correcting myths and misinformation that often exist in the highly interconnected academic ecosystem.

When hiring individuals who will both have their own portfolio of responsibilities and be part of a leadership team, it is important to judge candidates based on their expertise and experience related to their responsibilities and on the complementary strengths they bring to the larger team. I strongly recommend that team members participate in the review of job candidates for leadership positions, such as deans when hiring new deans or vice provosts when hiring a peer, and their input should be carefully considered. Finally, it is critical that the leader publicly acknowledges the good work of each contributor and is prepared to support them when there is pushback or setbacks.

One-on-One Meetings with Direct Reports

Because each direct report, such as vice presidents with the president, vice provosts and deans with the provost, or chairs with the dean, has their own portfolio of responsibilities as well as being part of a larger team, it is important for each leader to have regular one-on-one meetings with their direct reports. Such meetings will consume considerable time for leaders, depending on the number of direct reports, but the time spent is important, worth the investment, and empowering to those individuals. Making time for people, especially your closest colleagues, sends a powerful message that you value them and the work they are doing. As provost, I had monthly one-on-one meetings with each dean and typically met individually with each vice provost twice per month. Rather than using that time to share my issues or concerns, I asked everyone to generate an agenda of items they wished to discuss in their meeting. My role was largely listening, asking questions, offering advice and suggestions, and pledging support as necessary and appropriate. These largely informal one-on-one meetings, helped me remain informed, learn about the various issues, obstacles, and progress in their work, and get to know them as individuals in a casual setting distinct from structured group meetings.

Appointing and Empowering Committees and Task Forces

Most of the work of the university, whether it involves strategic planning, implementing a change agenda, or responding to a crisis, will likely be done by either standing committees, *ad hoc* committees, or task forces appointed specifically to address a timely issue. Presidents, provosts, deans, and chairs will often choose individuals to serve on task forces or committees to explore new and better ways of doing business within the department, college, or university. In appointing members of such task forces, it is important to include individuals with expertise and interests relevant to the issue at hand. In many cases, it is also best to include faculty from a range of disciplines across the university, unless the work of the task force is specific to a narrow set of disciplines. Finally, it is helpful if the task force members offer complementary perspectives and possess both problem-solving and interpersonal skills appropriate to group work.

There are almost always individuals with their own agendas who would like to be on such committees to push their agenda forward. Frankly, those individuals can be disruptive, unwilling to listen, and typically get in the way rather than help move the task force forward. Appoint a task force chair who knows how to and understands the importance of running effective meetings and engaging and giving voice to all committee members. An experienced chair will ensure a fair and thorough process and drive the work to completion. However, it is also helpful to not always rely on the same small group of individuals to lead each task force. While many academically focused task forces will comprise faculty and perhaps administrators, it is often helpful and inclusive to involve students, staff, and even a community member or two, depending on the nature of the work, because they will usually bring very different and valuable perspectives to discussions and recommendations.

As the leader, it is important to establish a clear charge for the committee, an approximate timeline for the work to be completed, and a process for interim reporting and responding to questions that emerge. The charge should make clear the importance of the work and why it is worth the time and efforts of the individuals asked to serve. The task force may be urged to speak with certain campus leaders to get their insights. It is also helpful to reinforce implementation plans and timelines associated with the outcome of the work. Folks are more likely to become deeply engaged in work that truly matters and leads to outcomes that will be implemented rather than another set of recommendations or plans that will gather dust on a shelf.

It is helpful if the individual appointing the task force checks in with the chair or the entire group periodically to respond to questions, react to early findings, demonstrate true interest in the work, and restate its importance to the university. Most importantly, effective leaders will carefully listen to issues of concern that emerge as well as recommendations and show their trust, respect, and confidence in those empowered to take on the important work of the university. See "Collaborative Crisis Management: Remote Teaching and Learning Task Force" for a description of the formation of an *ad hoc* task force established to provide guidance during the abrupt transition of classes to remote delivery over an eight-day period at the beginning of the pandemic.

Collaborative Crisis Management: Remote Teaching and Learning Task Force

After transitioning all classes to remote delivery at URI in the beginning of the pandemic, we established an *ad hoc* task force to ensure two-way dialogue with faculty and a network to both share information and listen and respond to concerns. The task force was chaired by the vice provost for academic and faculty initiatives. The charge to the task force included context and purposes statements as outlined below.

Context: This requires an unprecedented rapid response on the part of faculty who are currently teaching students in face-to-face or hybrid classes. We recognize that faculty provide instruction using a full range of pedagogical approaches appropriate to the distinctive attributes of the disciplines and course learning outcomes and have varying levels of familiarity with remote instruction tools and techniques. We are committed to working with faculty in making this transition, supporting their adoption of strategies best suited to achieve the learning outcomes for their courses, and doing our best to ensure that resources are available to assist faculty during this transition. The task force is intended to support the teaching community and serve as a liaison to faculty. The task force comprises faculty and key knowledgeable staff representing a cross section of disciplines, remote teaching skills, and pedagogical experiences in a broad array of course learning goals and approaches.

The *Purposes* are to serve as a faculty resource to:

- help identify and solve emerging problems that will arise during this abrupt transition;
- identify gaps in university resources and services, respond to existing challenges, and propose potential solutions or resources to help address those challenges;
- support open lines of communication regarding the needs of faculty, available resources, and student concerns; and
- offer ideas and expertise to address instructional needs in experiential, laboratory, studio, capstone, performance, etc.-based courses that are likely to be especially complex to deliver remotely.

The task force included faculty senate and union leaders, established a website and open communication lines; worked collegially to define immediate faculty development, support, and resource needs; assisted in developing an alternative grading scheme for the semester; created a faculty support network related to family care and remote teaching; served as a conduit of information for student emergency assistance concerns; developed provisions to address technology needs, including the availability of devices, internet access, and recording suites on campus; and, established community networks for sharing knowledge, socializing, and balancing demands. The task force quickly became an essential and effective resource to pull the faculty and academic leadership together during this time of crisis.

Creating and Engaging External Advisory Boards

External advisory boards or councils can be an asset if they are engaged and thoughtfully managed. Most deans and some department chairs have external advisory boards that offer insight and advice pertinent to the work of their units, and presidents typically have an external presidential advisory council who does the same for the entire institution. Such boards or councils also play an important role in fundraising through board member giving and helping to connect the college or university to others who can provide philanthropic support. Advisory board members are typically well-connected and very busy people who are asked to volunteer their time, energy, ideas, and money to help position and advance the school, college, or university. As such, it is critically important to engage members and use their time thoughtfully and respectfully. Some say advisory boards exist solely or primarily for philanthropy purposes and, therefore, only individuals with significant financial capacity should be invited. I don't buy that idea. While all members should be expected to make an annual gift, some who are not wealthy may be a real asset to the board and the college in other ways. For example, relatively recent alumni who may not yet have reached their peak earning level may provide valuable fresh perspectives on certain issues. Also, I am convinced that actively engaged board members will be more likely to donate at a higher level than those who are only passively involved.

As dean several years ago, I was fortunate to have a great advisory board that really helped move the college forward. In inviting individuals to join that board, my intention was to assemble a diverse group of constituents who connected to the work of the college, mostly through their current or former (if retired) employment. The connection might relate to students, research, practice, or to policy development at the state or federal level. Some members were alumni of the college, some brought corporate experience or ran their own businesses, while others worked for nonprofits or advocacy organizations, public agencies, or as lawyers or scientists at other institutions.

My goal was to cultivate this assemblage of smart, talented, well-connected individuals into a functional team. Collectively, that team would help advocate for the college; offer insights, internship experiences, and their networks to our students; share relevant ideas derived from the outside (i.e., nonacademic) world; and directly and indirectly provide philanthropic support for the college and university. While I emphasized the importance of the board having 100 percent participation in annual giving, I did not set a target amount for them to give. Several members were wealthy and gave generously, while others were not wealthy and gave at a level they could afford, but they also contributed enormously in other ways. We had 100 percent participation of board members donating every year, and we promoted their participation in our efforts to engage other prospects and donors. As the board became more and more engaged, their level of giving went up, as did their efforts to provide internships and career advice for students and outreach to others who might be helpful.

Creating an effective advisory board entails much more than simply inviting influential people to be on the board. Their engagement in substantive work is critical and is respectful of their time. In my years in higher education, and especially as a provost who met with many college-level advisory boards, I observed more ineffective than effective boards, mostly because of unclear purpose, insufficient goals for and planning of meetings, poorly run meetings, lack of follow-up discussions, and insufficient meaning or substance of the work to engage the board. These issues are not a reflection of the board members but rather are cases where the institutional leaders did not appropriately prepare or plan for the purpose and work of the board.

The following is my list of dos and don'ts to consider when creating and managing an advisory board at the department, college, or university level.

DO:

- Develop a thoughtfully written charter that articulates the purpose(s) of the advisory board, the expectations of board members, and highlights the *advisory* nature of the board.

- Assign a key staff member to serve as liaison to the board to ensure timely communication to and engagement of board members between meetings.

- Think carefully about a strategic mix of board members to invite, including the nature of their occupations; connections to fields relevant to the college or university; all forms of human diversity, including age and ethnicity; capacity and willingness to contribute philanthropically; and a strategic mixture of alumni and non-alumni.

- Plan two or three board meetings per year and ensure that the agenda is substantive and includes items for discussion and for board members to offer their ideas and advice.

- Make efforts to ensure all board members are engaged in discussions and that each member's voice is heard and respected.

- Be very thoughtful about who gets nominated to serve as chair of the board and ensure the chair has input into the agenda, understands the goals and desired outcomes for each meeting, and runs the meeting in a time-sensitive manner.

- Consider creating subcommittees within the board, such as advancement and student career and internship subcommittees.

- Invite the university president or provost to meet with the board to provide institutional updates and ensure there is time for board members to ask questions.

- Provide a strategically planned and timely communication specifically for board members in between meetings to keep them connected to the college or university, and ensure it includes follow-up to discussions, actions, or recommendations from previous meetings.

- Plan some social time, perhaps a lunch or a cocktail hour, during or immediately following each board meeting and organize it so that members can engage with each other as well as with key college leaders, such as deans, associate deans, and perhaps a few key faculty and students.

- Keep minutes of meetings, including action steps and follow-up needed, and ensure board members are informed of the many ways their advice and generosity are helping the college/university.

DON'T:

- Talk at board members for an entire meeting or parade one speaker after another to give mind-numbing PowerPoint presentations.

- Ask a question that you really don't want an answer to. If you ask the board for input or advice, the board will expect you to pay attention to their suggestions or it is a waste of their time—so be careful what you ask of them.

- Ask the board to review the curriculum or course content or to provide ideas for new majors, which are the purview of the faculty.

- Ask the board to make decisions or provide advice or input about funding, allocation of resources, personnel matters, or priorities for the college or university—remember they are advisory and do not have formal governance or fiduciary responsibilities.

- Ask or urge the board to lobby the president or provost for additional resources to the college, which will alienate the institutional leadership and do more harm than good because institutional investments should not be driven by advisory board advocacy. (By the way, I offer the same advice to visiting program accreditation teams.)

- Bludgeon advisory board members with a plethora of emails about everything going on in the college and university or add them to every newsletter listserv from the college and university.

There are many great opportunities for external advisory boards to be very helpful. Certainly, identifying new approaches to fundraising and individuals who might provide support and making introductions that might enhance philanthropic support are key areas. Also, opening their networks and making connections that might lead to partnerships of interest with industry, NGOs, or agencies can be very helpful. Board members bring key insights and experiences from their world of work and government that is different from and complement insights from faculty scholars. Sometimes board members are willing to host events that might draw in alumni and friends. Simply sharing contemporary issues they experience in their workplaces can be informative and valuable to students, staff, and faculty. Also, board members certainly can provide meaningful career advice and opportunities for students, and their companies, organizations, or employers may offer valuable internships for students. As external constituents, advisory board members are in an excellent position to offer advice on ways to enhance the visibility, image, and brand of the college to the outside world, which is something that most colleges struggle with and care about. There are so many ways to tap into the experiences of external friends that can enhance the well-being of a college or university.

Managing Conflict and Solving Problems

So much of the teamwork of advancing a change agenda and challenging the *status quo* is about problem-solving, continuous improvement, and driving to consensus or critical decision points. Given the diversity of personalities, perspectives, disciplines, and values among faculty and the complexity of the issues being discussed, there will always be disagreements, differences of opinion, and conflicts. Effective leaders understand that conflict is to be expected and that the friction associated with different perspectives can contribute to personal growth and more informed decisions. Very effective leaders are able to anticipate the areas of likely disagreement and may be able to defuse a situation before it occurs or, at least, before it becomes a major conflict. If potential difficult issues can be prediagnosed, it may be possible to discuss those early in the charge to a committee or the charter of a working group. While this doesn't make the problem go away, it reveals the necessary challenging work to be done, signals clearly that the leader is willing and able to engage in the conflict, and that failure to resolve differences about important issues is not an option.

When conflict arises, and it will, leaders at all levels must be willing to engage in the issues creating the disagreement. That is, they must listen carefully to all sides of the argument, truly work to understand the basis for the conflict through the lens of those with differing opinions, and find a way to resolve differences and build consensus, if possible, without compromising the integrity of the desired outcome. Active and empathetic listening is a critical element of leading through conflict. It may not make the disagreement go away, but all parties will understand that their concerns and positions were heard and considered before decisions were made. In the end, a decision must be made that reflects the best interests of the institution, even if there are differential implications for some individuals, departments, or groups.

In some cases, conflicts between or among individuals may be ongoing and create explosive and entrenched situations that interfere with everyday operations and programmatic advancement. In such cases, it may be necessary for a leader to engage an impartial, skilled, third-party mediator who can assist in resolving differences through careful negotiations. The mediator's role is not to determine who or what is right or best or to ascribe blame to a certain party, but rather to pull the opposing parties together, help identify the issues, and minimize, if possible, the obstacles that have created the conflict. Often the mediator will seek to establish concessions from each party to resolve or ameliorate the conflict and help shape a viable path forward.

There are occasionally individuals who seem to thrive on conflict with their peers or supervisors. Such chronically antagonistic people often have anger and discontent in their core being or need to prove that they are right, you are wrong, or that they are smarter or better informed than everyone else. In many cases, they thrive on getting attention and will sabotage teamwork and forward progress. Such individuals can create disruption and a chilling, even hostile, work environment. While I have encountered such individuals, I am not a psychologist and certainly not an expert in dealing with pernicious colleagues in the workplace. In my experience, however, engaging or arguing with such personalities is pointless and will only result in an acceleration of their behavior. I recommend that you refrain from point-counterpoint debates, especially on email, and do your best to minimize their role and negative impact on others. While you may refer them to the human resources office, an employee assistance program, or file a formal reprimand, they probably won't participate in a meaningful way or change their deeply embedded behavior. If, or rather when, they threaten to sue or resign in protest, you should refer their attorney to the Office of the General Counsel or politely accept their resignation.

As an academic leader, a major part of your job every day is creating and cultivating relationships and working with people. Every effort you make to better understand the human condition and character, including dysfunctional behaviors, will help you become a better leader and manager.

PART IV

ENERGY FLOW AND PRODUCTIVITY

Understanding How the Money Works

Energy creates the capacity to do work. In natural ecosystems, the sun is the primary source of energy for most living things and the major driver of natural phenomena, such as atmospheric circulation and the water cycle. In higher education ecosystems, money is the primary driver that creates the capacity to do work. Unlike energy from the sun, however, money is far less abundant. There is never enough to support all that we wish or need to do. As such, leaders must understand how to generate and conserve money and maximize the efficiency in converting and allocating financial energy into productivity (i.e., strategically important outcomes derived from investments). Just as in nature, productivity is dynamic with the potential to change over time. Effective leaders make strategic investments to enhance institutional productivity. Indeed, leaders must understand how the money works!

CHAPTER ELEVEN

Understanding Revenue Streams and Your Value Proposition

The Cost-Value Proposition

The it's all about people mantra extends to how the money works because salaries and fringe benefits often account for 70 to 80 percent or more of the annual base general fund operating budget of institutions of higher education. When you include student financial aid through tuition discounting and scholarships, it becomes clear that the budget too is largely about people. If human resources are the foundation of our institutions, then money must be the building blocks of that foundation.

Because expenditures associated with salaries, benefits, and financial aid are ongoing and almost always increase from year to year, *the connection between the people and the money in higher education is the major driver of the cost of a college education.* The true and full cost of a college education has become a serious societal concern that has led to a student debt crisis and questions on the part of some about the value of a college education and degree. Tuition increases at most institutions help cover part of these annual expense increases, but they also create a financial burden on students and families and prompt continuing financial aid investments to ensure the institution is accessible and affordable. Tuition increases, if not sensitive to the market and the institution's cost-value proposition, can also lead to enrollment losses, further exacerbating institutional challenges. When you add annual costs associated with maintenance and improvement of the expansive infrastructure on many campuses, annual increases in utilities, and information technology hardware and software upgrades needed to keep the institution contemporary and operational, it becomes clear that the sustainability of the higher education business model is strained. Money matters, and it frequently seems there isn't enough of it.

There is a constant pursuit of more revenue to cover growing expenses just to break even before one considers funds for strategic investments. Our colleagues in enrollment management carry the weight of the constant challenge of "bringing in the class," and they must push the limits of innovation in a highly competitive environment to attract applicants and yield a class of accomplished students. If revenue streams diminish, the focus shifts to increasing efficiency and cost-controlling measures, which often translates into budget reductions and sometimes quality and morale compromises. Throw a demographic decline in the number of high school graduates in most states and a pandemic into the mix, and the challenges can be daunting. Indeed, as reported in *The Chronicle of Higher Education*, net-tuition revenue declined at 61 percent of US institutions between 2019 and 2021 because of pandemic-induced enrollment declines creating financial challenges and a greater focus on recruitment and retention of students to restore financial stability.[45]

There are no simple answers, but there is certainly a need for strategic leadership, improvements in program delivery, relevance, and reputation, and ensuring value in a very competitive marketplace. Indeed, an understanding of the cost-value proposition for your programs and institution and how the money works is essential.

Revenue Streams

The revenue streams that support most higher education institutions in the United States are limited and relatively straightforward. Tuition and fees are essential for private institutions and increasingly interface directly with state appropriations to function as a critical revenue stream at public institutions as well. That is, as state funding declines, tuition revenue must rise. Tuition and fee revenue is typically the major revenue stream and is unrestricted, which means it can be used for any purpose. State appropriation funds vary by state and are frequently unrestricted, although portions may be restricted to specific items such as paying debt on state-issued general obligation bonds. These funds collectively make up most of the operating budget for most institutions, which is typically referred to as the ***unrestricted budget***, ***general fund***, ***operating budget***, or *education and general funds.* The operating budget or general fund is the primary source of unrestricted funds that supports the overall academic mission and most administrative support services of the institution. In addition, there may be endowment funds, research overhead funds, and auxiliary enterprise service funds, which may have restrictions on their use. Money from grants and contracts and gifts are almost always restricted and separate from the general fund.

Tuition and Fees and State Appropriations

For private institutions, and increasingly for public institutions as well, net tuition (tuition after financial aid tuition discounting) and mandatory fees are the primary revenue drivers, which means many institutions are largely enrollment dependent. Public colleges and universities also receive a state appropriation designed originally to subsidize the full cost of education for in-state students. Out-of-state students at public colleges and universities presumably pay the true and full cost less any financial aid tuition discount awarded. In a perfect world, the state appropriation or subsidy would be equivalent to the difference between the tuition charged to in-state students and the true cost of education. Over the past two decades or more, however, there has been a steady, or in some cases abrupt, decline in state funding to public institutions in many states, thereby underfunding the state subsidy. Such declines have been driven by a lack of availability of state funds due to limited tax revenue, the need or desire for legislators to prioritize other essential state funding needs, such as health care (e.g., Medicaid), transportation, corrections, debt service on bonds, etc., and increasing recognition that higher education can make up state funding reductions by increasing tuition and fee revenue. That is, many states have transferred the burden of supporting higher education from the citizens broadly to the student and their families individually.

As illustrated in Figure 11.1, for URI, the state appropriation in FY 2022 ($82.4 million) finally returned to the FY 2007 level of $82.5 million after sixteen years. If adjusted for inflation, the FY 2022 appropriation would have needed to be $111 million to break even with FY 2007. In FY 2022, the state appropriation was sufficient to cover the subsidy for approximately 4,600 in-state FTE students, but the institution enrolled approximately 7,100 FTE in-state students. State funding of approximately $127.5 million in FY 2022 dollars would have been necessary to fully fund the subsidy for the number of enrolled in-state students. This effectively means that the university loses money on every in-state student enrolled. This situation is certainly not unique to URI.

Despite insufficient state revenue to cover the tuition subsidy for in-state students, most public institutions continue to offer reduced tuition to in-state students in recognition of the critical state support they do receive. Reduced tuition for in-state students helps make a public college education accessible and affordable for resident students and is consistent with the state institution's mandate and mission. At the same time, public institutions continue to advocate for legislators and governors to restore state appropriations to the levels needed to minimize the tuition burden on families. With limited state funds available, however, that is an uphill battle in most states.

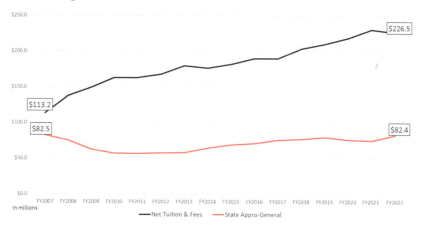

Figure 11.1. Changes in state appropriation and net-tuition and fee revenue (tuition and fee revenue less institutional student aid) at the University of Rhode Island from FY 2007 to FY 2022.

Because of annual increases in mostly personnel expenses, declining state funding at public institutions and/or diminished enrollment at many institutions creates financial challenges for both institutions and students. As shown in Figure 11.1, declining or level state revenue necessitates increases in tuition revenue to make up for the shortfall and/or budget reductions to reduce expenses on the part of the institution. Often this is perceived as unaffordable annual tuition rate increases contributing to greater student borrowing and the student debt crisis of today. Similarly, reducing expenses within the institution can create a negative perception or reality of reduced services, such as eliminating course sections or academic or career advising resources, and charging more while providing less support to students, which can lead to enrollment losses. It doesn't have to be this way.

The doubling of net-tuition revenue between FY 2007 and FY 2022 shown in Figure 11.1, for example, reflects growth in tuition revenue from multiple sources with only a small portion coming from actual tuition rate increases. The largest portion came from strategic growth in enrollment associated with recruiting slightly larger incoming classes, dramatic improvement in retention of continuing students, changing the mix of in-state and out-of-state students, reinvigoration of summer session, a new winter J-term program, and some new market-based online programs. In other words, the tuition revenue base was expanded while keeping tuition increases equal to or below the Higher Education Price Index (HEPI). Optimizing enrollment capacity relative to expenses is also important. Such efforts collectively not only grow tuition revenue with only small increases in tuition rates, but also dramatically improve degree completion and time to graduation, which saves families money, hastens the timely pursuit of a career, improves the university's reputation, and enhances the institution's value proposition.

Because of the interconnection of costs throughout the academic ecosystem, institutional leaders must be strategic and coordinated in their tuition policy, housing, dining, fee rate increases, and internal budget prioritization, and must truly understand their competitive position in the higher education marketplace. Raising tuition, room and board rates, and/or fees to levels that exceed the cost-value proposition and reputation of the institution, or inflation, will be totally counterproductive, as is accepting students that are not likely to be successful at the institution.

Leaders must also recognize and carefully manage academic indirect costs associated with delivering the core mission, such as IT infrastructure, libraries, classrooms, teaching laboratories, administrative costs, etc. Such costs are real, can be substantial, and are supported by tuition, fee, and state revenues from the operating budget. Administrative costs especially are sometimes overlooked and should be carefully managed to maintain an appropriate balance with mission-centric costs associated with academic and student programs.

Some states allocate funding to their public colleges and universities using a headcount or full-time equivalent student formula, and others have implemented performance funding models that provide funding in response to improvement in various performance measures, such as retention, graduation rate, degrees awarded, or perhaps even the number of students in certain majors with the promise of contributing to economic development in that state. While one can argue about the "best" or "right" metrics or criteria for states to use in making state appropriation allocations, an advantage of such models is that institutions understand the basis for their allocations and can plan accordingly. This, of course, assumes states will make their appropriation allocations based upon some identified and preferably agreed-upon criteria. In many cases, however, the level of the state appropriation is no longer, or perhaps never was, based on any specific measures, but rather a function of an annual request from the institution and a state allocation of whatever amount is affordable or can be negotiated with the state legislature or governor. Such apparently random allocation approaches are problematic, defy planning, and can easily become politicized. In moments of frustration during efforts to secure and justify needed annual state funding increases, I have often pleaded "please tell us the rules of the game so we can play." It is helpful for institutions to know the criteria to be considered in determining annual state allocations, even if they disagree with them, rather than meandering through an unknown allocation approach and attempting to negotiate without criteria.

Endowment Income

The annual interest generated from the investment of university endowments is allocated in accordance with the purpose of the gifts that collectively create the endowment. Most endowment funds from individual gifts are consolidated and invested in aggregate, and a portion of the annual interest (usually 4 to 5 percent) is allocated to the purpose of the fund, such as scholarships, endowed professorships, academic programs, lecture series, etc. These endowed gifts and funds provide support each year and allow an institution to make commitments into the future, which is a wonderful asset. While very helpful to certain programs and beneficial overall to the institution, such restricted endowment income may not bolster the institution's operating budget directly, although endowed scholarships certainly help students and extend the institution's base financial aid budget. Also, endowed professorships may cover a portion of a faculty salary, freeing up some operating funds for other investments.

Some endowments are unrestricted, and the annual interest can be invested to cover selected institutional operating expenses and may be used for financial aid purposes instead of, or in addition to, tuition discounting supported by the base general fund budget. Unrestricted endowment income is an incredible asset and can provide direct operating support in perpetuity, although it typically represents a very small proportion of endowment funds. In contrast to scholarships from unrestricted endowment income, tuition discounting reduces the tuition revenue the institution collects that would otherwise contribute to the base operating budget while enhancing affordability for eligible students. There still is, however, a net-tuition contribution to the operating budget. Tuition scholarships from unrestricted endowment income also meet the goal of making a college education affordable to students and simultaneously serve as a source of revenue because the scholarship funds provide a portion of the tuition to the operating budget.

Some prestigious private universities, such as several Ivy League institutions, and some very high-profile public research institutions have multibillion-dollar endowments. For such institutions, endowment income can be a significant contributor in multiple ways to the operating budget. Even for the wealthiest institutions, endowment income serves to supplement, not replace, annual revenue from tuition and fees and state appropriations. See "The Top Twenty-Five Institutions Ranked by Their Fiscal Year 2021 Endowments" for a list of universities with the largest endowments as reported by *Inside Higher Ed.*

Top 25 Institutions Ranked by Their Fiscal Year 2021 Endowments

Institution Name	FY 2021 Endowment (in $1,000s)	FY 2020 Endowment (in $1,000s)	Change in Market Value (%)
Harvard Univ.	51,900,662	40,575,027	27.9
Univ. of Texas System	42,906,847	31,958,313	34.3
Yale Univ.	42,282,900	31,201,700	35.5
Stanford Univ.	37,800,000	28,948,000	30.6
Princeton Univ.	37,697,509	26,558,643	41.9
MIT	27,527,204	18,495,905	48.8
Univ. of Pennsylvania	20,523,546	14,877,363	38.0
Univ. of Notre Dame	18,074,543	11,962,820	51.1
Texas A&M System	18,028,267	13,594,482	32.6
Univ. of Michigan	17,022,683	12,860,473	32.4
Northwestern	14,958,441	10,926,510	36.9
Columbia Univ.	14,349,970	11,257,021	27.5
Washington Univ.	13,536,003	8,420,497	60.8
Duke Univ.	12,692,472	8,474,071	49.8
Emory Univ.	11,031,029	7,936,988	39.0
Vanderbilt Univ.	10,928,512	6,917,371	58.0
Univ. of Virginia	10,532,651	7,255,701	45.2
Johns Hopkins Univ.	9,315,279	6,750,092	38.0
Dartmouth College	8,484,189	5,975,180	42.0
Rice Univ.	8,061,260	6,163,926	30.8
Univ. of Southern Calif.	8,008,443	5,769,643	38.8
Ohio State Univ.	6,814,413	5,287,131	28.9
Brown Univ.	6,520,175	4,377,466	48.9
Univ. of Pittsburg	5,647,017	4,172,380	35.3
New York Univ.	5,574,000	4,323,652	28.9

Figure 11.2. The top twenty-five endowments by value in FY 2021, annual endowment growth from FY 2020, and the percent change in market value.[46]

According to a 2021 report published by the American Council on Education, approximately 1,300 private nonprofit and 700 public four-year institutions reported endowment data at the end of FY 2018.[47] At that time, approximately 43 percent of private and 40 percent of public institutions had endowments greater than $50 million, and 104 institutions (64 privates and 40 publics) had endowments exceeding $1 billion. The median endowments for the 2,000 private and public four-year institutions that provided endowment data at the end of FY 2018 were $37.1 million and $35.4 million, respectively. At a typical endowment spending rate of 4 to 5 percent, these median endowments would support annual spending of about $1.4 million to $1.9 million at private and public institutions, which represents about 1 to 6 percent of the median total expenditures.

Recent 2021 and 2022 *Study of Endowments* surveys conducted by NACUBO and TIAA of approximately 700 institutions demonstrate that college and university endowments grew substantially in FY 2021, but then declined abruptly in FY 2022. Surveyed institutions posted a median return of 30.6 percent for FY 2021 compared to a 1.8 percent median return in FY 2020. For FY 2022, the median return was -8.0 percent, which highlights the potential annual volatility of endowment investments and the market. Despite year-to-year volatility, spending rates from endowments remain relatively constant over time (e.g., 4.8 percent in FY 2021 and 4.2 percent in FY 2022), even across a windfall year like FY 2021 and a challenging year like FY 2022. According to the NACUBO-TIAA study for FY 2022, 132 colleges and universities had endowments assets exceeding $1 billion, and the median endowment size among the 678 respondents was $203.4 million. Their analysis of endowment spending revealed that on average endowment spending was distributed as follows: 46 percent for financial aid, 16 percent for academic programs and research, 11 percent for endowed faculty positions, and 10 percent for campus facilities operations.[48]

While endowment income provides important stability and flexibility for institutions and has been especially helpful in providing financial aid to needy students through scholarships, the relatively small endowments at most institutions limit the impact of endowment income on the base operating budgets of all but a few. Given the incredible value of endowed funds, it is easy to understand why growing the endowment is a primary goal of fundraising campaigns at almost every institution of higher education in the United States.

The growing disassociation of state appropriations as a provision to directly subsidize tuition for in-state students highlights a parallel between the annual state appropriation to public institutions and annual endowment interest income in many private institutions. For example, at URI, the state appropriation of $82.4 million in FY 2022 would be roughly equivalent to the annual payout of a $2 billion endowment, while URI's true endowment is about $211 million. Furthermore, the $82.4 million is largely unrestricted and can be used to support the base operating budget. A portion of endowment income is restricted based on donor gift intent. When viewed through that lens, I find myself expressing gratitude for the state appropriation that we receive each year, even as we aggressively advocate for increases. Without that appropriation, the institution would be doomed. Perspective can be a powerful tool to create understanding.

Research Overhead Funds

Federal- and state-funded research is a prominent feature of American research universities today. Before World War II, however, federal funding for research was minimal to nonexistent. In the postwar era, the Office of Naval Research (ONR) began to initiate federal contracts with universities for special research projects. Through that process, it became evident that for university-based research infrastructure to grow and be successful it would be necessary for ONR to fund the full costs incurred by universities related to ONR contracts, including both institutional costs and the costs specifically associated with sponsored projects.

Thus, in 1947, ONR acknowledged the legitimacy of institutional costs, such as research facilities, utilities, and administrative infrastructure, above and beyond the direct costs of a project and agreed to fund both costs associated with university research.[49] Shortly thereafter, other federal agencies also recognized and agreed to fund those costs. Initially, these institutional costs were funded through flat-rate reimbursement of 8 percent, then 15 percent in the late 1950s, and 20 percent in the early 1960s. In 1966, the federal government agreed to remove the flat-rate ceiling and established policies to reimburse universities for the indirect costs incurred in conducting federally funded research projects, although some agencies have restrictions or caps on indirect costs for certain kinds of grants, such as educational or training grants or off-campus research.[50] What had been referred to as *institutional costs* became designated *indirect costs* associated with sponsored research.

Today, research indirect costs are built into research grants to partially reimburse the institution for costs that the institution incurs in carrying out its research mission. As such, research awards, especially federally funded research, generally include funds to support both the direct and indirect costs of research at universities. Direct costs are those specifically related to carrying out the research project activities and may include researcher salaries, graduate student assistantships, travel, supplies, and other direct research expenditures. Research indirect costs, often referred to as F&A for facilities and administration, support administrative costs, such as payroll, financial management, research administration, etc., and facilities costs, such as research space, building and equipment depreciation, capital improvements, maintenance, utilities, etc. The portion of the research grant funding associated with indirect costs (or F&A) is referred to as overhead funds, and it is accounted for separately from the overall university base general fund operating budget.

For major research universities, overhead funds represent a substantial revenue stream that can total many tens of millions of dollars each year. However, the indirect cost reimbursement for facilities and administration expenses rarely, if ever, covers the full indirect costs of the research mission, which therefore must be subsidized by the university. Indeed, research is an important, yet expensive, proposition. Research universities, for example, designate and fund through the operating budget a portion of faculty salaries and benefits dedicated to research, which is an appropriate investment in the research mission. Indirect cost reimbursement from grants is tied to direct cost expenditures from research projects. As direct project expenditures are incurred, a portion of the overhead dollars becomes available to cover F&A expenses. As such, if funded project expenditures are stalled because of unanticipated factors, as was the case during COVID-19 when travel was restricted and some projects had to temporarily shut down, then direct expenditures are reduced, and overhead dollars become unavailable. Such a situation can create short-term funding shortfalls for critical research infrastructure, including research administration personnel.

The amount of overhead charged to an agency on each grant is based on a federally negotiated indirect cost rate, which will vary from one institution to the next, but typically exceeds, or even greatly exceeds, 50 percent. That is, a negotiated indirect cost rate of 50 percent for an institution means that half of the total direct costs of a project will be added to the budget to cover research indirect costs. To be clear, 50 percent of the total cost of the project is not allocated for indirect costs, but rather 50 percent of the direct costs. So, a grant with direct costs of $1,000 and a 50 percent indirect cost rate would add indirect costs of $500 for a total project budget of $1,500 with one-third of that allocated to overhead funds. While the indirect cost rate is firmly established for each institution for a specified timeframe, some sponsors may choose to cap the indirect costs at a reduced rate (e.g., many state government-funded projects) or not pay overhead at all (e.g., many foundation-funded projects). As such, the effective overhead rate, or the amount of overhead generated as a proportion of total research expenditures during a year, is typically lower than the negotiated rate.

Because overhead funds are partial reimbursements for expenses that the university has already paid, there is flexibility as to how overhead funds can be spent. Most universities invest a large portion of these funds right back into the research mission by supporting research pre-award and post-award faculty support offices, start-up costs for new faculty hires, equipment purchases, seed money to increase research competitiveness, staff to operate core laboratories, and much more. These funds, however, might also flow into the base university operating budget to support a portion of utilities and insurance costs, fiscal accounting offices, etc., and therefore may provide some supplement to the base operating budget that would otherwise be totally dependent on tuition, fees, state appropriation, and endowment income.

Auxiliary Enterprise Services

Auxiliary enterprises at colleges and universities are distinct entities managed as self-supporting programs, including all personnel and operating expenses, maintenance of the plant, debt service on bonds, and any institutional support provided. Auxiliaries exist to provide goods and services to students, staff, or faculty and, at times, may serve the public as well, and they charge a fee specifically related to those goods and services. Typical auxiliary enterprises include housing, dining services, campus bookstores, operations of the student union, health services, parking and transportation services, and more.

While auxiliary services are largely self-contained and self-supporting, they typically pay direct and modest indirect costs to the university for services provided, which may be charged directly as expenditures or allocated as a proportional share of costs. While auxiliary enterprise services represent a significant self-contained financial operation, the contribution to the general operating budget through direct and indirect costs is comparatively small. If auxiliary departments fail to become self-sufficient, as they are intended to be, they can become a financial drain on the institution. As such, university leaders must pay careful attention to the pricing structures of auxiliary and enterprise services and the quality of those services because they contribute to the total cost of attendance for students and their families. To some extent, the auxiliary and enterprise costs to students compete with tuition and mandatory fees and can undermine financial aid packages provided by the university. While financial aid is officially a discount against tuition, families remain focused on the bottom line that they must pay each year. So, if housing, dining, health services, and student union auxiliary fees go up each year along with tuition indexed to the HEPI, the annual increase in real costs to students may be prohibitive, and the financial aid tuition discount becomes less impactful. Institutions must carefully position their tuition and fee structures in the very competitive higher education marketplace and must ensure that auxiliary costs and services don't compromise their cost-value proposition.

More importantly, however, auxiliary and enterprise services are critically important because they directly impact the student experience and can shape a university's reputation, in either a positive or negative way. The real asset and keys to success for campus auxiliaries are excellent service delivery and high-quality products. By placing emphasis on innovation, quality, and service, auxiliaries and enterprises positively impact the student experience and enhance their competitiveness relative to the myriad off-campus alternatives that exist for such services.

Institutional Reserve Funds

Institutional reserve funds are liquid assets that help maintain the financial health of an institution, provide a foundation for managing debt, allow for nonrecurring strategic investments, and protect the institution against volatility in external factors, such as pandemics, recessions, or declines in enrollment. Institutional reserves are not allocated to any specific unit within the institution but rather are held centrally. Maintaining central operating reserve funds represents sound fiscal policy to ensure the financial health of the institution, including maintaining or improving bond ratings.

Annual institutional operating budget surpluses represent additions to institutional reserve accounts, while the allocation of reserve funds to support construction projects, short-term strategic initiatives, or to respond to emergencies represents deductions from the reserve accounts. In any given year, surpluses might occur because some retired or departed positions are vacant, utility expenses are less than budgeted, or a funded project is delayed. These unplanned events result in a short-term surplus that can be transferred into a reserve account. Such accounts typically include a central reserve fund at the institutional level, but may also include college-based reserve accounts, research overhead reserve accounts, auxiliary reserve accounts, and perhaps cost center reserve accounts as well. Maintaining robust central reserve funds provides institutions with a financial cushion against unanticipated fluctuations in revenues and/or expenses and the potential to respond to emergencies. In fact, some states require their public institutions to maintain reserve accounts for exactly this reason.

University leaders must be cognizant of the need for and importance of reserve funds and resist the temptation to spend frivolously from them or routinely charge project cost overruns to reserve accounts and run the risk of depleting these critically important funds. Without an opportunity to transfer annual surpluses into reserve accounts, budget managers have a perverse incentive to simply spend out any surpluses at year-end rather than save for emergencies or strategic needs. The opportunity to transfer annual surpluses into reserve funds for strategic investment purposes encourages careful annual budget management because everyone benefits from the investments, especially if such strategic reserve investments generate new revenue for the institution.

In addition to creating a public health crisis of devastating proportions, COVID-19 represented a major shock to both the revenue and expense side of the ledger for most higher education institutions and serves as a reminder of the essential need for reserves as a provision against emergencies. At my institution, we were able to use reserves as bridge funds when faced with significant and abrupt COVID-19 expenses that allowed us to protect the health and safety of our community and to safeguard and sustain our human resources by preventing layoffs. In fact, some institutions designate a portion of their central reserves as contingency reserves for protection against unforeseen emergent catastrophic situations. Contingency funds differ from investment reserves that are held for one-time strategic investments, such as major information technology upgrades or capital projects.

It is important to understand that institutional reserves are one-time-only (OTO) funds—once spent they are gone. Therefore, these funds should only be used for nonrecurring expenses and should not be used to support salary and benefit increases or to fund permanent positions, unless they are serving as temporary bridge funds to a known retirement or new position. Also, if reserves become near depleted because of emergency or strategic spending, it is prudent to aggressively rebuild the reserves as quickly as is plausible. Operating with no or only a limited reserve is tantamount to balancing risk without a safety net.

While the essential nature of reserve funds is without question, there is not consensus about the optimum size or target for central reserve accounts. Often the target for the reserve is described as a proportion of the total annual operating expenditures of the institution. Many public institutions have operating reserve targets ranging from 3 to 12.5 percent of the annual operating budget with some outliers in the 20 to 25 percent range. In some cases, the maximum size of the reserve is based on recommendations about the number of weeks of cash on hand an institution should strive to maintain operations, including personnel, in an emergency. The Government Finance Officers Association has suggested a target of not less than two months.[51] NACUBO recommends that institutions should be able to cover about five months (twenty weeks) of expenses from reserves, equating to about 40 percent of the total annual operating expenses.[52] The latter would likely be challenging for many institutions, especially public institutions, with limited resources, small annual surpluses, and/or concerns about the optics of large reserve accounts.

While one might intuitively think the larger the reserve the better, there are potential issues of concern for institutions consistently carrying large annual surpluses, especially for public colleges and universities. For example, for public institutions in some states, some legislators may interpret the presence of annual surpluses or robust reserve accounts as indicators that the institution is overfunded by the state at taxpayers' expense and use that as a rationale for future budget reductions. In the interest of transparency, institutional leaders should educate legislators about the critical nature of reserve accounts, which protect both the institution and state from financial risks. The benefit of institutional reserves should have become abundantly clear during the COVID-19 pandemic and may serve to squelch any legislator angst about surpluses and reserves that may exist in some states.

In addition to potential state legislator concerns, it is important to remember that the largest revenue stream at all private and most public institutions comes from tuition and fees paid by students and their families. News stories referring to large institutional reserves may accuse universities of stockpiling funds while at the same time raising tuition. This sort of interpretation reflects a misunderstanding of the OTO nature, purpose, and strategic value of reserve funds, but nevertheless can create a public relations challenge. Also, because there is often a lack of clarity about the origin and purpose of reserve funds among constituents, questions about surpluses and reserve balances often emerge from faculty who will seek to use reserve funds to hire new faculty or add new programs, or from employees who wish to include reserves in collective bargaining negotiations to increase compensation. It would be highly inappropriate and irresponsible for institutions to use reserve funds for such recurring base budget investments. Board members may also not fully understand the nature of reserves and benefit from understanding how reserve funds are constituted and their purpose.

University leaders must strike a balance in building a reserve that is feasible, affordable, and that safeguards the institution and community, but not so large that it raises concerns from families about tuition being too high or from legislators believing that the institution is overfunded by the state. It is good practice for leaders to establish a fiscally responsible and defensible reserve target and make every effort to operate within that target budget. Finally, and most importantly, institutional leaders need to communicate clearly to constituents about the nature and limitations of reserve funds and why they are critical to the institution's financial viability and investment strategies to minimize confusion from both internal stakeholders and legislators.

Managing Enrollment Is Key to Managing Revenue

While there are multiple revenue streams at most institutions, enrollment is the primary driver at all private and increasingly most public institutions. Even for those relatively few remaining public institutions where state appropriations provide the largest proportion of the annual operating budget, enrollment often figures prominently in shaping the state appropriation. For most institutions, net tuition and fees contribute directly and substantially to the annual operating budget with endowment income, research overhead, and auxiliary enterprise overhead as important, but relatively minor, supplemental contributions. Institutional reserves serve as a cushion to secure financial health and support strategic investments critical to the institution's future. As such, thoughtful and creative management of enrollment, understanding the array of enrollment markets for different student populations (e.g., traditional-age students, adults, transfer students, veterans, graduate students), and acknowledging and understanding your institution's value proposition are essential for sustaining revenue, value, and the viability of each institution.

CHAPTER TWELVE

Managing Enrollment Means Managing Money

Enrollment management in higher education was traditionally viewed as the responsibility of the admission office to "bring in the class." The rest of us were expected to do our jobs by teaching and advising students, providing career guidance, ensuring that cocurricular activities are engaging, or providing quality housing and dining options for students. That is no longer the case. Because all aspects of the academic ecosystem are intertwined, institutional leaders must understand and convey that the responsibility for enrollment management belongs to all of us. Student outcomes, such as retention, graduation rate, time to degree, and the overall student experience, are as important as marketing, recruitment, and yield events to ensure the right size, academic profile, and make-up of the incoming class of new students.

Leaders must understand that strategic enrollment management drives student success and the institution's financial viability—and the two are inextricably linked. It is much more complex than simply recruiting and admitting students, although in the very competitive current marketplace recruitment and yield are by no means simple or unimportant. It involves a comprehensive process that relies on the entire campus community from those in buildings and grounds, student life, the bursar's office, and, of course, delivering a relevant and engaging learning experience that connects with students' academic interests and life goals. Let's face it, enrollment is a significant source of revenue for all institutions, and managing enrollment drives the upside or the downside of revenue, depending on how it goes.

Recent Enrollment Trends

As reported by the National Student Clearinghouse Research Center (NSCRC), total enrollment across all higher education sectors has been steadily declining for several years, even before the negative impacts of COVID-19.[53] For example, higher education enrollment declined year over year by 1.7 percent and 1.3 percent in 2018 and 2019, continuing a pattern of eight consecutive years of overall declining enrollment.[54] The pandemic, which began impacting most campuses in the spring of 2020, only served to exacerbate the situation with year-over-year total enrollment declines of 2.5 percent for fall 2020 and 2.7 percent for fall 2021, representing a total two-year decline of 938,000 students.[55] Undergraduate enrollment alone dropped 6.6 percent from fall 2019 to fall 2021, and the nation's fall 2021 class of first-year students was 9.2 percent smaller (213,000 fewer students) compared to pre-pandemic levels in fall 2019. The pattern of year-over-year enrollment declines continued for spring 2022. Following a 3.5 percent drop in spring 2021, total postsecondary enrollment declined an additional 4.7 percent, or 662,000 students, from spring 2021 to spring 2022, with most of that decline occurring in undergraduate enrollment.[56] As the impact of COVID-19 waned, so did the decline in enrollment. Fall 2022 enrollment declined by only 0.6 percent, or 94,000 students, and first-year student enrollment rose 4.3 percent compared to fall 2021. For fall 2022, however, total undergraduate enrollment remained down 1.2 million students, and first-year student enrollment was down 150,000 students compared to pre-pandemic levels in fall 2019.[57]

For the first time since the beginning of the pandemic, undergraduate enrollment grew by 2.1 percent in fall 2023 with most of that growth reflecting post-pandemic enrollment recovery in community colleges.[58] In sharp contrast, first-year student enrollment declined in fall 2023 by 3.6 percent across all sectors, reversing most of the gains in first-year students from fall 2022. Of even greater concern, enrollment of first-time, full-time bachelor's degree students declined by 6.2 percent across public and private nonprofit institutions with similar declines in highly selective, very competitive, competitive, and less selective institutions.[59] The fall 2023 decline in first-year, full-time students was most pronounced in the eighteen- to twenty-year-old student cohort. This abrupt decline in new incoming traditional-age students is troubling and may be a signal of challenging times on the horizon.

Recent surveys of more than 5,000 high school students between February 2020 and January 2022 further suggest the pattern of declining higher education enrollment may continue.[60] In September 2021 and January 2022, only 48 percent and 51 percent of the high school respondents indicated they are considering attending a four-year college, while 47 percent preferred a program they could complete with less than two years of additional education. The latter may include employer-based apprenticeships, internships, trade skills, and career and technical education programs. The cost of college tuition was the top concern followed closely by the magnitude of student loans that would be necessary. At the same time some high school students are questioning the value of a college education and degree, some private and public sector employers are migrating to skills-based rather than degree-based hiring of their future employees.

While these data paint a rather bleak picture of higher education enrollment, there is considerable variation in enrollment trends among the different higher education sectors and among some individual institutions within sectors. For instance, wealthy and highly selective private and many public flagships have fared better with some experiencing enrollment gains, and graduate enrollments have been steady or have increased at many institutions. Many of these are the same institutions that have recently experienced significant gains in their endowment investments, demonstrating that wealthy prestigious institutions are becoming wealthier as many others struggle and become increasingly enrollment and resource constrained. While many elite institutions continue to thrive, the remaining tuition-dependent institutions that serve the masses and many first-generation and underrepresented student populations struggle. Indeed, institutional income inequality is rampant in higher education today.

Current-day higher education enrollment challenges are driven by numerous factors, including a continuing demographic decline in the number of high school graduates, growing skepticism among some about the value of a college education relative to the cost, an expanding population of students from low-income families with no or limited college experience, growing mental health challenges in young people, and overall family financial challenges. Of course, the COVID-19 pandemic has exacerbated these drivers along with the deep polarization in society and the politicization of higher education. A June 2023 Gallup poll revealed that only 36 percent of Americans say they have a great deal or quite a lot of confidence in higher education as compared to 57 percent in 2015 and 48 percent in 2018.[61]

While the development and implementation of a strategic enrollment plan is not a guarantee for enrollment, it is a critical step toward stabilizing enrollment and tuition revenue for many institutions. *Each institution must develop a good understanding of its current and prospective student populations and their cost-value proposition and implement an adaptable plan to optimize enrollment and net-tuition revenue.* Because of enrollment challenges and intense competition for students, managing enrollment to generate revenue is a more viable path forward than large increases in tuition, given the current levels of student debt and societal concerns about the cost of a college education. In fact, tuition increases may exacerbate enrollment challenges.

Keys for Managing Enrollment and Tuition Revenue

Data Quality and Analysis

Collecting, analyzing, aggregating and disaggregating, and interpreting *accurate* enrollment and financial data is an essential element of any sophisticated effort to carefully manage and monitor enrollment and institutional financial information. All actions and initiatives must be evidenced-based (i.e., based on relevant data to devise strategies, inform decision-making, and measure outcomes). I highlight *accurate* data because data collection and analysis can be complex and must rely on data gathered and analyzed in a structured manner by centralized offices with the expertise and responsibilities for data accuracy and consistency. On most campuses, these are the Office of Institutional Research and the Office of Budget and Financial Planning. These offices understand the terminology, assumptions, and analyses and are held responsible for consistency in data quality and data analytics. It is not uncommon on many campuses for well-intentioned individuals from various other departments and divisions to create their own data sets and analyses, often based on different terminology, assumptions, databases, and analyses that lead to contrasting conclusions, confusion, and chaos. Institutional leaders need to be knowledgeable about the underlying constructs of data collection, analyses, and assumptions to make informed decisions about strategic priorities, enrollment management, and budget allocations.

The following quote from business leader C. William Pollard captures the essential nature of and need for quality data and information: "Information is a source of learning. But unless it is organized, processed, and available to the right people in a format for decision-making, it is a burden, not a benefit."[62] I have witnessed both the *benefit* of quality information and analyses and the *burden* of misinformation from incorrect or misdirected data, analyses, and interpretations. Insightful gathering and analysis of data are key elements in every aspect of managing enrollment and tuition revenue.

Financial Aid

College May Be More Affordable Than You Think

Given the rising cost of college education, financial aid is among the most important variables for institutions to understand and manage to shape their enrollment and financial stability. *The strategic allocation of financial aid provided by institutions is among the most powerful enrollment management tools available to maintain or enhance enrollment and stabilize institutional operating budgets.* While the cost of a college education has increased over time, most analyses and media reports suggesting that the cost of tuition and fees have "risen significantly" or are "out-of-control" equate the cost of attendance with the published tuition and fee rates from institutions (i.e., the sticker price), ignoring the substantial investments in institutional grant aid to offset tuition increases that have occurred in recent years.[63] Actually, only a small proportion of students pay the sticker price, and grant-based financial aid has risen faster than tuition at most institutions. For example, the College Board's *Trends in Pricing and Student Aid 2021* report shows that between 2006-07 and 2021-22, the average grant aid per first-time in-state student increased at public four-year institutions by $3,740 in 2021 dollars (from $4,360 to $8,100), while the published tuition and fees increased by $3,010 (from $7,730 to $10,740).[64] Between 2006-07 and 2021-22, the average net tuition and fees after grant aid paid by first-time, full-time students enrolled in public and private nonprofit four-year institutions was lowest in 2021-22. Investments in institutional student aid are critical and must not be ignored or undervalued. College is, indeed, more affordable than many think.

While university administrators should rely on their financial aid experts to develop allocation models, institutional leaders should have a good grasp of the interplay among tuition and aid and other costs, such as housing, dining, and mandatory fees, at their institution so they can articulate the nuances to prospective students and parents, legislators, donors, and even faculty and staff. There is little doubt that students and their families pay close attention to the financial aid package or scholarship they are offered by each institution, and it weighs heavily on their decision about which institution they choose to attend. Furthermore, society broadly, and legislators more specifically, are concerned about the perception of rising costs of a college education and the current level of student debt ($1.7 trillion). As such, the political as well as financial aspects of student aid are important to understand.

Aid from Loans versus Grants

While we often think of financial aid as support for students with financial need, 86 percent of first-time, full-time undergraduate students were awarded financial aid at four-year degree-granting institutions (79 percent at two-year institutions) for the 2018-19 academic year.[65] This includes aid from federal loans and grants as well as from state and local governments, institutions, and private sources. Contemporary financial aid models include both need-based and merit-based aid, and increasingly many students receive a combination of both types, which often include both loans and grants.

According to *Trends in College Pricing and Student Aid 2021*, the total amount of financial aid that students received in 2020-21 was $234.9 billion from all grants, federal loans, tax credits, and federal work-study.[66] Importantly, for the 2020-21 academic year, students borrowed approximately $96 billion, which represents the tenth consecutive year of decline in annual student borrowing, down from approximately $135 billion (in 2020 dollars) in 2010-11. This is encouraging given the growing concerns about student debt. *The largest portion of the total aid to students is in the form of grants ($138.6 billion), which unlike loans do not have to be repaid.* Federal Pell Grant expenditures (in 2020 dollars) declined from $42.3 billion in 2010-11 to $26 billion in 2020-21, while institutional grant aid for undergraduate students increased by $25.6 billion over that time, reaching a total of $71.1 billion. In 2020-21, grant aid provided by higher education institutions accounted for 51 percent of all grant aid, up from 35 percent in 2010-11, whereas federal grants of all kinds declined from

44 percent in 2010-11 to 27 percent of total grant aid in 2020-21. State and private and employer grants have consistently represented 9 percent and 12 percent, respectively, of grant aid over this time.

Institutional Grants via Tuition Discounting

With a decline in student borrowing and federal grant aid, private and public institutions have become among the most important sources of financial aid to students, which highlights the necessity for strategic financial aid planning and allocation and careful attention to both net revenue to institutions and meeting the aid needs of students. In fact, institutional aid is among the fastest-growing expenditures in higher education. Most institutional aid is in the form of grants and scholarships, typically implemented as tuition discounts, to offset all or part of the published tuition. The "discount" may be covered by institutional funds or from annual gifts or endowment income, although most of it is unfunded and represents tuition revenue forgone to incentivize enrollment.

While there are ongoing debates about the pros and cons of tuition discounting, it is occurring at almost every institution, and based on a 2022 NACUBO tuition discounting study, nearly 91 percent of first-year students and approximately 83 percent of all undergraduates attending private, nonprofit institutions received some form of institutional grant aid for the 2021-22 academic year.[67] Tuition discounts for private, nonprofit institutions approached 51 percent for all undergraduates and averaged 56 percent for first-time, full-time students in 2020-21, which means these institutions forgo more than half of the tuition revenue they would collect if they charged all students the published tuition, assuming those students chose to enroll. Of course, many would not enroll at the full published price, which is the point of tuition discounting. The discount rate for public institutions is more difficult to accurately discern because of differential in-state versus out-of-state tuition and is not directly comparable to that of private institutions. NACUBO's 2020 report has nevertheless estimated that the average tuition discount for the 2017-18 academic year at all public four-year institutions was approximately 24 percent, and 28.4 percent for doctoral/research institutions.[68]

Institutional Aid as an Enrollment Management Tool

Tuition discounting, used by both private and public institutions, is designed primarily to help make an institution more affordable. When done strategically and effectively, tuition discounting will increase enrollment and provide sufficient net revenue to operate the institution. The key is finding that sweet spot that addresses affordability for students and financial stability for the institution. Both the net price to the student and the net revenue to the institution is critical. With the strategic allocation of such aid, the institution can also shape the make-up of its student body in terms of meeting its diversity and academic quality goals, balancing enrollment across certain majors, and helping with retention. Hence, tuition discounting along with other sources of institutional grant aid is a powerful enrollment management tool.

While initially envisioned as a way of effectively transferring funds from those with greater means to those with lesser means, tuition discounting is now widespread, and most students and their parents have come to expect a "scholarship" from each institution to which they apply. In fact, anecdotal evidence suggests that the higher price tag of some institutions creates the perception or illusion of higher value, and students and parents take pride in receiving a scholarship from a high-priced institution. It is not uncommon for families to attempt to use scholarship offers from one institution as a bargaining chip with other institutions, which is a game that institutions should avoid playing. For families, what should matter is their bottom-line cost of attendance after aid, the quality of the educational experience, and the fit for the student rather than the size of the scholarship *per se*, which should be emphasized to inquiring families.

Institutional aid in the form of tuition discounts is a major investment. Discounting models must be carefully studied and monitored by each institution, including examining yield and net revenue at various discount rates and across various majors. Institutions need to keep one eye on student access and affordability and the other on net revenue to ensure that they don't discount away their needed operating revenues, which would threaten an institution's ability to deliver a quality education and fulfill its mission. As tuition is raised over time, institutions also need to increase their financial aid to keep pace while ensuring that their tuition increase generates new revenue for institutional investment. It's a very tricky balance.

Managing Costs and Optics

Even with tuition discounting, institutions need to be sensitive to their published tuition rate, or sticker price, which may discourage some students from applying. For example, low-income and first-generation college applicants, the exact populations that we hope to attract by making a college education more affordable, may not be aware that institutions offer discounts on tuition and, therefore, choose not to apply based on the sticker price alone. Also, raising tuition to generate additional revenue can be challenging. Tuition increases above the HEPI not only create financial challenges for students but are also a public relations issue. Front-page stories about tuition increases rarely highlight that aid will be increased to offset the tuition for needy students.

Finally, while strategic discounting of tuition is certainly helpful, the entire bottom-line cost associated with tuition—mandatory fees, housing, dining, books, etc., along with institutional reputation and quality—all influence the total cost of an education and a family's decision to attend. As such, annual increases in housing, dining, and fees can undermine an institution's significant investment in tuition grant aid and be counterproductive to the institution's enrollment goals and bottom line. Careful consideration of all proposed cost increases to prospective students, whether related to the operating budget, fees, or auxiliary enterprise services, should be coordinated through the enrollment management office to maximize the benefit to students and the institution.

Attention to Retention

Efforts aimed at growing enrollment to increase net-tuition revenue instinctively lean toward enhanced recruitment and innovative marketing strategies to grow the applicant pool, enhanced campus visits and yield events for prospective students and families, and increased institutional financial aid to first-time, first-year students. Such efforts are critically important, especially with intense competition among institutions for the shrinking population of college-bound high school graduates. Institutions spend considerable time and money recruiting new first-year students, as they should, considering the strong alignment with the mission and tuition-based revenue generation. Also, successful recruiting of first-time, first-year students hopefully leads to student participation at the institution for at least four years, and then engagement as alumni and donors in the future. So, the return on investment justifies the effort, although there is an important caveat.

Caveat: Retention Is Cost Effective

When analyzed across all higher education institutions, retention, or the proportion of the beginning fall 2020 cohort of full-time students who returned to the institution for their second year, averaged about 72.4 percent, a 0.7 percent decline from the previous year.[69] While the slight retention decline for the 2020 cohort may be attributed to the pandemic, retention of full-time students has consistently hovered between 72 percent and 73.5 percent over the past five years. Four-year public and private institutions have fared a little better at 78.5 percent and 78.2 percent retention for the 2020 cohort, respectively, although private institutions experienced a 1.6 percent decline from the previous year.[70] This means that 22 to 28 percent of students recruited as first-time, full-time students, the product of a significant recruitment investment a year earlier, leave their enrolled institution after only one year.

While first-year retention losses are usually the most prominent, additional losses occur in subsequent years as well. Retention losses not only represent lost tuition, fee, and auxiliary revenue for the institution and a lost recruitment investment but also often result in students with loan debt and no prospect of earning a degree, unless they transfer to another institution or return at some later date. So, while the recruitment of first-year students is certainly important, institutions should make every effort to bolster retention and have a significant financial incentive to do so. Even a 1 to 2 percent gain in retention represents a significant base budget gain for the institution. After all, the institution has already made an investment in these students, and they are presently at the institution and chose at least initially to be there. As noted by Hanover Research in their 2014 report entitled *Strategies for Improving Retention*, as higher education markets become increasingly competitive, it may be "more cost-effective to retain a student than to recruit a new one."[71] See "Retention Strategies Enhance Student Success and Institutional Investments" as an illustration.

Retention Strategies Enhance Student Success and Institutional Investments

As provost at URI, it did not take me very long to realize that gains in retention are critically important to both students and to the university. In fact, every 1 percent gain in retention at URI generates a base revenue gain of about $2.5 million. At URI, we have made significant gains in enrollment, partly through growth in the number of first-year students, but mostly by dramatically enhancing our retention rate, which increased from 78.5 to 85.5 percent from 2009 to 2019. To be clear, retention efforts were designed first and foremost to enhance student experience and success, but they also paid off substantially for the university. In fact, revenue gains from retention increases allowed us to strategically invest in sixty-three new faculty lines over a four-year period. This faculty investment paid off in multiple ways, including rejuvenating the faculty, expansion of our research enterprise and funding, building morale and pride on campus, staffing new programs, and further synergistic gains driven by new faculty building strong connections with students. Most of all, reinvesting retention revenue directly into the academic enterprise was an acknowledgment of the hard work by many and a responsible investment that built trust with the faculty. Our original plan was to add fifty new faculty lines from revenue gained by enhanced retention, but that was expanded to sixty-three when retention gains outpaced our projections.

Strategically Broadening the Student Population Base to Sustain Enrollment and Revenue

The demographic decline in high school graduates, shrinking interest among high school students in attending four-year colleges, growth in career and technical training programs, and the increasing cost of a college education and associated student debt, prompts us to think seriously about a shrinking population of prospective students to attend our institutions. College enrollments peaked in 2010 at approximately 20.5 million and have steadily declined to approximately 17 million in 2021.[72] Indeed, there have already been numerous closures of small liberal arts colleges or mergers with larger institutions. While each institution needs to acknowledge and respect its mission and niche in the higher education landscape, there may be opportunities to broaden the student population base and the potential for revenue at some institutions. That is, institutions that rely primarily on recruiting and retaining first-time, full-time students may wish to consider ways to diversify their enrollment and associated revenue portfolio just as you would your investment portfolio. Just as biodiversity creates resilient communities in natural ecosystems, broadening the student population base has the potential to strengthen the financial drivers in academic ecosystems.

When we refer to college students, our immediate attention is drawn to first-time, full-time students who have recently graduated from high school—the traditional college student population. There are, however, many populations of potential students, and each population has its own unique characteristics, interests, and needs. As such, historical information and expectations about academic and career interests, recruitment strategies, yield, retention, and drivers for choosing a certain type of institution and major will likely differ between recent high school graduates; transfer, international, and graduate students; and adult learners. If institutions wish or need to broaden the student base, they will likely need to rethink their strategies, program offerings and delivery, competitive position, and perhaps even brand, as Southern New Hampshire University did several years ago as it evolved into one of the most innovative organizations and fastest growing universities.

First-Time, Full-Time Students

This population of typically recent high school graduates represents a significant portion of enrolled college students at four-year institutions, but it is also the population that is shrinking in size and increasingly expressing disinterest in attending four-year colleges. As such, there is intense competition for these students among both private and public institutions. In recent years, approximately 78 percent of these students attend public institutions.[73] At one time, most would have been in-state students paying lower tuition because of state subsidies, but public institutions, especially flagships, are now aggressively recruiting out-of-state students who are charged the full cost of education, although many will benefit from tuition discounts. The out-of-state subpopulation, however, has several excellent alternative options for attending colleges, including flagship and comprehensive institutions in their home state with lower state subsidized tuition and many private institutions with higher tuition and discount rates that might be comparable in price to an out-of-state public flagship. As such, yield is likely to be much lower for these students, and they may also be more difficult to retain. Yield, financial aid awards, and retention are also likely to differ for Pell-eligible and first-generation college students. Clearly, there are multiple distinct subpopulations of first-time, full-time students, and the unique needs and options of all should be carefully studied and understood.

Both public and private institutions need to ensure their cost-value proposition is viable and must be prepared to dramatically increase their pool of out-of-state applicants to yield their class. However, the tuition revenue advantage can be substantial. At the same time, public institutions must recognize their state funding and honor their important access and affordability mission and commitment to in-state students and ensure they are not accepting out-of-state students at the expense of resident students. Clearly, such a practice would likely create a political hardship as well as a potential ethical dilemma. All in-state students with an academic record indicating they can be academically successful at their in-state institution of choice should be accepted.

Transfer Students

Students choose to transfer institutions for many different reasons. Over the past decade, greater than 9 percent, or about 240,000, of first-time students each year transfer to a different institution at the end of their first year.[74] A student that enrolled in an out-of-state public or an expensive private institution might transfer for financial reasons or just want to come home. A student that was initially denied or waitlisted at their school of first choice might transfer to that institution after accumulating credits and strengthening their academic record elsewhere. Some students may start at a community college to take some general education courses with a plan to transfer to an institution with a strong reputation in their major of interest. Others may have stopped out of college for academic or health reasons and are now ready to return to an institution close to home.

Regardless of the reason, there are several critical factors beyond reputation that help brand an institution as "transfer friendly" and that will be important to attracting transfer students. First and foremost is the seamless and efficient transfer of credits, including counting credits toward general education and/or major requirements in addition to elective credits that simply count toward graduation. While institutions need to maintain standards and consistency, students will be seeking flexibility in credit acceptance and will be discouraged if they must retake courses or learn their accumulated credits count for very little, thereby delaying the completion of their degree. This would suggest that they wasted their time and money, which is disheartening. Institutions that wish to be attractive to transfer students should work diligently to create and promote transfer pathways that are efficient and attractive to students and should be available to advise prospective transfers well in advance of their application.

Second, the availability of campus housing will be critical for many transfer students, particularly out-of-state transfers, who wish to live on campus or have no other choices. Often institutions allocate the bulk of their available housing, especially in the fall, to incoming first-year and returning students to secure their enrollment with limited availability for transfers. Institutions may wish to set aside housing for transfer students, assist them in finding off-campus housing, or develop a midyear January admission and enrollment plan when more housing is available. Third, financial aid will be as important to transfer students as it is to first-year students, so institutions should be prepared with competitive aid packages.

Finally, institutions should be careful to not treat transfer students as second-class citizens when advising, welcoming and orienting them to the campus, and ensuring course availability. Often, institutions focus on the first-year student experience, leaving returning students and transfers to fend for themselves. It is a common concern shared by transfer students. Transfers are an important source of students and revenue and, with some care and attention, can become a true institutional asset. At URI, a flagship public research university, nearly 25 percent of the graduating class each year transferred to the institution.

International Students

According to 2021 data released by the Institute of International Education (IIE), the total number of international students at US universities in 2020-21 was 914,095, a 15 percent decline from 2019-20.[75] In 2020-21, international students comprised 4.6 percent of the total college student population in the United States, down from 5.5 percent in 2019-20. Much of the decline reflects a 46 percent reduction in new, first-time international students, in large part due to the continuing effects of the COVID-19 pandemic. Follow-up data released by IIE in fall 2022 shows that international student enrollment has begun to rebound.[76] The number of new international students increased year over year by 80 percent over the fall of 2020, and the total number of international students increased by 4 percent. For fall 2022, there was a 9 percent increase in total international student enrollment and a 7 percent increase in new enrollments compared to fall 2021. This recovery is encouraging and likely reflects both the easing of pandemic restrictions and a renewed US commitment to international education captured in a Joint Statement of Principles in Support of International Education from the US Departments of State and Education.[77] During the hiatus of international enrollment due to an unwelcoming era in our country and pandemic travel restrictions, many international students discovered available and affordable options for study in their home country or elsewhere. This, along with a restricted immigration policy, may continue to pose challenges for international student enrollment in the United States.

While international students numerically represent a small portion of the US college student population, they are an increasingly important component. As important as the tuition revenue they generate, international students help globalize American campuses with contributions to the campus community through their language, culture, and religious affiliations. In the twenty-first century, we must be preparing students to become citizens in a global society and to navigate an increasingly global economy. Many, perhaps even most, domestic students will not have an opportunity to study abroad; international students broaden the cultural experience of our campuses for all students, staff, and faculty. From a financial perspective, most international students, whether funded by their families, their government, or through foreign university aid, pay full tuition, fees, housing, and dining costs and represent positive contributors to the institutional bottom line. Furthermore, according to a Migration Policy Institute report, international students contributed nearly $39 billion and 416,000 jobs to the US economy in 2019-20.[78]

Recruitment of international students is not without challenges, including some geopolitical obstacles with students from certain countries. More than half of international students in the United States are focused on STEM disciplines or business, with engineering among the most common majors at undergraduate and graduate levels. There are, however, many international students who choose to study in other fields, including the social sciences, the arts and humanities, health-care

202 | SUBSTANCE OVER STYLE

professions, and intensive English. Many international students are especially interested in institutional reputation. Some high-profile US institutions, mostly wealthy privates, offer significant scholarship funding.
International students often have geographic preferences and may be
attracted to certain states or cities that they know about or have visited,
such as California, New York, and Texas, or New York City, Boston, and
Chicago. Language preparation is an issue to consider as is standardized
testing, although many institutions becoming test optional will be helpful
to recruiting international students.

Enrolling international students doesn't just magically happen for
most institutions, especially for those that do not have a robust global
track record. Institutions seeking to increase international enrollment
should develop a plan that highlights specific programs of study and
countries. In addition to recruiting in STEM and business, there may be
opportunities to create niche programs that capitalize on the strengths
of the university and match the expertise needs of a particular country.
For instance, at URI, known for its programs in the marine sciences, fish-
eries, aquaculture, oceanography, and environmental sciences, we have
developed strong educational partnerships with the federal government
and several institutions in Indonesia that wish to expand expertise in
these areas.

Further, in most cases, institutions must be prepared to work with
and carefully vet international recruitment companies or consultants
(agents) to aid in recruiting. The use of agent-paid commissions for
recruiting international students has been somewhat controversial; but
it is an important recruitment tool and has gradually become an established and accepted practice. In addition, some institutions partner
with pathway programs, which recruit less well-prepared international
students to universities and then guide them through entry-level coursework and language development. Such partners, however, can be expensive because they typically retain all or most of the first-year tuition, and
there is no guarantee that the student will matriculate at your institution thereafter.

Finally, attending a US institution can be expensive for international
students. We are experimenting with a chronologically blended approach
to selected professional master's programs that encourage students
to take the first year of graduate coursework online from their home
country with language support provided as needed, and then attend in
person during the second year to interact with other students and faculty,

expand their cultural horizon and language skills, and complete their master's degree. Early indications are that this approach may have excellent promise.

Adult Students

About 38 percent of the US population aged twenty-five or above have completed a bachelor's degree or higher as of 2021.[79] In addition, more than 40 million Americans had some postsecondary education but had not completed a degree or formal certification as of 2021.[80] This represents an increase of 1.4 million over 2020 and approximately 4.5 million over 2019 and is more than twice the number of individuals enrolled in college in 2019. These students have been dubbed the some college, no degree (SCND) or, more recently, the some college, no credential (SCNC) population. About 7 percent of this population have accumulated at least two years' worth of academic credit at the time of their last enrollment and have a high potential for degree completion. They are referred to as *potential completers.*

While the typical SCNC population is near middle age and stopped out of college ten years or so ago after a short college experience, potential completers are a distinct subgroup of younger students (mostly under age thirty) who were enrolled more recently and followed a more diverse pathway involving multiple institutions and more stop outs. The NSCRC has tracked this subpopulation over the past five years; they have achieved greater re-enrollment and completion outcomes, with 25 percent completing college and 29 percent still enrolled.[81] Potential completers appear to be a good starting place for institutions looking to increase enrollment. For detailed information on the profiles, demographics, and distribution of SCNC and potential completer populations, I refer you to the recent NSCRC report.[82]

While the potential completers within the SCNC population may be a great place to start recruiting adult students, they are by no means the only population of adult or mature learners (i.e., learners aged twenty-five or older). According to data from the National Center for Education Statistics, adult learners make up a sizable proportion of undergraduate and graduate students enrolled in colleges and universities.[83] While 85 percent of full-time undergraduates are under age twenty-five, more than 40 percent of part-time undergraduates and the majority of full-time (66 percent) and part-time (88 percent) graduate students are twenty-five or older. In 2019, prior to the pandemic, it was projected that the number of students between the ages of twenty-five and thirty-four would increase by 21 percent. Most of the increase in enrolled adult learners is at four-year institutions because most believe a bachelor's degree is a good investment and an associate degree or certificate would not guarantee them a better job.

Adult learners are a diverse population that includes individuals with no experience in higher education, those that have taken a course or two, veterans, those in active military service, or individuals who have completed one or more degrees. Regardless of their backgrounds and experiences, a common thread that connects most adult learners is enrolling in an academic program that is relevant to their career interests and aspirations. Developing knowledge and skills relevant to the workplace is essential as they consider where to enroll. Many adult learners wish to expand their careers or hope to use a college degree to change professions or upgrade their skills and credentials. Affordability is a chief concern of most adult learners, including taking on too much debt. Many have current student debt, and some form of debt reduction or forgiveness may be crucial to their re-enrollment. Most adult learners work while they are enrolled in college, and many are also raising families. Their lives are complex and may not fit well with traditional college class schedules.

There is a substantial population of potential adult learners that would benefit from completing a college degree and would also help institutions struggling with enrollment of traditional students. Institutions, however, will need to reach out to potential adult learners, offer support and guidance, and ensure that academic offerings will be relevant to their needs and interests. Online or blended course offerings in compressed formats (five to seven weeks) may be necessary to accommodate work schedules and family responsibilities. Some institutions should explore employer partnerships both to help with recruitment and potentially to offset all or part of the cost. Veterans and those in active military service may be able to apply the GI Bill to cover costs. Institutions will need to offer financial aid as well and perhaps create flexible billing models that spread costs out over time. There may also be a need for some cost-sharing of previous unpaid bills for adult students who stopped out years ago to create an incentive for students to return to college and overcome existing obstacles to enrollment.

Finally, institutions need to offer robust opportunities for adults to earn meaningful credit for prior learning, work experiences, and/or military training and service. In addition to credit by exam options, this often includes some form of a student-prepared portfolio that translates meaningful work and life experiences into learning outcomes worthy of college credit. Such an accumulation of credits that satisfy academic requirements represents formal recognition of their experiences and wisdom as well as cost savings toward earning a degree.

Graduate Students

Graduate education traditionally engages a select number of students in advanced coursework, small classes, individualized programs of study, and substantial one-on-one time with a faculty mentor who serves as the major professor. At the doctoral and PhD level, students are engaged in sophisticated research or other projects and are guided by their faculty mentor and a committee of faculty who offer advice and input and evaluate the output of each student's work. Many master's programs also require research or a project leading to a thesis or major paper along with advanced coursework and individual programs of study. While such programs are important, they are expensive and often subsidized by undergraduate tuition revenue. The expense is compounded when the cost of university-funded graduate assistantships is added to the equation.

With undergraduate enrollment challenges continuing and a growing pool of international and adult graduate students interested in career advancement, it is time to reinvent graduate education. There is an opportunity to convert selected master's degrees into efficient, revenue-generating programs. Enrollment in graduate degrees, and recently graduate certificates, has been growing as individuals seek career advancement. Recent educational attainment data released by the US Census Bureau revealed that the number of people aged twenty-five and over whose highest degree is a master's increased by 50 percent from 2011 to 2021.[84] Furthermore, between 2021 and 2023, enrollment in graduate certificate programs has grown by nearly 10 percent.[85]

Many traditional master's degrees can be recast as professional master's, including Professional Science Master's degrees that incorporate learning in real-world situations. To enhance efficiency for both students and faculty, such programs should consider a cohort model rather than the traditional single mentor-mentee model and develop advanced core curricula along with some individualized elective choices. This, combined with a maximum of thirty credits including some project or experiential learning, would likely be attractive, efficient, and affordable. An individual faculty member could advise the cohort, which would be recognized in their workload, and that responsibility could be rotated among faculty members. Similarly, post-baccalaureate certificates in key fields consisting of twelve to fifteen credits are increasingly popular with individuals working full-time who wish to advance their skills and credentials.

Such master's and certificate programs could easily shift to online or hybrid delivery using compressed five-to-seven-week terms throughout the year. Full-time students could complete their master's in one year, while part-time students might take two years to complete a master's and one year to complete a certificate. Restructuring graduate degrees and certificates in this manner would be attractive to students and convert some graduate programs from expense generators to revenue generators. That revenue would contribute to the institution's bottom line or could be invested in institutional strategic priorities, such as the expansion of new in-demand interdisciplinary doctorates in critical areas.

Strategically Broadening Academic Delivery to Support Students and Generate Revenue

While many institutions offer summer sessions, winter J-term classes, and/or some online programs, there is value in strategically rethinking and promoting such programs to maximize the benefits to students and to revenue generation. From a revenue perspective, these programs collectively may pale in comparison with total tuition revenue and the annual operating budget at residential institutions. The additional revenue, even if modest, will nevertheless assist in keeping annual tuition increases in check and maintaining affordability for all students while providing institutional funding for strategic investments. See "Broadening Academic Delivery to Manage Revenue and Tuition Increases" for an illustration.

Summer Session

Careful analysis of student credit completion data from several years ago at my institution revealed that many matriculating students were transferring credits earned from other institutions in the summers prior to their junior and/or senior years. Because many students change majors, they often needed to take key courses for their new major or to complete their general education requirements. Students were taking these courses over the summer from institutions near their homes, often community colleges, and transferring them. We offered a robust array of summer courses, but our offerings were determined more by what faculty wanted to teach in the summer for extra compensation than what students needed or wanted. Also, many critical courses were only being offered in face-to-face modality, which precluded out-of-state students from taking them during summer and living at home. We were so focused on promoting our institution's academic year programs that marketing of summer session was essentially an afterthought. Summer sessions operated out of our continuing education program as an add-on rather than as a critical component of our educational delivery and revenue generation operation.

We made the strategic decision to create a new coordinator of summer programs position and moved the summer session into the Office of the Provost, reporting to the vice provost for enrollment management. The logic was that even a small increase in summer enrollment would more than pay for that position. We determined the courses needed and desired by students, and the coordinator worked with departments and colleges to recruit faculty to teach them and promote summer session options for students, including highlighting reduced tuition. Most of summer session offerings are now taught online, facilitating their availability to students living out-of-state and/or working during summer. The availability of federal Pell Grant funding for summer session classes is also helpful for students from low-income households. In recent years, summer session enrollment has been the highest in institutional history, and summer revenue is now a significant contributor to the institution's annual budget, despite, or perhaps because of, reduced summer tuition rates for all students. The reinvention and reinvigoration of summer sessions have been an academic success for students and a financial success for the institution.

Winter J-term

Winter J-term is an academic mini-semester during the three-week period between the first week of January and the beginning of the spring semester in late January. At URI, we implemented winter J-term in 2014 and chose to offer those courses at a significantly discounted rate to ensure affordability and accessibility to most students as a supplement to their academic year coursework. From an efficiency perspective, it allowed us to utilize the campus academic infrastructure that was otherwise dormant during winter break. From a student perspective, J-term allowed students to catch up on credits, take or retake a required course to stay on track, or participate in a value-added, credit-bearing experience that would not fit into a regular semester. For example, prior to COVID, we offered fifteen to twenty international travel courses led by faculty each J-term that provided students rich, life-changing, cross-cultural global learning experiences delivered in the context of disciplinary learning. Students flourished in J-term courses because they focused their time on one intensive course rather than attempting to balance four or five courses during the regular semester. J-term has been a phenomenal success for gains in retention, significant increases in graduation rate, shortening time to degree completion, and providing distinctive international experiences as well as generating additional revenue for the institution. In recent years, more than two-thirds of URI students have taken at least one winter J-term and/or summer session course.

Select Online Programs

Predominantly residential campuses catering to traditional-age students may benefit from offering alternative online programs in select fields aimed specifically at non-traditional student populations seeking career advancement or upskilling, including international, adult, and graduate student opportunities. Given the 50 percent growth in the adult population with master's degrees over the past decade, online or blended professional master's degrees and skills-based stackable post-baccalaureate certificates may be especially attractive and provide considerable flexibility for students. In addition, online degree completion programs aimed specifically at adults with SCNC and at students enrolled in or completing community college programs also have potential. As noted earlier, chronologically blended programs (i.e., first-year entirely online and second-year in-person) are attractive and cost-effective for some government-supported international students seeking to enhance their professional credentials while minimizing the expense and disruption to their families.

Broadening Academic Delivery to Manage Revenue and Tuition Increases

To be clear, the primary purpose for reinventing summer sessions and creating winter J-term and some select fully online programs at URI was to expand learning opportunities for students and to drive student success, including retention, graduation rate, and time to degree. At almost any level of success, these programs would easily cover their costs but would be comparatively minor contributors to the total annual revenue generated by tuition and fees. When viewed through the lens of annual tuition increases, however, the additional revenue generated, which totaled $10.3 million for the summer session and winter J-term in FY 2021, became an exceedingly important institutional asset even with reduced tuition in these terms. In FY 2022, for example, each 1 percent increase in tuition at URI with the current mix of in- and out-of-state students generated $1.9 million of new revenue. With the supplemental revenue from summer and J-term programs, we were able to increase tuition by just 2.5 percent, which generated approximately $4.8 million, helped maintain our competitive position in the marketplace, and minimized the financial burden on students and families. Figure 12.1 highlights the enrollment and revenue growth associated with broadening our academic delivery models.

Program Type	2015 Enrollment	2015 Revenue	2018 Enrollment	2018 Revenue	2021 Enrollment	2021 Revenue
Winter J-term	616	$0.7M	998	$1.1M	1,395	$1.7M
Summer Session	5,498	$6.3M	5,852	$6.8M	7,304	$8.4M
Total	6,185	$7.0M	6,850	$7.9M	8,699	$10.3M

Figure 12.1. Enrollment and revenue growth at URI after the implementation of expanded learning opportunities in the summer and during the January break.

Enrollment is the primary driver of revenue in higher education today. Apart from the elite, highly selective, and wealthy subset of institutions, there is intense competition for a shrinking population of prospective students. Most indicators suggest that enrollment will likely continue to wane across multiple student populations. At the same time, the cost of running an institution will continue to rise; and the cost of tuition and fees is stretching the pocketbooks of most citizens, even with generous institutional grant aid. The growing populations of students of color, first-generation college students, and those from low-income families, who deserve and will benefit most from a college education and who are a critical element of our nation's future workforce, run the risk of being priced out of an educational opportunity. Indeed, creatively managing enrollment and enhancing opportunity for all may be among the most important strategies shaping the future of higher education in the United States.

CHAPTER THIRTEEN

Strategic Planning Drives Strategic Budgeting

Strategic Planning—Why Does It Matter?

As a faculty member many years ago, I recall my disinterest, and that of many colleagues, about an announcement from the administration that the university would begin a strategic planning process. At that time, it seemed to me like a burdensome activity for someone else's attention. It must be some mandate from the board or governor, I thought. We were busy doing the important work of the university—teaching our courses, seeking grant funding, publishing, advising students, and working with colleagues to ensure the curriculum and student experience were contemporary and engaging. At the level of the department, the effort seemed uninteresting, detached from any tangible benefits, and mostly unrelated to the important work of the university at present.

In retrospect, what I didn't understand or think about is the constantly changing landscape of society, its reverberations across and within the academic ecosystem, and the critical importance of thoughtfully considering and shaping the future of my university. As with natural ecosystems, external forces impacting the academic enterprise are ever-changing and can powerfully constrain or accelerate institutional evolution and vitality. In my day-to-day routine, I just assumed all good things would simply continue, resources would be available to support all that we do, students would just continue to show up, and the university would go on as it had for hundreds of years. Clearly, I was naively misinformed.

In the context of today, strategic planning is essential—providing a framework to carefully shape the future of the university, identify important priorities to sustain the institution and its relevance to constituents (including students and faculty), engage the community to establish a vision and institutional values, and provide a construct for the allocation of resources and university investments. In this context, what was I thinking? To not participate is akin to not voting, not showing up, and not caring about the future—effectively choosing to remove my voice, ideas, and values from the important conversation about priorities and the future of the university. Do any of us really want to just step aside and leave decisions about future directions entirely to others? I think not. It is not only our responsibility to participate but also in our own best interest to do so.

Engaging the community in planning is essential and shouldn't just happen once every five years or so. Serious annual discussions about emerging challenges, changes, and opportunities, such as the annual academic summits discussed in chapter 4, create a culture of planning and improvement built around shared dialogue and forward-thinking practices being implemented on campus. As community engagement in self-examination and improvement becomes routine, even if at very modest levels, evolutionary change becomes embraced as part of the fabric of the institution, resulting in greater participation and ownership among faculty, staff, and students in planning processes and outcomes.

Finally, regional organizations responsible for the accreditation of our colleges and universities require our institutions to not only have strategic plans, but also to be able to provide evidence that meaningful self-evaluation informs planning, continuous improvement, and resource allocation. For example, one of the nine accreditation standards of the New England Commission of Higher Education (NECHE), the accrediting body for all higher education institutions in New England, establishes clear and specific expectations for strategic planning and evaluation as follows:

> The institution undertakes planning and evaluation to accomplish and improve the achievement of its mission and purposes. It identifies its planning and evaluation priorities and pursues them effectively. The institution demonstrates its success in strategic, academic, financial, and other resource planning and the evaluation of its educational effectiveness.[86]

Ambitious Aspirations for the Future

Strategic investments, *strategic resource allocation*, *strategic priorities*, etc. are terms purposely referenced repeatedly throughout this book. That's because in resource-constrained environments institutions must ensure that they don't simply spend, but rather *invest*, their limited resources on priorities that will advance the institution. What are those priorities, who determines them, and how should they be identified? The strategic plan is the formal articulation of the institution's vision, goals, and priorities for a period of time, often five years or so. It represents the university's carefully and collaboratively developed ambitious aspirations for the future and should build and expand upon the institution's comparative advantages and distinctive attributes. It also alerts the institution about areas of opportunity and pitfalls to avoid. **With a strategic plan as a road map, the budget becomes the visible and tangible manifestation of that plan and strategic investments moving forward.** That is, expenditures align with priorities. When done well, strategic investments will directly or indirectly generate additional revenue by increasing enrollment, retention, research funding, productive partnerships, donors and gifts, and institutional visibility and reputation.

The strategic plan charts a path forward for the institution. It establishes priorities, sets goals, lays out strategies and actions to attain those goals, and represents an investment plan in alignment with the budget. A set of carefully developed performance metrics track progress, investments, and return on investments. The investment plan relates not only to the future allocation of resources to strategic priorities but also to protecting high-priority programs and initiatives already in the budget during times of financial shortfalls. As such, across-the-board budget reductions, which are too often implemented during difficult times, are anathema to strategic planning and investment. Reductions, which may be inevitable in certain situations, need to protect priorities, even those that were recently funded and perceived as the easiest—least contentious—items to cut to save money.

Academic Strategic Planning

Given the primacy of the academic core mission, strategic plans frequently identify academic priorities relevant to advancing teaching, learning, and the student experience; research, scholarship, and creative work; and outreach opportunities and partnerships. Operational priorities are selectively established in the context of institutional effectiveness and advancing academic priorities. Certainly, input from staff, students, alumni, and members of the governing board is important in establishing priorities and shaping the strategic plan. Nevertheless, the institution's strategic plan is often first and foremost an *academic* strategic plan, and the primary architects of that plan must include the president and/or provost, deans, and faculty members. Referring to the university strategic plan as an academic strategic plan can be advantageous in highlighting the academic core mission as the primary purpose of the university and may be preferable in situations where previous planning was largely operational and deficient in an academic focus. That was the situation that existed when I began as provost. The drawback of emphasizing the academic focus, however, is that staff in units whose contributions are outside the primary academic mission may feel marginalized, even if they are actively involved in the planning process through task forces or divisional planning efforts. It is important for nonacademic staff to participate and share ownership of the plan as well.

The university strategic plan is not only an institutional road map essential to the core mission but also a template and framework for strategic plans to be developed by each college and other major budget units of the university, such as the divisions of administration and finance, athletics, student affairs, and research. While these plans address specific goals and priorities associated with the functions of these units, they must adhere to and support the overall vision, goals, and priorities of the institutional strategic plan. Alignment of the strategic plan with the budget and future allocation of resources provides motivation and incentive for colleges and major budget units to take seriously their responsibility to develop plans and establish priorities within the context of the university strategic plan. In our planning efforts between 2009 and 2020, our president clearly established the *academic* strategic plan as the *institution's* strategic plan, and the goals and priorities of all unit plans were designed to support the academic plan and core mission as well as charting a path forward for those units. This clarity was helpful to squelch confusion and competition about roles and responsibilities and to ensure strategic planning reflected a *one cohesive university* model.

Developing a Strategic Plan—Who, What, and How?

There is no single recipe or process for creating a strategic plan, although inclusivity is an essential feature that results both in stronger plans and better buy-in related to goals, priorities, and future directions. The process for developing a strategic plan will no doubt vary from one institution to the next based on the planning culture and history of the institution, the scale and scope of the plan, and the level of trust between the faculty and administration.

As a dean, I led efforts to create two college-level strategic plans. As provost, I led campuswide efforts to create two university strategic plans. College-level plans are focused on the distinctive role of the college in the university and may be more straightforward to develop because the constituents are limited and focused on the unique features of the college. University plans are invariably more broadly defined and capture directions, priorities, and values that extend across the university but may be more complicated to develop because university-wide consultation with faculty, staff, students, alumni, and board members is essential, but not always easy to attain.

While there will be variation in the planning process from one institution to the next, or even among colleges within an institution, there are some general common features that are helpful in driving the development of a strategic plan. The Society for College and University Planning (SCUP) is the recognized leader in "advancing the knowledge and practice of planning in higher education," and their publication, *Academic Design: Sharing Lessons Learned*, offers a useful road map to guide college and university strategic planning.[87]

Alignment with the Mission

First and foremost, strategic plans must emanate from and align with the institution's or college's mission. The mission of the institution defines its distinctive character and purposes and provides the foundation upon which the institution identifies its priorities and plans. The mission statement fundamentally describes the reason for the university's existence and characterizes its educational, research and scholarship, and public service dimensions, and often includes reference to core institutional values. Because university mission statements are so fundamental to the university's distinctive character and purpose, the mission state-ment should reflect the stability of the university's purpose and typically would not be modified on the same five-year rotating basis as a strategic plan. Universities should not be totally redefining themselves, their values, and their reason for being every few years. At the beginning of a strategic planning process, however, the mission should be revisited and reaffirmed and, as appropriate, refined, revised, or updated on a longer-term basis.

While university mission statements may seem rather generic and invariably pledge a commitment to advancing learning and discovery, the intellectual growth of their students, and diversity and inclusion, careful examination does highlight distinctive differences. For example, missions of public land, sea, and space grant institutions will no doubt reference their flagship status and special commitment to the citizens and the socioeconomic well-being of their state; research universities will typically refer to outstanding research that will transform the world, and those with medical schools may highlight their role in advancing health or health care; religious-affiliated institutions will typically empha-size building character and a commitment to service in their students consistent with a specific religious tradition; and, state comprehensive and community colleges may highlight their special commitment to access, affordability, and education for all students. While the language of mission statements may seem universal, these carefully crafted state-ments do capture in a few sentences the distinctive purposes of colleges and universities. Accrediting bodies require a contemporary and clearly articulated mission statement and fully expect that the mission will drive the direction of the institution and provide a meaningful basis for assess-ment and enhancement of the institution's effectiveness.

Identifying the Players and Roles

The overall development of the university strategic plan is the respon-sibility of the president, who will engage with and inform the governing board about progress and directions and seek their input and support at key steps in the process. Given the academic focus of the mission and the overall institutional goals, it is not uncommon for the president to dele-gate much of the details for developing the university strategic plan to the provost, who must ensure that the deans and faculty are engaged in the planning process. With college-level planning, the dean is the responsible administrator, who will engage the chairs and faculty of the college. Even if the university planning process is driven by the provost, it is essential that the president is a visible participant and that the president's vision and aspirations for the institution are clearly disseminated and ultimately reflected in the plan, after consultation and modification from the community, especially the faculty. This will ensure that the power of the presidency is behind the plan.

Beyond the president and provost, it is critical to engage a cross-section of the university community, especially faculty, in leading the strategic planning process. Sometimes the president or provost will invite certain individuals to form a planning steering committee, which may create various subcommittees or task forces to focus on certain aspects of the plan as it takes shape over time. As an alternative to forming a planning committee by special invitation, which sometimes creates some angst about insiders versus outsiders, it may be helpful to establish and engage a standing committee within the university with responsibility for academic planning, tracking implementation progress, and perhaps overseeing accreditation reports and reviews.

As provost, I worked collaboratively with faculty senate leadership to establish a joint committee on academic planning (JCAP) to fill the niche of a planning steering committee. JCAP became a permanent standing committee of the university—where *joint* conveys the coordination and collaboration of the administration and faculty. JCAP is chaired by the provost. The vice chair is the vice president of the faculty senate, and it includes four of the six members of the faculty senate executive committee, chairs of key standing faculty committees, the vice provost for academic and faculty initiatives, the special assistant for academic planning, the dean of the graduate school, vice president for research, and representatives from the Council of Deans, student affairs, administration and finance, the graduate student association, and the student senate.

While other steering committee models can be effective as well, JCAP serves very effectively as the planning steering committee and interfaces with specific *ad hoc* subcommittees to explore and develop specific aspects of the plan. A cross-section of faculty and staff thought leaders from across the campus and all disciplines, academic ranks, and roles in teaching and research participate in the work of the subcommittees. As the planning steering committee, JCAP serves as the conductor, compiler, and reviewer of drafts, and JCAP members often chair the subcommittees. Because the faculty senate is the formal elected body and voice of the faculty in shared governance, and senate leaders are key members of JCAP along with other constituents, this approach and process visibly and functionally reinforces collaborative leadership and its importance in establishing the direction for the future and strategic investment priorities. As such, it ensures that the representative voice of the faculty, in addition to the power of the presidency, is behind the plan.

While the planning steering committee plays a critical organizational role in the university's strategic planning process, it is also wise and helpful to engage regularly with the Council of Deans in the strategic planning process. As the academic leaders of the university, the deans and vice provosts are critical players—they are knowledgeable and experienced leaders and have a good sense of challenges and opportunities for the institution. The deans need to understand, however, that their role in university planning is not about advocating for their college, but rather about guiding what is best for the institution moving forward. In the end, the deans and vice provosts will play a key leadership role in the implementation of new initiatives, programs, research centers, etc. that emerge from the strategic plan. So, their active participation in the planning process secures their buy-in as well as captures their best ideas and insights.

Understanding the Dynamic Landscape

After reaffirming the institutional mission and identifying and organizing key players, an important and initial task of the planning steering committee is to conduct a landscape analysis of the external and internal factors that may be impacting the university. Typically, this consists of an *environmental scan* of societal and higher education marketplace factors and an *institutional scan* to identify internal challenges, opportunities, and comparative advantages and assets.

In my efforts leading strategic planning at both the institutional and college levels, I have found that an environmental scan provides useful societal and higher education context for establishing a forward-looking institutional vision as well as strategic goals and priorities. Environmental scanning involves examining key trends, forces, and issues that have the potential to impact the position of the institution (or college) and its attributes and assets. These may include political, economic, technological, or social factors as well as higher education trends and challenges and both national and global perspectives. A good environmental scan provides a much needed and valuable backdrop for strategic visioning and planning. It is also a very good initial activity to engage and inform the planning steering committee. A facilitated discussion among steering committee members of a few carefully selected trend and issue reports will provide helpful insights and ensure that strategic planning is not an entirely inward-leaning process conducted in a vacuum. The steering committee will understand contemporary societal issues impacting higher education as well as the comparative position of the institution relative to peer and aspirant institutions. An environmental scan conducted today would no doubt surface myriad potentially impactful issues that provide important context for planning, such as:

- the social, economic, and educational impacts of the pandemic;
- deep polarization toward and politicization of higher education in society;
- the resurgence of Black Lives Matter and issues of racial injustice;
- questions about the value of higher education by students, families, and some employers;
- student debt, the cost of education, and the impacts of inflation;
- the mental health crisis and increasing fragility of students; and
- the emergence and availability of generative AI (e.g., ChatGPT) in academic settings.

An *institutional scan* is an internal examination to identify issues and opportunities unique to the institution and connections between the mission and existing programs. This might involve a review of previous strategic plans and outcomes, accreditation reports, results of a campus climate survey, and analysis of key institutional performance metrics, such as retention, graduation rates, research expenditures, etc. Are there areas of strength that provide the institution with a distinctive niche in the higher education marketplace? The focus here is on identifying potential aspects of the learning and discovery enterprise that enhance the vitality, attractiveness, and competitive position of the institution in the future.

A challenge for the steering committee might be to maintain objectivity and an institutional perspective when identifying distinctive strengths and opportunities and identifying weaknesses or areas of less relevance that are low priorities going forward. Everyone wants their college, department, or discipline to be identified as a strength or area for investment. Sometimes needs and opportunities can be discussed without highlighting certain disciplines, but there are invariably growth opportunities in certain fields or professions that cannot be ignored. This may be tricky terrain for the steering committee to navigate, but the chair calling it out in advance of the discussion may go a long way toward addressing this concern. Frankly, in my experience, I have found that most faculty members, who are accustomed to critical peer review, can rise above self-serving behaviors when participating in university-wide committees, although sometimes division leaders struggle to do the same.

An institutional scan might identify the need to improve retention or graduation rates, better capitalize on opportunities for interdisciplinary research, bring greater visibility to distinctive programs in certain fields, expand and promote experiential learning opportunities, highlight a vibrant and engaging honors program, tout successful student employment data, build upon a very successful fundraising campaign, or many other possibilities. The results of the environmental and institutional scans should provide valuable context to establish a bold vision and strategic goals and priorities for the institution.

Vision Statement

A vision statement articulates the university's aspirations and establishes the institution's desired strategic position in the future. It should be both bold and achievable, and not simply an exciting sound bite with little meaning or substance. The vision should be inspirational as well as aspirational and sufficiently embraced by the community so that most can imagine how they might contribute to achieving that vision. If the strategic plan is the path forward, the vision is the ultimate and desired destination. While the president and provost (or dean for college-level planning) should certainly have a hand in establishing the vision, the planning steering committee must ultimately shape it, share it, and advocate for it, and the governing board needs to endorse it.

The vision should be informed by the environmental and institutional scans and what is truly a plausible and aspirational leap forward for the institution. At the same time, the vision should specifically address issues of real meaning and desire for the institution. That is, vision statements should not be interchangeable among institutions because each is built on opportunities and desires distinctive to each institution.

Contemporary university vision statements are typically short, eloquently worded, and convey bold and meaningful aspirations that the university community and external constituents can rally around. In recent years, it appears that university vision statements have become increasingly brief (often one sentence), perhaps to a point that they lose their distinctiveness. While I understand the upside of brevity, I also see advantages to visions that truly reflect the distinctive aspirations of the institution, especially if the vision is to inspire and coalesce the community moving forward. See "Examples of Contemporary University and College Vision Statements."

Examples of Contemporary University and College Vision Statements

University Vision Statements

THE PENNSYLVANIA STATE UNIVERSITY

Penn State will be a leader in research, learning, and engagement that facilitates innovation, embraces diversity and sustainability, and inspires achievements that will affect the world in positive and enduring ways.

UNIVERSITY OF MASSACHUSETTS DARTMOUTH

UMass Dartmouth will be a globally recognized premier research university committed to inclusion, access, advancement of knowledge, student success, and community enrichment.

MARQUETTE UNIVERSITY

Marquette University aspires to be, and to be recognized, among the most innovative and accomplished Catholic and Jesuit universities in the world, promoting the greater glory of God and the well-being of humankind.

We must reach beyond traditional academic boundaries and embrace new and collaborative methods of teaching, learning, research and service in an inclusive environment that supports all of our members in reaching their fullest potential.

Marquette graduates will be problem-solvers and agents for change in a complex world so in the spirit of St. Ignatius and Jacques Marquette, they are ready in every way "to go and set the world on fire."

College Vision Statements

COLLEGE OF ARTS AND SCIENCES AT THE UNIVERSITY OF ALABAMA

The College will be a forward-thinking leader in the creation, sharing, and application of knowledge. As it prepares the citizens of the future, the college will act on the principle that knowledge must serve humanity and our environment and be dedicated to global responsibility, justice, and ethics.

SCHOOL OF MEDICINE AT JOHNS HOPKINS UNIVERSITY

Johns Hopkins Medicine pushes the boundaries of discovery, transforms health care, advances medical education and creates hope for humanity.

LEAVEY SCHOOL OF BUSINESS AT SANTA CLARA UNIVERSITY

At the center of innovation, the Leavey School of Business cultivates ethical business leaders who transform the world.

GRAINGER COLLEGE OF ENGINEERING AT THE UNIVERSITY OF ILLINOIS URBANA-CHAMPAIGN

We are innovators who work at the forefront of science and engineering, leaders who turn the extraordinary into everyday reality, and partners who are trusted to transform the world.

Foundational Values

Institutions often articulate a set of foundational, guiding, or core values, sometimes referred to as principles, that are meant to characterize behavior and commitment for all within the university community. The institutional values should guide decision-making and shape the culture of the institution. While the nature and expression of values may vary from one institution to the next, they often include reference to some of the following principles: a commitment to excellence, responsibility, respect, integrity, compassion, freedom of inquiry and expression, diversity and inclusion, innovation, ethical behavior, etc. Some value statements are simply a list of attributes shared by the university community, while others provide some explanation of the specific importance of each of the stated values in the context of that institution's mission and culture. Such brief explanations add substance and veracity, in my opinion, to value statements. Some present their values diagrammatically; others may organize their list of values so that the first letter of each attribute spells a word with meaning to the community, such as INSPIRE or ASPIRE. While the list of values may seem obvious, the process of defining a set of institutional values, capturing them in writing, and highlighting them along with the institution's mission and vision has significance and makes a statement about what the institution stands for. A meaningful set of foundational community values may also serve as institutional guideposts for decision-making, assessing actions in difficult situations, and managing controversial issues, such as the consideration of rescinding an honorary degree.

Goals, Strategies, and Actions

The heart of the strategic plan is the list of **goals** that emerge from the planning process that reflect strategic priorities defined and embraced by the campus community, the planning steering committee, the academic leadership of the institution, and the governing board. The goals should be lofty, yet achievable, and should reflect the landscape analysis of societal drivers coupled with distinctive university strengths, weaknesses, and opportunities. The goals of the strategic plan are critical to the evolution of the university and serve as guideposts for the journey along the path to the future. Achieving or progressing toward these goals over the life of the strategic plan, five years or so, should be transformational and significantly raise the profile, reputation, impact, and sustainability of the institution. The goals should describe desired outcomes in various areas consistent with the university mission, vision, and values, such as enhancing student success; achieving high-impact, translational, and innovative research, scholarship, and creative work; embracing diversity and social justice; and growing a global presence.

While the *goals* describe desired outcomes, the *strategies* within each goal outline approaches toward achieving those outcomes. The *actions* within each strategy represent very specific tactical steps that might lead to the desired outcome. The goals are sacrosanct and should be adhered to throughout the plan. However, the strategies, and especially the actions may—and even are likely to—evolve over time. As such, the proposed actions might be viewed as suggested steps. The hope is that bold ideas encapsulated in each goal will inspire innovation and additional or alternative strategic approaches and actions to achieve the desired outcomes inherent in each goal. Thus, the strategic plan should not be thought of as prescriptive, but rather as a dynamic or "living" plan—one that is open to modification over time as progress is made, new opportunities emerge, and changes occur in the world. See "Illustration of Strategic Plan Goals, Strategies, and Actions."

Illustration of Strategic Plan Goals, Strategies, and Actions

Note: These goals, strategies, and actions are meant to be illustrative of a style and format for a strategic plan rather than content recommendations.

GOAL 1: Enhance Student Success.

Transform undergraduate and graduate student learning and academic support to produce knowledgeable, skilled, and engaged graduates prepared for an ever-changing world.

Strategy 1: Expand opportunities for experiential learning within all majors and restructure academic and career advising to better support students in meeting their life goals.

Proposed Actions:

- Adopt a model of professional advising in the early years of the student experience and assess the effectiveness of advising at all levels.

- Promote internships and experiential learning opportunities through knowledgeable advisors and strong collaboration with the Center for Career and Experiential Education.

- Expand efforts to make graduate students and faculty advisors aware of and prepared for both academic and nonacademic careers.

- Track student experiential learning participation in every major and in all graduate programs.

Strategy 2: Focus on access and affordability and improve student retention, credit completion, and degree completion rates for all undergraduate and graduate students.

Proposed Actions:

- Focus and expand efforts to ensure student success in challenging gateway courses.

- Target additional financial aid to support economically disadvantaged students and to retain out-of-state students.

- Ensure successful implementation of the new reinvigorated general education curriculum comprising, including interdisciplinary courses addressing "grand challenges" in the world.

- Identify and assess gaps in programs and services focused on student access, at-risk students, and overall student success.

Goal 2: Expand Research, Scholarship, and Creative Work.

Expand high-impact, translational, and innovative research, scholarship, and creative work that addresses state, regional, and world challenges to improve health, sustainability, economic development, and the human experience.

Strategy 1: Broaden support for significant growth in research opportunities and recognize the value of all forms of scholarship.

Proposed Actions:

- Ensure effective research infrastructure, including improved electronic workflow and grants management from proposal to post-award.
- Enlist senior research-active faculty to mentor, advise, and assist early-career faculty.
- Leverage federally supported small business funding mechanisms to support faculty research and translate research into commercial applications.
- Establish open lines of communication about scholarship in all disciplines and measure faculty research productivity.

Strategy 2: Develop high-performance research computing initiatives to facilitate research and advance "big data" analyses and applications across disciplines.

Proposed Actions:

- Provide incentives and infrastructure to foster a community of researchers in high-performance and research computing.
- Provide technical support for high-performance computing (HPC) for teams seeking external funding.
- Create incentives, such as seed grants, for the formation of interdisciplinary teams focused on HPC and research computing.
- Organize and complete a "big data" cluster hire of faculty in various departments across the university.

Goal 3: Implement a Bold Advancement Agenda.

Elevate the stature of the university through robust and bold strategic advancement initiatives to establish a strong and sustainable financial and marketplace position.

Strategy 1: Engender a culture of philanthropy by building strong university partnerships.

Proposed Actions:

- Identify, jointly develop, and disseminate strategic funding priorities for the university through collaborative planning and communication between the institution and the foundation.
- Ensure that fundraising effectiveness, success, and accountability are embedded in the responsibilities of deans, development officers, and foundation leaders.
- Establish that every university event is an advancement opportunity and the expectation that board and advisory council members participate in giving as a model to promote an advanced fundraising agenda.

Strategy 2: Leverage university relationships to expand the pool of individual, alumni, foundation, and corporate prospects and donors.

Proposed Actions:

- Identify emerging university constituents and friends as immediate or future development prospects.
- Develop and disseminate strategic fundraising messaging in all university and foundation communications.

Strategy 3: Develop and support a cutting-edge infrastructure that supports a robust advancement operation.

Proposed Actions:

- Enhance foundation-based prospect research, reporting, and capacity analysis and ensure that such information is timely, accurate, and utilized in developing prospect engagement strategies.

- Develop strategies and an actionable plan for integrating the work of the foundation and the alumni association and ensure a major focus of alumni engagement is advancement.

Implementation and Key Performance Indicators

The success of any strategic plan will depend on inclusivity in its development, abundant and transparent communication about the goals during implementation, adhering to and investing in the established priorities, fending off resistance, and measuring and reporting key performance indicators (KPIs). KPIs are metrics, usually quantitative but also qualitative, as appropriate, that track progress and outcomes for each goal. Sometimes the goals might include targets, such as increasing enrollment, retention, graduation rates, degrees awarded, or research awards by a specific amount, achieving a certain national or international competitive ranking, or meeting a specified fundraising goal.

Typically, the Office of Institutional Research will be responsible for gathering and analyzing KPIs for most goals, including comparisons with peer institutions, if appropriate. It is important, however, to not only gather data and information to track progress but also to share it with the community and the board to reinforce progress in strategically important areas and continue to build buy-in and pride in the institution. Progress toward meeting the goals and achieving the vision will no doubt also increase donor engagement and giving. At URI, the standing JCAP committee has reviewed and disseminated key performance indicators for each goal on an annual basis. The president and/or provost, and other leaders as appropriate, should be publicly reporting progress; internal communications should share key success stories; and a strategic planning website that includes KPIs should be established and updated regularly to ensure transparency, including areas where progress may not be evident.

Converting goals, strategies, and actions into desired outcomes and aspirations articulated in the vision is challenging work that requires leadership and persistence. Simply stating goals does not guarantee achieving them. The senior leadership must commit to advancing the goals of the university plan and accompanying unit-based plans, which means aligning investments with priorities and communicating regularly and consistently about priorities with all constituents. Furthermore, everyone needs to be prepared for the strategic plan to drive resource allocations, as that is ultimately the purpose of the plan. This is where the most pushback is likely to occur. If some programs or budget units do not see themselves as part of the strategic priorities and goals, they will likely express resistance. Hopefully, most will come to understand that the university's success benefits everyone. Such messaging will need to be conveyed consistently and clearly by institutional leaders.

Creative leaders will find ways to ensure their programs are contributing to advancing the goals of the plan and benefiting from strategic investments. That is, even if the plan calls for the expansion of investments in certain fields, such as engineering, nursing, or computer science, to maximize institutional revenue through enrollment or research, other programs can benefit by building collaborative partnerships, investments in the expansion of general education offerings, and new opportunities for interdisciplinary or interprofessional educational and research activities. There is room for many to benefit. An effective strategic plan will incentivize drawing the campus together around strategic strengths and opportunities rather than pulling it apart.

Symbolically, it is ideal if a pool of resources for strategic investments can be identified by the president or provost at the implementation phase for the strategic plan. These resources may come from university reserves and can be set aside in advance so that the implementation phase of the plan can highlight a few significant and especially strategic investments to kick off implementation. To the extent that the desired outcomes of the strategic plan goals result in revenue enhancements through enrollment gains, expanded research funding, translation of research to commercial applications, growth of gifts and endowment, enhanced auxiliary revenue, etc., the investment of reserve funds will produce an ROI as well as signal the administration's commitment to success right from the beginning. Perhaps the most important element is that the strategic plan is developed through a collaborative and participatory process and that everyone has an opportunity to provide input.

As such, the university's strategic plan serves as "our" plan for the future direction and vitality of the institution.

Why Does Process Matter?

I spent much of my first year as provost leading a campuswide effort to develop the university's first-ever academic plan, which served as the university's strategic plan. Previous institutional plans were mostly developed by the central administration, and they were rather general in scope and direction and neither very strategic nor controversial. As such, the campus was not accustomed to or trusting of the participatory process or the administration's role in leading the development of a university strategic plan, let alone one referred to as an *academic plan*. Throughout the process, the faculty referred to the evolving, and ultimately completed, plan as the "provost's academic plan." Each time I politely countered that the academic plan was developed by the community and for the university and that the plan did not belong to the provost or any other individual. I must have made that or a similar public statement hundreds of times. In fact, leaders of the faculty senate, who also referred to the plan initially as the provost's academic plan, publicly shared in a positive and supportive way that they could see their specific language in many facets of the plan, acknowledging faculty participation in the process. Nevertheless, reference to the provost's academic plan persisted.

Then, one day a few months later, as I sat quietly listening to a discussion in a faculty senate meeting, I heard the faculty senate president and other members of the executive committee repeatedly refer to the critical importance of the "AP." I was scratching my head wondering what this apparently very important AP thing was all about. After the meeting, I asked the faculty senate president what the AP was that she and others were referring to. She looked at me bewildered and responded—the academic plan. Oh, of course, I said, a bit embarrassed at not realizing it. I was smiling inside because that informal moment signaled the acceptance by the faculty of the academic plan as the university's strategic plan and recognition that participatory processes and transparency do indeed build trust and confidence. From that day forward, the academic plan and strategic investments aligned with it guided us through turbulent financial times and led to a major transformation of and positive trajectory for the institution.

CHAPTER FOURTEEN

Higher Education Budget Models: An Overview

Budgets Drive Institutional Goals and Priorities

In addition to allocating revenue and expenses, university budgets represent a visible manifestation of an institution's or college's strategic priorities, commitments, and mission. As such, a budget is a tool that drives and supports institutional goals as articulated in the strategic plan. At their best, thoughtful and effective budget allocation processes also shape behavior by aligning incentives and rewarding progress toward advancing priorities, generating new revenue, ceasing unproductive or outdated activities, and building institutional or program quality and reputation. Because of consistent growth in expenses, such as salaries, benefits, utility costs, and financial aid, budget processes should also build in mechanisms to ensure and incentivize the *reallocation* of existing resources to support strategic priorities. Sustained growth in tuition revenue, state appropriations, and philanthropic support is not likely, and budget reductions are counterproductive and demoralizing for all. As I have stated many times, you can't cut your way to excellence or success—you must strategically invest your way forward.

The operating budget, or general fund, is the central income and expense budget that supports the academic core mission and most day-to-day operating expenses of the university. For that reason, it is the primary focus of this discussion about budgets for aspiring leaders. There are, however, other important budgets as well.

The capital budget, for instance, is typically managed on a multi-year horizon, allowing for planning, design, and implementation of construction, renovation, and repair projects as well as major equipment purchases. Capital projects and budgets may be supported by institutional reserves, transfers from the general fund, state or federal appropriations, grants, and gifts. They often involve the university borrowing money, which requires interest payments, or debt service, over the duration of the loan. University borrowing for capital projects frequently involves bond issuances; in most cases, the debt service is paid from the operating budget or from revenue generated by the capital investment itself, such as with new residence halls or indirect cost recovery from grants. Because the operating budget is dominated by tuition revenue at most institutions, one can comfortably assert that students are paying most of the debt service on capital projects through their tuition and fees. As such, capital investments should be carefully analyzed and justified through the lens of student impact.

Auxiliary budgets fund self-supporting activities, such as housing, dining, campus stores, parking, and student unions, that provide fee-based services to the campus community. Leaders should be thoughtful about the value-added from services and amenities that they budget for in auxiliaries. Students pay for these amenities through fees, which drive student costs and loan amounts upward. While advanced recreational facilities and other amenities may be attractive, they cannot substitute for limited or marginal academic experiences. The remaining discussion of budget models will focus on revenue and cost allocation of operating budgets.

Budget Models

Budget models are nothing more than a description of a set of processes used to create a budget and, especially, to allocate revenue and expenses to various units and priorities within the institution. Because the largest portion of institutional resources is allocated to the academic core mission, budget models usually focus on mechanisms or approaches for the strategic allocation of revenue to the colleges, schools, and university libraries, which in turn allocate resources to academic departments, research centers, and other operating units within their purview. A very simple, but entirely nonstrategic budget model would be to increase the budget of each unit by a fixed percentage that aligns with the annual increase in institutional revenue from tuition and/or state funding each year. With this very simplistic model in mind, one can imagine how such a model can be adapted to provide differential increases or reductions to each college, school, or department based on measures of unit productivity, such as growth in enrollment and/or student credit hours, research successes, or to support the strategic development of new programs that will attract additional revenue to the institution.

Because money is a driver that connects all aspects of the academic ecosystem, there is room to enhance strategic thinking, allocation, and reallocation of resources within nonacademic units as well, such as administration, student affairs, and athletics. Those units must be supportive of and congruent with the academic mission and may benefit from greater strategic management of financial resources. As with academic units, central service units should be expected to reallocate resources across departments and/or implement differential increments or decrements based on appropriate measures of unit efficiency, productivity, and contribution to the overall mission rather than across-the-board allocations or automatic replacement of vacated positions without scrutiny.

While resource allocation is always a major driver of budget models, attention to managing or controlling expenses should also be incentivized by an effective budget model. Universities are notorious for struggling with managing the expense side of the ledger because units rarely cease existing activities, initiatives, or programs as they embark on new ones. In part, this is because most existing activities involve people (remember, universities are all about people) and stopping an activity may mean eliminating positions, letting people go, or possibly retraining existing staff for new roles, which is not always feasible.

While there is variation in definition, most higher education budget processes fall *roughly* into five or six budget model categories. I emphasize *roughly* because institutional budget approaches often capture desired elements of two or more of the budget models and function as hybrid models and are customized to meet the specific needs and goals of the institution. Remember, budget models don't dictate budgets, and they certainly are not capable of printing money. That is, the budget model alone does not create new revenue or uncover pools of funds already in existence. Thoughtful and effective models, along with excellent strategic management, may encourage or discourage (i.e., incentivize) certain types of budget manager behaviors, help inform decision-making by institutional leaders, and lead to new revenue or reduced expenses. Simply put, if done well, they provide a transparent framework for the allocation, investment, and utilization of resources.

Each model offers some potential advantages and disadvantages that may be unique to each institution. There is no single "best" or "right" model for all institutions, although it is not uncommon for leaders to ascribe financial shortfalls to the budget model rather than to a disconnect between available funds and spending. The budget model that best meets the needs of an institution will likely be influenced by the specifics of the institutional budget situation, such as declining or expanding enrollment and/or state appropriation, along with budget history, campus culture, and strategic goals and priorities. Key historical and campus culture issues undoubtedly relate to trust and transparency, as discussed in chapter 3, which are especially critical in relation to resource allocation. That is, does the community trust that resource allocation has been equitable, strategic, and transparent or that a new budget model and allocation strategy will reflect these attributes? If the answer is no, choosing a new budget model alone will not address the paramount campus concerns.

There is extensive literature addressing elements of university budgets and budget models. Dean Smith's book entitled *How University Budgets Work* includes a chapter on budget models and is an excellent and very readable reference.[88] In addition, informative pieces from Hanover Research and the Educational Advisory Board offer valuable insights.[89] Budget models run the gamut from highly centralized to highly decentralized revenue allocation models. Below is a brief overview of five common budget models from most centralized to most decentralized.

Incremental Budgeting

Incremental budgeting is a commonly used centralized model in which the current fiscal year's budget serves as the base for the next fiscal year. Funding increments or decrements are added or subtracted to the previous year's base. Budget increments or decrements may be differential by budget unit or across-the-board, although differential allocations to academic and administrative units offer strategic advantages.

- **Advantages:** easy to implement; provides budgetary stability; allows multi-year budget planning by units; and assumes goals are consistent over time

- **Potential Issues:** in strict implementation, it may lack incentives and rewards for performance; may not reflect changing institutional priorities or enrollment patterns; limited cost accountability may perpetuate low-performance expenditures; and depends on revenue growth and reallocation to support budget increments

Zero-Based Budgeting

Zero-based budgeting is a seldomly used model in which each year the previous year's budget is erased, so units must justify all expenditures from scratch each year. Annual budget hearings serve as performance reviews.

- **Advantages:** controls unnecessary costs; focuses all spending on priorities; and minimizes waste and discretionary spending

- **Potential Issues:** seriously hampers long-term planning; requires substantial time and labor from units and administration in conducting extensive performance reviews; likely impossible to manage for all units each year; and directly conflicts with the stability of tenured faculty positions, multi-year contracts, and other fixed costs

Performance-Based Budgeting

In performance-based budget models, funding allocations are typically based on performance in quantitative productivity measures, such as semester credit hours taught, retention, and graduation rates, using multi-year rolling averages. Models are often formula-based with potential for differential weighting related to varying costs to deliver programs and outcomes. Performance-based models are often used by states in making appropriations to public institutions.

- **Advantages:** increases transparency and objectivity; more intentional and incentivizes specific behaviors; creates accountability for results in areas of institutional importance; and aligns allocation of resources with tangible results

- **Potential Issues:** requires time-consuming performance reviews and measures against expectations; often does not include qualitative factors in resource allocation decisions; may inadvertently favor high producing less strategic programs at the expense of high strategic priority investments; and could create perverse incentives to achieve productivity outcomes

Activity-Based Budgeting

Activity-based budgeting awards funding to activities that produce the greatest return on investment in the form of increased revenue, such as tuition and indirect cost recovery. Most of the revenue from specific activities (e.g., instruction, research, outreach) is returned to the unit responsible for generating the revenue from that activity.

- **Advantages:** clearly identifies streams of revenue; aligns incentives for greater revenue-producing activities; and empowers effective local strategic planning and accountability at the unit level

- **Potential Issues:** requires imposing a central "tax" on revenue generated by units to fund central expenses, such as administration, infrastructure, libraries, and strategic investments; may also require "subsidies" (subvention) for strategically important programs that generate insufficient revenue to be self-supporting; and can be complex to implement and manage

Responsibility-Centered Management (RCM)

RCM is a highly decentralized or distributed model that delegates operational authority and budget management responsibility to colleges, schools, and other units within the institution. Each budget unit functions as a "responsibility center" and is accountable for managing its expenses and generating its own revenue, thereby incentivizing deans and chairs to explore creative ways to generate additional revenue. Decentralization of responsibility and authority is a primary feature of this model. Responsibility centers pay for administrative services, including space, financial services, IT, human resources, etc. from their revenue generated.

Incentive-based budgeting (IBB) is a form of RCM that incorporates incentives as a decision-making tool. As with any RCM model, incentive-based budgeting should promote transparency and accountability across units; use of trusted and reliable data in planning and decision-making; entrepreneurial activity and innovation within and among units; efficiency and support of institutional priorities; and an equitable model for revenue and cost allocation.

- **Advantages:** increases accountability and creates powerful incentives for both revenue generation and expense reduction; units must live within their operating margins; positive and negative fund balances stay with the units as reserves; provides deans and chairs with investment resources and stimulates multi-year strategic investment planning, including capital investments; leads to more informed decision-making at the unit level, including efficient use of space; makes visible otherwise hidden costs of operations, such as space allocation, administrative functions, and overhead; and assigns responsibility for such costs

- **Potential Issues:** implementation is complex and likely to require several years of institutional focus; requires a more sophisticated skill set of staff and unit managers, including deans, and may force staff turnover; requires units to pay a central tax to pay for university administrative costs and subsidies (subvention) to supplement units and other institutional priorities needing financial assistance; subsidies from revenue-generating units to revenue-limited units can create angst, a class structure, and undermine university collaboration; produces competition among units for revenue that may undermine institutional integrity and lead to duplication of services and instruction, reduction of standards to gain enrollment, and discouraging students to transfer to majors outside the unit

Exploring Alternative Budget Models

Concerns about declining enrollment, reductions in state funding, and challenges associated with tuition increases and student debt have prompted many institutions to revisit their processes for allocating resources and costs (i.e., their budget model). The desire or hope is that an alternative model might help uncover or incentivize new revenue, expense reductions, or innovative opportunities. While examining alternative budget models is certainly logical and warranted, it is important to remember that no single budget model is going to address all university financial challenges. As emphasized by Mehta, there are numerous rational budget design choices an institution can consider, and none of them are "inherently right or wrong."[90] Choices will vary based on the needs and priorities of different institutions. Regardless of the budget model, transparency and aligning incentives to drive behavior change are key. Focusing on revenue allocation, distributing costs, identifying and investing in important institutional priorities, creating incentives, and removing disincentives are essential for successful budget redesigns.

Mehta suggests several basic principles for leaders to consider in budget model redesign analyses.[91] Prominent among them are:

- Effective budget models are intuitively understandable; complexity leads to less transparency, weaker incentives, and reduced likelihood of behavior change.

- A small group of leaders with a good understanding of complex financial matters should drive critical early decisions, including the president, provost, chief budget officer, budget director, dean of the largest unit, a financially savvy dean, and a college business manager.

- Deans should be assured of skilled financial staff and accurate program-level and market data so they can make informed and successful decisions.

- Cost allocations to central service units are among the most contentious issues; as such, cost allocation discussions should include expectations of administrative outputs and services to ensure academic unit needs are being met.

Historically, incremental budgeting was the norm at most institutions, especially in public universities. Incremental budgeting should not, however, operate through the implementation of across-the-board increases or decreases to all budget units, including academic and administrative units. Such an approach is nonstrategic and effectively penalizes productive and efficient units. There should be plenty of room for differential increments and decrements in alignment with strategic priorities, unit productivity measures, and the efficiency and effectiveness of service units.

Over the past two decades or so, there has been a trend away from incremental budgeting and toward various adaptations of RCM and hybrid models in both public and private doctoral universities.[92] In 2016, EAB indicated that about two-thirds of institutions were using some form of incremental budgeting.[93] In many cases, exploration or pursuit of alternative budget models occurs as institutions anticipate or begin to grapple with budget challenges, which may not be ideal timing. Simultaneously attempting to actively pursue critical strategic priorities while implementing a transformation of the institution's financial practices during a budget crisis may be daunting. The flip side argument, of course, is that financial challenges may highlight the potential need for change, although the dynamic of the inevitable winners and losers with new models may be more acute during challenging times.[94]

As institutions consider tackling a major budget model transformation, they need to keep in mind that the budget model itself does not directly produce or guarantee revenue. Insufficient funding must be met by new or expanded revenue streams, expense reductions, and reallocation regardless of the budget model. So, the question becomes can a new budget model incentivize such progress?

The Upside and Downside of RCM

The primary drivers in the trend toward RCM models, including IBB and other hybrid models, are the desire to incentivize revenue growth, control costs, and improve transparency.[95] There is often initial enthusiasm among some deans and others because they perceive, perhaps somewhat naively, that they get to keep all the revenue they generate, such as tuition and indirect cost recovery dollars from grants. While this is mostly true, the enthusiasm is usually tempered when they realize they will be taxed for central services, must pay for the space they occupy, and are expected to subsidize via subvention allocations to low-revenue-generating/high-cost units and services, including some less than optimum ones they may not care about or utilize. Or, when they learn that they have several high-cost/low-revenue programs.

Of course, funding of low-revenue/high-cost or underperforming administrative units from the general fund may occur with centralized budget models as well, but it is largely hidden and less evident. A potential advantage of an RCM model is that it brings low-revenue/high-cost and underperforming units out of the shadows. That advantage is only realized, however, if the institution is prepared to address those challenging units. As such, it should prompt discussions about whether some of those units should be retained and highlight the urgency to improve underperforming administrative units that may be costly and ineffective.

RCM has the potential to raise awareness of financial issues among unit budget managers, including both potential revenues and costly expenses, but it also requires a higher-order skill set in financial management. The challenges in adopting an RCM model are the time, efforts, and resources required for implementation and the potential, or even likelihood, for significant turnover among academic and administrative leaders during or after implementation, including deans and business managers. EAB reports that institutions need three to four years to transition to RCM, and the full benefits may not be realized for several years beyond that.[96]

Time and resource investments are necessary to upgrade financial tools, redesign positions, and train existing leaders and budgetary personnel as well as to develop the specific structures of the RCM model unique to institutional circumstances. Such structures include creating viable central tax and subvention models and striking the right balance in the allocation of tuition revenue between units of instruction and enrollment or perhaps even graduation rates (i.e., between credit hours taught versus the number of majors versus degrees awarded). Also, because net-tuition revenue largely remains with colleges, thoughtful analysis should be conducted about institutional financial aid through tuition discounting that is usually allocated centrally and applied differentially across colleges, resulting in the potential for differences in net-tuition income per student in each college.

The RCM revenue generation model incentivizes the delivery of relatively low-cost, high-enrollment courses and programs to maximize revenue. It may also intentionally or unintentionally compromise certain mission-critical programs or initiatives that may not be revenue generators, such as PhD programs and some programs in the arts and humanities that are critical for the institution and student success. Because tuition revenue is largely retained within colleges in most RCM models, there can be challenges in generating sufficient strategic central reserve funds and encouraging potentially important cross-unit interdisciplinary programs and initiatives, although accountability for these issues may be addressed by strong central leadership. Further, there are no guarantees that RCM, or any other model, will lead to enrollment or revenue gains. Despite such challenges, institutions generally report satisfaction with the implementation and outcomes of their RCM or hybrid models.

In analyzing RCM models across multiple institutions, the EAB reported the primary motivating factors that drive institutions toward shifting their budget model are the potential to enhance revenue and improve transparency.[97] Comparing enrollment and revenue growth before and after a change to RCM for an institution in relation to similar growth in the state in which they are located, the EAB offered an informal assessment of the impact of the budget model on enrollment and revenue growth.[98] Results were mixed. As shown in Figure 14.1, enrollment increased after RCM adoption in seven of the nine institutions examined, but only five of the nine outpaced state average enrollment growth, and only four of nine institutions witnessed revenue increases that outpaced the state average revenue growth after the budget change. While EAB acknowledges that the state average is an imperfect comparative measure, the analysis nevertheless shows that RCM does not always lead to enrollment or revenue growth.

EAB Analysis of Enrollment and Revenue Impact of RCM

	Enrollment[1]		Revenue[2]	
	Increased After RCM Adoption	Outpaced State Average	Increased After RCM Adoption	Outpaced State Average
Duke (1991)	✘	✔	✔	✔
Univ. of Michigan (1995)	✔	✘	✘	✘
Central Michigan Univ. (1999)[3]	✘	✘	✔	✘
Univ. of Minnesota (2000)	✔	✘	✘	✔
Univ. of Utah (2000)	✔	✔	✔	✔
Brandeis Univ. (2001)[4]	✔	✘	✘	✘
Univ. of New Hampshire (2001)	✔	✔	✔	✔
Ohio State (2003)	✔	✔	✘	✘
Syracuse (2006)	✔	✔	✘	✘

[1]*Enrollment was measured using total full-time equivalent enrollments.*
[2]*Revenue was measured as total revenue excluding auxiliary enterprises.*
Figure 14.1. Summary of enrollment and revenue growth of nine institutions following their transition to an RCM budget model between 1991 and 2006 compared to enrollment and revenue growth at other institutions in their state over the same period.[99]
Reprinted with permission from Educational Advisory Board (EAB)

These results highlight the principle that there is not one best budget model for all institutions or circumstances and that changing budget models does not guarantee enrollment or revenue growth. Regardless of the budget model, it is critical to align incentives for strategic growth and understand and promote the institutional value proposition. It is important to remember that the budget model does not recruit, enroll, or retain students, although it may incentivize behavior that is helpful or reveal inefficiencies and costly operations that must be adjusted or improved.

There are challenges to overcome in every budget model. Leaders considering budget redesign should have a good understanding of what's not working in their current system, a clear set of goals about desired elements from a new model, an appreciation of the impacts for and engagement of the campus community associated with the change, and anticipation of unintended consequences that may emerge and undermine progress. See "Potential Unintended Consequences with Budget Allocation Models" for a few examples.

Finally, before engaging in a campuswide budget model transformation, leaders should ensure that they can confidently and consistently generate trusted and reliable data centrally as well as in the units. Experienced, capable, and adaptable financial personnel, including deans and business managers, efficient and skilled administrative support units, and staff that function at a high level and engender confidence from the community should also be in place.

Potential Unintended Consequences with Various Budget Allocation Models

Budget allocation model policies and processes shape behavior, incentivizing positive outcomes and/or negative unintended consequences. Such unintended consequences can occur with any budget model. See examples with various budget models:

Incremental Model

Budget Process: Annual budget surpluses in colleges and divisions flow into a central reserve fund managed by the president and/or provost to ensure there are central funds for strategic investment in institutional priorities.

Potential Unintended Consequence: Units spend out their budgets late in the year because they perceive the central reserve fund doesn't benefit them.

Budget Process: Institutional budget challenges trigger across-the-board reductions for all units to contribute equally on a proportional basis to meet the necessary budget reduction target.

Potential Unintended Consequence: Highly productive, over-producing units are forced to reduce sections, increase class sizes, and compromise quality to meet their target, exacerbating the budget problem, while overfunded, underperforming units have only minor impacts.

Budget Process: All units are instructed to streamline administrative or instructional processes for cost savings.

Potential Unintended Consequence: Units resist efficiency improvements and cost-cutting because savings will be captured centrally, and they fear they will lose positions.

Performance Model

Budget Process: Supplemental performance funding is promised by the board, legislature, or administration for enhanced retention and graduation rates and to incentivize efforts to improve timely degree completion.

Potential Unintended Consequence: Institutions and programs increase academic selectivity, marginalizing students from first-generation families and underserved communities who would benefit from a college education, thereby undermining the mission.

RCM Model

Budget Process: All or most revenues and costs are allocated back to colleges and schools who then pay for central administrative services, decentralizing authority and responsibility for managing all unit revenues and costs.

Potential Unintended Consequence: Directors question the cost, quality, and value of central administrative services and develop their own duplicative structures within their units.

Budget Process: Tuition revenue is allocated back to colleges that teach courses and enroll students to incentivize growth in enrollment, revenue, and control over managing their academic and financial resources.

Potential Unintended Consequence: Increased competition among colleges for internal enrollment leads to colleges offering duplicative teaching of certain courses (e.g., writing, math, statistics, etc.) and recruiting students from other majors to enhance college resources with no new revenue to the institution.

While these and many other unintended consequences may emerge with any budget model, strong central leadership along with carefully developed and implemented strategic policies, such as signed memoranda of understanding (MOUs), service level and/or revenue sharing agreements, etc. may serve to maximize benefits and minimize contentious behavior. Regardless of the budget model, institutions need to focus on ways to incentivize revenue growth, how best to allocate and reallocate revenue, how to control and distribute costs, and how to establish and support strategic priorities at the unit level and centrally. To the extent possible, these key issues should be incorporated into the implementation of any models, whether highly centralized or decentralized. Finally, at the heart of all budget models is a central repository of accurate data that is shared broadly, particularly when changes in budget models are being considered.

While much time and discussion may be directed at exploring or arguing about the pros and cons of budget models, it is at times easy to forget that budgets are simply a way for institutions to organize and understand their revenues and expenses and ensure that resources align with strategic priorities and the institution's mission. In so doing, the budget highlights the institution's bold ambitions and exposes its limitations. Most importantly, an effective budget serves as a visible manifestation of the institution's strategic investment plan.

CHAPTER FIFTEEN

Strategic Allocation of Resources: Principles, Practices, and Incentives

In his 2019 book *Provost,* Larry Nielsen, referring to the importance of the budget, states that "money is way ahead of whatever is in second place."[100] Indeed, that is the case. Money is the primary energy driver in academic ecosystems. The budget is a major force that shapes the university community. Budgets support every aspect of academic life, including teaching, research, outreach, faculty and staff salaries and benefits, facilities, and administrative activities. Change the budget by adding, subtracting, or shifting funds and the activities change as well—for better or for worse. As such, the budget also impacts morale, motivation, and behavior, especially during challenging times. For these reasons and more, budget processes, especially the allocation of resources, are critical to the operations, optics, and image of the institution as well as to the delivery and nature of the curriculum and services. When the community believes the university is significantly underresourced, always seeking to minimize spending on important priorities, and constantly cutting budgets, confidence and enthusiasm wane and negative energy becomes infectious and is passed on to others, including students, alumni, and donors. On the flip side, when the community becomes accustomed to at least modest growth and strategic investment and progress is evident, institutional enthusiasm and support can be palpable, even during some difficult budget years. Indeed, the budget exerts a major influence in both tangible and intangible ways.

Regardless of the budget model, it is important that the operating budget and resource allocations and investments be *strategic, sustainable,* and *transparent* and that *incentives align* to reinforce these essential aspirations. The budget should be a visible manifestation of the strategic and institutional investment plans. Many institutions struggle to simultaneously address these four overriding goals, especially in times of limited resources, and frankly, most institutions are pretty much always in times of limited resources. Departments, colleges, centers, and entire institutions will always say they could do more or better if they had more resources, and no doubt they are correct. In fact, we make that claim to our funders (e.g., state legislatures) each year.

Basic Framework for Budget Processes

For budgets to be *strategic*, resource allocation must reflect institutional priorities, including functional and efficient administrative services, and college plans must align with the institutional academic strategic plan. Strategic priorities must include investments in programs of high demand and initiatives that drive student success as well as improved academic and administrative programs essential to the institution. Central and college-based reserve funds should be developed for strategic investments with the potential for a return on investment, such as high-demand new programs, contemporary research centers, and facility improvements.

For budgets to be *sustainable*, revenue potential and expenses must align so that investments support and encourage revenue growth in select areas, new high-demand programs, and efficient and effective central services. In addition, central recovery mechanisms must be in place to ensure financial stability over time, despite annual increases in salaries, benefits, utilities, and financial aid, and create the potential for reallocation across and within colleges and administrative support units.

For budgets to be *transparent*, the budget process, including any metrics used to measure progress or establish needs, should be straightforward, accessible, and understandable. Deans and other budget managers must ensure they engage departments about strategic needs and communicate clearly about unit priorities. Deans should also be made aware of the strategic needs, directions, and allocations of the other colleges. Central data providing unit productivity measures should be made available and shared annually to guide understanding of revenue growth, performance, and expenses, including enrollment, research, and other priorities.

For budgets to *align incentives*, allocations need to support top institutional and college priorities that are revenue and/or reputation-enhancing and recognize programs for progress toward advancing institutional goals and streamlining administrative operations. Mechanisms to encourage the cessation of already funded low-priority or outdated initiatives should be established, including ensuring that funding released is available for reinvestment within units. Annual budget increments and decrements should be sensitive to unit productivity, progress, and efficient service delivery.

Budgets should not remain stagnant silos of funding by divisions, colleges, departments, and central support services each year. The dynamic nature of strategic plans, resource allocations, operating expenditures, and investments typically result in differential year-to-year budgets to support a vibrant and evolving institution. No two budget years will be identical, and opportunities may occur some years for one-time strategic investments to enhance instruction, address research needs, and/or upgrade equipment, service centers, or facilities.

Potential Budget Principles to Operationalize Process Frameworks

The principles outlined below represent an approach one might consider and adapt to operationalize frameworks for a strategic, sustainable, and transparent budget process that incentivizes investments, revenue growth, and reallocation. While these principles have been implemented with centralized budget models, they are not meant to endorse any specific model or to discourage the pursuit of more decentralized models, such as activity-based budgeting or RCM. In fact, adaptations of these or other principles may be applicable to almost any budget model and could be applied to administrative as well as academic units. Too often administrative units seem to minimize strategic approaches to annual resource allocation, assessments of unit effectiveness, and processes to encourage the reallocation of resources across units.

These principles are meant as an illustration of elements that might help establish a transparent and sustainable strategic resource allocation process.

Principles to Guide Strategic Investments and Reinvestments

Principle #1: Funds and lines associated with vacated positions (retirements and departures) will be recaptured centrally each year as a budget recovery mechanism and purposefully reallocated, mostly at entry-level salaries, in areas of high demand, strategic opportunity, and revenue potential.

PRINCIPLE IN ACTION:

- Central budget recovery is necessary to control institutional expenditures over time and create an internal pool of revenue for reallocation across colleges, departments, and administrative units.

- Recovering and reallocating vacant faculty and staff lines prioritizes reinvesting resources in underfunded, high-demand programs, new priority programs to ensure revenue growth, or bolstering staff in high-demand service units.

- Such reinvestments not only support revenue enhancement in growing areas but also improve cost-effectiveness by shifting base resources from low-demand areas.

- Phased retirement programs may offer a gradual and respectful approach to incentivize individuals to retire, thereby freeing up resources for reallocation or reinvestment.

- Lines from tenure denials are exempt from central recovery to ensure incentives are aligned to maintain and enforce standards; deans reallocate these lines in concert with needs and the college plan.

Principle #2: Resource allocations, both increments and decrements, will be guided by the alignment of unit priorities with institutional goals as well as unit productivity, cost-effectiveness in teaching, research, outreach or service activities, and student success.

PRINCIPLE IN ACTION:

- Resources should flow preferentially to programs and initiatives of high strategic priority and revenue generation potential as evidenced by credit hour production, number of majors, and research productivity to ensure that resource constraints do not limit potential.

- Initiatives aimed at enhancing student success, including retention, productive grades in gateway classes, and timely graduation, are encouraged and rewarded.

- Decisions regarding the allocation of resources to colleges will be shared among all deans to ensure transparency.

- Central data providing unit productivity in teaching and research should be straightforward, updated annually, consistent, transparent, and considered along with strategic considerations in allocation decisions.

- A distinct FTE student-to-faculty ratio (or credit hours generated per faculty FTE) target should be established for each college that reflects its unique mission, strengths, and program delivery model; deans must then manage to those targets, and resource allocations should strive to sustain those targets. Parallel processes and metrics should be established for administrative units.

Principle #3: Prior to requesting additional resources, colleges will internally examine existing programs and initiatives and identify low-priority or outdated activities that can be reduced, eliminated, or phased out over time; resources released from such efforts will be retained by the college and matched centrally for reinvestment in high priority areas within the college.

PRINCIPLE IN ACTION:

- In a rapidly changing world with an abundance of technological innovations and potential for new initiatives, eliminating existing low-priority and outdated activities is important for financial stability, generating additional revenue for high-priority contemporary reinvestments, and streamlining processes.

- Assuring that resources freed up from eliminating such programs will be retained within the college and matched with central funds (effectively doubling that resource) incentivizes strategic management, the evolution of programs and initiatives, and innovation.

Principle #4: New fully online programs in selected areas, especially professional master's programs, stackable post-baccalaureate certificates, and degree completion programs aimed primarily at adult learners and career advancement, are a high priority; seed grants help develop programs, and tuition revenue-sharing opportunities may incentivize participation.

PRINCIPLE IN ACTION:

- This is meant to incentivize the development of fully online programs in certain areas to grow enrollment and expand revenue primarily from adult learners, including those with some credits, active military, veterans, and individuals upskilling or reskilling.

- Seed grants to cover costs to develop such programs and tuition-based revenue sharing offer incentives for departments and colleges to participate.

Principle #5: Across-the-board budget adjustments, including both increments and decrements, will be avoided, except for mandated annual negotiated faculty and staff salary increases.

PRINCIPLE IN ACTION:

- Across-the-board equal proportion budget additions and reductions are inherently nonstrategic.

- Proportional budget increases and reductions potentially damage highly productive but underfunded units, exacerbating financial challenges and draining morale.

- The negotiated and agreed-upon annual salary increase pools must be covered and are often managed centrally.

- When necessary, budget reductions will be differential across colleges and divisions, and should consider unit priority, productivity, and faculty workload while ensuring the delivery of the curriculum and academic mission.

- Recently funded strategic initiatives, although at times the easiest to cut because they are new, should be exempt from budget reductions because they represent strategically vetted investments with beneficial impacts.

Principle #6: Across-the-board hiring and spending freezes should be minimized as a budget control mechanism.

PRINCIPLE IN ACTION:

- Across-the-board hiring and spending freezes are inherently nonstrategic.

- Hiring and spending may be temporarily constrained during times of severe budget challenges, but critically important and time-sensitive hires and expenditures should be allowed with justification on a case-by-case basis if in the best interests of the institution.

- Even during the most challenging financial times, it may be important that select critical positions (e.g., the director of IT security) can be hired, and the institution continues to invest in key personnel. (Remember: you can't cut your way to excellence or success.)

- Institutions with freezes in place invariably violate their own policy as they make exceptions without an equitable and transparent justification process, which diminishes trust and morale.

Principle #7: Carryforward of annual surpluses in college budgets should be used to establish on a shared basis college-based and central reserve funds available for nonrecurring (i.e., one-time-only) strategic investments in revenue- or reputation-enhancing activities or facility upgrades.

PRINCIPLE IN ACTION:

- Carryforward of annual surpluses is strategic and allows the deans, provost, and president to make important tactical investments and provides short-term budget protection; investment of college-based reserves requires approval of the provost.

- Allowing carryforward of surplus funds incentivizes careful annual spending of resources and minimizes end-of-the-year nonstrategic spending.

- Unallocated fringe from open positions will be directed on a one-time basis to the central reserve.

- Annual surpluses generated in nonrevenue producing units will flow into the central reserve fund.

Principle #8: Investments in new initiatives within units should include an investment of noncentral resources (e.g., from reserves, overhead accounts, gifts, etc.) from the units and internal reallocations; central co-investment reflects mutual support of the initiative.

PRINCIPLE IN ACTION:

- The unit's commitment to and strategic analysis of a new initiative is exhibited by their willingness to invest their own funds at least on a short-term basis.

- Central co-investment for new unit-based initiatives incentivizes and rewards innovation and efficiency and provides ongoing support.

- The provost and deans should establish a standard cost-sharing agreement from central reserves and college funds for start-up packages to attract the highest quality new faculty.

Principle #9: The budget process will include an annual college submission articulating recent accomplishments and unit strategic investment priorities and individual college budget hearings to discuss budget challenges and opportunities, and an annual summit for deans/unit leaders to share their progress, priorities, and needs with their peers.

PRINCIPLE IN ACTION:

- Annual written budget submissions prompt regular analysis and reinforcement of priorities and needs, assessment of recent investments and accomplishments, a multi-year (usually three years) budget planning horizon and ensure that all requests are considered at the same time, minimizing concerns about private side deals during the year.

- Budget hearings allow for thoughtful discussion of needs and sensitive financial or personnel issues and ensure open lines of communication.

- The annual summit for unit leaders ensures transparency, informs potential areas of mutual interest across units, and often stimulates multi- and interdisciplinary investment in new initiatives and programs.

Principle #10: Once allocations are made, units are expected to operate within the framework and constraints of their annual budget, unless justified emergencies (e.g., midyear state appropriation reductions, sudden dramatic shifts in enrollment, etc.) occur during the year.

PRINCIPLE IN ACTION:

- Units are expected to spend allocated resources as justified in their request and approved; any proposed changes are subject to reconsideration.

- Units are held responsible for any annual budget expenditures that exceed available unit revenue and must use internal reserves to balance, or the negative fund balance will carry forward within the unit budget to the next fiscal year.

- Special circumstances related to potential emergency situations must be discussed, and any alternative funding approaches must be approved.

These principles are meant to serve as guidelines to be modified for the situation and culture on various campuses. More than anything, they illustrate that there are ways to connect resources to strategic priorities, incentivize behaviors you wish to encourage, build sustainable budgets, and reallocate resources to ensure that revenue-producing units and activities are not or only minimally constrained by resource limitations. During times of resource constraints, the ability to reallocate resources to areas of greatest need and impact is essential and beneficial to the entire university community because of revenue enhancements in particular programs. With reallocation, there certainly can be a lag time in getting resources from where they currently sit to where they are needed. Building in a multi-year college-based planning horizon, however, can help create timely investments. At times, central or college-based reserves may be used as bridge funds to future retirements or new positions to ensure that growing programs are supported and revenue growth is sustained.

As is always the case, the details of implementation, availability of new and reallocated revenue, and the actual outcomes of budget allocation practices will significantly impact the translation of budget principles into meaningful institutional investments. While none of this is simple or easy, the community generally adapts to budget principles and practices in place, appreciates consistency in process, timing, and transparency, and budget requests become increasingly thoughtful and focused over time. Unique situations or exceptions will certainly arise and must be addressed transparently on a case-by-case basis. Following these budget principles and practices, many tens of millions of dollars were strategically allocated and reallocated to the colleges over the course of a decade. These investments led directly to significant enrollment and revenue growth, more than doubling of research funding, enhanced student retention and timely graduation, investment in graduate student support, and increased diversity and reinvigoration of the faculty, even though state funding diminished or remained flat over time and tuition increases remained at or below the HEPI.

Moving from Budget Principles to Budget Practices

In addition to providing a basis for budget requests and resource allocation decisions, annual budget request submissions from each college or budget unit should prompt self-reflection on what is working well and what is not, review of college and institutional strategic plans, and identification and justification of the highest priority needs of the unit. Furthermore, the effort in preparing a formal budget request annually is also a reminder that allocations of limited resources are not automatic or entitled. Resources are always constrained, and units must justify their requests and be prepared to explain how such investments benefit the university as well as the college/division.

As a dean for many years, preparing an annual budget narrative submission always seemed a bit laborious. When it was completed, however, I learned so much each year about challenges and opportunities in the college. For example, it instigates an annual review of the unit's productivity data (gathered centrally and shared broadly), triggering an assessment of patterns in enrollment, credit-hour production, research activities, etc. by program. Of course, knowing that the provost will have reviewed this data and that it will be discussed at budget hearings also prompts careful analysis and explanation.

Finally, even during times of major financial challenges, it is important for units to identify their most pressing needs, even if the institution is unable to address those needs because of insufficient revenue at that moment. It is plausible that other opportunities may emerge outside the normal budget cycle to address some of those critical issues. An ongoing budget submission practice is a healthy exercise for units and is an important step in ensuring requests and allocations align with strategic priorities and that incentives drive investments toward areas of need and growth.

Budget Narratives

The budget request narrative process should be straightforward and consistent from year to year, although it may be appropriate to customize additional questions related to recent university investments, reorganizations, or other contemporary issues, such as changes in curriculum delivery or unit-related business in a post-COVID world. The process should respect the distinct missions, purposes, and plans of each unit while at the same time clearly focusing on strategic areas for institutional investment that should be addressed by each of the units in the context of their needs as well as the best interests and investments of the institution. Most importantly, requests should be prioritized and accompanied by a strategic rationale and justification for each position and non-personnel financial request. To prompt multi-year planning on the part of each unit, the budget narrative submission should project anticipated needs at least two years beyond the immediate year of request.

Below is a brief overview of a budget request narrative framework to serve as an example that could be modified based on strategic priorities, needs, cultures, and important issues at other institutions.

I. Accomplishments and Innovations: Provide a summary of recent accomplishments and innovations of the college/unit and a brief overview of goals for advancing the unit and university strategic plan next year.

II. Diversity Progress: Given the prominence of the overriding goal to embrace diversity and social justice in the university's academic strategic plan, complete the annual college diversity progress accountability report using the standard template for reporting (see chapter 5).

III. Strategic Requests for New Positions: Criteria for prioritizing requests must align with the goals of the university and unit strategic plans. Prioritize each faculty or staff position request and provide a clear and concise rationale and justification for the position and priority. The justification must demonstrate how each position addresses one or more of the bulleted areas in each of the criteria outlined below and must designate one of the criteria as a major driver for each position requested. These criteria are meant as an illustration and should be modified to fit your department, college, or institution's priorities.

Criterion 1: Advance student success and alignment with documented student demand.

- Position provides quality teaching and learning for rapidly growing majors/programs at the undergraduate and/or graduate levels.

- Position provides quality teaching and learning in programs with exceedingly high student credit hour production.

- Position will improve student success in challenging gateway classes.

- Position's expertise will enhance strategic learning outcomes and inclusive pedagogy focused on diversity, equity, inclusion, and social justice.

Criterion 2: Foster strategic innovation and excellence.

- Position bolsters new majors or the transformation of existing majors with evidence-based student demand; emphasis on developing professional masters' programs.

- Position aligns with and substantially enhances cross-cutting institutional priorities, such as interdisciplinary programs, global partnerships, diversity, experiential learning, and workforce and economic development.

- Position enhances the success of selected fully online programs that contribute directly to revenue generation and revenue-sharing with the sponsoring college/unit.

- Position contributes to institutional centers of excellence, and supports existing cluster themes or new strategic areas with substantial potential positive impact.

Criterion 3: Enhance research and scholarship.

- Position contributes expertise in priority areas of research, scholarship, and creative work aligned with important state, national, or global issues.

- Position adds expertise in areas with the potential to significantly enhance external research funding, including generating overhead funds critical to the research enterprise.

- Position focuses on research that will enhance economic development, business incubation and acceleration, and facilitates partnerships with external constituents, including businesses and other institutions.

- Position expands scholarly contributions that will enhance the quality of life and prominence of the university in the state and beyond.

- Position contributes scholarly expertise that advances progress in diversity, equity, inclusion, and social justice.

IV. Strategic Requests for Operating Resources (if applicable): Provide a justification for any requests for non-personnel operating funds. Such needs should first be addressed through internal reallocation, and any such requests must provide a compelling rationale and justification related to advancing student success or the research enterprise.

V. Low-Priority Activities (if applicable): Identify funded low-priority or outdated activities within your unit that can be reduced, eliminated, or phased out over time. Resources released will be

retained in the college, matched 100 percent, and available to the
unit for reinvestment in areas of high priority to the unit. For
activities to be phased out over time, funds will become available
and matched at the time of elimination, although identifying such
areas in advance is beneficial.

VI. Future High-Priority Position Needs: Project anticipated high-priority position needs for the next two fiscal years by listing position titles, departments, and areas of expertise, recognizing they
are subject to change given the dynamic nature of higher education. Provide a list of retirements and anticipated retirements
this year and over the next two years.

Budget Hearings

College unit budget hearings involve the dean/director and additional
appropriate college/unit representatives, such as the business manager
and associate deans, meeting with the provost, vice provosts, budget
office director, and budget specialist. The meetings explore budget
requests in detail, including strategic justifications and alternatives, and
discuss any other budget and personnel matters, issues of concern, and
emerging opportunities.

Budget Presentations Annual Summit

To promote transparency and clear communication across colleges/units,
each dean or unit head is asked to make a fifteen-minute public presentation (plus five minutes for Q&A) that includes a general summary of
unit accomplishments, strategic needs and requests, and overall direction, opportunities, and challenges. Such presentations need not include
detailed budget information or discussion of any pressing personnel
matters. Discussion of mutual or potential cross-college interests, collaboration, and possible joint appointments or shared positions among
colleagues are appropriate.

Budget Decisions and Impacts

Following a review of the budget narrative, discussions at budget hearings, and unit budget presentations, resource allocation decisions are
ultimately made by the provost in consultation with the vice provosts

and director of the budget office. In a more decentralized budget model, I expect a similar process might lead to resource allocation decisions by deans or directors of units to departments, but strategies and approaches could be parallel. Decisions are shared in writing with the unit leaders and resources are allocated to base budgets of units at the beginning of the fiscal year and can be used on a one-time-only basis for that year while searches are conducted. Deans have appreciated the advanced allocation of funds supporting positions that allows them to make one-time-only short-term investments.

Allocation decisions have mostly favored programs of high demand, promising new and innovative initiatives, and focused areas of research where the institution can build excellence. In so doing, such investments lead to a ROI in revenue, reputation, and prominence, all of which help the institution broadly. Of course, not everyone agrees with or is pleased with the resource allocation decisions. Some disciplines are defined by having an array of faculty scholars in many unique and distinct subfields and believe they are deficient if they are missing expertise pertinent to certain time periods, geographic perspectives, or subdisciplines in their faculty, regardless of enrollment patterns in their department, strategic institutional goals and priorities, societal needs, and the potential ROI for the institution. While the frustration is understandable, such investments are not always affordable, although we remain sensitive to the needs and desires of all disciplines.

Finally, an effective process shapes behavior and incentivizes the development of and investments in new interdisciplinary programs popular with students, advancement of online programs, and encourages deans to work with their faculty and across colleges to identify and invest in critical and lucrative areas of research. One college, for example, developed high-priority college-based research themes that cut across rather than focused within departments. Following a few years of strategic investments, the college established two nationally prominent, externally funded centers of excellence borne directly from those investments. Strategic allocations have incentivized thematic cross-college cluster hire investments in interdisciplinary areas, such as neuroscience, data science, and high performance and research computing, that have expanded research funding and capabilities and led to new undergraduate and graduate programs, major gifts, and enhanced institutional visibility.

Leading during Crises—Addressing Budget Shortfalls

In a perfect world, the challenge may appear to be deciding which institutional priorities warrant financial investment in any given year because there is never enough money to fund the many legitimate strategic requests put forward. We simply do the best we can. A much larger and substantially more unpleasant challenge occurs when anticipated revenues do not materialize or when significant unanticipated expenses emerge that exceed revenue projections. For example, significant reductions in state appropriations and/or tuition and fee income, or market fluctuations that dramatically impact the endowment payout would likely result in budget shortfalls across the university that must be addressed through base budget adjustments to each unit. That is, each budget unit will need to reduce its expenditures so base budget funds can be recaptured to address the deficit.

If the revenue shortfall or expense increase is certain to be temporary, it may be possible to cover the shortfall on a one-time-only (OTO) basis with reserve funds, although that can be a risky proposition because it reduces contingency funds that protect the institution against sudden emergencies. For the most part, budget deficits must be met with base budget reductions across all or most budget units. This includes central administration units that should not be exempt from reductions. In fact, it may be more important to protect revenue-generating units, such as the academic units, so that the financial challenges are not exacerbated by further enrollment losses. Nevertheless, the necessity for base budget reductions invariably creates heartache for all.

To address budget reductions, institutional leaders should establish guidelines for the implementation of strategic budget reductions. While across-the-board budget cuts (e.g., a 5 percent reduction to all units) may seem to be the most straightforward to implement, they are inherently nonstrategic and assume that all units are equally well-funded, equivalent in tuition and research revenue generation, contribute similarly to institutional vitality, and have similar access to other discretionary funds, such as research overhead, gift accounts, reserves, or other restricted funds that may serve as a short-term buffer. Such assumptions are rarely true. As such, I have recommended as a general operating guideline avoiding across-the-board proportional cuts and implementing differential budget reduction targets across units predicated largely on unit productivity based on credit hour generation (i.e., tuition revenue generation) and/or other revenue generation.

Because the academic mission receives most of the operating budget, it invariably will absorb the largest reduction. It is, however, the major revenue generator through tuition and fees. Protecting the ability to deliver the curriculum with quality and preserve revenue-generating capability must be paramount in establishing reduction targets as failure to do so will further exacerbate the financial challenge. As such, under-producing academic units and administrative or service units that are not revenue-generating may absorb a disproportionally large share of the reduction. Within each unit, strategic priorities that are already funded should be protected to the extent possible. Once guidelines are established, unit leaders will need to identify items to meet their reduction target. This is best done in consultation with internal budget advisory teams that can offer advice and perspective, ensure transparency, and perhaps assist in delivering the unpleasant message and rationale for the specific areas that are being reduced. See "A Possible Set of Guidelines for Implementation of Budget Reductions" for some suggested guidelines.

Under the most severe financial situations, consolidation or elimination of programs, services, or functions may be deemed necessary, which invariably involves temporary or permanent reductions of personnel. Frequently, underenrolled, low-priority, and underproducing programs or services are targeted for elimination. Such consolidations or eliminations are always very difficult and fraught with challenges from both internal and external constituents, especially in institutions with staff and faculty unions. Because of commitments to existing students, tenured faculty lines, and multi-year contracts for certain staff and administrative positions, cost savings from program consolidation or elimination may be minimal, spread over multiple years, and insufficient in the near term to address the immediate budget shortfall. While program elimination or consolidation may be necessary or appropriate at times, it should be a last resort as an emergency budget reduction strategy. The time to carefully consider phasing out unproductive or nonstrategic programs and services is during solvent financial times so that recovered funds can be either strategically reinvested or placed in reserve for future challenging times. Such decisions should be informed by structured evidence-based academic reviews of programs rather than by last-ditch efforts to respond to an abrupt financial crisis. A substantive academic program review process provides an excellent mechanism to do just that.

A Possible Set of Guidelines for Implementation of Budget Reductions

- Avoid proportional across-the-board reductions.
- Sustain a quality education and experience for all students to the extent possible.
- Protect primary general revenue streams (tuition and fees) by ensuring timely delivery of the curriculum and student support services.
- Protect strategic investments in alignment with the strategic plan.
- Be careful not to compromise safety of students, staff, and faculty.
- Sustain financial aid investments critical to attracting and retaining students and supporting student success.
- Sustain mission-critical diversity initiatives and programs as a strategic priority.
- Strategically invest in initiatives and programs that enhance revenue.

While the specifics of the principles, practices, and guidelines outlined here may not be appropriate for all institutions, I am convinced that strategic allocation of resources, controlling costs leading to sustainable budgets, and creating incentives to craft and sustain new high-demand programs, interdisciplinary research centers, and revenue growth is essential for institutions to remain vital in a complex and ever-changing world.

PART V

POPULATION DYNAMICS

Empowering Progress and Overcoming Obstacles

Population dynamics relate to the growth and regulation of populations and communities that reflect a net balance of positive potential and constraints imposed by internal and external factors. Without limitations, populations exhibit exponential growth, but limitations always exist or emerge over time. Depending on conditions, disturbances, and advancements, population density may be constant or may fluctuate widely over time. Leaders need to understand, and even predict, potential disruptions and opportunities for advancement that may serve to spawn or resist progress and relevance to ensure institutions are maximizing their potential. Indeed, engaged leaders recognize and overcome existing and emerging obstacles and empower forward progress!

CHAPTER SIXTEEN

Driving Change and Continuous Improvement: You Get What You Measure

Key Indicators of Improvement

In chapter 1, I proposed that effective leaders identify and address key institutional challenges and mobilize the community to pursue bold aspirations. That is, leaders work collaboratively with the campus community to develop and embrace a change agenda that leads to continuous improvement in the relevance and value of a college education and university research. This is in the best interests of current and future students and society but also enhances the value proposition, reputation, and future financial viability of our institutions.

We live in a dynamic world where the value and meaning of education are evolving, as are the learning needs and demands of students, the knowledge and skills expected by employers, and the critical societal needs for new information, interpretations, and discoveries uncovered through the research, scholarship, and creative work of faculty and students. *Universities must always be adapting, evolving, and improving organizations to remain vital and relevant.* Leaders must create an environment of continuous positive change in teaching, research, and societal outcomes driven by collaborative contributions from the university community.

The dynamics of a vibrant and resilient academic ecosystem are reflected in community stability or growth, even when confronted with demographic challenges, societal demands, or external disruptions. To track improvement, institutions must first gather data and other qualitative information to monitor their performance in key areas. Such measures must be both accurate and consistent to provide a reliable and useful assessment. Universities collect an abundance of data that are used for many purposes and by multiple constituents, both internal and external. Some of the routinely collected institutional data is submitted to the US Department of Education National Center for Education Statistics (NCES) for comparative institutional tracking of the "condition of postsecondary education in the United States."[101] This Integrated Postsecondary Education Data System (IPEDS) is the core federal government data collection program required of all institutions that participate in federal student financial aid programs. IPEDS is a comprehensive system built around a series of interrelated surveys designed to collect institution-level data in several areas, including enrollment, admissions, retention, graduation rates, degree completions, student financial aid, tuition and fees, faculty and staff, and institutional finances.

The power of IPEDS is its comprehensive nature across thousands of institutions and its clear definitions of all survey components, thus allowing helpful comparisons for certain measures of interest. For instance, governing boards, legislatures, etc. frequently call into question the cost-effectiveness of institutions, speculating an institution is inefficient in its utilization of resources. Because IPEDS includes both financial and performance data, costs of specific functions, such as instruction and student services, can be expressed on a cost-per-credit hour basis to allow spending comparisons (i.e., cost-effectiveness) among regional peer institutions with similar missions and educational outcomes.

Figure 16.1 presents a hypothetical comparison of institutional spending per credit hour for various institutional functions captured in IPEDS data allowing an institution to evaluate spending patterns compared to peers. In this example, Peer #1 spends the most per credit hour across most functional categories. Peer #4 generally spends the least but prioritizes academic support and student services. One might conclude that Peer #4 is more efficient regarding resource utilization, or Peer #4 is underfunded and forced to spend less in providing essential services. Either way, this type of simple comparative analysis can be helpful in informing boards and legislatures about institutional spending patterns, cost-effectiveness, and financial challenges.

Institution	Instruction $ per credit hour (rank)	Public Service $ per credit hour (rank)	Academic Support $ per credit hour (rank)	Institutional Support $ per credit hour (rank)	Student Services $ per credit hour (rank)	Total annual expense $ per credit hour (rank)
Peer #1	545 (1)	96 (1)	187 (1)	132 (1)	62 (3)	1834 (1)
Peer #2	524 (2)	40 (2)	101 (4)	112 (2)	87 (1)	1362 (2)
Peer #3	390 (3)	23 (3)	114 (3)	74 (4)	44 (4)	1195 (3)
Peer #4	291 (4)	22 (4)	116 (2)	96 (3)	85 (2)	1093 (4)

Figure 16.1. Comparison of spending (on a per credit hour basis) among four hypothetical peer institutions on several functions included in IPEDS surveys of institutions.

While interinstitutional comparisons may be helpful for cost analyses, reputation-building, and learning about other institutions, driving improvement in institutional performance and productivity should largely rely on internal comparisons of key performance indicators over time. In fact, many of the interinstitutional comparisons derived from IPEDS are compromised as assessments of achievement because they are subject to many interpretations with little to do with direct institutional performance or quality. This is not a function of the accuracy or quality of the data, but rather many confounding variables that impact interpretations of comparative performance metrics among institutions. For example, the near-perfect retention rates (95 to 99 percent) of highly selective Ivy League institutions are more likely a reflection of the previous education, academic stature, wealth, and family history of their students than specific institutional programs. In comparison, access-focused public colleges and universities with lower retention engage a high proportion of Pell-eligible, first-generation students, or those representing historically underrepresented populations with high unmet financial need.

To drive a change agenda, each institution should monitor improvement in key metrics of importance to that institution, especially in response to initiatives or investments designed to enhance performance. Assessment of outcomes should carefully consider drivers that enhance or detract from improvement and incorporate that information to implement targeted interventions to ensure forward progress. Accrediting agencies often refer to the integration of information learned from outcome assessments in making improvements as "closing the assessment loop."

Interpreting Key Performance Metrics

So, which institutional performance metrics deserve your attention? The answer will vary from one institution to the next, although there are common measures that will be important across most institutions. First and foremost, institutions, colleges, and departments should be generating and monitoring metrics to assess progress toward the goals stipulated in their strategic plan. Presumably, those goals are major areas of importance and investment for the institution, and there should be a high expectation for continuous improvement and return on those investments. If not, a change in course is likely necessary.

While performance metrics may be excellent indicators, the true value in measuring performance is **understanding the drivers behind those indicators and institutional responsiveness**, or the lack thereof. As a simple and obvious example, it would be important to discern an abrupt drop off in retention in response to COVID-19 as very different from a similar drop not associated with the pandemic. Often careful disaggregation of data by, for example, Pell eligibility, race/ethnicity, and first-generation status can help provide meaning or explanations for shortcomings or changing patterns in performance and guide an institution to targeted interventions leading to improvement. Below I discuss several key performance metrics that institutions often consider and offer potential interpretation commentary.

Retention

Most institutions, possibly apart from highly selective elite ones, carefully track retention with a keen focus on improvement as well as revenue generation (see chapter 12). Improving these metrics is certainly critical for students as well as institutional reputation. As defined by the NSCRC, *retention* refers to the proportion of students returning to the same institution for their second year, and *persistence* refers to the proportion of students returning to any institution for their second year.[102] While first-year retention is the standard metric reported, retention often continues to decline following the second and third year. Institutions should consider tracking these metrics as well and, if necessary, implementing interventions to retain students.

The average retention for full-time, first-year students in the 2020 cohort at public and private nonprofit four-year, two-year degree-granting institutions and private for-profit institutions was 78.5 percent,

78.2 percent, 59.5 percent, and 45 percent, respectively.[103] Retention of Latinx, Black, and Native American students on average lags that of other students by approximately 10 to 15 percentage points, creating an equity gap that must be addressed. Retention of part-time students and those aged twenty-one years and older at these institutions range from approximately 37 to 50 percent.

For four-year institutions, full-time, first-year retention averaged 93 percent for selective institutions with acceptance rates of less than 25 percent compared to 59 percent for the least selective institutions.[104] Citing statistics from his book *Who Graduates from College? Who Doesn't?*, Mark Kantrowitz reports that about three-quarters of those who drop out of college are first-generation students, and more than two-thirds are students from low-income families with an adjusted gross income (AGI) under $50,000.[105] In contrast, students from families with an AGI of more than $100,000 are 50 percent more likely to graduate from college than those from low-income families.[106] Evidence strongly suggests that low retention is shaped as much by historical educational inequities and socioeconomic factors for students and their families as it is by institutional standards or inherent student ability.

Dropping out of college is not only a missed opportunity for those students but also frequently creates an added economic hardship of student loan debt without the economic mobility employment benefit of earning a college degree or certificate. Thus, it is imperative that institutional leaders develop a good understanding of the academic, demographic, and financial profile of their students and disaggregate their data so that targeted interventions can be implemented.

Reasons Students Leave

There are numerous reasons students choose to leave an institution. Some students may transfer to another institution for financial reasons or a better fit for their interests or needs. According to NSCRC, approximately 9 percent of first-year students have transferred to another institution over the past decade.[107] Others might be struggling academically or have not discovered an academic major or courses of interest. Financial concerns, social isolation, and increasing mental health challenges can certainly be important contributors as well.

The factors are numerous, and institutions cannot control all variables. Institutions can, however, implement a series of initiatives that are good practices and beneficial to all students. It is well-known that engaged students who are academically successful and feel a sense of belonging to the university community have a very high likelihood of being retained as do students who feel supported by faculty or academic advisors. Institutions should develop a good understanding of who their students are and what they need to be successful, and then implement initiatives supportive of their students. For instance, it is well-established that retention of many first-generation college students, students of color, and students receiving Pell grants may lag that of other students on some campuses. Particular attention to the needs of those students, including targeting additional aid if appropriate, can be very helpful to enhance retention and reduce equity gaps.

Enhancing Retention

There is no one-size-fits-all model for enhancing retention. Each institution will need to analyze student needs, culture, and campus climate. Clearly, highly selective wealthy institutions offering robust financial aid and support programs have very high retention, typically well above 90 percent. Most institutions, however, have room to improve retention rates, which will be beneficial both to the institution and to the students. Institutions should establish realistic retention goals and then strategically develop and implement initiatives to achieve those goals. The revenue and reputational gains will more than pay for the initiatives. Furthermore, such efforts demonstrate the institution cares about its students, educational quality, and timely degree completion. To overcome equity gaps and continuously improve retention, institutions must offer guidance for students navigating the mysteries of college for the first time and create a sense of belonging for all students. There are numerous strategic initiatives that can be helpful, depending on the specific circumstances at the institution. A few examples are:

- monitoring student credit completion by semester or year;
- tracking retention by program;
- developing guided pathways or curriculum maps;
- providing robust academic support, including strong advising, a writing center, study skills, and tutoring programs, especially for challenging gateway courses;
- early identification of and support for at-risk and undeclared students;

- career development guidance;

- ensuring the general education curriculum and courses are contemporary, engaging, and accessible, including in the evening;

- offering selected summer and/or winter J-term courses at reduced cost;

- offering high-impact active learning opportunities, such as internships, service learning, short-term global experiences, and undergraduate research;

- offering alternative delivery models, such as active, hybrid, or adaptive learning and/or a math emporium, especially for gateway courses; and

- targeting financial aid specifically at retention, such as supplemental scholarships, delayed bill payment plans, or cost-sharing unpaid bills.

Graduation Rate and Degree Completion

Graduation rate, typically reported as the percentage of first-time, full-time students who complete their bachelor's degree within four or six years from their original four-year institution (or within two or three years at two-year institutions), is the most common measure of student success. The 1990 Student Right to Know and Campus Security Act requires postsecondary institutions to report the percentage of first-time, full-time degree-seeking students who complete the program within 150 percent of the normal time of completion—hence the reference to six-year and three-year graduation rates at four-year and two-year institutions, respectively. Despite this requirement, from a student affordability standpoint, it is essential to improve the four-year as well as the six-year graduation rate. According to the 2022 NCES report, the average four-year and six-year graduation rates for the 2014 cohort from four-year degree-granting institutions were 46.6 percent and 64 percent, respectively.[108] That is, less than half the first-time, full-time students attending four-year institutions graduate within four years.

While the standard first-time, full-time four-year and six-year graduation rates reported through IPEDS are the most widely reported measure of student success, they are also misleading. First-time, full-time students who graduate in four or six years are interpreted as an indicator of a "graduation success" for the institution. Students who start part-time or who transfer to or from an institution, regardless of the outcome, are excluded from this measure. That is, students who transfer and complete their degree in a timely manner from another institution are labeled "non-completers" at their original institution and are often interpreted as an indicator of a "graduation failure" for that institution with no recognition for the receiving institution from which they graduated. For institutions with a relatively high proportion of students who transfer in or out, their reported graduation rate may not accurately reflect their overall contributions to student success. Nearly half a million students each year who transferred and graduated are not counted by the federal graduation rate.

In addition, there are certain majors, including some very prestigious double majors, that require students to invest five or even six years to complete the program. At URI, for instance, our distinctive and highly acclaimed International Engineering Program is a five-year program that leads to two degrees—a BS in an engineering discipline and a BA in a selected foreign language—and it includes a year of study and a paid corporate internship abroad. This program produces culturally competent, bilingual engineers, who are in high demand and hired immediately upon graduation. The five-year program, however, officially lowers the institution's four-year graduation rate. Similarly, a six-year Doctor of Pharmacy program supports students from their first year through their graduate Pharm D degree but is not reflected in the institution's IPEDS graduation data, despite a very high retention and graduation rate. Indeed, you get what you measure, including unintended consequences. So, while quality data is important to track progress, leaders need to be data-informed rather than data-driven.

Institution Type	Four-Year Graduation Rate	Six-Year Graduation Rate
Public Nonprofit	42.4 percent	63.0 percent
Private Nonprofit	56.8 percent	68.0 percent
Private For-Profit	22.9 percent	29.0 percent

Figure 16.2. Comparison of four-year and six-year IPEDS graduation rates among institution types.

IPEDS Reported Graduation Rates

As highlighted in Figure 16.2, the average four- and six-year graduation rates vary by institution type. The average three-year graduation rates of the 2017 cohort from public, private nonprofit, and for-profit two-year colleges are 29.3 percent, 51.8 percent, and 61.5 percent, respectively.

Four- and six-year graduation rates have steadily improved at public and private nonprofit institutions since 1996, but there has been no improvement at private for-profit institutions (Figure 16.3). The four-year graduation rate for public universities nearly doubled over that time, although it is still only 42 percent. While there is variation among institutions, the low average four-year graduation rate is a major issue fueling the concerns about the value of higher education and the cost-value proposition for students. There is substantial room for continuous improvement.

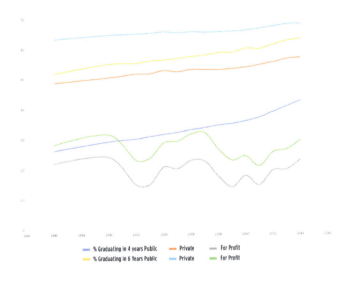

Figure 16.3. Four- and six-year graduation rates (percent) for public, private nonprofit, and private for-profit institutions for students in cohort entry years 1996 to 2014.[109]

Not surprisingly, graduation rates increase with institutional selectivity at both public and private nonprofit four-year institutions. Those with acceptance rates of less than 25 percent of applicants have six-year graduation rates greater than 90 percent compared to 28 percent for the least selective institutions.[110] Elite, highly selective Ivy League institutions, such as Harvard and Yale, have graduation rates of 98 percent and

97 percent, respectively. As expected, academic preparation and performance significantly impact graduation rates. Kantrowitz reports that more than 80 percent of students with a high school GPA greater than 3.5 graduate within six years compared to 49 percent with a high school GPA in the 2.0 to 2.9 range and 25 percent for those with a high school GPA less than 2.0.[111] Six-year graduation equity gaps based on race/ethnicity, gender, and family income are also pronounced. Average graduation rates for students of color across institutions lag those of all students by 10 to 20 percentage points, and male students lag female students by about 10 percentage points.

Third Way conducted a detailed analysis of six-year graduation rates of first-time, full-time Pell Grant recipient students from 1,566 institutions. When analyzed across all institutions, Pell students graduate at a rate 18 percentage points less than their non-Pell peers.[112] When comparing at the institutional level, the Pell graduation gap shrinks to an average reduction of 7 percentage points, with 81 percent of institutions graduating Pell students at a lower rate than their non-Pell counterparts. On average, 49 percent of Pell recipients graduate within six years, and many carry a significant debt burden whether they graduate or not. Because Pell students are more likely to be older, independent, or with their own dependents, first-generation college students, and students of color, there are added challenges to their path to degree completion. Higher education institutions that enroll Pell students have a responsibility to ensure support services are in place to help them succeed.

Other Measures of Degree Completion

Other measures of degree completion may help guide institutions on a path to continuous improvement. Each of these measures provides useful information beyond the standard IPEDS-reported graduation rate.

Student Achievement Measure (SAM). The SAM tracks student movement across institutions and provides a comprehensive picture of undergraduate student progress and degree completion. Students are increasingly mobile across institutions; more than one in five students that earn a degree in six years do so at an institution different from the one where they started. SAM tracks student movement and counts all students in calculating graduation rates, including transfer students. The NSCRC collects student data from more than 600 participating colleges and universities. The SAM categories for reporting are shown in Figure 16.4, illustrating the six-year graduation rates for the 2015 cohort for four-year institutions. The "graduated reporting institution" category is analogous to the IPEDS graduation data, while the SAM graduation rates add transfers that graduated from a different four-year or two-year institution as well as those still enrolled or that have stopped out.

Student Achievement Measure (SAM)
National First-time, Full-time Bachelor's Model
Data are current as of 2022, reflecting the Fall 2015 Cohort

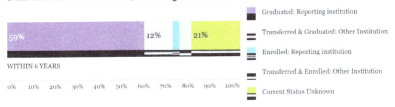

Figure 16.4. The Student Achievement Measure (SAM) tracks undergraduate student mobility across postsecondary institutions and provides a more thorough assessment of student progress and six-year degree completion within the higher education system.[113]
Reprinted with permission from Student Achievement Measure (SAM)

Number of Degrees Awarded. In 2009, President Obama declared that the United States should "once again have the highest proportion of college graduates in the world,"[114] a necessary ingredient to sustain an economy that will be increasingly dependent on an educated workforce. At that time, 41 percent of twenty-five- to thirty-four-year-olds in the United States had completed at least an associate's degree and the United States ranked fifteenth in college degree attainment among the thirty-five Organization for Economic Cooperation and Development (OECD) countries. Joined by many governors and major funding initiatives from the Lumina and Gates Foundations, a national movement was underway to increase college degree attainment.

As a nation, we remain far from reaching the attainment goals established by President Obama. According to OCED, in 2021 51 percent of US adults had completed at least an associate's degree, and the United States ranks fourteenth among OECD countries.[115] As a result, greater attention has been placed by boards of trustees, academic leaders, politicians, and students and their families on monitoring degrees awarded by institutions each year. The result of efforts to increase enrollment and retention, close equity gaps, and shorten the time to degree completion should result in increases in degrees awarded by institutions. Annual counts of undergraduate and graduate degrees awarded per institution are straightforward but important metrics for maintaining focus on educational attainment and contributing to the nation's goal of ensuring the human capital needed in a competitive global economy.

As a nation, employers are already observing a shortage of workers that may be limiting productivity, and higher education institutions have two million fewer students now than they did when President Obama established the goal. Because of demographic shifts and the perceived declining cost-value equation for higher education, we are losing ground. Institutions must continue to improve the value proposition of a college education and degree attainment to ensure we as a nation have an educated workforce. Concerted efforts do make a difference. See "Growth in Undergraduate Degrees Awarded from 2009 to 2019" for an example of a dramatic increase in degree production over time.

Growth in Undergraduate Degrees Awarded from 2009 to 2019

At URI, an institution of approximately 14,500 undergraduate students, the number of undergraduate degrees awarded increased annually from an average of approximately 2,020 in the 2003-08 timeframe to 3,471 in 2019—approximately 10,000 additional bachelor's degrees above the 2003-08 baseline over the course of the decade. The dramatic gains in the number of degrees awarded reflect a strategic focus on enrollment, retention, credit accumulation, and timely degree completion. Enrollment increased by 989 FTE students over that period due to a combination of recruitment of new students and a 7-percentage point increase in retention. Focused efforts do make a difference.

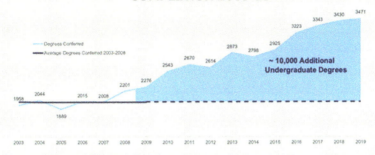

URI UNDERGRADUATE DEGREE COMPLETION 2009-19

Degrees Conferred
Average Degrees Conferred 2003-2008

~ 10,000 Additional Undergraduate Degrees

1958 2044 2015 2008 2201 2276 2543 2670 2614 2873 2798 2925 3223 3343 3430 3471

1849

2003 2004 2005 2006 2007 2008 2009 2010 2011 2012 2013 2014 2015 2016 2017 2018 2019

Figure 16.5. Focused efforts at URI resulted in dramatic gains in undergraduate degrees awarded each year from 2009 to 2019.

Degrees Awarded Per 100 FTE Students. While annual counts of degrees awarded track degree production over time, they do not necessarily reflect institutional performance in degree completion productivity. That is, increases or decreases in the number of degrees awarded may simply track enrollment rather than reflect improved effectiveness in granting degrees through such measures as increased retention, closing equity gaps, enhanced credit accumulation, and/or hastened degree completion. Degrees awarded per one hundred full-time equivalent students is an alternative and better measure that reflects institutional productivity and efficiency in advancing graduation and degree attainment that is independent of total enrollment. For example, for the total degrees awarded shown in Figure 16.5, the degrees awarded per one hundred FTE students grew from 18.1 in 2009 to 25.1 in 2019. That is, a higher proportion of the larger student population in 2019 completed their degrees compared to the smaller proportion in 2009, illustrating the power of this measure and reflecting that the gains in degrees awarded resulted largely from improved institutional effectiveness rather than enrollment growth alone.

Because this measure is scaled on a per FTE student basis, it includes all students, including part-time and transfer students, and is a more inclusive and representative measure of degree productivity than IPEDS first-time, full-time graduation rates and simple annual degree counts.

For context, one can think of the rate of degree completions per FTE as the proportion of the total FTE enrolled students that graduate each year. In a perfect world, twenty-five degree completions per one hundred FTE students would mean about one-quarter of the students graduate each year, a desirable outcome. Degree completions exceeding twenty-five may occur because transfer students typically spend two to three rather than four or more years at their transfer institution before graduating. Degree completions of say eighteen to twenty per one hundred FTE students are indicators of lower efficiency or productivity and demonstrate room for improvement.

Annually monitoring four-year and six-year graduation rates is important but will not itself lead to improvement without first identifying obstacles that impede timely progress toward degree completion and implementing strategies to overcome those obstacles. Regardless of measures used to track student success, retention and semester-by-semester credit completion are key elements to timely degree completion. Steps must be taken in the first and second years to increase four-year and six-year graduation rates. Obviously, students must remain enrolled to complete their degree, so retention is critical. For those students who are retained, degree completion will depend on timely credit completion and accumulation, which is a challenge for many students with cost implications for additional time needed to graduate. The lack of or delayed degree completion, along with escalating tuition and fees and the student debt crisis, are major factors shaping the perception of the declining value of a college education.

Credit Completion and Accumulation

Monitoring credit completion and accumulation by semester is among the most useful measures to track student progress toward degree completion and graduation. While monitoring graduation rates informs us of the proportion of students who progress to graduation, the lack of timely credit completion and accumulation can be detected early and offers possibilities for adjustments to get students on a path to timely degree completion. Students in most majors need to earn on average fifteen credits per semester or thirty credits per academic year (120 credits in total) and complete all general education and major course requirements to graduate with a bachelor's degree in four years or an associate degree in two.

A comprehensive study of credit accumulation and completion rates among first-year college students conducted by the NSCRC demonstrates that timely credit completion and accumulation is a substantial barrier to retention and degree completion at many institutions. In a study of more than 905,000 first-time, first-year degree-seeking students from 342 institutions, only 51.2 percent and 27.5 percent of students on average earned twenty-four and thirty credit hours, respectively.[116] So across many institutions, nearly 75 percent of first-time, full-time students were already not on track to graduate in four years by the end of their first year. Male first-year students completing thirty credits lagged females by nearly 5 percentage points, and first-time, full-time transfer students lagged slightly behind first-time college students.

There were substantial gaps in the proportion of first-year students completing thirty credits across racial/ethnic groups. For example, while 35.9 percent of Asian and 29.9 percent of White students completed thirty credits or more during their first year, only 19 percent of Native American, 19.6 percent of Black/African American, and 25.6 percent of Hispanic students did so, highlighting yet another equity gap that leads to lower graduation rates for vulnerable populations. For full-time, first-year students from private and public four-year institutions and public two-year institutions, 43.1 percent, 32.5 percent, and 18.0 percent, respectively, completed thirty credits or more.

Why are so many full-time, first-year students earning so few credits? While there are many individual stories and struggles that contribute to this problem, there are two prominent explanations.[117] First, the average full-time student does not even attempt enough credits to complete their bachelor's degree in four years. The average first-time, full-time college student attempts fewer than twenty-seven credits during their first year. The second part of the problem is that on average, first-year, full-time degree-seeking students only earn about 76 percent of their credits attempted and, therefore, successfully completed fewer than twenty-two credits. Only 51 percent of all students earn 100 percent of the credits they attempted. At that rate of credit completion, it would require about five and a half years to complete a bachelor's degree, which is costly as students are forced to pay additional tuition and fees while completing their degree. In addition, there are large equity gaps in credit completion rate and credit accumulation, especially across gender and racial/ethnic groups.

Institutional Efforts to Increase Credit Completion and Accumulation

To drive a change agenda toward continuous improvement, institutions should monitor credit completion and accumulation by semester and disaggregate data to better understand credit completion equity gaps among different student populations on their campus. While recognizing that a fifteen credit per semester course load may not be optimum for every student, an initial step is to increase the number of credits attempted by most students and ensure that tutoring services are in place to support student success in challenging courses. Many institutions have created credit completion awareness campaigns with t-shirts and slogans, such as "Take 15—Finish in Four," and curriculum maps or plans aimed at guiding students beginning at freshman orientation and continuing with academic advising throughout the student's four years.

Professional advisors, especially during the first two years, can be helpful to consistently reinforce the importance of timely credit accumulation and degree completion. Promoting both the academic and financial benefits of completing thirty credits can be compelling to students and their families. For students who need to carry a lighter credit load, retake a course, or pick up an additional required course because they changed majors, developing and promoting a vibrant and cost-effective winter J-term during the January break and enhanced summer session provides opportunities for students to catch up on credits and progress toward timely graduation. See "Credit Completion and Accumulation: Keeping Students on Track to Graduate in Four Years at URI" for an example of a dramatic turnaround in student credit completion and a description of some of the drivers of that transformation.

Credit Completion and Accumulation: Keeping Students on Track to Graduate in Four Years at URI

In the mid-2000s, the university was unaware that less than half of first-year, sophomore, and junior students had earned enough credits and were on a path toward timely graduation and that only 57 percent of seniors had completed 120 credits. Not surprisingly, four- and six-year graduation rates were abysmal. In 2008-09, we began examining student credit completion by semester. Figure 16.6 shows yearly credit completion rates of student cohorts from 2005 to 2019 by credit threshold targets. The proportion of students achieving or exceeding their threshold credit accumulation increased across all four years: 33 percentage points for first-year students, 27 percentage points for sophomores, and 22 percentage points each for juniors and seniors. These gains translate into a 74 percent increase in credit accumulation for first-year students, a 59 percent increase for sophomore students, and steady progress for upper-level students.

Keeping Students on Track to Graduate in Four Years

Credit Completion Rates by Academic level

- 30 Credits by the end of the First year
- 60 Credits by the end of the Sophomore Year
- 90 Credits by the end of the Junior Year
- 120 Credits by the end of the Senior Year

Figure 16.6. Increased yearly credit completion and accumulation resulting from targeted strategic actions and leading to improved graduation rates.

Many factors contributed to the problem and the solution. The main driver of the initial problem was a well-intentioned policy that allowed students to drop classes through the ninth week of the semester without advisor or instructor consultation or approval. A quick study revealed that many students at all levels routinely dropped one or more classes between weeks five and nine. This option likely compromised student work commitment in challenging classes and led to students falling behind in credit accumulation. It became part of the student culture. With great student opposition and some faculty concerns, the faculty senate amended the drop policy to the end of the third week of the semester beginning in 2010. Increased failure and withdrawal rates feared by many students and some faculty never materialized, and student credit completion and accumulation immediately increased in 2011.

Shortly thereafter, a multifaceted campuswide campaign was initiated to promote fifteen credits per semester for timely graduation, which also saved students money. The following new initiatives were implemented starting in 2013: curriculum maps and plans for each major, transition to professional advisors for the first two years, expansion of credit-bearing experiential learning across programs, a new undergraduate research funding initiative, the implementation of winter J-term, and the revamping of summer session offerings. From 2008 to 2019 collectively, these initiatives enhanced credit completion and accumulation resulting in moving the four-year graduation rates from 38 to 59 percent and the six-year graduation rates from 58 to 71 percent.

Gateway Courses

One major challenge at many institutions is the high proportion of students receiving unproductive grades, such as D, W, or F, in certain gateway courses, which are often but not always, in the sciences, mathematics, and other quantitative disciplines. These typically introductory, large enrollment prerequisite courses are taken by every student in certain disciplines, and high failure rates limit both major options and credit accumulation for students as well as requiring rework that is inefficient and expensive for students and the institution. The proportion of students receiving unproductive grades may be as high as 25 to 50 percent of enrolled students in some courses and even higher for first-generation, Pell students, and students of color from economically disadvantaged communities. Students with unproductive grades not only fall behind in credit accumulation but also are at higher risk of not graduating at all. Unproductive grades in gateway courses often relate to weak pre-college (elementary, middle, and/or high school) academic preparation of students and their lack of college readiness in certain disciplines, especially mathematics, which may be exacerbated by large class sizes and pedagogical challenges.

Improvement in retention, graduation rates, and time to degree will depend on institutions focusing attention on and making strategic investments to address the intractable problem of unproductive grades in gateway courses. While there are a few simple solutions, there is little evidence that colleges offering remedial course sequences is a viable solution. In fact, Complete College America (CCA) reports only 10 percent of students that start non-credit developmental remedial courses go on to graduate.[118] In contrast, in a corequisite support model, students are immediately enrolled in credit-bearing college courses and receive additional support to ensure success in challenging classes, leading to dramatic increases in the completion of gateway classes and graduation. Some possible areas worthy of consideration are as follows:

- targeted tutoring support for less well-prepared students;

- faculty training in high-impact and corequisite teaching practices, such as active and problem-based learning, supplemental instruction, and inclusive pedagogy;

- faculty support for course redesign, as appropriate;

- implementation of adaptive learning courseware and strategies in select courses;

- expanded teaching assistants and training for recitations in certain courses;

- reducing class sizes and adding additional sections; and

- summer intensive boot camps aimed at students not prepared for college-level coursework, especially in STEM fields.

Finally, the first year of college is a time of transition and personal growth for many traditional-age students. Some students, especially in STEM disciplines, are guided to enroll in five courses, including many with laboratories, that may not allow time for personal development and mental health. A more flexible first semester with a combination of courses in and outside their major and delaying some laboratory courses until the second semester may be important to improve credit completion, grades in gateway classes, retention, and overall student success.

Experiential Learning

Traditionally, higher education has been largely organized around credit-bearing courses that include lectures, recitations, laboratories, discussions, or seminars and various forms of examinations, projects, and class assignments, including research papers and presentations. As institutions respond to the desires of both employers and students to better prepare students for the working world and the future of work, many institutions are ramping up credit-bearing experiential learning opportunities for their students. When done well, learning by doing outside of traditional classroom settings, along with deep reflection on those experiences, provides high-impact learning with the power to reinforce principles discussed in courses and bridge the fundamentals of a liberal arts education with workforce preparation. Through experiential learning, students build technical and professional skills, learn how to apply knowledge in real situations, and navigate the workplace and uncertainties of problem-solving in the real world. Most forms of experiential learning can be organized and delivered in a highly efficient manner that truly engages students and enables them to earn academic credit toward degree completion.

Experiential learning increasingly includes a broad array of learning opportunities for students. Experiences may include internships, service learning, undergraduate research, problem-based learning, clinical experiences in health fields, student teaching in education, global experiences, community-based projects, entrepreneurship projects, and more. Each institution should provide its own guardrails in describing meaningful experiential learning outcomes for students, awarding academic credit, and ensuring that the experiences, reflections, and learning are substantive. By tracking the number of students engaged in experiential learning each semester or year, institutions are effectively tracking high-impact learning opportunities and the expansion of deep learning and application across disciplines. This information will be helpful in recruiting future students and in promoting the institution as an important contributor to workforce development. It will be necessary to ensure such opportunities are available to all students not just those plugged in with faculty members who may agree to oversee their project or internship. As such, disaggregating experiential learning opportunities data by student population and major will help inform and enhance equitable learning opportunities.

Research and Scholarly Productivity

Institutions typically track total annual research grant and contract awards and expenditures as measures of research productivity. These data reflect research funding from external sources, including federal, state, corporate, and foundation grants. Because annual research expenditures reflect the actual spending of grant funds, it can be expected to lag research awards by a year or two. That is, if research awards rise in a given year, research expenditures can be expected to increase a year or two later as the funding is used in carrying out the research. At most research institutions, funding from federal sources represents the largest proportion of external research funding and is a good indicator of the institution's position in securing financial support in a highly competitive federal research funding marketplace.

Institutions should also track the number of proposals submitted and the funding requested annually, which reflects the continued efforts of the faculty in pursuing grant funding in a competitive environment. Because research programs often address societal challenges and lead to high-impact, translational, and innovative discoveries, institutions often track technology transfer and business development, such as invention disclosures, new patent applications and awards, intellectual property agreements, and start-up companies formed. Institutions should also measure the economic impact of the research enterprise and the university more broadly on the state and surrounding communities, which is often substantial and should be shared publicly to demonstrate institutional impact.

As with retention and graduation rate, tracking gains or losses in research funding over time is likely to provide greater meaning for an institution than interinstitutional comparisons as the latter is confounded with many other variables. For example, the size of the faculty, the array of disciplines represented, the proportion of primarily research versus teaching faculty, and whether the institution includes a medical school will significantly influence levels of research funding. At research universities, medical school research funding could easily exceed that of the rest of the institution combined.

While research funding is a commonly used measure of institutional research productivity, it ignores substantial and impactful scholarly and creative contributions in the arts, humanities, social sciences, and other fields that do not typically depend on external grants and contracts for scholarly productivity. In so doing, it undervalues the critically important work of faculty and students that leads, for example, to a better understanding of the human condition, analysis and development of federal, state, and local economies and policies, and exhibitions and performances that enhance the quality of life for citizens and local communities. The work and contributions of faculty in these areas are important and reflect the comprehensive mission of every research university, especially land grant universities that have a special commitment to contribute to the vitality of their state. Attempts at cataloging these types of important contributions by reporting scholarly publications, single- or multi-authored books, or numbers of concerts, performances, and exhibitions are always difficult because of the broad array of venues and outlets for sharing scholarship across disciplines and the qualitative nature of impacts that are difficult to measure. Nevertheless, institutions need to recognize and celebrate the broad role of scholarship in defining the university, shaping the intellectual environment of the campus, and sharing the many ways the university contributions enrich society.

University leaders mostly emphasize faculty publications in high profile refereed journals and large competitive grants from major federal agencies, such as the National Institutes of Health and the National Science Foundation, as primary indicators of the quality of university scholarship. Traditional measures of academic scholarship typically include citation counts or indices, journal impact factors as a surrogate for journal prestige, google scholar profiles, and author h-index, which equals the number of papers (h) cited a certain number of times. These metrics may be helpful in judging the scholarly impact of individual faculty but are often invisible outside the academy and do not lend themselves to monitoring institutional productivity or societal impact. As scholarly outlets and impacts become more diverse, altmetrics (i.e., alternative metrics) measure the impact and reach of public-facing scholarship through various online activities, such as the number of downloads of articles, databases, or software, scholarly bookmarks or downloads, news agency or blog coverage, exhibition visits, and references in public policy documents.

By providing measures of how university research outputs are being used by agencies, legislators, researchers, and the public to solve real problems and shape public policy, selected alternative metrics provide an additional nontraditional measure of research impacts and institutional reputation. Given enhanced scrutiny about the value and contributions of higher education and declining trust from the public, legislators, and politicians, forward-thinking leaders should incorporate meaningful alternative metrics along with traditional measures to highlight the many ways that university research is impactful and benefits society. To do this, leaders and faculty must become liberated from the shackles of conventional thinking, structures, and practices that stifle nontraditional, but highly impactful, measures of research while still maintaining high standards.

Student, Staff, and Faculty Diversity

Given the mission-critical focus on diversity, equity, and inclusion at many institutions, it is important to monitor progress in expanding diversity within the community, despite anti-DEI sentiments and legislation in some states. Given demographic projections, the educational benefits of diversity, and the promise of equal opportunity to education for all, institutions should strive to increase the proportion and number of students of color in their undergraduate and graduate student cohorts. Given the recent Supreme Court ruling banning race-conscious admission, student recruitment, admissions, and financial aid strategies may need to be adjusted at some selective institutions to ensure continuous progress.

Because you get what you measure, monitoring faculty and staff diversity helps bring attention and focus to the pursuit of parallel growth of faculty and staff racial/ethnic diversity along with student diversity. In addition to tracking the proportion and number of faculty and staff of color each year, it is also important to monitor the proportion of new hires who are people of color each year. That is, what proportion of searches each year hired candidates of color? While the availability of applicants of color will no doubt vary widely by academic discipline and professional employment categories, tracking the diversity of new hires each year along with careful monitoring of retention of diverse faculty and staff, may provide insights into the effectiveness of efforts to enhance the diversity of faculty and staff.

Innovation Aimed at Continuous Improvement

Too often, when we think or speak of innovation, we immediately make connections to applications of advanced digital technologies, such as artificial intelligence or augmented reality, or to innovation in the context of entrepreneurship and discovering ways to develop new products or ideas that lead to patents, companies, and revenue. These narrow interpretations exclude the efforts of most faculty and disciplines and frame the concept of innovation for many faculty as an ill-defined and overused buzzword. I admit to some fault here as our recent academic strategic plan was called *Innovation with Impact* and emphasized the many ways we can and should innovate to improve, but the innovations did not all depend on technology or refer to entrepreneurial efforts. After all, most would agree that the emergence of MOOCs as an "innovation" a decade ago did not transform higher education as predicted.

Maybe we need a fresh start in thinking about innovation in relation to continuous improvement in higher education. As humorously depicted in Figure 16.7, substantive innovation is more than a buzzword and requires individuals willing and able to think out of the box. Innovation is about creating and implementing new and improved products, systems, and/or services that add value and address a real challenge. Innovations help us improve what we are already doing and/or do new things, thereby making us better and more relevant. This certainly might include reducing costs, enhancing efficiency, and hastening the path to degree completion, but not at the expense of quality or a goal of creating high-impact, deeply engaging, and more relevant learning for students. A technological quick fix usually is not helpful or innovative. New ideas that don't lead to improvement, add value, or address a real challenge are nothing more than gimmicks, which are likely to be short-lived.

During the COVID-19 pandemic, the abrupt shift of all classes to online delivery was necessary, but hardly an example of widespread innovation. Everyone did what they could to get by, but the level of student engagement and quality of the learning environment was no doubt compromised. The terms *remote, distance,* and *online* were typically used to describe teaching and learning with references to *synchronous, asynchronous,* or *hybrid* modes of delivery—hardly enticing descriptions of engagement or innovation. Unfortunately, these approaches may have become embedded in the teaching and learning repertoire and in the mindsets of some faculty and students. Alternatively, applications of "technology-enriched teaching and learning" are potentially more innovative and palatable as conveyors of improved approaches to creating an engaged learning environment by blending useful technologies with a human interface. To be clear, many experienced faculty did implement such modernizations.

"What a coincidence!
I'm finding it hard to think out of the box, too!"

Figure 16.7. Innovation can be stifled by our own lack
of imagination and internal trappings.
Copyright Timo Elliott; Printed with permission from Timo Elliott

While some innovations may incorporate technologies or lead to entrepreneurial activities, they are equally likely to refer to improvements, such as the reinvigoration of the purpose and learning outcomes of general education; the development of efficient and novel skills-based micro-credentials (e.g., badges or certificates) aimed at workforce reskilling or upskilling; incorporating experiential learning as a centerpiece rather than an afterthought in the curriculum; creating active learning spaces and inclusive teaching strategies that equalize learning opportunities for students from all backgrounds; or reorganizing academic structures to encourage interdisciplinary learning and discovery to address the major challenges of our time.

At the beginning of this chapter, I suggested that universities must always be adapting, evolving, and improving organizations to remain vital and relevant. In this context, the curriculum, educational delivery models, degree requirements for almost every major as well as academic and career advising and support services should be reconsidered through the lens of "innovation with impact" (i.e., improvements or new models that add value and relevance to student learning and preparation for the rapidly evolving global economy and society). From this perspective, innovations can be transformational—not just efficiency tweaks. See "Innovation in General Education for the Twenty-First Century" for a description of the reinvention of a general education program.

Innovation in General Education for the Twenty-First Century

At many institutions, traditional general education programs consist of a grab bag of introductory courses from disciplinary lists, which are often thought of as uninteresting and uninspiring requirements. Yet, such programs typically comprise one-third of the academic experience for all students. The focus for students and faculty was "to get gen ed courses out of the way." At URI, a faculty academic summit and a student summit a decade or so ago provided pervasive critique of the general education program. The vocal concerns triggered a comprehensive and innovative reinvention and reinvigoration of general education under the leadership of the general education committee of the faculty senate. It was challenging work for many reasons; the faculty and the faculty senate leadership deserve enormous credit for their perseverance and creativity. Their efforts transformed the teaching and learning experience for all.

In 2016, an innovative new general education program was launched and envisioned as every student's "second major" to explore interests, spark intellectual curiosity, and assure efficiency of transferring across majors. Modeled after Liberal Education-America's Promise, the program was built around twelve learning outcomes viewed as essential by students and faculty, which reflect four overriding objectives.

- *Knowledge:* STEM, Social/Behavioral Science, Humanities, Arts and Design
- *Competencies:* Writing, Communication, Mathematical/Computational, Information Literacy
- *Responsibilities:* Civic Knowledge, Global Responsibilities, Diversity and Inclusion
- *Integration and Application:* Connections of knowledge and ideas to complex situations

Grand Challenge courses focus on complex societal problems that challenge students to grapple with big questions and issues of global significance are the centerpiece of the program. The program is led by a newly created director of the Office of Innovation in General Education position that guides faculty in the development of new course proposals, leads learning outcomes assessment, offers support for course enrichments, and oversees an Excellence in General Education Award that celebrates faculty offering stimulating and dynamic general education experiences for students.

As leaders, how do we encourage innovation to ensure continuous improvement, adaptability, and relevance? This is an important and timely question given the perception of the declining value and rising expense of higher education increasingly prevalent today and the emerging student disengagement and transactional approach to learning. Leaders must find ways to engage and support the community in creating a culture of innovation that addresses some of the big challenges we face. To do so, leaders at all levels must encourage and embrace innovation as an opportunity rather than as a burdensome extra effort. This may mean overcoming the cultural inertia to resist change, defend the *status quo,* or tinker with glitzy toys of little real educational value. In *Building a Culture of Innovation in Higher Education: Design and Practice for Leaders*, Setser and Morris suggest that a culture of innovation refers to "an environment that continually introduces new ideas or ways of thinking, then translates them into action to solve specific problems or seize new opportunities."[119] Such an environment where new ideas and experiments aimed at improvement are encouraged, supported, and become the norm should be an exciting place to work and learn.

To nurture a culture of innovation, leaders need to work in a collaborative and transparent manner with the community, especially the faculty, to establish a framework aimed at continuous improvement that addresses the needs of the institution. This might include:

- collaboratively developing a working definition of innovation in relation to improvement specific to the discipline, college, or university;

- dispelling prevailing myths about innovation as largely technocratic or moneymaking ventures;

- establishing a set of unit- or institutional-level parameters for identifying tangible challenges or problems that must be addressed to improve the institution;

- resisting the temptation to establish an "innovation guru" position; instead, encouraging and incentivizing faculty and staff *writ large* to generate new ideas that address real problems;

- establishing an innovation fund to support worthy ideas or projects with the potential to add substantive value; funds may come from reserves, efficiency gains, or revenue from new programs or initiatives;

- encouraging experimentation, pilot projects, and feedback mechanisms and acknowledging that innovation comes with risks and some worthy projects may not add value, create scalable improvement, or be cost-effective; and

- communicating a commitment to the pursuit of strategic innovation aimed at improvement as not just a fashionable fad of the moment but a necessary path toward institutional adaptability, relevance, and sustainability in the future.

Striving to establish and sustain a culture of innovation is not only about recognizing the need for continuous improvement and relevance in an ever-changing world but also a reflection of the essence of the scholarly foundation upon which our institutions were founded and function today. As hubs for learning, discovery, and new ideas, universities must be places that build and expand upon existing knowledge, practices, and applications, and pursue research and scholarship designed to improve the human condition and add value to society more broadly. Simply put, we have no choice—we must continuously innovate to become what we are intended to be.

CHAPTER SEVENTEEN

Building Partnerships and Bold Advancement Initiatives

Effective Partnerships Provide Multiple Benefits

Forging partnerships is an essential strategy for colleges and universities to address the multidimensional needs of students and the increasingly complex challenges facing society today and in the future. By building symbiotic partnerships, universities leverage their own institution's distinctive strengths and resources with those of other organizations or individuals in mutually beneficial ways to achieve goals that would be difficult to attain independently. When partnerships are done well, they build powerful coalitions that advance the goals of the institution in a manner consistent with the mission of the partnering organization. University partnerships might involve collaborative relationships with corporations, public agencies, nonprofits, communities, school districts, and other universities. Furthermore, philanthropic partnerships with donors represent an increasingly critical revenue stream and are essential for higher education institutions. As such, this chapter especially focuses on fundraising as an essential skill set for higher education leaders in the twenty-first century.

The nature and breadth of university partnerships are diverse and support or expand university administrative operations, academic programs, research opportunities, economic development, international connections, or student opportunities, such as scholarships, internships, experiential learning projects, and workforce development. Such partnerships may involve a specific department, college, or administrative office or the entire institution. Finally, there are also important partnerships built across units within institutions, such as interdisciplinary academic programs, research centers, interprofessional education in the health professions, and partnerships between central and distributed IT.

Effective partnerships often provide financial benefits through increased efficiency in operations and facilities, new revenue generation, student recruitment via articulation agreements, philanthropic support through gifts and grants, or cooperative public-private partnerships (P3s), such as ground leases of university land to developers to construct buildings or joint ownership projects. The American Association of State Colleges and Universities (AASCU) has published a handbook entitled *Making Partnerships Work: Principles, Guidelines, and Advice for Public University Leaders* that provides details about the types of university partnerships and potential benefits, risks, legal, and policy consider-ations.[120] In addition, the Council of Independent Colleges (CIC) brochure titled *Building Partnerships with College Campuses: Community Perspectives* offers insights into core elements of effective partnerships, bene-fits and costs, and practices and policy recommendations that lead to successful partnerships.[121] Messmore suggests best practices for devel-oping authentic partnerships grounded in humility and respect in "How to Establish Powerful Campus Partnerships."[122] Gleaning from these ideas and my own experiences in developing partnerships and collab-orations, I offer the following as core ingredients of effective university partnerships:

- The partnership aligns with the missions of the institution and partners.

- The partnership is mutually beneficial, and goals are collabora-tively derived from a shared vision rather than established by a single dominant entity.

- Roles and responsibilities are based on each partner's unique assets, capacities, and resources.

- Partner relationships are authentic and acknowledge the exper-tise and experience of all contributors along with mutual under-standing and appreciation for the efforts of all partners.

- Criteria for tracking results and a system of accountability are established to promote quality outcomes in accordance with the jointly determined plans.

- Evaluation criteria includes mechanisms to assess the partnership, make changes, and/or collegially dissolve the relationship if one or more partners find it is no longer aligned with its mission.

Philanthropic Support—A Lucrative Outcome of Authentic Relationship-Building

Commonly referred to as *development* or *advancement* in the world of higher education, philanthropic relationships are among the most important and lucrative of the many types of institutional partnerships on college and university campuses. With declining government funding, the rising cost of higher education, the growing student debt crisis, and widely disparate incomes among families, philanthropy has the potential to play a vital role to enhance access to and affordability of public and private institutions. As such, there is a strong case for fundraising and private giving in higher education to improve social and economic mobility and strengthen higher education institutions and our democracy. It is essential that contemporary higher education leaders understand the power of and develop the skill set for effective fundraising.

Philanthropy is a distinctly American phenomenon. Americans donate more than any other nation. According to *Giving USA 2022: The Annual Report on Philanthropy for the Year 2021*, Americans gave $485 billion to charitable causes in 2021, and 67 percent of all philanthropic gifts came from individuals.[123] While religious giving topped the list with $136 billion (27 percent of total giving in 2021), educational giving at $71 billion represented the second largest share (14 percent) of charitable dollars; and higher education institutions were recipients of $52.9 billion, or 75 percent of the total educational giving. Philanthropic support for education represents an investment in the greater good for the present and future and is driven largely by donor passion and a belief in the value of higher education for individuals and for society. Private giving supports facilities, research, curriculum, and faculty as well as financial aid to ensure student access and degree completion.

As with other partnerships, successful fundraising is dependent upon establishing strong and authentic relationships and a shared vision between institutional leaders and prospects or donors who share an interest and passion in some aspect of the institution. I emphasize *authentic* relationships because some academics assume that fundraising is a form of schmoozing, and they are inherently turned off by playing that role. In fact, successful fundraising is about honest relationship-building with individuals and organizations to establish mutually beneficial partnerships. In higher education today, inspiring, securing, and stewarding philanthropic support through gifts and private grants of various kinds is essential to the operations and activities of all institutions, including private and public institutions ranging from community colleges to the highest profile research universities.

Leaders must be comfortable engaging prospects, articulating a compelling vision, directly asking for money, and reporting back to donors on the outcomes and impacts of their gifts. Fortunately, leaders don't need and should not attempt to do all of this on their own. Development officers are professionals with specific training and experience in working to identify and build relationships between potential donors and institutional leaders, including. deans, athletic directors, provosts, and presidents. Leaders do have a responsibility, however, to learn how to best work in tandem with the development office to help cultivate relationships with individuals or entities that share a common interest in one or more aspects of the university and who have the capacity and inclination to make a gift. To facilitate that learning, organizations such as Academic Impressions and the Council for Advancement and Support of Education (CASE) offer workshops and conferences, including online boot camps, aimed at training academic leaders. Aspiring leaders—especially new deans, provosts, and presidents—should consider attending such workshops because fundraising will be a key component of your leadership position whether it is highlighted in your position description or not.

Organization of Advancement Functions

The art and science of successful fundraising is a collaborative tripartite venture involving academic leaders, the fundraising office or organization affiliated with the institution, and, of course, prospects and donors. Professional development officers, sometimes referred to as constituent development officers (CDOs) if they are assigned to a specific fundraising unit like the athletics department or an academic college, usually are employees of and report to the fundraising office or organization. For most private universities, fundraising activities operate from an advancement or development office that exists as an administrative unit within the institution, usually led by a vice president who reports to the president and oversees both advancement activities and alumni relations.

For most public colleges and universities, all fundraising functions usually operate as a separate, independent nonprofit foundation established specifically to support the college or university. In the latter case, the foundation serves as the fundraising arm and the investment bank for the public institution separate from all institutional activities and independent of the many restrictions on sources and uses of funds imposed by state governments. Fundraising foundations are typically led by their own independent president who reports to a distinct foundation governing board. Because alumni are integral to fundraising at most institutions and alumni giving and messaging should be coordinated with other fundraising efforts, it is best practice for alumni relations activities to also operate from the foundation. The operations of such foundations, including salaries, travel, third-party management arrangements, etc., are typically funded in part by the university through a negotiated contract, but also by a portion of the income from the endowment and sometimes a small surcharge on gifts, although the latter is not popular with donors.

Regardless of organizational structure, the fundraising office or foundation typically serves the following functions:

- cultivating and vetting a pool of prospects with the potential to become donors, including researching their financial capacity through public records, identifying potential areas of donor interest, and facilitating relationships with key institutional leaders;

- organizing events that engage alumni and friends with the institution;

- working collaboratively with institutional leaders and, as appropriate, with faculty and students to engage and nurture interested prospects with the institution;

- organizing and facilitating the "ask" of major gifts, including determining the timing of and who is best to make the formal solicitation and establishing appropriate gift language to represent the donor's wishes and institutional best interests;

- providing oversight of the spending of gift funds to ensure consistency with donor interests, established gift language, and institutional spending policies;

- careful and strategic investing of the endowment to ensure a satisfactory return on investment and an annual endowment payout to purpose in support of endowed gifts, such as endowed scholarships, professorships, institutes, or colleges; and

- conveying appreciation through continuous stewardship of donors—may include remembering birthdays and anniversaries, thank you letters from scholarship recipients, and/or reports on the extraordinary impact of their gifts.

Institutional leaders at all levels must work collaboratively rather than at odds with the fundraising office. While this may seem obvious, it is not uncommon that individual leaders either don't make sufficient time for cultivating relationships or become possessive of certain prospects to the extent that they exclude the development office from connections to donors. Similarly, development officers at times may express a level of angst about who will get "credit" for a gift. These types of issues are unproductive, a distraction, and can lead to missed opportunities. Effective fundraising must be donor-centered. The primary interests of the donor should drive fundraising strategies, prospect management assignments of development officers, and institutional liaisons. While donors often have programmatic preferences and interests, donors don't belong to any specific department, college, or program, and many may have multiple affiliations with the institution. For example, while every alumnus donor graduated from a specific college and major, their philanthropic interests might involve other university activities, such as intercollegiate athletics, the honors program, multicultural student scholarships, a college connected to their current employment, a favorite faculty member from their days at the university, or some entirely new university initiative.

While development officers help facilitate relationship-building between institutional leaders and prospects, most donors don't make gifts to development officers. They make gifts to a program of interest and to an individual that they know and trust. Working with the fundraising office, leaders must devote time and energy toward:

- cultivating meaningful relationships with prospective donors;

- listening carefully to donor interests;
- articulating an exciting and compelling vision;
- establishing a clear set of fundraising priorities and institutional needs relevant to that vision; and
- making a strong case for a prospect to proudly become a donor.

University leaders and development officers should work as a seamless team in building a strong and personal connection with prospects. When that happens, prospects with the capacity to give will often gladly make an investment that can have a positive impact on some aspect of the institution. Cultivating genuine relationships with donors and asking them to make a gift to a program that you believe in is both satisfying and important work. While it may seem a bit awkward initially, you should not be intimidated about asking for money. Most wealthy donors fully understand and expect that they will be asked to make a gift. They are interested, however, in making impactful investments rather than simply giving their money away. That's how they became or remained wealthy in the first place.

Your role is not to be a smooth-talking salesperson trying to hoodwink someone into making a gift, but rather a genuine and enthusiastic spokesperson for programs and impacts that you care deeply about and that you believe will be transformative for students, faculty, and the university. In my experience, the most effective academic fundraisers are not so much charismatic icons, but rather steadfast leaders that have established and can articulate a compelling vision and set of carefully crafted strategic investment priorities that advance that vision. When done well, donors will want to invest in advancing the vision and, in return, will enjoy both the personal satisfaction of giving to a worthy cause and the recognition that comes with inclusion in the inner circle of university donors. Of course, they also receive a tax benefit in return for their gift, a value and impact that should not be overlooked or underestimated.

Who Makes Gifts and for What Purpose?

Types of Donors

While every institution may have its own unique profile of donors and gift purposes, overall patterns of giving are worth understanding. Each year CASE releases a Voluntary Support of Education (VSE) key findings report based on an annual survey of fundraising outcomes in higher education institutions in the United States. Data from the survey are used to estimate total charitable support for all institutions, including nonrespondents, and represent the definitive source of information on philanthropic support for US institutions. The annual report recognizes two broad donor categories—individuals and organizations—and five donor types—alumni; non-alumni individuals (e.g., parents, faculty, staff, friends); foundations; corporations; and other organizations (e.g., religious organizations, fundraising consortia, donor-advised funds).

Based on the 2021 CASE VSE report on giving to higher education, individuals overall (alumni and non-alumni) are the largest source of donors, accounting for nearly 40 percent of philanthropic giving, while foundations account for about one-third of higher education giving.[124] Foundation giving, however, outpaces alumni giving, highlighting the importance of institutions actively partnering with foundations for philanthropic support of projects and initiatives. It is important to understand that foundations, unlike individual donors and corporations, are required by law to serve charitable purposes, and their primary business is donating money to good causes and meaningful projects. That's why they exist. Foundations often establish their own funding priorities, so institutional leaders and faculty should work with their development/foundation office to identify foundations with priorities that converge with institutional needs and aspirations. The distribution of gifts across the five donor types based on the CASE VSE 2020 report is illustrated in Figure 17.1.

VOLUNTARY SUPPORT OF HIGHER EDUCATION BY SOURCE, 2020
(DOLLARS IN BILLIONS)

Alumni
$11.06 (22.3%)

Corporations
$6.63 (13.4%)

Other Organizations
$6.74 (13.6%)

Total Support
$49.50

Foundations
$16.44 (33.2%)

Nonalumni Individuals
$8.63 (17.4%)

Figure 17.1. The distribution of gifts in 2020 across five donor types.[125]
Reprinted with permission from the Council for the
Advancement and Support of Education (CASE)

Institutions often intuitively focus on their alumni as the prime source of philanthropic giving, which makes sense given their existing connection to the institution, friendships developed in college with peers and faculty, and the career-launching impact of their education. The pattern of donor giving to higher education institutions, however, is gradually changing. In 1998, alumni (31 percent) and other non-alumni individuals (22 percent) were collectively responsible for nearly 54 percent of higher education giving, while foundations and corporations represented 21 percent and 18 percent of higher education giving, respectively. As illustrated in Figure 17.2 from the CASE VSE 2021 report, the proportion of giving from alumni, non-alumni individuals, and corporations have steadily declined over the past two decades, while foundation giving has risen.[126] The category "other organizations," while still comparatively small, has also increased. In fact, giving from that donor category has had the largest relative increase, more than doubling over the past two decades and increasing by more than 53 percent since 2011.

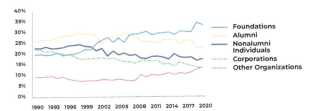

Figure 17.2. Changes in the source of voluntary support as a percentage of total voluntary support between 1990 and 2020.[127]
Reprinted with permission from the Council for the Advancement and Support of Education (CASE)

The declining trend in the proportion of alumni giving reflects a faster pace of giving growth from foundations and other organizations accompanied by a slower rate of growth and a recent decline in alumni giving.[128] Overall, however, alumni still represent an important donor population for most institutions. Nevertheless, the comparative decline in alumni giving is concerning and may reflect a cultural change about giving back among millennials who graduated after 2005, increasing disengagement of graduates from their institutions, income limitations for those graduating during or after the Great Recession, or a consequence of the increased cost of education experienced by recent graduates. That is, some recent alumni may feel they have already "given" to the institution by paying comparatively high tuition and fees as students. At the very least, waning alumni giving should prompt institutional leaders to strategically engage students on the importance of giving back and to make extra efforts to stay connected with graduates over time.

The increase in giving from the other organizations category is driven largely by increases from donor-advised funds (DAF),[129] which may reflect individual donors becoming more sophisticated in their giving and explain some of the decline in alumni and non-alumni giving. A DAF is essentially an investment account through a public charity for the sole purpose of supporting charitable organizations; it is a flexible and tax-beneficial way to make gifts. DAFs are the fastest-growing charitable giving vehicle in the United States, especially since the 2017 changes in tax policy. Individuals make an irrevocable contribution of cash or other appreciated assets (e.g., stocks or bonds) to a DAF and are eligible to get an immediate tax benefit. Those funds are then invested and grow tax-free. The individual can then recommend grants from the DAF to any qualified public charity over time until the fund is depleted. It represents a win-win for donors and recipients—the donor realizes an immediate upfront tax benefit for the whole amount invested in the DAF, and the charitable organization(s) receives the gift benefits from the interest accrued in the DAF investment account. Development and foundation staff are knowledgeable about such investment vehicles that help shape donor giving, but leaders also benefit from a basic understanding of innovative investment strategies available to donors to support their philanthropic interests.

Purpose of Donations

There are generally two broad purposes or designations for donor gifts to higher education institutions—current operations and endowment/ capital support.[130] Current operations refer to expenses for a broad array of ongoing institutional operations. Gifts in support of current operations may be further subdivided as unrestricted or restricted based on the wishes of the donor. Unrestricted gifts can be applied to any purpose at the discretion of the leader responsible for managing the gift account and allocating resources. Restricted gifts must be used to support a specific purpose, function, or initiative designated by the donor.

Because donors want their gift to matter, their restrictions are usually, but not always, in response to certain needs or priorities defined by the institution that are also of interest to the donor. A donor may restrict their gift to some favorite program or activity whether it is an institutional priority or not. If that purpose is not antagonistic to institutional goals or activities, the institution will likely gratefully accept the gift and apply it consistently with the donor's wishes. Restrictions on the use of gifts may be rather general, such as gifts restricted to supporting an academic division, a college, a library, or athletics broadly; alternatively, the restriction can be narrowly defined, such as in support of a specific student program in the history department, the women's basketball program, the distinctive collections within the library, or for need-based financial aid for undergraduate students. While unrestricted gifts for current operations are highly desirable because they have no strings attached, restricted gifts are also beneficial as they provide opportunities for growth and distinction in designated areas.

In contrast to gifts for current operations, gifts to endowment provide long-term financial stability that sustains and supports educational and research programming into the future. An endowment is a collection of assets that are invested by an institution to support its mission in perpetuity. The institution's endowment consists of numerous individual gifts for different purposes as designated by donors. The endowed funds are collectively invested as a consolidated endowment, and a portion of the interest generated from the investment is made available to support the stated purpose of each endowed fund. At most institutions, gifts to endowment must exceed a certain minimum threshold level, say $50,000 or $100,000, to establish an endowed fund to support, for example, an endowed scholarship, professorship, honors program, or student study abroad fund. The interest applied to the stated purpose of the endowed fund is usually equivalent to between 4 and 5 percent of the principal (an average of 4.6 percent between 2011 and 2020) for each endowed fund. That amount is available on an annual basis for institutional spending in support of the fund.

Because investment returns may be volatile (median return on endowments was 1.8 percent for 2020, 30.1 percent for 2021, and -8.0 percent for 2022), institutions usually apply a spending formula to a three-year, or twelve-quarter, rolling average of the endowment to smooth the volatility and provide predictability in spending. For example, according to the ACE 2021 report *Understanding College and University Endowments*, the ten-year average annual return on endowments from 2011 to 2020 was 7.5 percent, although the range was -1.9 percent in 2016 to +19.2 percent in 2011.[131] As such, when returns on investment are strong, spending represents a relatively small share of the endowment value; during lean years, spending is a larger share. The endowment principal typically cannot be spent, and a portion of the interest in any given year that exceeds the 4 to 5 percent payout to purpose will roll into the principal, allowing the endowment corpus to grow over time.

Endowments provide stability, allow institutions to achieve their educational goals, supplement financial aid, support faculty, and strengthen academic programs. According to the *2021 NACUBO-TIAA Study of Endowments*, higher education endowment spending for FY 2020 was allocated as follows: 47 percent for student financial aid, 15 percent for academic programs, 11 percent for endowed faculty positions, 9 percent for campus operations and maintenance, and 18 percent for other purposes.[132]

The TIAA Institute recently conducted a thirty-year analysis of donor giving to higher education across hundreds of institutions that offers keen insights on trends in donor giving by purpose.[133] In that analysis, the purpose of donations is categorized as gifts to either current operations or endowment/capital with further breakdowns of unrestricted versus restricted gifts and a distinction between gifts directed to capital/property versus endowment. The capital portion of that category includes gifts of personal property or gifts to purchase buildings or land as well as for construction or renovation. In general, donors are increasingly making restricted gifts to current operations; gifts to endowments have gradually declined in recent years. Unrestricted giving to current operations now represents a small portion of total giving to current operations and an almost negligible proportion of giving to the endowment. See Figure 17.3 and "Distribution of Donations to Higher Education by General Purpose Between 1988 and 2020" for the trend in the purpose of donations over that thirty-year period.

Distribution of Donations to Higher Education Institutions by General Purpose between 1988 and 2020

Donation Purpose	% Distribution of Donations				
	1988	1998	2008	2018	2020
General Purpose					
Current Operations	56.0%	49.8%	53.1%	57.2%	61.6%
Endowment/Capital	44.0%	50.2%	46.9%	42.8%	38.4%
Current Operations					
Unrestricted	24.6%	17.2%	13.1%	10.4%	na
Restricted	75.4%	82.8%	86.9%	89.6%	na
Endowment/Capital					
Property/Buildings	36.%	29.1%	29.6%	28.7%	na
Unrestricted Endowment	12.1%	3.7%	5.0%	3.0%	na
Restricted Endowment	50.8%	66.7%	65.4%	68.3%	na

na = data not available

Figure 17.3. Changes in the percent distribution of donations between current operations and endowment/capital property and unrestricted and restricted gifts between 1988 and 2020.[134]

While overall giving to higher education continues to rise, there is a general trend toward increasing donor giving to current operations rather than endowment. In 1998, donor giving to current operations and endowment/capital were evenly split. By 2018 and 2020, 57 percent and 62 percent, respectively, of donor giving was to current operations. More than ever, donors are restricting their current operations and endowment gifts rather than providing funds for discretionary spending. By 2018, nearly 90 percent of donor gifts to current operations were restricted, with the largest proportions going to research (33 percent), academic programs (21 percent), student aid (9.4 percent), and athletics (7.9 percent). Despite the increasing importance of gifts to student financial aid, the percentage of higher education giving directed to restricted operating and endowment combined for financial aid purposes has grown slightly from 10 percent in 2003 to a high of 13 percent in 2018.[135] There is, however, evidence that some foundations have recently begun prioritizing funding for economically disadvantaged students and for social justice, which is encouraging given the need for additional aid to offset the rising cost of a college education. Gifts of property and in support of buildings and construction have gradually declined, and almost all giving to endowment is restricted.

Types of Gifts

Categorizing gifts by type can be tricky because there are dramatic differences among institutions in the size and impact of gifts received and in the level of experience, sophistication, and importance of their fundraising efforts. That is, a major gift for one institution may be considered routine for another accustomed to receiving seven- or eight-figure gifts on a regular basis. Nevertheless, there is some common language used by advancement offices, and it is helpful for institutional leaders to have some familiarity with the terminology. From my non-advancement perspective and experience, I think of gifts of the following types: annual gifts, major gifts, principal gifts, and planned gifts. No doubt, fundraising professionals might divide these differently, and there certainly may be overlap between types, but I think this taxonomy of gift types will serve the interests of aspiring higher education leaders delving into the world of fundraising.

Annual gifts are typically solicited on a regular basis and usually provide general support for current operating needs of a program or institution. These are typically relatively small and are often, but not always, unrestricted gifts that tend to come from individuals, although foundations and corporations may also participate in annual giving. Alumni should be a particular target for annual giving, which can be a great way to introduce recent alumni to philanthropic giving to their alma mater. Depending on the donor base of the institution, annual giving often includes many gifts, perhaps in the $50 to $500 range, plus a few larger ones in the $1,000 to $10,000 range and will depend on the volume of giving to generate impact.

Most institutions organize an annual giving solicitation that reaches out to new prospects while also encouraging existing alumni and friends to give on a regular basis. Annual giving programs often have a catchy theme or title that captures some special feature or tradition associated with the institution that resonates with alumni, parents, and friends. Funds raised through annual giving are referred to as the *annual fund*, which may be a misnomer because there are often many annual fund accounts within an institution. For instance, each college and the athletics department will likely have their own annual fund accounts, even if annual giving is organized centrally through the advancement office or foundation.

While the size of the gifts may be relatively small and the total amount raised may pale in comparison to major and principal gifts, a vibrant annual giving program is vitally important to the institution for several reasons. First, the funds raised support day-to-day needs that typically can't be covered by restricted gifts or university base budget funds, especially for public institutions that have many restrictions on spending. Second, a significant part of fundraising is about donor participation, which can be as important in some ways as the total amount raised. Annual giving is a vehicle to connect individuals to the institution and its mission. When colleges report that 100 percent of their advisory board or institutions boast that 100 percent of the board of trustees or 25 percent of their alumni participated, or donated, each year, it sends a positive message of enthusiasm to others that encourage additional giving. And, finally, donors almost always make a small gift before they make a large gift. As such, annual giving is often a vehicle to uncover new major or principal gift prospects and a pathway for introducing new donors to the institution.

In contrast to annual gifts, *major gifts* typically involve larger amounts of money and are likely to be more future-focused. In most cases, major gifts are restricted funds, and the donor will stipulate where and how the gift funds are invested, such as for scholarships, professorships, facilities, or specific programs. There is no universal threshold level for major gifts, and it will vary from one institution to the next, but it is not uncommon for major gifts to be at the level of $100,000 or more. While major gifts for use as unrestricted operating funds are welcome, they are uncommon. Major gifts may contribute to an existing endowed fund or establish a new one. Most major gifts to establish or grow endowments will come from individuals rather than from foundations or corporations, although foundations and corporations may certainly make restricted major gifts to support certain programs of interest.

While annual giving involves annual solicitations, securing major gifts takes more time, strategy, and resources, including research about donor wealth capacity, personal and family interests, previous giving patterns, and inclination to give to the institution. Major gifts may come as cash directly from a donor's income, but frequently include the transfer of other donor assets and may involve multi-year pledges. Depending on the size of the major gift, it is not uncommon for such gifts to include a written proposal that describes how the funds will be used. As such, major gifts are inherently more complex, and relationship-building between prospects and institutional leaders and development officers may take many months or years before a major gift is requested and realized.

Also, while there may be hundreds or even thousands of donors to the annual fund, major gift prospects represent a much smaller pool, although they are collectively responsible for a very large proportion of the funds raised. Some major gift prospects will surface through their annual giving, while others, namely parents of students, may emerge through the university application and admission process. A review of the names and zip codes of applicants to some institutions may reveal families with financial capacity and interest in the university. While one should refrain from interacting with parents of applicants about giving during the application review process and perhaps even with parents of current students, it is important to identify individuals that may be cultivated for gifts later or after their student has graduated.

Principal gifts are essentially very large major gifts. Because of their distinctive impact and complexity, they warrant separate recognition and designation. While perhaps rather subjective, principal gifts are often defined as gifts that are "transformative" for institutions, which of course will vary substantially in size from one institution to the next. The recent groundbreaking gifts of $1.8 billion from Michael Bloomberg to Johns Hopkins University and the $500 million gift from Phil and Penny Knight to the University of Oregon certainly fit the transformative definition of principal gifts.

Again, while there is no universal threshold, it is common for principal gifts to be defined as gifts exceeding $1 million or more, which are increasingly common in recent years.[136] In recognition of the growth in gifts of more than $1 million, many advancement operations employ principal gift officers focused exclusively on high-capacity principal gift prospects in addition to those focused on major gifts. Because of the size of these gifts, which often include multiple appreciated assets, stock or property transfers, and complex legal issues, such gifts are inherently complicated and will likely involve a team of accountants, attorneys, and financial advisors as well as development staff and institutional leaders. For principal gifts, institution presidents and chief advancement officers will typically play an important role with the donor and developing the gift proposal.

Cultivating and closing a principal gift may take several years, or even a decade or more, but the investment is worth it. For both major and principal gifts, cultivation of relationships will likely involve personal visits with donors and the solicitation for the gift will no doubt be a personal face-to-face request made by the individual with the closest relationship with the donor along with a written proposal. Furthermore, a thoughtful stewardship plan that conveys the institution's appreciation and includes reports to donors on the benefits and impact of their generosity is essential and will involve input from institutional leaders in its development and implementation.

According to the *CASE Study of Principal Gifts to US Colleges and Universities*, family foundations, trusts, and other private philanthropic vehicles are the most common funding source for principal gifts, contributing 60 percent of gifts with cash a component for 40 percent of these gifts.[137] About two-thirds of principal gifts were designated in whole or part for endowment, while support for capital projects and restricted current operating uses are also sometimes included. More than half of principal gifts include encouraging additional giving as a formal goal of the gift, suggesting that institutions and donors view transformational principal gifts as having the potential to stimulate giving by others.

Interestingly, non-alumni donors made half of the principal gifts in recent years. There are many reasons for non-alumni to develop a philanthropic connection with institutions, which include family relationships with students or alumni. Some non-alums, however, who reside near a university may have a particular passion for certain topics, such as environmental issues, social justice, athletics, or health care, that are especially high priority and reputable areas of strength for the university. Institutional leaders need to recognize and broadcast the distinctive strengths of their institutions and seek to establish partnerships with

310 | SUBSTANCE OVER STYLE

philanthropists who resonate with those topics. For example, UVM's distinctive reputation in lake studies, including a state-of-the-art laboratory on Lake Champlain, a world-class research vessel, and acclaimed faculty and endowed professors, attract gifts from non-alumni who live near, sail, or otherwise care deeply about Lake Champlain and view UVM as stewards of the Lake Champlain ecosystem. Similarly, URI's world-class Graduate School of Oceanography connects with the passions of sailors, yacht owners, and homeowners who care about Narragansett Bay or oceans more broadly. Connections like these should be cultivated and celebrated.

Finally, the opportunity for *planned gifts,* often referred to as *legacy giving,* may sometimes be overlooked by institutional leaders, who tend to be focused on gifts for today rather than the future. From an institutional perspective, this is a mistake. Planned giving may enable donors to contribute at a level that they could not afford today because the gifts are not dependent on one's ordinary annual income. Planned gifts are frequently in the form of life insurance, equity, real estate, or personal property. As such, a donor who cares about the institution and may be a regular modest contributor to the annual fund may be willing and able to make an estate gift at a much higher level.

A planned gift is a donation made through a formal financial or estate plan that is designated for a charity at a future date, usually at the time of death as conveyed through a will. While there are many variations on planned giving, planned gifts usually are in the form of a bequest and involve individual rather than organizational donors. While planned giving programs may target major or principal gifts, planned gifts can be any amount, and the funds may be unrestricted, restricted to a particular purpose, or directed toward the endowment, which enhances the long-term financial position of the institution. Because it is not known exactly when a planned gift will be received, it is not useful for such gifts to be directed at specific projects where the timing of support is critical. Planned giving is a sensitive and specialized area of fundraising, and there are many planned giving options that donors may wish to consider. Most advancement/foundation offices will have specially trained staff able to assist prospective donors and the institution in navigating the details to respectfully honor the donor's wishes for their estate and ensure family members understand the positive impact of the gift.

Creating a Culture of Philanthropy

Developing a successful long-term fundraising program is much more than periodically asking donors for money and figuring out interesting and important ways to spend it. Perhaps that's why the term *advancement* is used to encapsulate the much larger and ongoing process to truly *advance* the institution by sharing points of pride, telling its most revered stories, building genuine partnerships with and among constituents, and recognizing that the heart of the institution is its community. As emphasized in earlier chapters, universities are all about people, so a vibrant university is one in which the people in the community care about and enhance each other's well-being. In an article entitled "Creating a Culture of Philanthropy," Lindsay Cavanah shares a definition of philanthropy as "an effort to promote human welfare," meaning it is much more than the simple act of donating money. It is about giving "to help make life better for other people."[138] James Langley, president and founder of Langley Innovations and former vice president for advancement at Georgetown and UC San Diego, emphasizes that "fundraising does not in itself engender philanthropy," but rather it "harvests philanthropic goodwill."[139] A culture of philanthropy emerges when the larger community cares, embraces the value of giving, and recognizes the importance of building relationships and garnering resources to support the institution and empower new possibilities.

Building such a culture begins with institutional leaders valuing the roles of and input from the broader university community, motivating students, staff, faculty, alumni, and friends to embrace continuous improvement and change, building enduring relationships with friends and partners, and supporting a climate where generosity, whether of spirit, time, or money, is valued and celebrated. Effective leaders do this work little by little one day at a time. This may sound a bit Pollyannaish. Nevertheless, goodwill, community spirit, and pride are important ingredients to building a culture of giving because philanthropy is not just about giving money but giving to help make life better for other people or make a better world in some small way. The community too should reflect those values to engage and sustain long-term donor interest and giving.

So, what does it take to create a culture of philanthropy? While there is not a simple formula and shifts in culture come about slowly, there are some characteristics of institutions that reflect a culture of philanthropy. Some of those attributes are listed below.

- **There is a seamless working relationship between university and advancement staff.** Development officers and university leaders share the responsibility to promote the university, engage prospects, ensure up-to-date prospect contact reports, understand each other's roles and responsibilities, and refrain from finger-pointing when missteps occur.

- **Strategic coordination protocols for managing prospects are in-place and followed.** Protocols for managing prospects with multiple affiliations, the potential for major, principal, or planned gifts, or from corporations and foundations are known and embraced by all.

- **A donor-centered focus drives relationship-building with prospects.** Cultivation strategies, prospect management assignments, and information-sharing are driven by the primary interests of donors.

- **All university events are recognized as advancement events.** All university functions, whether a student orientation or a black-tie alumni celebration, convey a message about the institution's values, sophistication, and service orientation and are friend-raising and impression-making moments, even if not designed directly as fundraising events.

- **Donor participation is celebrated to create and sustain momentum.** Growth in giving participation, whether to the annual fund, a celebratory day of giving each year, or major gifts, reflects success in engagement and retention of donors and pride in the institution.

- **Continuous cultivation, stewardship, and recognition of long-term donors are paramount.** While all donors are important and deserve recognition and appreciation, long-term donors are loyal to and invested in the institution and are your best prospects for future major, principal, and/or planned gifts.

- **Student giving and volunteerism are encouraged and recognized.** Early and consistent student participation in giving and/or community service builds relationships and a sustained bond to the institution.

- **Boards understand their larger stewardship role to strengthen the culture of philanthropy.** University and foundation governing boards understand their philanthropic role is not only to give and monitor fundraising progress but also to ensure the institution continuously evolves, remains distinctive, and sustains a strong culture of philanthropy.

- **Authentic expressions of gratitude are consistently extended to all donors.** Donors deserve to receive genuine appreciation, to learn about the impact of their generosity, and to be acknowledged by those who benefit from it, such as scholarship recipients, endowed professors, and athletic teams.

If effective fundraising is about building authentic relationships, then a culture of philanthropy is about building such relationships with internal constituents as well as with alumni, friends, corporations, and foundations. That is, the extended university community understands that each of us by doing our jobs well plays an important role in securing resources to advance the institution. Thus, leaders need to understand and value the engagement of the entire community and create a climate where embracing the institution's mission and vision is a shared experience, and success is recognized as a shared success. This not only builds pride but also creates an exciting place to work and learn.

Comprehensive Fundraising Campaigns—Once in a Campaign, Always in a Campaign

Strong evidence indicates that fundraising campaigns are the most effective means of achieving accelerated and sustained growth in private giving to colleges and universities. As such, most contemporary colleges and universities engage in fundraising campaigns as a means of raising money to address high-profile institutional priorities and needs. In addition to raising money, effective campaigns create positive momentum, raise the visibility, stature, and profile of the institution on- and off-campus, and build long-term capacity, infrastructure, and know-how for fundraising in the future.

A fundraising campaign is a large-scale targeted effort over a multiyear timeframe to achieve a specified financial goal that is usually publicly broadcasted. Traditionally, college and university campaigns were referred to as capital campaigns and were designed to raise money for specific projects, often new buildings, major renovations, or large-scale equipment purchases. In a contemporary context, there has been a shift to inclusive comprehensive campaigns that are more broadly focused and include funds raised for several purposes, including annual operating support, endowments, scholarships, professorships, planned gifts, and capital projects. Comprehensive campaigns appeal to a wide audience of donors because all gifts count toward achieving the campaign goal. These campaigns offer an opportunity to engage new donors, thereby expanding the potential donor base for the future.

Planning a Campaign

Planning a comprehensive campaign is a major undertaking that requires careful and detailed analysis and research, including a feasibility study often conducted by an independent consultant. The feasibility study objectively evaluates the potential of the campaign, including wealth and inclination to give analyses of the institution's donors based on inter-views with the largest donors. The information gleaned advises the pres-ident and advancement leader about selecting a viable fundraising goal for the campaign and helps the institution develop its most compelling case for support.

Selecting an achievable, yet aspirational, goal for the campaign is a delicate matter. The institution should have to stretch to meet the ambi-tious fundraising goal, but it cannot run the risk of falling short of the widely publicized campaign goal, which would deflate prospects, donors, the board, and the campus community and cast a shadow of doubt over the next campaign as well. There is, however, some wiggle room in that the timeframe is usually loosely defined so there may be flexibility to quietly extend the duration to ensure the goal is met. Ideally, however, institutions want to exceed the established campaign goal and publicly announce at some point that progress has been so phenomenal that the goal has been elevated to a higher level. As a general frame of reference, it is not uncommon for a campaign goal to be at least twice the amount raised from the previous campaign.

Following the feasibility study and the establishment of a working campaign goal, there are usually two overlapping phases for comprehen-sive campaigns—the *quiet* phase and the *public* phase. The quiet phase (although there is nothing quiet about it), also referred to as the *discovery* phase, focuses on securing lead major gifts for the campaign from top donors. This is a critical phase expected to produce gifts equivalent to approximately 50 to 70 percent of the campaign goal, and it serves to generate interest, attention, and credibility among other donors. Typically, the largest gifts to the campaign will be solicited and closed during this phase. The late stages of the quiet phase provide an opportunity to evaluate progress toward the campaign goal, adjust the goal up or down, and revisit the campaign timetable before the official public announcement of the campaign goal.

The public phase is launched with the fanfare of a campaign kick-off celebration. The kick-off celebration may honor many of the lead donors and officially announce and promote the campaign goal, including highlighting the plan to extend the goal, if appropriate, because of the early success of the campaign. The public phase expands fundraising efforts to energize and solicit wider audiences of donors and may include a focused effort reaching out to faculty and staff to contribute to the campaign. This phase leverages the success of the quiet phase to draw in other donors. First and foremost, the public phase must generate sufficient dollars to achieve or preferably exceed the campaign goal. In the current world of almost continuous institutional fundraising campaigns, a final aspect of the public phase may be the beginning of laying the groundwork for the next campaign by identifying and qualifying new prospects with the potential to become the major or principal gift quiet phase donors of the future. For many institutions, each comprehensive campaign delicately transitions into the next one; so, indeed, once in campaign mode, always in campaign mode.

Where to from Here?

Bold advancement initiatives, especially comprehensive campaigns, have been highly successful in generating resources and partnerships in support of the needs and priorities of many colleges and universities. Recently, many high-profile private and public institutions have successfully completed campaigns with multi-billion-dollar goals, and individual mega-gifts in the multi-million to greater than a billion-dollar range have gained in frequency and national visibility. These are impressive results and encourage less experienced institutions to ensure that they too are building their capacity to cultivate and harvest philanthropic goodwill to secure the resources necessary to support their neediest students and guide students to degree completion.

Some have posed that too much private support is directed to wealthy institutions and students who need it least with too little aid directed toward students with the greatest financial need. This is a legitimate concern, although not an inherent problem with philanthropy *per se*, as evidenced by Mackenzie Scott's recent multi-billion dollar unrestricted gifts to institutions and other nonprofits that have been historically underfunded and overlooked, including several community colleges, HBCUs, Hispanic-serving institutions, and Tribal Colleges and Universities (TCUs) as well as students of color and others from low-income communities.[140] Scott's extraordinary generosity is unusual, but nevertheless an inspirational model of the power of philanthropy at creating opportunities for those who might otherwise be excluded from a college education and the potential for social and economic mobility.

In recent years, comprehensive fundraising campaigns have become prevalent at many institutions, including small private and community colleges with modest campaign goals of a few million dollars and high-profile public and private research universities with multi-billion-dollar goals. Recognizing increasing student financial need, it is encouraging that most institutions now list student aid, student access and success, and scholarships among their top campaign priorities. Aspiring university leaders must develop the comfort, understanding, and tools to successfully build partnerships with prospective donors, and passionately convey their best case for donor giving, student access and support, and sustaining their institutional value proposition. Simply put, fundraising is an essential part of your job—enjoy it!

CHAPTER EIGHTEEN

Intercollegiate Athletics: A Source of Pride, Expense, and Headaches

Just as with philanthropy, college athletics is a uniquely American phenomenon. Many colleges and universities are better known nationally for their intercollegiate athletic programs—especially football, men's and women's basketball, and ice hockey in certain regions—than for their academic programs, although there are many exceptions to this generality. Certainly, many institutions participating in the National Collegiate Athletic Association (NCAA) Division I athletic programs, including about 350 institutions in the Football Bowl Subdivision (FBS), Football Championship Subdivision (FCS), and Division I Subdivision (schools without football programs) routinely pack stadiums and arenas and benefit from widespread television coverage, endorsements, and high-profile student-athletes that bring enhanced visibility to the institutions. In this respect, athletic programs, especially winning programs in high-visibility sports, may help promote the institution to prospective students as well as donors and build long-term bonds with many alumni and non-alumni sports fans. Such positive impacts, however, are countered by numerous issues of concern that represent ongoing challenges for many institutions. Indeed, intercollegiate athletics is a highly complex, enigmatic, and costly endeavor that simultaneously stimulates public engagement, both positive and negative, pride in the institution, and potential headaches for institutional leaders at multiple levels, especially presidents.

318 | SUBSTANCE OVER STYLE

According to the NCAA, the total revenue reported by NCAA athletic departments across all three divisions in 2019 was almost $19 billion with several campuses topping $200 million in annual revenue, especially from football.[141] See "Top 25 Revenue-Generating Division I College Athletics Programs for 2022-23."[142]

These are impressive numbers and reinforce the notion that intercollegiate athletic programs are a lucrative business for colleges and universities. Nevertheless, most institutions are not making money from their athletic programs and require institutional athletic subsidies to break even each year. Among the so-called sixty-five autonomy Division 1 schools within the Power Five conferences—the Southeastern Conference (SEC), Atlantic Coast Conference (ACC), Big Ten, Pac-12, and Big 12—the NCAA reported that only twenty-five realized positive net revenue in 2019 with a median per institution net revenue of $7.9 million for those twenty-five programs.[143] The term *autonomy* refers to a 2014 NCAA decision to allow athletic programs in the top five conferences to establish their own rules on things such as scholarships, recruiting rules, and staff sizes.[144]

Based on NCAA financial reporting, the remaining forty schools in Power Five conferences had a median negative net revenue in 2019 of about $16 million, and each of the sixty-four non-autonomy FBS (i.e., outside the Power Five conferences) schools experienced a median shortfall of $23 million per school.[145] Each of the 125 FCS and the ninety-seven additional Division 1 Subdivision institutions without football programs reported negative net revenue in 2019 with median losses of $14.3 million and $14.4 million, respectively. In addition, none of the Division II (approximately 310 institutions) or Division III (approximately 438 institutions) campuses had positive net revenue. All in all, twenty-five of the approximately 1,098 institutions across 102 conferences in the NCAA were net-revenue positive in 2019.[146] That number dropped to twenty in 2020. Between 2005 and 2020, the number of schools with positive generated net revenue ranged from sixteen (in 2009) to twenty-nine (in 2018). From a purely financial perspective, it is not a pretty picture. Some degree of angst among institutional leaders is certainly understandable and justified.

USA Today's Top 25 Revenue-Generating Division I College Athletic Programs for 2022-23

1. Ohio State University: $251,615,345
2. University of Texas: $239,290,648
3. University of Alabama: $214,365,357
4. University of Michigan: $210,652,287
5. University of Georgia: $203,048,566
6. Louisiana State University: $199,309,382
7. Texas A & M: $193,139,619
8. University of Florida: $190,417,139
9. The Pennsylvania State University: $181,227,448
10. University of Oklahoma: $177,320,217
11. Auburn University: $174,568,442
12. Michigan State University: $172,799,513
13. University of Indiana: $166,761,471
14. University of Virginia: $161,916,231
15. Florida State University: $161,141,884
16. University of Kentucky: $159,079,024
17. Clemson University: $158,283,618
18. University of Tennessee: $154,566,935
19. University of Oregon: $153,510,555
20. University of Arkansas: $153,513,755
21. University of Iowa: $151,483,092
22. University of Wisconsin: $150,100,977
23. University of Louisville: $146,225,965
24. University of Illinois: $145,735,330
25. University of Washington: $145,184,864

Potential Benefits of College Athletic Programs— Fact or Fiction?

The financial picture of athletic programs, however, may not tell the whole story. College sports and athletic rivalries are popular with many college and university constituents and lead to the engagement and education of many student-athletes. Community building is an especially positive outcome of intercollegiate athletics at all levels. Fans across many backgrounds, perspectives, identities, and political leanings come together to share their enthusiasm and support for their team, especially when competing against rival schools. Successful sports teams often promote school spirit and ignite a passion for and pride in one's institution and alma mater. This bond is foundational for building community on campus, regionally, and often nationally, and should not be overlooked or undervalued.

Student-Athlete Success

About 500,000 student-athletes, many receiving athletic scholarships, representing nearly 20,000 teams in up to twenty-four different sports participate each year in NCAA-sponsored athletic programs across 102 conferences in three athletic divisions (Division I, II, and III). About 16 percent of those student-athletes are first-generation college students.[147] Although the educational experience and graduation rate for athletes in high-profile sports (e.g., football and men's basketball) are often questioned, the NCAA reports that the overall six-year graduation success rate (GSR) for all Division I student-athletes was 89 percent in 2021.[148]

The GSR calculation used by the NCAA tracks the six-year progress toward degree completion for all student-athletes, including student-athletes that transfer and those who have not received an athletic scholarship. While the GSR is not directly comparable with graduation rates reported by the federal government using IPEDS data (see chapter 16), direct comparisons using the federal calculation show student-athletes in Division I, II, and III graduate at rates on par with or exceeding the general student body. This is especially true for female student-athletes in most sports. The argument can be made that intercollegiate athletics enhances, or at least does not detract from, overall student success while also providing student-athletes the opportunity to compete in their sport, enhance their athletic prowess at the highest level, and hone life skills that help prepare them for the working world.

Value-Added of NCAA-Sponsored Sports Programs

The NCAA is well-known for the financial support it distributes in support of NCAA institutions, conferences, and nearly half a million student-athletes. What is less well-known, however, are the academic support, leadership, and professional development programs sponsored by the NCAA. Such programs support and enhance the institutions and serve the best interests of many student-athletes and are value-added benefits worthy of recognition. These include annual investment in the Academic Enhancement Fund to assist institutions with academic programs and student-athlete support services. Some of the NCAA professional development programs available to student-athletes or athletic program staff are:[149]

- After the Game Career Center—preparation to transition into life after college sports
- Student-Athlete Leadership Forum—designed to enhance professional growth and help build networking connections
- Emerging Leaders Series—equips graduate assistants and interns with the skills needed to accelerate their career progression in college sports, including as athletic administrators and coaches
- The Pathway Program—an experiential learning program aimed at elevating athletics administrators to the next level as directors of athletics or conference commissioners

It is also important to acknowledge the positive impact of Title IX, which recognized gender equity in education as a civil right, creating opportunities for female students to participate in college sports programs. In 1972, Title IX of the Educational Amendments Act was passed establishing that "no person in the United States shall, on the basis of sex, be excluded from participation in, be denied the benefits of, or be subjected to discrimination under any education program or activity receiving federal financial assistance."[150] Now, some fifty years later, women's teams outnumber men's teams across the NCAA and have done so since 1996-97; more than 10,000 women's teams compete in NCAA championship sports. Indeed, this is a tangible benefit of college athletics that has ensured educational opportunities and scholarships for female student-athletes as well as the opportunity to participate in sports at the highest competitive level.

Institutional Name Recognition—the "Flutie Effect"

The success of athletic programs may lead to ancillary benefits for the institution. For instance, college athletic programs, especially winning programs, can lead to increased visibility, name recognition, reputation enhancement, as well as community spirit on- and off-campus. Anecdotal evidence suggests at least short-term modest growth in applications for admission, donations, or even state funding following high-profile athletic successes, such as a national football or basketball championship, a major bowl game victory, or a deep run to the Elite Eight or Final Four in the NCAA March Madness basketball tournament. In this context, a football or basketball game can be viewed not only as engaging sports entertainment but also as several hours of valuable institutional advertising that may draw students and others to that institution. Even though the financial picture associated with most athletic programs may be challenging, it is often asserted that athletic programs can be justified because of these ancillary contributions to the institutional greater good— although evidence in support of that assertion is mixed.

The phenomenon of surging student applications following sports success is commonly referred to as the *Flutie Effect*, named after Boston College quarterback Doug Flutie who threw a successful Hail Mary touchdown pass as time ran out to beat powerhouse Miami in a nationally televised game in 1984. Apparently, applications to Boston College surged for a couple of years following that game. While many attributed the surge in applications to the Flutie Effect, Boston College attributed it to mid-1980s investments in residence halls, academic facilities, and financial aid.[151] In a story published in *The Washington Post*, Mayes and Giambalvo highlight several observations of surges in student interest following major sports victories, such as Auburn and Alabama's national championships in football, the UCONN women's string of basketball national championships, and No. 16 seeded UMBC's upset victory over No. 1 seed Virginia in the NCAA basketball tournament.[152] They also emphasize, however, that such a boost in student interest following significant sports accomplishments does not always occur.

Increases in Applications for Admissions—Yes, No, or Maybe?

Rather than relying on observational information, Pope and Pope conducted a quantitative analysis of the relationship between NCAA Division I school sports success and the quantity and quality of student applications to those schools.[153] Their findings indicate that football and basketball success increased the number of applications with estimates ranging from 2 to 8 percent for the top twenty football programs and top sixteen basketball programs. Private institutions experienced larger increases than public institutions. They found little evidence supporting the notion that successful teams increased the quality of enrolled students. The positive impact on applications, however, was short-lived with no positive effect after two to three years.

Conducting econometric analyses of relationships between football success and outcomes for FBS schools from 1986 to 2009, Anderson found that unexpected wins—upsets—were associated with increased application numbers and SAT scores, but only for teams in the Power Five conferences within the FBS.[154] The remaining FBS conferences and teams did not show this relationship. Furthermore, improving season wins by five games (8 percent over one year and 13 percent over two years) or by three games (20 percent over one year and 27 percent over two years) is associated with a 5 percent and 3 percent increase in applications and 1 percent and 0.2 percent increase in incoming twenty-fifth percentile SAT scores. Once again, the positive effect of unexpected wins was short-lived. Applying quantitative models, Chung also found that athletic success had a significant impact on the quantity and quality of applications.[155] However, students with lower-than-average SAT scores had a stronger preference for schools with athletic success, while students with higher SAT scores had a greater preference for schools with a reputation for academic quality.

Analyzing data from 2006-2016 for sixty-five institutions that partic-ipate in the athletically prominent Power Five conferences, Baumer and Zimbalist found that winning a national championship in football or basketball was associated with a subsequent approximately 10 percent increase in applications two years later, which dissipated by year three. Also, an additional win per year for three consecutive seasons was asso-ciated with an approximate 1 percent increase in applications for foot-ball, but not basketball.[156] These data confirm a limited and short-term positive relationship between sports success and applications largely confined to the Power Five conferences. Indeed, most of the suggested cause-and-effect associations between athletics success and application increases relate to very high-profile sports events and athletically prominent institutions. These do not appear to translate into increased interest, applications, or enrollment in lower profile, mid-tier athletic programs or conferences, and Division II or III institutions that depend on athletic subsidies. Thus, direct institutional advertising may be as or more effective to increase applications than investments in athletic program success.

Funding from Alumni and/or State Governments

Intuitively, one might expect that alumni and athletic booster donations to athletics and/or the institution more broadly would increase because of enhanced visibility and the celebratory impacts of athletic program success. Most, but not all, evidence supports this notion. For example, Anderson found that NCAA Division I FBS football teams that are eligible for postseason bowl games experience increased athletic donations, especially for those in the Power Five conferences.[157] He estimated that an additional unexpected win during a season would increase alumni giving to athletics by $136,400, and three additional wins would increase alumni athletic donations by approximately $409,000 with no significant increase in nonathletic donations, total donations, or the alumni giving rate.

Similarly, Walker compared 129 schools participating in either the Final Four of the NCAA men's basketball tournament or the Division I FBS Bowl Championship Series over a ten-year (2002-2011) period to 1,003 other higher education institutions over the same period.[158] The mean percent increase in athletic donations during a two-year period was 5.4 percent for all institutions (the control) compared to 12.8 percent for those that were athletically successful. Increases associated with athletic success were evident for both basketball and football successes and were more pronounced at private than at public institutions. These data reinforce a positive outcome of athletics success on donor giving, at least for high-profile institutions playing at the highest levels of college sports. In contrast, Baumer and Zimbalist, analyzing data from 2006 through 2016 for the sixty-five schools in the Power Five conferences, reported no significant effect of football and men's basketball success on funding to institutions through either alumni donations or increased state allocations.[159]

There are other dimensions of donor giving connected to athletics worthy of attention. For instance, there are major donors who are avid fans of athletics, even though their philanthropy is directed to scholarships, endowed professorships, or academic programs rather than or in addition to athletics. For these individuals, athletics plays a prominent role in sustaining their connection to the institution. This is a true value that may not surface in econometric analyses. On the flip side, however, some major donors may exert influence that interferes with the academic mission or pressures institutions to make athletic investments, such as hiring high-profile coaches or building new facilities, simply to keep up with the competition. The latter can create headaches for presidents.

Anderson conducted an interesting, but admittedly limited, "back of the envelope" calculation to get a rough idea of the ROI in alumni donations and increased applications associated with increased team investments. He notes that it has been reported that a $1 million increase in football team expenditures is associated with a 6.7 percent increase in winning percentage, which translates into 0.8 additional games won.[160] He speculates that if that relationship is causal, based on the positive outcomes projected, a $1 million investment in football expenditures would result in a rather modest increase in athletic donations of $109,000 and an increase in applications of 108. Such ROI effects on their own would be hard-pressed to justify the additional investment, although it is possible that the increased success might stimulate additional direct athletic revenue through ticket sales, conference revenue, television contracts, etc.

Finally, it is worth noting that most studies examining the ancillary benefits are seeking evidence of incremental gains from recent athletic program successes. It is possible, perhaps even likely, that some high-profile athletic institutions, such as those in the Power Five conferences, are already benefiting in applications and donations from their perennial high-visibility athletic programs and household reputation, even if they are not regularly winning national championships.

Financial Challenges and Athletic Subsidies—An Ethical Dilemma?

At a time when college affordability is viewed as the greatest challenge facing higher education, student debt is deemed a crisis, and the cost-value proposition of a college education is being questioned by many students and their families, elected officials, and employers, intercollegiate athletics is one of the fastest growing expenses at many institutions. Just twenty to twenty-five or so NCAA athletic departments generate enough revenue each year to cover their expenses, which means that almost all programs are heavily subsidized from direct institutional general fund allocations and/or student activity fees directed to athletics. Despite annual shortfalls of generated revenue versus expenses for almost all athletic programs, athletic expenditures seem to be continuously rising in what is commonly referred to as an "arms race" in athletic spending, often related to coach's compensation and facilities improvements. With declining state appropriations at most public institutions, tuition and fees is the predominant source of funding comprising athletic subsidies. That is, whether they know it or not or choose to attend games, students are covering the cost of institutional athletic subsidies through their tuition and fees. For some, this is not only a serious economic issue but also an ethical dilemma.

The Nature and Scope of Athletics Program Financial Challenges

Recently, the NCAA released multi-year financial trend reports for 2005-2019 and 2011-2020 focused on revenues and expenses for mostly Division 1 athletic departments.[161] These detailed reports provide deep insight into the financial challenges and structures associated with Division I athletic programs. University leaders, especially presidents and provosts, should carefully examine and digest these data to better understand the nature and scope of the financial issues associated with college athletics at their institutions.

Athletics departments across the NCAA reported total revenue of $18.9 billion in 2019, the year prior to the pandemic. Of that amount, 56 percent, or $10.6 billion, was generated by athletic departments through ticket sales, NCAA and conference distributions, broadcast rights, royalties, and donations from alumni and other boosters. The remaining 44 percent, or $8.3 billion, was subsidized by institutions through student activity fees and/or direct general fund allocations.[162] Division I schools accounted for 96 percent of generated revenues, while Division II and Division III schools accounted for 3 percent and 1 percent of generated revenues, respectively. The sixty-five FBS autonomy schools accounted for approximately 72 percent of all revenues. Thus, institutional athletic subsidies represent an increasing proportion of the total athletic department revenues for all the remaining non-Power Five FBS, FCS, Division I Subdivision, and Division II and III conferences and schools. That is, about 6 percent of the approximately 1,098 NCAA institutions generate nearly three-quarters of the total revenue, and most of that comes from football.

While median revenue has grown steadily between 2005 and 2019 for schools in each of the Division I subdivisions, growth in expenses has outpaced the growth in revenue, leading to a steady decline in net generated revenue for athletic departments at most schools. For example, over the fifteen-year period, the median growth in revenue versus expenses for the four categories of Division I programs was 149 percent versus 159 percent for the FBS autonomy schools; 47 percent versus 92 percent for the FBS non-autonomy schools; 114 percent versus 130 percent for the FCS schools; and 120 percent versus 130 percent for Division I Subdivision schools. Furthermore, the ratio of athletics expenses to overall institutional expenses has steadily increased over time, reflecting faster growth in athletics compared to academic expenditures. The Delta Cost Project reports that athletic costs have increased at least twice as fast as academic spending on a per capita basis across Division I schools.[163] In 2005, the median ratios of athletic to institutional expenses were approximately 4.5 to 5.5 percent compared to approximately 6.5 percent to greater than 8 percent in 2019. The FBS autonomy schools, however, were about 95 percent self-sufficient in 2019 compared to the FBS non-autonomy, FCS, and Division I Subdivision schools, which were 40 percent, 27 percent, and 19 percent self-sufficient, respectively. The top half of the FBS autonomous schools were mostly fully self-sufficient.

These data reflect two important patterns. First, there is a need for continuing increases in direct institutional athletic subsidies over time for most schools. With expenses exceeding generated revenue, most programs are becoming increasingly reliant on institutions allocating more and more tuition and fee revenue for athletic subsidies. This is likely not sustainable. Second, there is an increasing independence of the Power Five conference schools, especially as compared with the other FBS non-autonomy schools. In fact, the median revenue–expense gap between Power Five and other FBS schools increased from approximately $26 million in 2005 to approximately $80 million in 2019.

The working model appears to be that increased investment, or expenditures, in athletics leads to stronger recruitment and increased success (i.e., wins), which will return greater self-generated revenue. This model may be viable for some schools in the Power Five conferences but does not appear workable for the remaining Division I programs. So, while the top Power Five schools have the highest spending, they represent less of a financial drain on their institutions because of their ability to generate revenue from lucrative television contracts and conference distributions as well as ticket revenue from filling large stadiums and arenas. As such, the rich are getting richer and better or, at least, staying rich and continuing to dominate in athletic success, especially in football. It may not be possible for others to catch up, regardless of the level of investment.

Driven by the pursuit of more lucrative television contracts, recent geographically dubious conference realignments involving institutions from the soon to be decimated PAC-12 and the Big Ten, Big 12, SEC, and ACC conferences will increase travel time and expenses for players and some fans and disrupt some traditional regional rivalries. It will likely also change the competitive landscape within and among the realigned conferences. Whether the potential for enhanced television revenue for a few athletic programs will somehow benefit college athletics or further compromise the integrity of and enthusiasm for college sports is yet to be determined. What is apparent, however, is the recent conference realignments will further concentrate money and power in a small number of institutions with high-profile football programs in even fewer increasingly dominant conferences.

Athletic Subsidies

Athletic subsidies refer to funds allocated by institutions to athletic departments to make up for the annual shortfall in net generated revenue (NGR)—the difference between generated revenue and total expenses. Figure 18.1 offers a snapshot overview of the median athletics subsidies across the four Division I Subdivisions for 2019.

	FBS Autonomy	FBS Non-Autonomy	FCS	Division I Subdivision
Median NGR	-$6.9M	-$22.9M	-$14.3M	-$14.4M
Range in NGR	-$45M to +$44M	-$6M to -$65M	-$2M to -$42M	-$4M to -$43M
Median Subsidy	8%	56%	71%	76%

Figure 18.1. Median and range in net-generated revenue (NGR) in millions and median institutional athletic subsidies across the four Division I athletics subdivisions in 2019.[164]

While median net generated revenue shortfalls for each Division I subdivision offers some insight into the scope of the athletic subsidy financial challenge to institutions, there is a substantial range among schools within each subdivision. Some schools within all four Division I subdivisions require institutional athletic subsidies of approximately $40 million to $65 million each year to break even. Such subsidies probably exceed the budget for one or more entire colleges that are tuition revenue generating and serving several thousand students across many academic departments, disciplines, and majors at those institutions. In contrast, according to the interactive Knight-Newhouse College Athletics Database, which includes 2021 financial data and athletic subsidies for Division I public institutions, the ten largest earning athletic programs on average serve the interests of about 632 student-athletes (range 558 to 1,004).[165]

While the median expenditure per student-athlete for 2019 was highest in the FBS autonomous schools at approximately $218,000, they receive the smallest subsidies on average because of their greater self-sufficiency. Even though the median expense per student-athlete is much lower for FBS non-autonomy (approximately $90,000), FCS (approximately $48,000), and Division I Subdivision schools (approximately $56,000), they require on average larger athletic subsidies because of the restricted capability to generate revenue. Not surprisingly, athletic departments spend far more per student-athlete than institutions spend to educate the average student.[166]

Cost-Effective Approaches to Consider

Let's face it, despite the significant expense, athletic subsidies are not going away anytime soon. While some athletic departments may occasionally eliminate a team to reduce expenses—which is usually followed by protests or lawsuits—athletics spending, for the most part, appears to be sacrosanct. So, is there anything institutional leaders can do to reign in the costs? Well, my best answer is *perhaps* rather than a definitive yes.

First, we need to accept the reality that subsidizing athletics is necessary, part of the cost of doing business, and not inappropriate. Then, it is going to take courage and leadership to ask difficult questions and strategically develop solutions that are both cost-effective and sustainable. Whereas university auxiliary–enterprise operations, such as housing, dining, and parking, are required to be totally self-sufficient and supported by student fees, most athletic programs cannot operate as auxiliaries. Those that can—such as about half of the Power Five conference schools—should, even if a modest student activity fee is necessary to provide a subsidy. For the remaining schools across the three NCAA Divisions, institutional athletic subsidies at some level will be necessary to sustain the programs.

Recognizing that athletic subsidies come largely from student tuition and fees and often as part of student loans, whether from general fund allocations or a designated student fee for athletics, some key questions for leaders to consider in grappling with growing athletic subsidies may be as follows:

How much should institutions spend on athletic subsidies?

If not already doing so, university and athletic department leaders have a responsibility to collaboratively devise a carefully planned strategy and set of expectations for determining the level of athletic subsidy to be covered centrally by student tuition and fees. Such an analysis should be objective and transparent, and must carefully consider institutional affordability, student debt, the cost-value implications across the institution, and potential opportunity costs associated with deferring alternative investments that support teaching and research—the academic core mission.

This effort should integrate athletic department goals with institutional needs and priorities rather than view them as independent or competing. To be clear, the goal of such an analysis should *not* be to simply minimize the athletic subsidy, but rather to ensure that everyone understands the rationale and performance expectations associated with the investment and the importance of stability over time. No doubt, one-time needs will periodically emerge, but if warranted they should be funded as one-time-only strategic investments. Once the subsidy level has been determined and agreed upon, the athletic department should then be expected to manage within that level of subsidy, and the institution should commit to it as well to the extent possible.

Should athletic departments be held accountable for their spending and performance?

At most institutions, vice presidents, deans, directors, chairs, and other unit budget managers are held responsible to manage and balance their budgets each year. If there is a shortfall, they must reduce expenses. If the enrollment/admissions department consistently does not bring in the class, it is held accountable, and it is likely personnel changes will be made. While there may be some unpredictable elements in athletics that can influence generated revenues, it is reasonable to expect athletic departments at most institutions to manage their resources effectively and efficiently, maintain balanced annual budgets, and live within the allocated athletic subsidy, which may mean reducing expenses some years. In so doing, agreed-upon athletic subsidies can become sustainable rather than ever-increasing. Evidence suggests that this is often not the case at present. To be sure, reductions in athletic spending and eliminating sports, if necessary, will be met by pushback from some student-athletes and parents, coaches, boosters, etc., so leaders must be prepared. As with the admissions example, athletic performance expectations have the potential to create a positive or negative ROI. So, it is not unreasonable for athletics to be held accountable for the success of their programs as well, especially for potential revenue-generating sports.

Finally, recognizing that coach compensation makes up the largest spending category (19 percent of total spending) across Division I and the NCAA, athletic departments need to be especially careful about and responsible for renegotiated coach contract increases and extensions. Coaches often wish to renegotiate the terms of their contract following one or more successful seasons, which is important to retain successful coaches. If, or perhaps when, those same coaches are fired following one or more losing seasons, the institution may become responsible for the payout of millions of dollars associated with the extended renegotiated contract on top of absorbing the salary of the new coach.

Should there be a revenue-sharing model so that the financial successes of athletic programs reduce the athletic subsidy?

The goal of institutional investments in athletics is to create and sustain winning programs that serve the best interests of the student-athletes and the athletics department and advance the mission of the institution. When teams win, whether consistently or even an occasional great season, ticket sales, NCAA and conference revenue, sponsorships, television contracts, and school spirit often spike upward and generate more revenue back to the athletic department. While it is important to ensure that incentives are aligned to encourage and reward success, it may be justified to devise a revenue-sharing plan that would reduce the athletic subsidy during years when self-generated revenue increases due to program success. The details of such a plan should be worked out in advance and should ensure that there is a net financial benefit to the athletics department in recognition of their success. The institution should also have a plan for how it would invest what might be short-term athletic subsidy savings to advance the institution, such as supporting needy students through short-term scholarships or assistance with outstanding tuition bills to aid student retention.

Management Challenges and Headaches

My Italian grandmother often claimed we grandchildren gave her *agida* when we were arguing or roughhousing with each other. *Agida* refers to feelings of anxiety, aggravation, or uneasiness, and is derived from the Italian word *acido* for acid, referring to the heartburn or indigestion after a spicy meal. Or, perhaps to heartburn, aggravation, or anxiety many leaders experience in reaction to athletic scandals, recruiting and/or Title IX violations, academic fraud, or dubious activities of a few overzealous boosters or abusive coaches. While there are certainly admissions and academic honesty issues that periodically plague some institutions (e.g., the Varsity Blues admissions scandal), it seems the frequency, visibility, and impact of athletic scandals and violations are pronounced and can tarnish institutional reputations quickly. Indeed, the fortunes and positions of some presidents have been turned upside down over athletic scandals.

Common Faculty and Student Concerns

While presidents and other senior leaders may feel the major brunt of the management challenges connected to intercollegiate athletics, chairs, deans, and trustees are often also lured into the fray. For example, it is not uncommon for faculty to complain to their chair and dean about the exorbitant salaries of some coaches or rising athletic subsidies, especially during difficult times when faculty and staff salaries are frozen or when significant cuts are made to academic programs to balance shrinking budgets. As provost, I heard those concerns on a regular basis from deans and faculty senate and union leadership as well as concerns about the perception among some of lowered or different academic expectations or standards for some student-athletes to ensure their eligibility. Furthermore, the persuasive power of strong athletic programs through popular coaches, wealthy donors, and high-profile student-athletes is seen by some as having an undue influence on decisions made by presidents or trustees. These are real issues that rightly create *agida* for leaders, undermine trust and transparency, and raise questions about institutional values and priorities.

Many students are attracted to, fully engage in, and enjoy college athletic programs at their school. This is a wonderful benefit. Students, however, often don't know how much they are directly paying to support the athletics department. With increasing concern about college affordability, loans, and debt, some students have begun to examine the details of their tuition and fees and voice concerns about being charged a designated fee for athletics. A recent example at the University of New Orleans (UNO) illustrates this point. As reported by Alonso in *Inside Higher Ed*, students at UNO overwhelmingly voted against a proposed new $300 per semester "student experience fee" that would have provided funding to support several new intercollegiate athletics programs.[167] In the largest UNO student voter turnout in over a decade, 69 percent of the students voted against the proposed fee.

Writing for *NBC News*, Enright, Lehren, and Longoria reported that four out of five Division I public universities charge students a designated fee to finance intercollegiate sports teams, excluding club sports and intramurals.[168] In 2018, the athletic fee varied from a few hundred to a couple of thousand dollars per year. Many schools with designated student athletic fees also provide an additional subsidy from the general fund, which also comes largely from tuition revenue at most institutions. Their article includes a searchable database for specific athletic fees per school. Most institutions with no designated student athletic fee, simply wrap the cost into the tuition and fee sticker price, and the athletic subsidy is allocated from the general fund. Without designated fees, it is difficult for students to discern how much of their tuition and fee payment, or student loan, is directed to subsidize athletics. This issue of cost transparency and student concerns about costs and affordability

is only going to increase and is likely to become a growing cause of headaches for leaders in the future.

Commitment to Educational Values

Despite encouraging GSR data published by the NCAA as referenced
earlier in this chapter, some question the commitment on the part of
athletic programs to ensure a quality education for student-athletes,
especially in Division I football and basketball programs. The Drake
Group, a nonprofit research-based academic think tank working to
educate the US Congress and higher education decision-makers about
critical issues in intercollegiate athletics, has boldly stated that "Division I colleges and universities are not providing the college education
promised to the athletes they recruited."[169] In support of this statement,
they report that 15,782 (40 percent) of the 39,495 Division I basketball
and football student-athletes will not graduate, including 52 percent of
Division I men's basketball, 38 percent of football, and 38 percent of
women's basketball players. Only a few make it to the professional level.
They further assert educational and economic exploitation as graduation
rates of Black football and men's and women's basketball players lag their
White peers by 6 to 10 percentage points in those same sports. Finally,
they project that many of the 23,495 who graduate may not accrue
the financial benefits of a bona fide college education because many of
these elite student-athletes were specially admitted and placed in less
demanding majors and courses to keep them eligible.

These data and assertions are deeply troubling and should be of
concern to institutional and athletic department leaders and current and
prospective student-athletes. Some will argue that many student-athletes, especially those in high-profile athletic programs, come to college
primarily to compete in their sport. Otherwise, they would have little or
no interest in attending college. Thus, they claim that the fact that they
graduate with a degree is life-changing. Rather than defaulting to such
an excuse, there needs to be increased pressure and responsibility on
institutions to ensure that athletes mature as students and get a meaningful degree that aligns with their interests. Failing to do so highlights
the tragedy of exploitation and undermines the value of education and
athletic programs. University leaders and trustees must hold athletic
departments accountable to carefully examine and report with transparency student-athlete graduation rates disaggregated by sport and

ethnicity. To the extent that problems exist, the leadership is responsible for correcting the deficiencies and providing a viable pathway for students to complete their degrees. Through a combination of a robust general education curriculum and substantive majors, student-athletes should graduate with the knowledge and skills needed for success, beyond ever making a cent as a professional athlete.

NCAA Transfer Portal and NIL: Opportunities, Risks, and Confusion

In October 2018, the NCAA Transfer Portal was created as "a compliance system to create a more efficient transfer process for student-athletes who are looking to compete for a different institution."[170] With modifications made in April 2021, the NCAA Transfer Portal allows student-athletes to maintain immediate eligibility the first time they transfer to another school provided they follow notification-of-transfer protocols and are academically eligible. Prior to the transfer portal, players that transferred schools had to sit out an entire season before being able to compete. Theoretically, they must sit out a year before playing after a second transfer, but waivers focused on student-athlete well-being or circumstances beyond their control can allow immediate eligibility. From an athletic perspective, the ability to transfer is viewed by many as positive for student-athletes, although it is unclear what the educational implications are for the students.

The portal provides an opportunity for athletes to get broad exposure and leverage their athletic skills. As such, the number of athletes entering the portal has skyrocketed. According to the January 2023 NCAA Transfer Portal Data, 11,902 student-athletes across all NCAA divisions entered the transfer portal in 2022—about 57 percent enrolled in a new school, 43 percent had not found a new school, are still looking, or have left their sport completely. For 2021, 10,129 entered the transfer portal with a similar split between those transferring or not. Of concern is the overall well-being of the student-athletes during the process, especially the 43 percent that have not found a new school. There are risks associated with entering the portal and transferring schools. Some student-athletes may not be receiving adequate guidance to make informed decisions in their own best interests regarding both their academic and athletic pursuits. For coaches and athletic programs, it has dramatically changed the landscape. Teams may have drastically different rosters of players each year. Coaches may need to teach their system from scratch each year, rebuild team spirit, continuity, and chemistry, and adopt totally new approaches and strategies toward recruiting. Emerging elite athletes coming from high school may now be competing for positions, scholarships, and playing time with experienced transfer students. There are many unknowns yet to be sorted out.

In June 2021, the Supreme Court ruled unanimously (*NCAA v. Alston*) that the NCAA could no longer restrict member institutions from offering educational-related compensation and benefits to student-athletes. Effective July 1, 2021, the landscape of intercollegiate athletics became much more complex with the adoption by the NCAA of an interim policy that allows student-athletes to benefit financially from their name, image, and likeness (NIL).[171] Players can profit from endorsements, signing autographs, selling apparel, corporate partnerships, teaching camps, starting their own businesses, and more.[172] Effectively, players have an opportunity to monetize their brand. Furthermore, they can hire professional service providers to help develop and promote NIL opportunities. Student-athletes are still considered amateurs, so schools remain prohibited from paying players directly, using money as an enticement when recruiting, or compensating student-athletes for their athletic achievements. Because NIL rules vary among states, however, and there is little transparency regarding NIL deals, it is difficult for the NCAA to enforce the rules and detect infractions by individuals or programs, including boosters and sponsors. Nevertheless, players can now be financially compensated through NIL deals, and collectives are being formed to help create NIL packages for players.

Collectives are organizations independent of the institution that pool money from boosters and businesses, facilitate NIL deals for athletes, and help athletes monetize their skills and reputations. It is unclear at this time whether such booster and business contributions to NIL deals aimed at individual student-athletes will detract from or be in addition to donations made to athletic departments or institutions. When combined with the one-time transfer rule, NIL financial packages, player interests in expanded media markets, and building their brand are analogous to "free agency" in professional sports. Star players are being lured to bigger markets by guaranteed money and playing time. While NIL has created financial opportunities for student-athletes, it has also created massive changes in college athletics and headaches for some fans, coaches, and university administrators.

The money from NIL is likely a positive outcome for many student-athletes, but are they fully prepared to manage the details of their arrangements and commitments? Student-athletes have always struggled to manage conflicts with classes, studying, travel schedules, practice, and workouts. Now they must balance NIL responsibilities along with their athletic and academic activities. While the highest-profile athletes have agencies to represent them and search for opportunities, most student-athletes are left to fend for themselves and to navigate contracts, interpret school and state regulations, and ensure compliance with tax policies. This is new and complicated terrain for the athletes, athletic departments, and university leaders, and the landscape is only likely to get more complex.

Some are advocating that colleges be required to compensate student-athletes directly, at least in lucrative sports like football and basketball, or for a revenue-sharing model among student-athletes, their institutions, and/or the NCAA. Others, such as the National Labor Relations Board, argue that student athletes should be considered employees eligible to receive benefits, such as workers compensation. The College Athlete Protection Act in California, designed to provide rights, benefits, and safeguards for college athletes, would allow, if enacted, college athletes in some California institutions to be compensated directly by their schools in alignment with revenue generated by their teams.[173] Although specific to California, its potential passage will likely have national implications. NIL has opened the door, and it is unclear how the future will unfold. The NCAA is urging Congress to develop national policy to regulate NIL.

In this new world of NIL and quasi-free agency, universities must remain committed to caring for the well-being of the student-athletes they have recruited, including those who choose to transfer elsewhere. Institutions should provide NIL education resources to inform and protect student-athletes and prospects. Failure to do so is tantamount to shifting from one form of uncompensated educational and economic exploitation of student-athletes to another built around eager businesses promising fame, fortune, and dreams of long-term prosperity. Leaders must be prepared to manage the headaches to minimize the heartache of athletes who might be led astray.

The Ball Is in Your Court

College sports can add substantial value to a university's visibility, reputation, and brand and are fundamental to building community on- and off-campus. The cost, however, to most institutions is substantial. There is little evidence to date to suggest that college spending on athletics will abate in the near term. Schools strategically switching conferences, negotiating new media contracts, and NIL-infused free agency is aimed at bringing even more money into the system. From an institutional financial perspective, this is not sustainable. From a student-athlete perspective, there are pros and cons. With increasing concern about college affordability and growing student debt, university leaders must strategically regain control of athletic subsidies generated largely from student tuition and fees. As aspiring leaders—the ball will be in your court.

PART VI

EVOLUTION OR EXTINCTION

Emerging Unknowns in a Changing Climate

Perturbations and disturbances occur in all ecosystems and are to be expected. Just as pollutants or climate change degrade natural ecosystems, enrollment declines, budget reductions, or inability to adapt or respond to stressors destabilize higher education ecosystems. Stable systems resist disruptions, persist despite the disturbance, or exhibit sufficient resilience to recover and return to their equilibrium condition. Communities must undergo continuous change or succession from less stable phases to those characterized by fresh new strategies to acquire resources and respond to emerging challenges. In some cases, whole new systems better adapted to the disruptive conditions must evolve. The nature of the disturbance may be less important than the responsiveness of leaders (i.e., how leaders anticipate and respond to stress signals). Indeed, effective leaders are prepared to address the emerging unknowns in an ever-changing climate!

CHAPTER NINETEEN

Navigating the
Political Quagmire

The intersection of politics and higher education is not new. Higher education institutions have always been engaged with issues relevant to society and active participants in divisive political issues. Whether related to the Red Scare from Senator Joseph McCarthy in the 1950s, the Vietnam War and civil rights movement protests of the 1960s and 1970s, or issues of race and racism on campuses in recent years, colleges and universities have long been engaged with and often criticized for their front-page involvement, commentary, and protests about highly partisan issues. Such issues invariably involve both faculty and students protesting, frequently together and mostly peacefully, to express their contrary voices about divisive issues. The partisan issues of today, however, are more pervasive, mean-spirited, and extend from partisan politicians to a growing proportion of the citizenry—the voters.

Universities are also well-known for their own brand of campus politics. To be clear, the campus politics I am referring to here is not so much about partisan political differences, although there is that too. Campus politics usually centers around faculty governance or competition among colleges and departments for attention or resources, and the interpersonal squabbles among faculty related to their ideas, workload, personalities, and seniority. *The Chair*, a recent Netflix series, illustrates this latter campus politics through a satirical depiction of faculty and campus cultures, including coverage of serious issues such as racism, sexism, ageism, and free speech.

While the campus political issues highlighted in *The Chair* are important and worthy of attention, external interference and regulation imposed on colleges and universities by highly partisan state and federal legislative bodies, and individual politicians have the potential to undermine the meaning, purpose, and impact of higher education, especially for public institutions. To be sure, higher education leaders and institutions can't singlehandedly solve the political divide that exists today. They must, however, find a way to communicate clearly and persuasively about the importance and benefits of higher education to state and local communities, society broadly, and students without becoming embroiled in damaging political discord. At times leaders must take a stand on issues consistent with core institutional goals and values. Identifying and walking this fine line is a critically important and delicate challenge for campus leaders.

Politics and Higher Education

We now live in a highly polarized society; every issue and opportunity, including a college education, divides along partisan lines. Prior to 2016, according to survey data from the Pew Research Center, a majority (60 to 63 percent) of people of both political parties had positive perceptions of higher education.[174] By 2019, only 50 percent of American adults felt colleges were having a positive effect on the country, and 38 percent, up from 26 percent in 2012, believed colleges were having a negative effect. This change was distinctly linked to partisanship, as Republicans' positive perceptions dropped from 54 percent to 33 percent between 2015 and 2019, while Democrats' positive perceptions remained stable at nearly 70 percent.[175] A recent 2022 survey conducted by New America found that 73 percent of Democrats and 37 percent of Republicans believe that higher education is leading the country in a positive direction, although Democrats and Republicans share concerns about the cost of a college education.[176] Confidence in higher education is eroding, and there are substantial partisan differences in the rate of that decline. A recent Gallup poll released in June 2023 shows that US adults' confidence in higher education among Republicans declined from 56 percent in 2015 to 19 percent in 2023, while confidence among Democrats declined from 68 to 59 percent.[177]

So, what is the basis for this clearcut partisan divide, and are there institutional implications? Writing for *The Chronicle of Higher Education,*

Eric Kelderman persuasively asserts that the college degree is dividing the country.[178] That is, education level has become equated with political party affiliation and voting patterns. Society has drifted apart along educational lines. The recent Gallup poll shows a steep 25 percentage point decline in confidence in higher education from 2015 to 2023 among those without a college degree compared to a 10 percent decline among those with a college degree. There is a recent pattern of many White voters with less formal education embracing a populist agenda and aligning with Republicans, while more college-educated White voters and most Black voters have favored Democrats. In 2022, for example, 63 percent of Republican voters did not have a college degree compared to 49 percent of Democrat voters, and White voters without college degrees comprise 54 percent of Republican voters compared to 27 percent of Democrat voters.[179] Higher education has become a fulcrum for resentment that has resonated in Republican politics and become fodder for culture wars, creating a conservative backlash against higher education. This is partly about perceptions, but also economic realities, among some of the working class who feel they have been left behind by an economy favoring the educational elite.

At the same time, Kelderman notes that political rhetoric is feeding a perception that liberal faculty are trying to indoctrinate students through their teaching by telling them what to do, say, and think and squelching free speech on campus, thereby influencing students' political affiliations. While there is certainly evidence that most faculty and students are somewhat left-leaning, faculty ideology is not uniform and varies to some degree regionally and by discipline.[180] As noted by Abrams and Khalid, largely left-leaning professors should not automatically be interpreted as colleges being unwelcoming to right-leaning students and colleagues.[181] Most faculty make a concerted effort to expose students to a range of viewpoints, and research has shown there is little evidence of grading bias for conservative versus liberal students.[182]

Nevertheless, Abrams and Khalid share that most students regardless of ideology are reluctant to express their opinion on controversial topics (i.e., they self-censor).[183] More Republican students self-censor than Democrats, but the primary reason for self-censorship among all students is concern that other students will criticize their views. In summarizing research on campus political bias, Jaschik suggests that "student beliefs are surprisingly resilient," and the "vast majority complete their education with their views largely intact."[184] There is little evidence that faculty or campus politics is changing the political views of students. Yet that perception is pervasive among many conservatives, leading to further societal polarization and an erosion of support for higher education among elected Republicans in state and federal governments. Higher education has already struggled with reduced state and federal support and can ill afford further disinvestment stimulated by political discord.

Furthermore, some public institution and system governing boards, often selected by governors or legislatures, have become increasingly partisan and are expected to carry out the political agenda of the party in office, including selecting chancellors and presidents sympathetic to political leaders. This can be especially problematic in situations where increasingly closed searches for institutional leaders allow no or limited input about candidates from the academic community. To be clear, this can occur in both parties and compromises the board's critical governance role to ensure fulfillment of the mission and act in the best interests of the institution. Leaders need to find ways to expand access to higher education, support student success and degree completion, carefully manage the fine line of politics, and demonstrate the benefits of a college education not only to individuals earning degrees or other credentials but also for economic development and quality of life in states and local communities. While higher education leaders may need to refrain from direct antagonistic politicization of issues, they must vocally stand up for institutional values, shared governance regarding curricular content and pedagogy, academic freedom of inquiry and expression, and a core belief in factual information derived from sound science and thoughtful analysis.

Challenging Academic Freedom and Tenure

Academic freedom is a hallmark of the American system of higher education. Academic scholars have the freedom and responsibility to develop and share important new ideas, encourage critical analysis and thinking, challenge conventional wisdom and leaders, and promote innovation and opportunity. Political interference that constrains such freedom of inquiry and expression threatens democracy as well as a basic tenet of higher education. Neither our universities nor the country benefits by constraining the unbridled pursuit of new knowledge and understanding. A scholar's role is not to protect the ideas, agendas, or policies of elected officials and institutional leaders, but rather to objectively seek and advance truth, bold new perspectives, and informed learning. This is not a privilege of the teacher-scholar, but a responsibility. Just as a free press is essential to democracy, integrity, and accountability of elected leaders, academic freedom is an essential ingredient for civil democratic society and economic prosperity.

Academic leaders must understand and reinforce, however, that the responsibility that comes with academic freedom flows in two directions. Faculty have a responsibility grounded in their academic and scholarly competence to seek and disseminate truth. That is, professors have the "freedom to pursue the scholar's profession according to the standards of the profession" as articulated by former Yale Law School Dean Robert Post.[185] Equally as important, however, they also have a responsibility to refrain from misusing the power of their positions and academic freedom to exploit or manipulate students, espouse hate or violence, or publicly and purposefully attack, demean, or harm those whose views differ from their own. In fact, the latter behavior, although perhaps permissible under the first amendment right to free expression, is incompatible with academic freedom and opens the door to the exact political interference and attempts to silence scholars that we rightly find so intrusive.

In contrast with academic freedom, Post describes freedom of speech as an individual right of citizens and academic freedom as the right of the profession to determine what is true or not "by a scholar's method and . . . a scholar's spirit."[186] Thus, academic freedom is not unconditional and applies to a "community of inquiry" that serves "a public trust to create and disseminate knowledge" distinct from individual rights. Freedom of speech, too, has become highly politicized with assertions by some that liberal ideology curbs the free speech of conservative faculty and students. To effectively defend academic freedom, leaders must have the courage to support faculty members' academic freedom of thought and inquiry and, at the same time, condemn any blatant manipulation and misuse of that privilege and uphold standards of professional ethics.

As captured in the 1940 *Statement of Principles on Academic Freedom and Tenure* formulated by the American Association of University Professors and the Association of American Colleges (now the Association of American Colleges and Universities), "the common good depends upon the free search for truth and its free exposition."[187] As part of the politicization of higher education, this "common good" is being challenged by some aggressive legislatures, governors, and board members who are attempting to control, regulate, or censor through legislation or intimidation the subject matter that faculty can teach or the scholarship that they can share. Among many issues, this includes politically motivated prohibitions of public health-recommended mask or vaccine mandates during pandemics, banning of books, limitation of academic scholars testifying about proposed new voting laws, or restrictions on the teaching of so-called "divisive concepts," including diversity training programs, systemic racism, the nation's racial history, and critical race theory. Such politically charged interference restricts educational opportunities, compromises truth, and undermines democratic governance.

The partisan politics of higher education has also led to direct attacks on the tenure system, which has been the foundation of US higher education for nearly a century. Once awarded, tenure allows for lifetime faculty appointments, except in rare cases of institutional financial exigency or just cause, such as incompetence, violation of institutional policies, immoral conduct, or negligence. In spring 2023, the Texas Senate approved a bill that would ban tenure for all new hires, although the House voted to reform rather than eliminate tenure. As reported in *Inside Higher Ed*, the reformed tenure system added "unprofessional conduct that adversely affects the institution" as a reason tenured professors can be terminated without providing clear definition of such conduct.[188] Such vague language may open the door to termination of tenured faculty for doing or saying things at odds with state or university leaders, which is the type of threat that tenure is supposed to protect. Legislatures in several other states have also introduced legislation to weaken or ban tenure in their public institutions. The largely partisan rationale often involves assertions that the tenure system limits budgetary and programmatic flexibility and organizational efficiency. That is, resources get locked in areas that may no longer be strategic or relevant at the expense of investments in new student learning needs and programs of societal or economic importance. In addition, there are old arguments that tenure allows underperforming faculty to persist and liberal faculty to somehow indoctrinate students politically.

Academics argue that tenure is necessary to protect academic freedom and to fend off the exact partisan attacks and attempts at censorship of teachers, scholars, and academic leaders that are occurring increasingly today, especially surrounding DEI issues. That is, tenure ostensibly protects faculty members from political interference or recrimination for academic work that may be viewed as controversial, unpopular, or challenging to the administration or elected officials. As originally established, the rationale for tenure was also explicitly to offer "a sufficient degree of economic security to make the profession attractive to men and women of ability."[189] This latter rationale should not be overlooked. If some state legislatures are successful in undermining tenure, faculty positions in public institutions in those states will be less attractive, and many highly productive faculty will be lured to tenure-track positions at private institutions or public institutions in other states. Also, to remain competitive in attracting faculty talent, institutions without the possibility of offering tenure will likely have to pay substantially higher salaries to attract new hires with the potential for a tenured position elsewhere.

The academic freedom and economic security arguments are relevant and compelling but may not carry the day with conservative legislatures and governors in the future, especially for those who view academics as the enemy. After all, currently, there are more nontenure track than tenure track faculty in the higher education workforce. In 2021, 32 percent of faculty were either tenured or tenure-track compared to 53 percent in 1987.[190] Nontenure track faculty too are afforded academic freedom, although their job security is more malleable. To bolster the argument for tenure, academic leaders and faculty must work together to ensure that tenure does not become an entitlement and that tenured faculty remain engaged, contemporary, and productive in the future. Ensuring fair, thorough, and objective evidence-based review is a positive step toward accomplishing this goal (see chapter 9). Given job security, tenured faculty need to exhibit the courage to explore new and different modalities and strategies in teaching and compelling new avenues of relevant academic scholarship. Ensuring expectations for excellence in teaching, research and scholarship, and service along with maintaining high standards in faculty reviews and the awarding of tenure may be the best way to recognize our most consistently productive faculty and sustain the protections of academic freedom and economic security afforded by tenure.

Issues of academic freedom and tenure must be responsibly managed on campus by knowledgeable parties, not by partisans in state houses, governor's mansions, or in board rooms. Courageous leaders will need to persuasively defend this principle, as the fundamental protections of tenure are worth preserving. Given the gradual erosion of tenure and the imminent political threats, however, the next generation of leaders should work collaboratively with faculty to explore bold new approaches to tenure that preserve the essential protection of academic freedom and the recognition of faculty expertise and accomplishments. This might include, for example, tenure with covenants between the institution and faculty or long-term fixed period (e.g., twenty-five years) tenured appointments with periodic reviews (e.g., every five years) that might address concerns about complacency and programmatic rigidity while still protecting academic freedom. There are no doubt other viable models as well. What doesn't appear viable is simply observing the gradual demise of tenure and hoping that voicing concerns will reverse course.

The Politics of Higher Education Policy

Title IX Regulations

Partisan politics is also shaping higher education policy and practice. Perhaps there is no better example than Title IX regulations, which have undergone a decade of political flip-flopping as each new administration reverses previous policies and changes rules and guidance, leaving institutions struggling to comply in a constantly changing political landscape. Writing for *The Chronicle of Higher Education*, Bellows highlights the partisan dynamics leading to changes to Title IX over time and key elements of the Biden administration's latest proposal.[191] In 2011, the Obama administration issued guidance requiring colleges to respond to sexual violence, including protections for transgender students, under Title IX or risk investigation by the Office of Civil Rights and the potential to lose federal funding. In response, many institutions created Title IX offices and hired new staff. In 2017, the Trump administration codified protections for accused students, drawing criticism from victims' rights groups, and threw out the Obama directive to protect transgender students, even though they are disproportionately affected by campus sexual misconduct.

The Biden administration's proposal reverses many of the Trump-era policies, adds protections for sexual orientation and gender identity, restores a pro-victim approach, and broadens the definition of sexual harassment under Title IX to "all forms of sex-based harassment." The Trump administration narrowed the definition to behavior that is "severe, pervasive, and objectively offensive." Biden's proposed regulations would reduce the live-hearing requirement of the previous administration that allowed cross-examination of both victims and the accused and balance the rights of survivors and the accused. Instead of focusing efforts on preventing sexual assaults on campus and sensitively responding when they do occur, the constant politically motivated rule changes and compliance regulations continue to upend how colleges handle sexual misconduct complaints and leaves institutions and victims caught in a political tug-of-war.

During the 2020 presidential campaign, Biden pledged to overturn Trump administration changes to Title IX in response to pleas from advocacy organizations for immediate action. Now, more than two and half years after Biden took office, his proposed new rulings still have not been codified, leaving the Trump-era rules in place. There is growing frustration among schools, who will once again need to invest time and resources on training, and advocates for survivors of sexual assault about the delays and partisan rulemaking processes for issuing new Title IX regulations.

Race-Conscious Admissions Policy

Race-conscious admissions policy has once again become a hot-button partisan issue at the level of the Supreme Court. At issue is whether it is constitutional for selective institutions to consider a student's race as one factor in a holistic review process to create a more diverse student body that enriches the learning environment for all students. While the Supreme Court ruled in 1978 in *University of California v. Bakke* that the use of racial quotas in admissions is unconstitutional, it has consistently ruled in *University of California v. Bakke, Grutter v. Bollinger* in 2003, and *Fisher v. University of Texas* in 2016 that race may be considered in the admissions process along with other factors because it serves a "compelling interest" in promoting and supporting a diverse student body on campuses.

Empirical information reinforces the efficacy of those rulings. The elimination of affirmative action due to bans in several states led to persistent declines in the proportion of racially and ethnically diverse students admitted to and enrolling in public flagship universities in those states, despite the implementation of alternative policies designed to replace race-based affirmative action in admissions and demographic growth of underrepresented students in those states.[192] For example, proposition 209 banned race-conscious admissions at California public universities in 1998. Following the ban, Black and Hispanic student enrollment dropped at selective public institutions, such as UCLA and

UC Berkeley. At UC Berkeley, Black and Hispanic student enrollment dropped 50 percent immediately following the ban.[193] Other states also experienced reductions in Black, Hispanic, and Native American enrollment at selective institutions after state bans. At the University of Florida, for example, Black student enrollment dropped to 6 percent twenty years after the ban, which is 15 percentage points below Florida's college-age Black population in 2020.[194] Over the long-term, the California ban relegated many Black, Hispanic, and Native American students to less selective institutions, leading to poorer education outcomes, such as lower graduation rates, degree attainment in STEM fields, graduate school enrollment, and reduced economic mobility.[195]

In October 2022, the Supreme Court heard arguments in *Students for Fair Admissions, Inc. v. President and Fellows of Harvard College* and *Students for Fair Admissions, Inc v. University of North Carolina at Chapel Hill (UNC)*. Lower courts had upheld the admissions processes at Harvard and UNC and rejected claims that the institutions discriminated against White and Asian American students. The Supreme Court agreed to hear the case despite strong support for continuing race-conscious admissions from the higher education community and compelling evidence of the positive impact of race-conscious admissions on student diversity. According to a Pew Research Center survey, even though 85 percent of Americans say it is very or somewhat important for colleges and universities to have a diverse student body, 73 percent believe race should not be a factor in admissions decisions.[196] Despite this belief, a May 2023 poll from the Associated Press—NORC Center for Public Affairs Research found that 63 percent say the Supreme Court should not prevent colleges from considering race or ethnicity in admissions.[197]

Forty higher education organizations signed a brief of *amici curiae* making the case for the value of considering race and ethnicity as part of a holistic admissions process in colleges and universities. The brief was filed by the American Council of Education (ACE) and thirty-nine other higher education organizations to the Supreme Court for their consideration on August 1, 2022.[198] Emphasizing that "racial and ethnic identity plays a role in life experiences, leadership skills, and potential campus contributions," the brief argues that excluding race and ethnicity "would chill student expression, deprive a subset of applicants of the full benefits of holistic review," and confront students of color with "the unenviable choice of declining to speak of their ethnicity or race or speaking and being ignored."[199] At the same time, students discussing "socio-economic status, gender, age, disability, or experiences as veterans, musicians, or first-generation learners, all could speak freely."[200] In support of furthering the consideration of race and ethnicity in admissions, the higher education organizations emphasized that "it is the pluralism of institutions across the country that makes our system of higher education the greatest in the world."[201]

Reversing more than four decades of legal precedent, the Supreme Court, on June 29, 2023, ruled that race-conscious admission processes used at Harvard University and the University of North Carolina at Chapel Hill violate the equal-protection clause of the Fourteenth Amendment to the US Constitution. The ruling, however, isn't really about Harvard or UNC Chapel Hill. That is, while alumni, donors, and faculty offspring, who are mostly White, and athletic recruit status can continue to be considered as factors in admissions, applicant race and ethnicity can no longer be considered a factor, creating additional obstacles for many vulnerable students. This contradiction is disturbing. The decision has nationwide implications for selective private and public institutions that have considered race as a factor in admissions. For reasons that are not entirely clear, military academies were exempted from the ruling. Although silent on consideration of race in awarding financial aid or scholarships, it is possible, even likely, that interpretations of this ruling will be extended in some states to eliminate race-influenced financial aid, which would be devastating to efforts to diversify the student body. While banning consideration of race in admissions impacts selective institutions, financial aid and scholarships that consider race are offered at many more institutions.

Given such persuasive arguments from leading higher education organizations and the documented efficacy of race-conscious admissions toward enhancing diversity, student success, and economic mobility, why would the court change its position now after forty-five years? The answer once again appears to be rooted in partisan politics. The Supreme Court ruling was divided along ideological lines with six conservative justices ruling to strike down race-conscious admission and three liberal justices dissenting. At a time when institutions need to do even more to recruit, retain, and educate diverse populations of students and the future societal workforce, a powerful tool proven to enhance educational value and opportunities for underrepresented student populations has been taken off the table.

At the time of this writing, it is unclear how institutions will respond to this ruling. Because the ruling does not preclude students from discussing experiences related to their race and ethnicity in the admission process, some institutions may craft essay prompts for students to address their experiences overcoming challenges, whether related to discrimination, financial or health difficulties, or personal traumas. I expect, however, that efforts to glean an assessment of student "character" from race-related experiences in student essays will be litigated at some point. In addition, some may choose to eliminate or make optional the use of standardized tests in admissions, sometimes referred to as *the wealth test*, to help level the playing field among applicants. Institutions wishing to capture the benefits of a diverse student body may refocus recruitment efforts and strategies on communities of color and transfer students from community colleges and ensure a welcoming climate on campus for all students. Furthermore, institutions may need to provide enhanced support for first-generation students and applicants from economically disadvantaged backgrounds and discontinue preferences for legacy applicants that give an unfair advantage to children of wealthy alumni and donors.

Higher Education Funding

While there is a uniform concern across political party lines about the cost of college education, there are highly polarized perspectives about the responsibility for funding higher education. Based on a Pew Research Center survey, 85 percent of Democrats and Democrat-leaning independents favor free public college tuition for all American students, while only 36 percent of Republican and Republican-leaning independents support free tuition at public colleges.[202] More specifically, the New America Varying Degrees 2022 survey asked US adults who should fund higher education—government, because society benefits, or students, because they benefit personally.[203] Not surprisingly, Democrats and Republicans remain deeply divided in their response; 77 percent of Democrats believe government should fund higher education because it is good for society, while 63 percent of Republicans say students should fund their education beyond high school because they personally benefit.

This major partisan divide in values about who benefits from and should be responsible for higher education gets to the core of the "high cost" problem in higher education and the challenge of devising an equitable and rational national or state-based funding model. Ramping up federal Pell Grant funding would be a critical first step in a revised funding model. Leaders must, nevertheless, tackle this issue to override partisan perspectives and demonstrate the many ways that a college education and higher education research and development benefit society, including contributions to local and state economic development, employment, and quality of life.

Recognizing student loan debt as a significant societal problem, the Biden administration proposed one-time student loan debt relief of up to $20,000 for Pell Grant recipients with loans held by the Department of Education and up to $10,000 in debt relief to non-Pell Grant recipients with individual income less than $125,000 or $250,000 for households. The debt relief would apply only to loan balances prior to June 30, 2022. The plan was politically charged and controversial and would only be helpful to individuals with current student loans. That is, it does not address the overall cost of higher education or provide a solution for prospective students considering college in the future. Some saw it as politically motivated on the part of Democrats to attract student support. Others believed it was too costly, unfair, and a "good management penalty" of sorts (see chapter 3) for families that either saved for college, had no loans, and now would have to pay through their taxes to bail out others or for those who were unable or unwilling to take out loans to attend college—all compelling arguments. Of about 43 million qualified for the student debt relief program, 26 million people had applied and 16 million were approved before it was curtailed by a federal court ruling that the administration did not have the authority to forgive student loans to eligible applicants. The loan forgiveness program would have cost about $430 billion. An appeals court issued an injunction in response to a legal challenge brought by six states claiming the administration does not have the legal authority to cancel student loan debt and that the plan may harm state revenues and organizations that service student loans.

In *Biden v. Nebraska*, the Supreme Court ruled in a six-to-three decision along ideological lines on June 30, 2023, that President Biden does not have the authority to forgive student loans under the Higher Education Relief Opportunities for Students (HEROES) Act of 2003. The Secretary of Education argued that the HEROES Act allowed the Department to "waive or modify" the student loan program so that borrowers affected by a national emergency, such as war, military operations, or the COVID-19 pandemic, are not negatively impacted financially. The court rejected that argument. While support for the debt relief plan was divided among the public as well as politicians, it nevertheless illustrates the politicization of the Supreme Court as the six conservative justices sided with the Republican attorneys general from the six states that challenged the plan.

As political machinations played out in government and the courts, student borrowers were left in a financially vulnerable position. Whether you support the plan and court outcome or not, some of the 43 million student borrowers deemed qualified for debt relief under the plan, and especially the 16 million who were already approved, may now be subject to economic harm as they resume their loan payments in fall 2023 after a three-year pandemic pause. The Consumer Financial Protection Bureau reports that about 8 percent of student loan borrowers are behind in other payment obligations (e.g., credit cards), 20 percent have two or more risk factors that indicate they will struggle to make their student loan payments, and median scheduled payments on other debt obligations have increased by 24 percent.[204] Rising costs due to inflation and higher interest rates certainly have contributed to these challenges. The rise in non-student loan delinquencies now exceeds pre-pandemic levels, which means more borrowers will be at risk of defaulting when student loan payments resume in fall 2023. It is feared that millions of student loan borrowers will default and experience serious financial distress, blocking their path to social and economic mobility, such as earning advanced degrees, purchasing a home, or starting a business. Indeed, it appears that politics may exacerbate financial challenges for many already economically disadvantaged students.

To provide some student debt relief for low-income borrowers, the Biden administration announced a new income-driven payment plan—Save on a Valuable Education (SAVE)—in August 2023. The plan determines payments based on a borrower's income and family size rather than loan balance, prevents balances from growing due to unpaid interest, and may forgive remaining balances for some after a certain number of years. The administration asserts it is the "most affordable loan repayment program ever that will lower monthly payments" and "benefit 20 million borrowers."[205]

Bans on Teaching "Divisive Concepts"—Systemic Racism and Critical Race Theory

Partisan politics rather than academic goals, student learning outcomes, and scholarly content and expertise is attempting to drive teaching, learning, and scholarship related to race, racism, and social justice. Perhaps there is no better example of partisan political attempts at hostage-taking than political machinations related to DEI, which seems to have become synonymous with critical race theory (CRT) to some politicians. This discussion is not intended to demonize any individual or political party or praise or denigrate CRT, but rather to highlight the danger and dysfunction of attempts at politically sponsored censorship, historical revision, and content agenda-setting in relation to higher education. That is, the process of using legislation and political threats, such as withholding funding or direct attacks on institutions or individuals, or political appointees to boards to prevent teaching about race and racism or ban DEI programs. At present, legislatures in twenty-two states have proposed legislation that would minimize or eliminate DEI efforts on public college campuses.[206]

On September 22, 2020, then-President Trump signed a highly partisan and controversial executive order "Combating Race and Sex Stereotyping" (EO 13950) that directly threatened efforts to address racial disparities in the workplace. The order was aimed at government agencies, nonprofits, and any institution that has federal contracts or plans to apply for them in the future, including educational institutions. The stated purpose of the executive order was "to combat offensive and anti-American race and sex stereotyping." The target of the executive order was to ban the use of "divisive concepts" in diversity training programs and, in particular, to disallow the teaching of CRT, a body of knowledge and scholarly work with intellectual origins in place for more than forty years. This so-called "equity gag order" from the administration was a direct attack on academic freedom and freedom of expression as well as significant partisan political interference aimed at scholarly content and curriculum based on political viewpoints rather than expertise.

On January 20, 2021, on his first day in office, President Biden signed an executive order "Advancing Racial Equity and Support for Underserved Communities Through the Federal Government" (EO 13985) that revoked the Trump executive order and rescinded the restrictions on diversity training. The Biden order went further to instruct the federal government to "pursue a comprehensive approach to advancing equity for all, including people of color and others who have been historically underserved, marginalized, and adversely affected by persistent poverty and inequality, . . . recognize and redress inequities in their policies and programs that serve as barriers to equal opportunity." While the Biden executive order may have reversed the Trump mandate, it did not bring an end to political assaults on curriculum, teaching about race and racism, CRT, and efforts to ban DEI initiatives in higher education. Many states jumped into the fray.

In April 2023, North Dakota enacted without fanfare anti-DEI legislation referred to as a "specific concepts" bill that bans numerous DEI programs and concepts in public higher education. Similarly, the Texas legislature approved a bill in May 2023 that would ban universities from having or creating diversity offices, hiring employees to conduct DEI work, requiring DEI training, or asking job applicants how they consider diversity in their work. At the same time, the governor of Florida signed legislation prohibiting public colleges and universities from spending on DEI programs unless required by federal law. The new law also politicizes the curriculum by banning institutions from offering general education courses that "distort significant historical events," teach "identity politics" or are "based on theories that systemic racism, sexism, oppression, or privilege are inherent in the institutions of the United States." Is highly partisan legislation really the best way to determine teaching and learning priorities at our institutions and to establish a local or national education agenda?

A year earlier and with much fanfare, the governor of Florida signed the Individual Freedom Act, a.k.a. the Stop Woke Act, into law. The Florida law prohibits teaching that one race is morally superior to another, teachers making students feel guilty for past discrimination, and portraying color-blindness as racist. A basic premise is that teachers are "forcing discriminating concepts on students." It also portends to "protect Florida workers against the hostile work environment that is created when large corporations force their employees to endure CRT-inspired training and indoctrination." Because the Individual Freedom Act is state law, instructors perceived to be in violation of the law might have their jobs threatened or face legal risks, and institutions may lose their state funding.

Another bill (HB 233) was passed in Florida in June 2021 purportedly to protect "intellectual freedom and viewpoint diversity" at public higher institutions, which requires an annual assessment of students and employees at those institutions. The premise and concern are that faculty are indoctrinating students with liberal ideas and squelching alternative viewpoints. It seems contradictory, however, that efforts to protect "intellectual freedom and viewpoint diversity" would aim to stifle the teaching of purported "divisive concepts." The Florida Department of Education took further steps in January 2023, prohibiting the offering of a new pilot Advanced Placement (AP) high school course in African American Studies developed by the College Board claiming that it "lacks educational value." The College Board describes the course as a "rich and inspiring exploration of African American history and culture." It seems any subject matter related to race, ethnicity, and gender in Florida, and many other states as well, has become synonymous with indoctrination and CRT and has become a target of state government. This form of censorship is not only a violation of academic freedom but also deprives students of comprehensive learning about history and culture, which undermines educational opportunity and the ability of young people to establish their own independent and informed beliefs and values.

The first annual assessment of students and employees in Florida's public universities, which some claimed was a politically motivated and biased survey with relatively low response rates (2.4 percent for students; 9.4 percent for employees), was released in August 2022.[207] The results were made publicly available online.[208] "Intellectual Freedom and Viewpoint Diversity 2022 Survey at Florida's Twelve Public Universities— Selected Results" highlights the results from some of the many questions designed to elucidate the nature and extent of the so-called indoctrination problem. While one may draw their own conclusions from these results, it certainly appears that most students and employees that responded across the twelve public institutions believe their campuses provide an environment for the free expression of ideas, which raises questions about the real purpose of the Individual Freedom Act. The answer to those questions is buried in the morass of mean-spirited politics driving higher education policy today. At the time of this writing, seven states have approved legislation restricting their public higher education institutions from teaching or training programs related to DEI. Several other states have passed similar content restrictions for K-12 education, state agencies, and/or employers.

Intellectual Freedom and Viewpoint Diversity 2022 Survey at Florida's Twelve Public Universities—Selected Results

Surveys were distributed to 368,120 students; of those, 8,835 responded for a response rate of 2.4 percent. In addition, surveys were sent to 98,704 employees, including faculty and staff; of those, 9,238 responded for a response rate of 9.4 percent.

Student Question: "My college or university *campus* provides an environment for free expression of ideas, opinions, and beliefs."

Results: A total of 62 percent of respondents strongly agreed (32 percent) or agreed (30 percent), while a total of 20 percent of respondents strongly disagreed (8 percent) or disagreed (12 percent).

Student Question: "My college or university *classes* provide an environment for free expression of ideas, opinions, and beliefs."

Results: A total of 60 percent of respondents strongly agreed (31 percent) or agreed (29 percent), while a total of 22 percent of respondents strongly disagreed (8 percent) or disagreed (14 percent).

Employee Question: "Students at my institution are encouraged to consider a wide variety of viewpoints and perspectives."

Results: A total of 60 percent of respondents strongly agreed (32 percent) or agreed (28 percent), while a total of 20 percent of respondents strongly disagreed (7 percent) or disagreed (13 percent).

Employee Question: "I see examples of free and welcomed expression (such as speeches, debates with other students or instructors, class assignments, etc.) on my campus regularly."

Results: A total of 56 percent of respondents strongly agreed (28 percent) or agreed (28 percent), while a total of 21 percent of respondents strongly disagreed (6 percent) or disagreed (15 percent).

Faculty Question: "Students in my classes are exposed to competing arguments and multiple perspectives on a topic."

Results: A total of 74 percent of respondents strongly agreed (43 percent) or agreed (31 percent), while a total of 9 percent of respondents strongly disagreed (3 percent) or disagreed (6 percent).

Order Date	Phone #	Customer PO	Order
9/23/2024	7814398368	ECOM-12047868-1	ECOM-120

Quantity	SKU	Title
1	9798986282176	Substance Over Style: A Field Guide to Leadersh
		ECOM-12047868-1 1

Total Quantity: 1

Ship To:

Quenby Olmsted Hughes
90 Brown Street
PROVIDENCE, RI   02906

Shipping Order No.
74261907-70465JS

DI   L1Q1   70465JS

Page: 1 of 1
9/25/2024

Ship To #: 25

...er	Ref#			CTN Type	CTN Qty
8-1	Don D Hardcover for	Ship Via: USPS Media Basic			
n Higher Ed				1	NA

Regardless of your perspective about CRT, most colleges and universities offer courses that address issues related to race and ethnicity, as they should. Some offer majors, minors, or certificates in social justice or related themes. These are topics with a deep body of scholarly literature gathered through research that has been debated and critiqued, which should be shared to inform and create learning leading to a better world. Frankly, education on these subjects is sorely needed in society. We live in a multicultural world, and our institutions of higher education have a responsibility to develop and inspire an informed workforce for the future prepared to contribute to a global economy and society. This includes understanding the history of race and racism, respect for difference, and the ability to work collectively to create a better world. This is exactly why many agencies and corporations have developed and invested in diversity training programs for their employees—a diverse and informed workforce is a more productive and creative one.

Finally, opening the door to curricular content dictated by Democrat or Republican partisans through executive orders or federal or state laws is frightening and fraught with problems. What's next? Might some political leaders, state legislatures, or extremist board members ban teaching and research about the holocaust, evolution, vaccines, or climate change because these topics make them uncomfortable, clash with their worldview or upbringing, or are counter to their personal agenda or economic well-being? It is not only possible but likely given the polarization in society today and the disdain that has emerged among partisans. Higher education leaders must be responsible voices for essential learning and, at the same time, ensure that ideas challenge students to think and debate responsibly rather than force them to conform to a singular line of reasoning and thought.

Walking the Fine Line—Finding Your Voice in the Political Morass

Higher education leaders not only have the responsibility to protect their programs and institutions, but also the responsibility to profess with clarity and integrity and role model behavior that inspires students, staff, and faculty on their campuses. Does that mean leaders should engage directly in political discourse and partisan politics? Not necessarily! To be clear, there must be room for leaders and board members with an array of political viewpoints—Republicans, Democrats, Independents,

Progressives, and Conservatives—in our institutions. Their political ideology, however, should be separate from their leadership roles and responsibilities. In private they get to cast their political vote any way they wish, but as university leaders, they should not be publicly advocating for or against certain candidates or parties and should remain independent from any formal political association. It is neither necessary nor helpful to do so and inappropriately conflates an individual's perspective with an institutional political position. Furthermore, board members who place their political affiliations over institutional priorities and well-being compromise board functionality and create difficulty for the senior leadership and management of the institution.

Higher education leaders, however, must speak openly and clearly about issues, proposed legislation, or assertions that directly impact their mission, operations, core values, or community. That certainly would include politically motivated infringements on academic freedom; interference in curricular content, educational delivery, or independence of scholarly research; mandates regarding criteria for awarding academic credit and degrees; and compromises to the pursuit and sharing of truth, even when it is counter to staunch partisan positions. The leader's role is not just to advocate for these mission-central positions, but to make clear to the public and the politicians the reasons why such positions are integral to the mission, student learning, work of the faculty, and democracy. Our goal in speaking up or calmly offering lucid testimony to state or federal legislative bodies should be to create an understanding of the academic core mission and the issue at hand, not simply to defend a counter viewpoint—always the mark of a good teacher. For instance, this might include illustrating the importance of students understanding systemic racism and social justice as preparation to live and work in a multicultural world; the benefits of technology-enriched teaching and learning; the devastating human resource and educational implications of budget reductions; the compelling data and stories that demonstrate opportunity and equity from race-conscious admissions; and the many ways that the unbridled pursuit of truth through scholarly research has changed the world for the better.

Simply stating we are right, you are wrong is not sufficient. In fact, such strident advocacy mimics the accusations being made about our institutions that we find so frustrating. We must do better. We may not change the minds of partisan politicians who refuse to listen to our explanations, but, if done well, we will *teach* the public about our institutions' thoughtful work and enormous impact. Indeed, our leaders must be thoughtful teachers who have earned the right to profess because of their integrity, staunch belief in the value of education and its purpose, and persuasive eloquence.

What about the larger societal impacts of extreme partisan political positions that extend far beyond our institutions? Should higher education leaders weigh in as prominent citizens to stimulate discourse and inform the public good? Once again, it's tricky and there is a fine line to walk. Knowledgeable leaders should certainly speak out in favor of facts and scientific knowledge that confronts misinformation that has become purposely entangled in local or national dialogues. Leaders have a bully pulpit and academic credibility and should use that platform to squelch dangerous politicized misinformation, such as the extremist rejection of the public health benefits of masks and vaccines, strong evidence for climate change, evolution in favor of creationism, or the devastating implications of slavery, the holocaust, and mass shootings in schools and other venues. While leaders may be speaking as experts on these and other matters, they also are representing their institution, which is fine when they are conveying factual information.

It becomes trickier, however, when the dialogue is about an opinion or one's viewpoint, which reflects a value judgment. When any members of the university community broadcast their opinion on contentious matters, they should make it clear that they are speaking for themselves and not for the institution. That space, however, becomes murky when it is the president, provost, trustee, or dean speaking because their institutional title and role become conflated with their opinion whether they intend for it to do so or not. Like it or not, their opinion is viewed as representing the institution's position on the contentious issue, which may be offensive to some or many within their own community with different deeply held convictions. Such opinion statements can create internal dissension and a social media firestorm that serves to further empower the partisan divide, which is counterproductive. Indeed, there is a very fine line to be carefully navigated.

There is perhaps no issue that has been more contentious over the past fifty years than a woman's reproductive health and her right to choose her own reproductive health-care services. After the Supreme Court overturned *Roe v. Wade* in June 2022, there were and continue to be numerous protests of that decision and advocacy for states to implement and enforce new laws to protect the right and access to an abortion at the local level. While many university leaders may have opposed the recent Supreme Court decision, few released bold statements of disagreement for fear of negative repercussions for speaking out on behalf of their institution on this highly contentious and politically charged topic perceived by many as a values-laden issue.

A few leaders did produce carefully worded and thoughtful public statements in support of abortion rights to their campus community or to broader audiences. In a letter to the campus community, Mary Sue Coleman, then president of the University of Michigan, firmly stated, "I strongly support access to abortion services, and I will do everything in my power as president to ensure we continue to provide this critically important care. . . . I am deeply concerned about how prohibiting abortion would affect U-M's medical teaching, our research, and our service to communities."[209] Similarly, the presidents of six colleges that were founded for women jointly published an opinion letter in *The New York Times* expressing their deep concern about the effect the overruling of *Roe v. Wade* will have on women's lives. They emphasized that "history and research suggest that this ruling will have a negative influence on college access, . . . people of color and those with limited incomes" and they pledged to "continue to provide reproductive health care on our campuses."[210] These leaders, all in states where reproductive health care remains possible, boldly and effectively communicated their support for abortion rights and the importance of participation in our democracy.

In a thoughtful and compelling piece in *The Chronicle of Higher Education* entitled "The Dumbing Down of the Purpose of Higher Education," President Patricia McGuire of Trinity Washington University eloquently calls on university leaders to confront "the corruption of truth that spreads through politically expedient lies" and "the daily toxic stew of 'fake news' that makes it difficult for citizens to understand the real threats to our democracy."[211] She emphasizes that democracy requires a well-educated citizenry and that universities are central to the ideals of freedom and justice in society. She reminds us that higher education is a "force to elevate society and educate true citizen leaders" and warns that institutional leaders in our silence around contentious issues in American life "become compliant, even complicit, in the dumbing down of the purpose of higher education."[212] She concludes that "leadership demands that we take the risk to raise up issues that must compel dialogue."[213] I urge all aspiring leaders in higher education to read her article and, whether you agree with her position or not, discuss and debate the details with your colleagues and students. There will always be a next crisis challenging higher education looming on the horizon. Soon it will be your turn in the ring. Be prepared!

CHAPTER TWENTY

Challenges on the Horizon

All natural and human-based ecosystems are periodically confronted by disturbance, disruption, or stressors. The ability to resist the disturbance or persist when faced with stress and recover—resilience— is critically important for long-term survival. For natural systems, the level of resistance, persistence, or resilience depends on the complexity and vulnerability of the system and the nature and magnitude of the external disruptive forces. Similarly, higher education ecosystems exhibit varying levels of buffering capacity and depend on how leaders anticipate and respond to the challenges in front of them and on the horizon. Those institutions with strong enrollment, a deep and diverse financial portfolio, and strategic approaches to confronting challenges may be adaptable, well-buffered, and able to resist or overcome stressors. Those that are inflexible, tuition-dependent, resource-limited, narrow in perspective, and unable or unwilling to adapt to stressors are highly vulnerable. Leaders that understand their institutional value proposition, assets, and challenges and who are willing and able to engage the community in strategic responses to stressors will ensure the stability and viability of their institution during difficult times.

Colleges and universities may be facing unprecedented difficult times. The challenges and unknowns on the horizon are abundant, multifaceted, and difficult but also represent opportunities for authentic leaders to step forward, confront the *status quo*, and collaboratively devise pathways to a vibrant and sustainable future—not only for their institution but also to fulfill their commitment to education as a path to economic and social mobility and an essential element of a democratic society. In this chapter,

I focus on emerging complex, multidimensional student, faculty, and information technology issues that academic leaders will need to address in the near term and in the foreseeable future.

The Looming Enrollment Cliff

Demographic Shifts

Although exacerbated in recent years because of the pandemic, higher education enrollments have been declining for more than a decade. In fall 2021, there were nearly 16 percent (3.6 million) fewer enrolled undergraduate students in higher education than in fall 2011.[214] A recent enrollment report from the NSCRC shows continued enrollment declines for spring 2022, which was down approximately 4 percent—685,000 students—compared to spring 2021.[215] The COVID-19 pandemic no doubt contributed to the accelerated undergraduate enrollment decline. Losses have been especially steep in for-profit four-year and public two-year institutions but persist across all sectors. While overall undergraduate enrollment grew by 2.1 percent in fall 2023 due mostly to post-pandemic community college recovery, enrollment of new first-time, full-time bachelors-seeking students declined by 6.2 percent at public and private nonprofit institutions largely independent of institutional selectivity, which may foreshadow enrollment challenges on the horizon.[216]

Most of the enrollment losses have been at the undergraduate level, as graduate enrollment has been largely stable, or even growing slightly over the past decade. According to the Council of Graduate Schools 2011 to 2021 report, first-time graduate student enrollment increased substantially between fall 2020 and fall 2021, especially at doctoral universities with very high research activity.[217] Most of that increase, however, is attributed to the return of international graduate students following the easing of COVID-19 restrictions and previous COVID-induced declines in international student enrollment. International graduate student first-time enrollment increased across all fields of study by 94.5 percent from 2020 to 2021, while domestic graduate enrollment declined across most fields, especially business, during that period. While the rebound in international student applications and enrollment is encouraging, the decline in domestic first-time graduate student enrollment is concerning.

Enrollment of male students has declined significantly, with male students now representing approximately 41 percent of enrolled college students—an all-time low.[218] In fall 2020, the drop in first-time male enrollment was seven times greater than the drop in female enroll-ment, and male students were ten percentage points less likely to grad-uate within four years than female students. These existing enrollment patterns are certainly disturbing—although there is nothing "looming" about them. The looming enrollment challenge, a.k.a., the enrollment cliff, is still a few years in front of us.

As illustrated in Figure 20.1, the projected abrupt decline in the number of eighteen-year-olds and high school graduates beginning in 2026 is startling and likely to lead to dramatic enrollment declines in many colleges and universities.[219] In his book *Demographics and the Demand for Higher Education*, Nathan Grawe forecasts a 15 percent decline in the college-going population between 2025 and 2029 and a continued drop of a few percentage points thereafter. Using projections from the Higher Education Demand Index, CUPA-HR reports that the number of eighteen-year-olds will peak at about 9.4 million in 2025 and abruptly decline to slightly more than 8 million in 2029.[220]

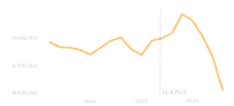

Figure 20.1. The projected number of eighteen-year-olds between 2012 and 2029.[221] *Reprinted with permission from the College and University Professional Association for Human Resources (CUPA-HR)*

Grawe attributes this abrupt decline, the "birth dearth," to reduced fertility triggered by economic uncertainty associated with the Great Recession beginning in 2008. Birthrates dropped precipitously from 2008 to 2011 and then did not rebound with the subsequent economic recovery. As a result, there will be fewer young adults reaching college age beginning in 2026, and college enrollments are projected to decline. The enrollment cliff, however, will likely vary by institution type with elite, selective institutions holding their own or even gaining slightly in enrollment by 2029, while regional bachelor's granting institutions and community colleges are projected to experience enrollment losses.

The declining college-age population is expected to vary regionally with northeastern and midwestern states hardest hit and modest growth in the mountain west.[222]

The recent decline in domestic first-time graduate student enrollment, if persistent, will exacerbate enrollment and revenue challenges associated with declining undergraduate enrollment patterns at many institutions. Fewer enrolled undergraduates will translate into fewer domestic students available to continue their education in graduate school, which will have to be compensated for by increasing the number of adults and international students seeking advanced certificates and degrees. Furthermore, the traditional population of predominantly White non-Hispanic high school graduates is expected to exhibit the greatest demographic decline, resulting in future students from increasingly diverse racial, ethnic, and socioeconomic backgrounds and first-generation college families. This pattern is already evident. Between fall 2021 and 2023, there was an 11.6 percent decline in enrollment of first-time White students compared with 6.7 percent and 3.7 percent growth in Latinx and Asian students, respectively, and a 3.9 percent decline in first-year Black student enrollment.[223]

The emerging combined demographic changes associated with further declining birth rates, differential population growth patterns across racial/ethnic groups, growing gender differences in college interest, and geographic variation in the proportion of high school graduates superimposed on top of the pre-pandemic and pandemic-induced enrollment declines may represent the greatest challenge facing higher education and society. Colleges unable to sustain enrollments will struggle financially, and the recent pattern of colleges being forced to close or merge with other institutions to survive will likely continue. These are difficult challenges for leaders to address, but there is more to the looming problem.

Affordability and Accessibility

Based on a survey of high school sophomores and juniors considering undergraduate programs, affordability is the top concern for prospective college students along with an institution's ability to improve employability and earning potential after college.[224] About half of these prospective college students want to earn four-year degrees, while a growing number are seeking online programs, alternative credentials, and flexible scheduling. The rising cost of college, growing student debt, and declining

Pell Grant funding have further complicated matters for many students and their families, creating an affordability crisis that is deterring some students from pursuing a college education. Declining federal and state funding on a per-student basis at many public institutions, especially since the Great Recession, along with continuous investments in the latest technology and additional student support services, such as innovative advising, career counseling, childcare, and expanded mental health services has increased the sticker price of a college education.

Education is a people-intensive business, and faculty and staff salaries and benefits, especially health-care coverage, have also contributed to rising costs. Despite cost increases, tuition costs have largely stabilized in recent years mostly because institutional aid in the form of tuition discount grants has grown steadily over the past fifteen to twenty years. Nevertheless, the average price of tuition, fees, housing, and dining adjusted for inflation for an undergraduate increased by 159 percent between 2000 and 2020.[225] This growth is largely driven by housing and dining charges, which increased by 9 percent and 6 percent above inflation rates from 2010 to 2015 at public and private institutions, respectively,[226] along with other ancillary costs, such as technology and books. While tuition increases are usually accompanied by tuition discount grants, housing and dining and other fees are not. Institutional grant aid through tuition discounting has increased substantially in recent years and helped counter affordability challenges for many students. It is not clear, however, that institutions will be able to continue to increase tuition discounts as a viable strategy to address the affordability challenge.

In 2022, student loan debt grew nationally to approximately $1.76 trillion with $1.6 trillion as federal student loan debt and the remaining as private student loan debt. Total student loan debt has doubled since 2010, although the rate of accumulated student loan debt has gradually slowed over the past decade.[227] The slower rate of debt growth is a function in part of reduced enrollment but also increased tuition discounting by many institutions. Nevertheless, by the end of 2022, student loan debt represented about 35 percent of all non-housing debt in the United States, followed by automobile loans (34 percent) and credit card debt (21 percent).[228] About 44 million US citizens currently have outstanding student loans. The average debt for undergraduate and graduate students with federal loans in 2022 was $37,574, which is more than double the average student loan debt of $18,233 in 2007. According to the National Center for Education Statistics, average cumulative debt from federal loans at graduation was $19,270 for graduates with an associate degree, $26,190 for those with a bachelor's degree, and $50,290 for those with a master's degrees, leading to average monthly loan payments of $197, $267, and $567 on a standard repayment plan.[229] These costs are likely prohibitive for many new graduates who are trying to establish their professional and personal lives. Prospective students, including new high school graduates, potential returning and transfer students, and adults are increasingly concerned about and steering away from taking on student debt, which may exacerbate enrollment challenges for some institutions.

Ambiguity of Purpose and a Flawed Funding Model

The affordability challenge is partly about rising costs, but it is also about inconsistent and flawed higher education funding models. The "high cost" problem relates indirectly at least to who benefits from a college education and who should pay for it. That is, is a college education a personal benefit or a public good? A corollary question is what is the fundamental purpose of a college education. The latter is not meant to reopen the tired old debate about whether a college education should be about a broad-based liberal arts education that engages the life of the mind or career preparation. In the modern world, both are essential to address the cost-value proposition demanded. And, yes, the value must accrue not only to individuals personally but to society *writ large*. That is, students benefit from developing skills and competencies necessary for certain jobs and from a broad education that teaches them to think critically, analyze problems, communicate clearly, and develop strategies and an informed set of personal values.

These attributes come not only from the curriculum but also from the socialization, maturation, networking, and exposure to diverse people and cultures inherent in a college education. This combination of specific skills and broad-based learning drives economic and social mobility and a vibrant democracy capable of developing new innovations and competitive strategies necessary to navigate an increasingly competitive global society. Of course, this leads to more questions: How well do our colleges and universities deliver these individual and societal benefits? Does anyone (i.e., families, legislators, and citizens broadly) value these broader attributes beyond career-based skills? Leaders must lead this dialogue on our campuses, in state houses, and in public forums and ensure that our institutions are delivering a quality and contemporary education that serves students and society.

As a nation, we have not proactively addressed these questions and devised a funding plan for higher education consistent with that goal. If one values a predominantly college-educated society and university research and development as assets that advance economic opportunity, quality of life, national security, and democracy broadly, then one might expect that state and federal governments would heavily subsidize higher education so the opportunity and benefits are broadly available. Alternatively, if the benefits of a college education accrue primarily to individuals by creating the potential for greater income, wealth, and access to more goods and services, then the financial responsibility would be expected to largely sit with individuals and families.

At present, US higher education falls by default mostly in the latter category. Colleges are increasingly providing major subsidies through tuition discounting with shrinking support from state and federal governments for the most vulnerable and disadvantaged. In fact, we often refer to the value of a "college degree" rather than a "college education," emphasizing the tangible value of the *degree* over the *educational benefits* to society from a learned citizenry. There is no strategic national funding model for higher education today. At best, we have a mixed model that varies by state and political affiliation with many families priced out of the opportunity. Leaders across institutions need to address these fundamental questions about who should benefit and why and then propose and advocate for a new rational and affordable higher education funding model consistent with those values.

Viable Alternative Pathways

Given growing concerns about costs and debt, many students and families are questioning the value proposition associated with a bachelor's level college education. As reported by Lederman for *Inside Higher Ed*, a recent *Wall Street Journal* survey of adults found that 56 percent of Americans across all ages believe that a four-year college degree is not worth it because people often graduate with significant debt but without specific job skills. Only 42 percent believed a college education was worth the cost. In 2013, the response was reversed—53 percent were positive and 40 percent negative.[230] Whether correct or not, such perceptions influence behavior. An increasing number of high school graduates are now exploring alternative, cheaper, and quicker pathways to pursue career interests. There are many technical training options emerging that lead to solid careers and salaries and appear to be a good return on investment at least in the short term. These include coding and programming boot camps, trade schools, apprenticeship programs, industry certification programs, and low-cost, accelerated online programs that may employ competency-based learning and credit for prior work and life experience. Education technology companies are developing and offering micro-credentials, including micro-bachelor's programs, that may lead to college credit at partner institutions. While undergraduate and graduate enrollment was essentially flat between 2021 and 2023, enrollment in undergraduate and graduate certificate programs increased 13.4 percent and 9.9 percent, respectively, reflecting growing interest in short-term, affordable, skills-based credentials.[231]

Employers migrating to skills- and experienced-based rather than degree-based hiring practices have served to further dissuade some students from seriously considering attending college and taking on additional debt. For example, the state of Maryland recently eliminated bachelor's degrees as a requirement for most state jobs, emphasizing experience, training, and competencies rather than four-year degrees. Maryland estimates that more than half of the 38,000 state workers can substitute relevant experience and skills for a bachelor's degree. Similarly, 92 percent of approximately 65,000 positions in Pennsylvania will be open to individuals regardless of whether they have a college degree. At least a dozen other states have recently eliminated or limited degree requirements for most state positions. Many companies, including IBM, Google, and Apple, have also moved to skill-based hiring and support upskilling and reskilling to ensure a competent workforce. The perception is that a college degree bias shrinks the talent pool and diversity in the workforce.

While earning degrees still signals a certain level of education and set of abilities, the changing nature of work is raising questions among some, perhaps many, whether traditional higher education is the best way to provide people with the skills and competencies necessary for emerging job markets. As reported in *Education Week*, a recent national survey entitled the "Purpose of Education Index" revealed that families now place a higher priority on preparing K-12 students for careers and basic life skills rather than college readiness.[232] In 2019, preparing students to enroll in a college or university was the tenth highest priority for K-12 schools. In 2022, that fell to forty-seventh out of fifty-seven total priorities. Preparing students for careers was sixth on the list in 2022, up from twenty-seventh in 2019. No doubt, affordability and the perception of the declining value of a college education may further accentuate the enrollment and financial challenges created by the demographic shifts described above.

Addressing Enrollment Challenges

If demographic projections are correct, the enrollment cliff will be steep, especially for tuition-dependent institutions. A recent survey representing 1,252 institutions shows that 89 percent of college leaders are concerned about future enrollment, as they should be.[233] While elite selective private institutions and many public flagships are likely to experience minimal impacts or perhaps even modest enrollment increases, many other institutions will struggle and may not be able to simply recruit their way through this challenge by more aggressively reaching out to the shrinking population of new traditional-age students. The eighteen- to twenty-two-year-old population is an increasingly endangered species. Enrollment-dependent institutions may be better served by focusing on retention of existing students, improving time to degree completion to four-years or less, and reconnecting with students who have dropped out of college, including the 40 million some college, no credential (SCNC) population discussed in chapter 12.

Building a diverse enrollment portfolio of transfer, international, adult, and professionally focused graduate students along with traditional undergraduates may help stabilize enrollment. To be successful with these populations and to offer flexible options for all students, institutions will need to ramp up online and blended course instruction as well as fully online program delivery and transition from so-called remote delivery to approaches that support technology-enriched teaching and learning, which focuses on engaging students and maximizing learning rather than simply teaching from a distance. Tuition-discounted and fully or mostly online summer programs along with abbreviated winter J-term course offerings can embellish revenue streams while at the same time assisting in retention and hastening time to degree completion—a financial win-win for students and institutions.

With the rising cost of a college education and increased dependence on student loans to fund a college degree, most students are increasingly interested in education as a conduit to their career goals and a lucra-tive ROI. While many faculty express concern about their role in job training compared to critical thinking, analysis, communication skills, and subject area mastery of major-specific knowledge and skills, there is a need and opportunity to blend these fundamental aspects of learning with skills and experiences that students will need to be successful in an array of career paths. SCNC and adult students are loan averse and seek potential career advancement value associated with their investment in education. Short-term upskilling and reskilling micro-credentials, such as micro-bachelor's, certificates, or badges, are viewed positively by both underemployed adults and their employers. Traditional student popula-tions are increasingly seeking the same relevance and value proposition.

It is also time to rethink the curriculum. The traditional model devel-oped *by the faculty for the faculty* often leads, in the words of former Harvard President Derek Bok, to undergraduate programs where "the whole is smaller than the sum of the parts."[234] That is, the curriculum often reflects faculty members academic experiences, perceived disci-plinary dogma, and research interests with little attention to societal needs and practitioner expertise. This must be replaced with student-cen-tered learning that ascertains and addresses what students need to know, be able to do, and stand for—knowledge, skills, and values—to thrive and contribute in a diverse and ever-evolving society. The reference to values doesn't mean faculty impose their values on students, but rather students are exposed to different ideas and develop their own informed personal philosophy and set of values. Leaders will need to step up and urge or cajole each academic program to re-examine and reinvent its curriculum and pedagogical delivery to ensure it is contemporary and includes analytical, communication, and writing skills, data and tech-nology applications, and meaningful experiential learning.

This can be done by weaving credit-bearing internships, undergrad-uate research, project-based learning, and/or leadership development experiences as central curricular features in each major. It is also crit-ical to modernize general education programs to ensure that courses meet clearly defined and meaningful learning outcomes rather than simply courses faculty want to teach. Skills-based micro-credentials that can stand alone or be combined with an array of academic majors can help prepare students for the working world and give them a competi-tive edge in the marketplace. These might include certificates in social justice, project management, coding and programming, leadership, or innovation and entrepreneurship. The opportunity for stackable certificates that lead to a master's degree may be especially attractive for individuals interested in upskilling and advancing their careers. Strategic partnering with educational technology companies that offer micro-credentials will likely become attractive.

Finally, there are new rapidly expanding interdisciplinary areas, such as neuroscience, data science, artificial intelligence, entrepreneurship, digital communications and marketing, and more that are important and attractive to a growing number of both traditional and nontraditional student populations. Each institution will need to choose programmatic offerings consistent with its mission, purpose, and ability to efficiently deliver a quality experience to students. The message here is not meant to dictate the next steps, but rather to emphasize that simply sitting pat or holding on to past curricular and pedagogical models during a time of major enrollment upheaval is neither a viable survival strategy nor a productive step toward the promise of higher education to shape a vibrant democratic society.

The Changing Behavior of Students

A Student Disengagement Crisis

Student populations are diverse, always evolving, and cannot be described in a singular fashion. Nevertheless, there are well-documented patterns of behavior emerging among many students that seem misaligned with the purpose of higher education teaching and learning that are potentially concerning and worthy of attention. A May 11, 2022, article in *The Chronicle of Higher Education* coined the phrase "student disengagement crisis," referring to a disconnect in student learning, sense of purpose, and overall college experience.[235] Symptoms include chronic absenteeism, failure to complete assignments in a timely manner, lack of motivation and participation in classes, and sometimes dropping out of college altogether. Many have attributed the disengagement to the impacts of the pandemic health crisis, misalignment between a generation of digital natives and higher education learning models, or a shift in responsibility to students for a greater portion of their own learning associated with online course delivery. While these and other factors have likely contributed to the so-called disengagement crisis, it is not a new or exclusively recent phenomenon and represents a divergence in the fundamental purpose of a college education between what many current students and their families expect and what institutions offer. This fundamental clash in educational values and expectations is a challenge that students, faculty, and university leaders must confront.

Fischman and Gardner made an evidenced-based case that the student disengagement crisis was not a pandemic-induced phenomenon and is, therefore, not going to simply go away.[236] Prior to the pandemic, they conducted a major study that included interviewing more than 1,000 students, 500 faculty and administrators, and 500 parents, trustees, and young alumni. Based on their hour-long conversations with those 1,000 students, they discovered a startling lack of engagement with academic work and greater disenchantment with their college experience over time. The student self-reported very limited studying time per week reinforced this lack of engagement with learning. Nearly half of the students interviewed did not see value in what they were learning and did not understand why they were expected to take classes in different fields or read books that were not directly related to their major.

According to Fischman and Gardner, many students have a transactional view of college—their primary goal is to build a strong resume using any means necessary to help them secure a job after college, which may even include cheating.[237] Many are "more concerned with the pursuit of earning than the process of learning," which reflects a lack of understanding about the purpose of college. There is nothing wrong with student interest in future employment, especially given the high cost of and significant investment in their college education. The concern is the apparent lack of commitment among many students to the pursuit of learning and expanding one's worldview as both a pathway to employment and as a central tenet of a college education and societal value.

This narrow more transactional purpose of college has been shaped by family members and early educational experiences. It is also being reinforced by colleges emphasizing amenities, a comfortable lifestyle, and other shiny objects as part of their student recruitment strategies rather than highlighting the foundational mission, purpose, and value of learning and intellectual growth as keys to their future. I raise this issue not to ascribe blame or disparage students or their families, but rather to describe a pervasive challenge that is potentially damaging to students, higher education institutions, and society more broadly. This is a fundamental issue that needs to be discussed and debated among leaders in higher education and society as it is inextricably linked to our collective future.

In addition to a career readiness focus, concerns about major problems in the world, such as climate change, income inequality, cyber warfare, racial reckoning, and the potential of a nuclear war, along with rampant social media can be overwhelming and lead to further disengagement. Student distraction from the primary educational purposes of learning, discovery, and application of knowledge, along with the rising cost of education, is likely contributing to students' pursuit of short-term training and career preparation programs discussed above. Perhaps that's the right path for some students, but it may have long-term consequences for their social and economic mobility and for society.

This transactional view of college also contributes to a growing disconnect between many students and faculty and expectations that faculty need to somehow do more to meet the needs and desires of their students. Fischman and Gardner suggest that many students don't understand or appreciate the expertise and role of faculty. I know many very caring, capable, and committed faculty who share this same perspective. Rather than viewing faculty as experts and mentors who teach, guide, and inspire their students and ignite their passion for learning, many students increasingly expect them to bend over backward to address their individual demands related to grades, class attendance, assignments, and making classes easier. At times institutional leaders inappropriately reinforce those same expectations of faculty in the interest of keeping students happy, enrolled, and progressing toward their goal of degree completion.

Leaders are facing a barrage of complaints from students who are condemning faculty for making classes too challenging, demanding changes in their grades, and seeking leadership support to force faculty to make classes easier or even step down. This is unfortunate and counterproductive to student learning, curiosity, and intellectual development as well as to the faculty's role in creating and nurturing meaningful learning. Certainly, leaders should expect faculty to employ best practices in teaching, engaging, and demonstrating empathy toward students and provide support for their professional development to do so, but they must also reinforce high expectations of students as keys to deep learning, which is the ultimate purpose of a college education. Indeed, this pattern of behavior is driving some faculty to leave the profession.

The Mental Health Crisis

Over the past decade or so, before the COVID-19 pandemic, universities faced a surge in student demand for counseling services that far outpaced most campuses' capacity to provide those services. In October 2021, the American Academy of Pediatrics, the American Academy of Child and Adolescent Psychiatry, and the Children's Hospital Association jointly declared a National Emergency in Children's Mental Health in recognition of steadily rising rates of childhood mental health concerns and suicides between 2010 and 2020 and the emergence of suicide as the second leading cause of death for youth ages ten to twenty-four in 2018.[238] The pandemic has further disrupted the safety and stability of families and has intensified the youth mental health crisis. The increased premature loss or serious illness of loved ones, racial reckoning and social injustice, questions about sexuality, visible imminent threats of climate change, mass violence, societal polarization, hate speech, and tangible threats of nuclear war have resulted in a generation of young people on and off college campuses experiencing soaring rates of depression, anxiety, trauma, loneliness, and suicide ideation.

According to a National Healthy Minds Study including data from more than 350,000 students from 373 campuses nationwide, more than 60 percent of college students met the criteria for at least one mental health problem during the 2020-21 academic year, a nearly 50 percent increase from 2013.[239] The American College Health Association's fall 2021 National College Health Assessment reported that approximately 72 percent of students reported moderate or severe psychological distress.[240] College counseling centers have experienced dramatic growth in demand, caseloads, and need for an ever-increasing investment in counseling center staff. Many centers are simply not able to keep up with the expanding challenge and are implementing new innovative approaches, including telehealth, group therapy, crisis hotlines, and teaching faculty and staff to spot student distress signals and refer students for counseling.

Institutional leaders must address the student mental health crisis to ensure that students needing assistance get the help they need. Indeed, support for mental health challenges is rapidly emerging as a new fundamental purpose of college education, whether recognized or valued by families or not. This will require an increased investment of already limited resources on many campuses as well as efforts to create a culture of wellness across campuses reflected in the curriculum as well as student, staff, and faculty support services. Leaders need to engage the community to inspire a shared responsibility to create and sustain wellness as a campus priority. Staff and especially faculty are rapidly becoming first responders to help identify students in distress, placing an increased burden on already overwhelmed faculty who have limited tools and skills to support students with mental health or substance abuse issues. Indeed, the challenge is complex and multidimensional; leaders need to be informed and prepared to modify policies, practices, and protocols to ensure the health and well-being of the community.

COVID-19 Coattails

Pandemic-Induced Declines in Fourth and Eighth Grade Math and Reading

Many American college students struggle academically in certain gateway courses, especially mathematics and quantitative sciences. The most recent results from the National Assessment of Educational Progress math and reading exams, commonly referred to as the Nation's Report Card, suggest that the problem is likely to get worse.[241] The NAEP exam is administered by the National Center for Education Statistics and samples 450,000 fourth and eighth graders in more than 10,000 school districts. Average scores in math and reading for both fourth- and eighth-grade students declined sharply between 2019 and 2022.[242] Students experienced the steepest declines ever in mathematics since the exam was initiated in 1990, especially among eighth-grade students. None of the fifty-three states and jurisdictions or the twenty-six largest urban school districts in the nation posted gains in math in either grade, and only 26 percent of eighth graders were proficient in math, down from 34 percent in 2019.[243] Only about one-third of fourth and eighth graders met proficiency standards in reading.[244]

The eighth graders who took the NAEP exam are already in high school, and many are likely missing foundational skills in algebra and geometry necessary to successfully pursue college majors and future careers in math and science. These alarming results are attributed to educational and learning disruptions caused by the pandemic, which worsened an already widening pre-pandemic gap in math and reading between higher-performing and lower-performing students with a disproportionate impact on the most vulnerable students.

At present, a high proportion of college students receive unproductive grades, such as D, W, or F, in certain introductory mathematics, science, and other quantitative courses. Such high failure rates limit major options and credit accumulation for students and require rework that is inefficient and expensive for students and institutions. The proportion of college students currently receiving unproductive grades can be as high as 25 percent to 50 percent of enrolled students in some courses and even higher for first-generation, Pell students, and students of color. Unproductive grades in gateway courses often relate to weak pre-college academic preparation of students and their lack of college readiness in certain disciplines, especially mathematics.

These latest NAEP results are a heads-up for higher education leaders about yet another challenge on the horizon. Lack of academic preparation, including poorly developed study and test-taking skills, may further inhibit less prepared and vulnerable students from attending or completing college, thereby accentuating the looming enrollment cliff. The national average ACT composite score for the 2023 high school graduating class dropped for the sixth consecutive year and was the lowest since 1991. Only 21 percent of the 1.4 million ACT test takers met college-readiness benchmarks in math, science, English, and reading, while 43 percent met none of those benchmarks.[245] These data highlight the need for creative new approaches for colleges to provide academic support for a new generation of students not academically prepared for college and to address the mathematics and reading learning deficiencies that are increasingly prevalent across the nation. Colleges and universities have no choice but to address these deficiencies in substantive ways.

Traditional-Age Students Shift to Fully Online Learning

Following the pandemic-induced abrupt shift to entirely online learning at most institutions in the spring of 2020, many traditional-age college students expressed frustration, dissatisfaction, and compromised learning opportunities associated with fully online learning modalities. In fact, several class action lawsuits were filed against institutions by disgruntled students and families claiming the shift to fully online teaching and services was a breach of contract, arguing they should be reimbursed their tuition and fees to compensate them for lost learning and services. Now, just a few years later, there appears to be substantial growth of that same population of traditional-age students choosing fully online programs rather than largely in-person, residential college experiences. To be sure, national online institutions, such as Western Governors University (WGU) and Southern New Hampshire University (SNHU), have and continue to primarily serve working adult students.

In a recent article in *Inside Higher Ed*, D'Agostino reports that enrollment of traditional-age students at SNHU has increased by approximately 10,000 to 43,750 since the pandemic began, and traditional-age students have more than doubled from 6,000 in 2017 to 15,000 students in 2022 at WGU.[246] Similarly, at the University of Maryland Global Campus, which has largely catered to active military, the population of fully online traditional-age students grew by 33 percent and is the fastest-growing population of students. It is likely that young people are drawn to the convenience, flexibility, and affordability of these fully online programs, which are priced lower than most residential institutions and often offer opportunities to accelerate progress to degree completion through competency-based and prior learning experience credit. As many students became accustomed to online learning during the pandemic, it appears it may now be viewed more favorably among many traditional-age college students as well as by many employers. At this point, it is unclear if this trend will continue or fizzle over time.

These three online institutions alone have enrolled more than 20,000 new traditional-age undergraduates over just the past few years; many of these students would have otherwise enrolled in traditional four-year or community colleges. In the big picture, these numbers represent a small proportion of the traditional-age student market. Across all demographics, however, the number of undergraduate students enrolled entirely in online courses at four-year institutions increased by nearly two million between 2019 and 2021.[247] Most of these increases were at public four-year institutions, which almost doubled in fully online undergraduate enrollment while experiencing an in-person enrollment reduction of about three million students and an overall net enrollment loss of about one million students between 2019 and 2021. For two-year institutions, the proportion of fully online students increased from 15 percent to 41 percent over that time, an increase of one million fully online students despite an overall enrollment decline of 1.1 million students.[248] Undoubtedly, the COVID-19 pandemic contributed to these enrollment shifts. With a projected declining demographic of traditional-age students and the possibility of continued growth of students in fully online programs, academic leaders at many traditional institutions cannot afford to lose an additional market share of students.

Enhancing Faculty and Staff Diversity

As a result of concerted recruitment and retention efforts by some institutions and demographic changes in race and ethnicity, the population
of undergraduate students of color has increased from approximately
30 percent to approximately 47 percent across the nation over the past
twenty years.[249] This is important and good news for those students
and communities and for society more broadly. Demographic projections indicate further growth in the diversity of prospective student
populations. Given overall expected enrollment challenges, undergraduate students of color will represent an increasing proportion of
college students in the future, although it's possible that historically
Black colleges and universities may become a preferred choice for Black
students following the Supreme Court ruling to ban race-conscious
admission. However, race and ethnicity-based equity gaps in retention and time to degree completion and uneven access across academic
disciplines and professional pathways have been persistent obstacles to
success for many students of color. Furthermore, faculty, staff, and graduate student diversity has not kept pace with the growth in undergraduate student diversity, resulting in a paucity of strong mentors and role
models for students of color and less inclusive campus communities and
climates. According to the NCES, racial and ethnic diversity of faculty
averaged approximately 26 percent in 2020, while graduate student
diversity averaged 39 percent, compounding the challenges to increasing
diversity of faculty and staff.[250]

A recent study has demonstrated that the increase in faculty diversity
is barely keeping up with the steady growth in racial and ethnic diversity in the US population. The implications are enormous. A new study
from The Education Trust offers compelling evidence that faculty diversity supports student success and positively impacts students' sense of
belonging, retention, and persistence, and students of color are more
likely to graduate when they interact with diverse faculty members.[251] The
benefits extend to all populations of students. Engaging with racially and
culturally diverse faculty and exposure to multiple perspectives builds
empathy, inspires creativity, enhances problem-solving skills, and better
prepares students from all backgrounds to become global citizens and
successful contributors to an increasingly multicultural workforce and
world. *The bottom line is that educational diversity enhances educational
quality for all populations of students.* Given projected declines in overall

enrollment and expected increases in the diversity of students in the future, leaders must develop plans and strategies to ensure more inclusive, welcoming, and equitable environments for all on our campuses.

Boosting faculty and staff diversity is necessary to help create a diverse and equitable campus community and to enhance student success and graduation rates, especially for students of color at predominantly White institutions. Faculty diversity is a pressing issue in all fields, especially in STEM disciplines. Investing in faculty, staff, and graduate student diversity will not only enhance academic success for students of color across disciplines but also expand the pipeline for more diverse faculty and campus leaders in the future. Enhancing faculty and staff diversity, however, won't simply happen on its own using the same approaches and search practices that have been ineffective in the past. Also, wealthy institutions poaching successful faculty of color from other institutions, while perhaps personally beneficial, is not a viable wholesale strategy to advance diversity in the academy. Investments will be necessary to recruit, enroll, and mentor graduate students of color through doctoral degree completion as well as for workshops for faculty and staff search committees to eliminate implicit bias in search and candidate review processes and ensure diverse applicant pools. The preoccupation of faculty with the academic pedigree of candidates and the use of traditional colleague networks in recruiting and vetting applicants typically work against candidates of color in the faculty search process. There is an urgent need to transform search and hiring processes and prioritize recruitment, hiring, and retention of faculty and staff of color.

Innovative approaches, such as recruiting high-achieving students of color into graduate programs, cluster hires of faculty in areas that contribute to diversity, annual funding of post-doctoral fellows' programs that segue into tenure-track faculty positions, and build-your-own-pipeline programs to produce PhDs in underrepresented disciplines are just a few examples of efforts that have been successfully implemented. In particular, the American Council on Education has shown that formal and informal mentoring programs are effective at encouraging historically minoritized students to pursue graduate education by demystifying pathways to graduate programs, offering exposure to research skills, developing social networks with faculty and other graduate students in their field, and providing opportunities to reflect on their academic journey.[252] The Education Trust and the Southern Regional Education Board reports on faculty diversity offer additional strategies to diversify university faculties.[253] While investments will be necessary, most progress will be made by establishing priorities, re-evaluating the decision-making process, and holding deans, directors, and faculty accountable for advancing diversity across faculty, staff, and graduate student populations. It is time for leaders at all levels to creatively and courageously implement new innovative and effective strategic best practices to create a diverse talent pool of new faculty, staff, and institutional leaders.

Faculty and Staff Dissatisfaction—The Great Resignation

COVID-19 created a variety of stressors for faculty and staff, including personal and family health and safety concerns, an abrupt shift to virtual teaching, endless Zoom meetings, and demands to cater to the needs of stressed-out students, colleagues, and family members. It also raised questions for many about the meaning of their work, their work-life balance, and their priorities. Many institutions asked faculty and staff to do more work and to work in new, different, and challenging ways during the pandemic. As a result, many feel undervalued and are experiencing mental exhaustion and increasing levels of dissatisfaction with their positions.[254] An October 2020 nationwide survey of 1,122 faculty members conducted by *The Chronicle of Higher Education* found that more than two-thirds felt "extremely" or "very" stressed, compared to one-third a year earlier.[255] Furthermore, 60 percent of respondents to a CUPA-HR survey of more than 3,800 higher education staff reported they are likely to look for alternative employment in the next year.[256]

Anecdotal information also suggests that faculty are retiring or leaving higher education at higher rates than in the past, although data on faculty departures are incomplete. Most institutions report having more open positions in 2022 than the year before, and most are having difficulty filling them. For many, higher education is perceived as a less attractive place to work than in the past when the mission and the opportunity to work with young people were viewed positively. "Burnout," "disillusionment," "overworked," "undervalued," and "lack of support" were among the common descriptors used by faculty who say they are leaving their positions.[257] Faculty and staff have shared that these concerns are not new but are exacerbated by the pervasive twin pandemics of COVID-19 and racial injustice along with the mental health challenges of students that many faculty are ill-equipped to manage. While the impacts have been challenging for everyone, female faculty consistently report feeling more overworked and overwhelmed than their male colleagues.[258]

As emphasized throughout this book, the work of colleges and universities is *all about people*, and the human resource is our greatest asset that must be nurtured, supported, and now rejuvenated. Strong evidence indicates that this essential asset—our talent pool—is struggling with burnout, which can lead to low morale, dissatisfaction, a loss of meaning in one's work as well as the turnover of personnel. The responsibility to address the conditions contributing to faculty and staff burnout and mental health challenges at the organizational level sits with the leaders of our institutions. The American Council on Education (ACE) produced an in-depth and informative analysis entitled *Addressing Burnout Through Cultural Change: How Leaders Can Stem Attrition and Support Employees* that offers thoughtful insights and recommendations for leaders to consider.[259]

While some critics of higher education periodically accuse faculty and staff of being unproductive with cushy jobs, the reality is that higher education is often associated with a culture that promotes excessive work and expectations of faculty and staff to always be available and work long days. Indeed, these are the conditions that lead to burnout. In addition to excessive work hours, employee concerns often include the following: salaries not keeping up with inflation, limited advancement opportunities, lack of flexibility in work schedules and meaningful work, technology overload, and extra work related to unfilled positions.[260] Recognizing that faculty and staff are the direct lines of support to students, addressing these and other concerns that constrain the pursuit of the institution's academic core mission is also an investment in student success and the financial viability of our institutions. Truly listening to and acknowledging these concerns may be a place to create an opportunity to rebuild the trust that has been compromised at some institutions.

Leaders need to ensure that human resources departments are contemporary and forward-thinking and that supervisors have the skills to ensure that their direct reports are respected, supported, and have the resources to perform their jobs. The ACE report offers several suggestions for leaders to consider in support of their employees. While there are no doubt limitations, there are numerous areas where progress may be feasible and important, such as:

- ensuring adequate cost of living increases for faculty and staff, especially during times of high inflation;

- modernizing the classification and responsibilities of positions and offloading uninteresting and repetitive functions to automation technologies;

- developing career paths and professional development and advancement opportunities where possible;

- considering hybrid or flexible work arrangements while ensuring in-person office coverage where necessary;

- communicating trust in employee competence to perform their jobs;

- promoting a healthy work-life balance for employees;

- reducing meetings and establishing meeting-free days so employees have time to get their work done; and

- recognizing that employee time—in their professional and personal lives—is a limited and valuable commodity that must be carefully managed and respected.

Many faculty and staff choose a higher education career path because they are inspired by the academic mission and the opportunity to work with students and colleagues with similar interests. Institutional leaders are ultimately responsible to ensure that they create and sustain workplaces that are supportive and respectful of their employees and allow them to thrive in the work that they have chosen to pursue.

Cybersecurity and Digital Transformation

Improving Data Security

The education sector is the top target for cyberattacks, and data security was among the highest risk areas in higher education in 2022.[261] Information technology risks include data breaches, phishing attempts, disclosure of personal information, hacking, and ransomware attacks. Despite numerous counter-ransomware initiatives, these attacks have not decreased, and education sector cyberattacks exceeding 170,000 malware encounters per day have recently been reported. Educational institutions have unique challenges because their purpose is largely to share rather than secure information, and they are dynamic communities of student, staff, faculty, and administrator users each with their own personal devices functioning in a world of ever-evolving security challenges. They also have large volumes of personal identity information and sensitive research and intellectual property. Many institutions are using outdated technology systems and have many users who lack security awareness or use unsecured wireless networks that may unknowingly introduce malware into their networks through their devices. A 2022 survey of campus chief information officers (CIOs) conducted by *Inside Higher Ed* in partnership with Hanover Research revealed that only 22 percent of the CIOs from 175 responding institutions were extremely or very confident that their institutional policies can prevent such attacks.[262] University leaders working closely with CIOs will need to ensure data security training and regular risk assessments along with updated data governance strategies and consistent investments in updated software and hardware cybersecurity systems.

Embracing Digital Transformation

Digital opportunities in support of student success, teaching and learning, research, and improved business functions are abundant and expanding. Many universities now use predictive data analytics to assist with student retention, online and blended course delivery is common and improved following pandemic-induced course conversions, and high-performance supercomputing power has been bolstered on campuses and in the cloud. Indeed, much progress has been made. The next major step for higher education is digital transformation (Dx). The opportunities are enormous, as are the challenges. Higher education is accustomed to slow and steady change and an internal siloed mentality of work. A Dx transformation involves institution-wide changes and new approaches to all aspects of campus functionality, including interactions with the IT organization, improved student outcomes, and new teaching and learning models, research capabilities, and business functions. A Dx culture triggers opportunities to create new functional cross-campus partnerships to address needs, inform decisions, and increase institutional agility to ensure new innovations and improvements can be introduced quickly. Such changes are a deviation from the historical glacial pace and incremental approaches to change in higher education.

Educause, a nonprofit dedicated to advancing higher education through information technology, is a leading voice and source of information and resources to advance Dx in higher education institutions. Educause defines Dx as "a series of deep and coordinated culture, workforce, and technology shifts that enable new educational and operating models and transform an institution's operations, strategic directions, and value proposition."[263] The goal is to ensure that faculty, staff, students, administrators, and other constituents have the tools and capacities to advance education, research, communications, and operations in an integrated and coordinated manner. To capture the strategic benefits of Dx, leaders must prepare for shifts in culture, workforce, and technology leading to greater agility, a new approach to everything, and collaboration at all levels throughout the institution. "Getting Ready for Digital Transformation: Change Your Culture, Workforce, and Technology"[264] provides a detailed description of the critical roles of leaders in implementing a digital transformation strategy focused on institutional goals and aspirations, including:

- establishing a cross-campus culture of collaboration, trust, and accountability;

- promoting greater use of data and an IT organization that empowers new digital strategies that address institutional goals and challenges;

- increasing reliance on data analytics to inform decision-making, track progress, and ensure continuous improvement in business management;

- prioritizing institution-wide data governance and platforms that utilize artificial intelligence (AI) and mobile technologies;

- supporting a university-wide workforce with technological and data skills, including faculty capable of adapting pedagogical approaches and researchers applying computation, analysis, and visualization across disciplines; and

- preparing for rapid advances in technology, greater personalization, and the use of emerging technologies, such as extended reality (XR), robotics, generative AI, and Internet of Things (IoT) technologies.

While this may seem a long way from reality for some, Dx is underway at many institutions. Based on results of the recent CIO survey, approximately 42 percent of CIOs viewed Dx as an "essential" or "high priority," and two-thirds have set specific goals toward becoming more digitally focused.[265] The greatest obstacle to progress, according to CIOs, is not surprising—insufficient financial resources and faculty and staff resistance. Leadership support and cross-organizational collaboration will be necessary to implement strategic elements of Dx to remain competitive in the higher education marketplace. According to Educause, "even if institutional leaders take no action, Dx will remake colleges and universities from the ground up through inexorable external changes. Leaders will need to become the change agents who guide this transformation and "prepare their institutions now to take advantage of the coming shifts in culture, workforce, and technology."[266]

Based on the CIO survey, the top priorities for digital transformation are leveraging data for better retention and student success, transitioning business processes, and improving teaching and learning. Most CIOs report opportunities for expanded use of and investment in the application of cutting-edge technologies, such as quantum computing, machine learning, AI, adaptive learning, and virtual reality/immersive learning. For example, adaptive learning and AI have the potential to reinvent teaching and learning by creating personalized learning models that meet students where they are. Course-customized AI teaching assistants can assist with grading, respond to student questions with real-time feedback, and determine the extent of student knowledge and understanding using probing assessments, allowing for more personalized learning content and pace for students.

On November 30, 2022, OpenAI launched ChatGPT, a free AI-empowered interactive chatbot that can understand and respond to natural language. A few months later they introduced GPT-4, an updated version. The good news is it produces very good, often shockingly good, text responses in seconds that may be structured as essays, blogs, poems, letters, computer code, websites, etc. The bad news is students are already submitting papers and essays written by ChatGPT for class assignments, and there are risks associated with misuse of the technology, such as organized dissemination of misinformation. In most cases, the chatbot generates articulate text responses to short prompts and follow-up probes. It is a dynamic tool that is learning and improving every day. While this might frustrate some faculty, it also challenges us to find alternative pedagogical approaches to use this technology to create better and deeper learning. Many examples are already emerging from creative instructors, such as having students discuss critical questions and subsequently analyzing and critiquing ChatGPT's response to the same questions. One can imagine developing in students the use of chatbots as a valuable analytical skill to be fine-tuned with practice rather than viewing it largely as a cheating platform or a devious source of misinformation. Perhaps this represents a significant challenge, but one with the potential for a positive learning payback. OpenAI has recently released a new tool that may help instructors detect if students used ChatGPT for exams or assignments. See "Example of ChatGPT Text Response" for an immediate ChatGPT response to a prompt I posed about the tool and its potential applications and limitations related to teaching and learning.

As Dx in higher education progresses, there is potential for AI-empowered adaptive learning models to serve as tutors, improve learning outcomes, lighten faculty workloads, and improve overall student success. These outcomes are well-within reach through the strategic application of emerging technologies in support of the institutional mission and priorities. Resistance will most certainly emerge. Institutional leaders, including collaborative efforts by chairs, deans, CIOs, provosts, and presidents, must become skillful change agents and shift from risk aversion to addressing the challenges and opportunities of the twenty-first century.

Example of ChatGPT Text Response

Prompt: Explain how ChatGPT works and how it can be used to enhance student learning in college courses. In what aspects of teaching and learning is ChatGPT not effective?

ChatGPT Response: ChatGPT is a large language model that has been trained on a vast amount of text data. It uses a deep learning technique called Transformer, which allows it to generate human-like text. When given a prompt, ChatGPT can generate a response that continues the conversation or provides information relevant to the prompt. ChatGPT can be used to enhance student learning in college courses by providing instant feedback and personalized explanations. For example, it can be used to answer students' questions, provide summaries of complex texts, or even generate practice problems. By using natural language processing, ChatGPT can understand the student's question and generate a personalized response. Additionally, it can be used to generate essays, research papers, and other written assignments.

However, ChatGPT is not effective in certain aspects of teaching and learning. For instance, it is not able to provide hands-on experience, which is essential for some subjects like laboratory sciences or engineering. ChatGPT's ability to provide individualized instruction is limited by the fact that it is based on pre-trained models and it does not have the ability to adapt to the student's learning style or pace. It also does not take into account the student's prior knowledge or understanding of the subject matter. Additionally, it is not able to provide the same level of personal interaction and feedback that a human instructor can provide. Therefore, while ChatGPT can provide some level of individualized instruction, it is not a substitute for human instruction and it is more effective when used as a supplement to traditional instruction.

Leadership for a Changing World

Leading in a changing world is certainly not a new phenomenon. What is new is the pace and complex interactive nature of the changes confronting academic ecosystems and the necessity for institutions to adapt, adjust, and evolve in response. The current day challenges are multifaceted. For example, enrollment challenges today are not simply a transitional demographic phase, but the product of numerous interconnected factors—affordability, alternative competing educational pathways, growing mental health issues, and employers and families questioning the value proposition of a college education. Superimpose the implications of a global pandemic, the changing behavior of a new generation of students, technological advancements, political headwinds, and the needs of a diverse population of students and the necessity for institutional adaptation and evolution becomes evident and urgent. Proceeding with more of the same will not chart an effective path forward for most institutions.

Historically, a growing population of traditional-age college students was accepted as the norm, government funding was generally available, and a college education was recognized as an essential asset for economic and social mobility and a societal as well as personal benefit. Institutions could continue doing what they had always done with some tweaking around the edges to keep up with the times. Traditional thinking and structures were largely workable. People and programs were entrenched, and little personal discomfort and real change were necessary. Survival was rarely questioned. In those days, leaders had the luxury to espouse a charismatic vision to highlight elements of higher education perceived to raise the institution's profile and prestige, such as greater selectivity, perceived higher standards, climbing in meaningless rankings, securing gifts from wealthy alumni, and increasing external research funding, often by releasing tenured faculty from teaching and hiring inexpensive contingent labor to support the teaching mission.

In contrast, modern-day and future leaders will need to boldly lead collaborative efforts on their campuses to address declining enrollment, perceptions of diminished value and relevance, diversity demands and equity gaps, and a large array of associated financial challenges. They will need to lead a real change agenda to remain competitive, contemporize programs, delivery, and impact, and improve efficiency and effectiveness. The agenda will certainly include important and relevant research and scholarship along with, rather than instead of, a focus on student learning and success. As is always the case, there are enormous opportunities embedded in these challenges for the transformational change needed in higher education.

Leaders today have an array of tools available to transform and improve educational delivery, personalize the learning experience for students, and pursue interdisciplinary solutions to the most compelling issues facing society. We need leaders prepared to use those tools to meet the mission and the challenges on the horizon. This will demand transitioning from old-school approaches of simply lobbing information at students to applying emerging technologies to improve educational delivery and learning outcomes. It will call for new interdisciplinary approaches to address the grand challenges of our time. Student learning, health, and well-being, and that of faculty and staff, should be at the center and serve as the highly relevant and charismatic vision of the next generation of leaders who care more about the community and learning than image. That is, bold leaders released from the shackles of traditional thinking in favor of a new era for higher education centered on students, advancing economic and social well-being, and contributing meaningfully to the betterment of society.

CHAPTER TWENTY-ONE

Departing Gracefully

It's Time to Move On

Leadership roles are challenging, and no one should do them forever, or even for a long time. Of course, what represents a long time is ill-defined. One of the biggest unknowns for almost all of us is knowing when it is time to move on. To be clear, sometimes it's obvious because one may be terminated for cause, informed that their contract will not be renewed, or asked to resign as a new leader rebuilds their entire leadership team. Of course, health and family issues may also influence one's decision to step down. These situations are rather obvious and don't require a lot of complicated analysis, although there may be some angst depending on the details. There are also times when the individual in a leadership position has become exhausted or frustrated and therefore decides to quit or seek a new position with new challenges. While being tired or disheartened and eager to step down is a clear indicator that it is time to go, it is also likely an indicator that the leader stayed in their position too long. There is little doubt that if you are sick and tired of the work, it is likely that the community you are charged to lead has similar feelings about you. Many otherwise impactful leaders, however, stay in these roles too long; and either their effectiveness wanes over time, whether they know it or not, or they end up burnt out and going through the motions as they close out their administrative career. Both scenarios can be damaging to the institution and perhaps to the leader as well. So, how do leaders who have been successful and impactful know when it is time to move on before their effectiveness and mindset turn sour? There is no simple formula, but there may be signs one should pay attention to.

When Should Successful Leaders Step Down?

A key to knowing when to step down from your leadership position is remembering the purpose, roles, and responsibilities associated with leadership, which are easy to forget over time. As emphasized in chapter 1, *effective leaders identify and address key institutional challenges and mobilize the community to pursue bold aspirations.* To do so, leaders must regularly challenge the *status quo* and push the institution toward strategic change and advancement—encouraging new ideas and innovations and stimulating a state of productive restlessness (see chapter 4). Institutional leaders catapult, or at least nudge, the university forward by asking tough questions, pushing expectations, challenging all of us toward continuous improvement, and inspiring a culture of achievement and pride. At some point, however, individuals (i.e., both the leaders and the community) become too comfortable in their positions and roles, and the drive to move the institution forward is gradually diminished. Everyone settles into a comfort zone much like a well-seasoned rocking chair that is familiar and comfortable, even though it doesn't rock anymore. At that point, the state of restlessness transitions to a state of complacency, which undermines the academic enterprise that depends on intellectual capacity, innovative potential, and entrepreneurial spirit for its success and resources. Often the largely community-wide comfort zone may not initially notice the difference or may even enjoy the sense of calm.

As nuanced and abstract as this may seem, this rather subtle loss of edge or tension is a signal that it is time for new perspectives, new energy, a paradigm shift—new leadership. Over time, institutions often settle into a cultural paradigm consisting of a broad set of norms and practices that shape behavior and decision-making. Such well-established paradigms may no longer fit the organization's operations and need to be disrupted so that the institution can continue to advance and accomplish its mission. University leaders often miss those signals and overstay their welcome and effectiveness because their own increasing self-comfort overwhelms their capacity for honest self-reflection (see chapter 2) and ability to continue to inspire forward progress. The implications can be perilous to the institution and the individual.

Excerpts from Prime Minister Jacinda Ardern's Surprise Resignation Speech on January 19, 2023

I am entering now my sixth year in office. And for each of those years in office, I have given my absolute all. . . . This summer, I had hoped to find a way to prepare for not just another year, but another term. . . . I have not been able to do that. . . . I am announcing today that I will not be seeking re-election and that my term as prime minister will conclude no later than the 7th of February. This has been the most fulfilling five and a half years of my life. But it has also had its challenges. . . . But I am not leaving because it was hard. . . . I am leaving because with such a privileged role comes responsibility—the responsibility to know when you are the right person to lead, and also, when you are not. . . . I am not leaving because I think we can't win the election, but because I believe we can and will, and we need a fresh set of shoulders for that challenge. . . . Politicians are human. We give all that we can, for as long as we can, and then it's time.[267]

This latter assertion is true not only for politicians but for all leaders in complex organizations, including in higher education.

There may be many reasons why higher education leaders overstay their effectiveness, including a lack of self-awareness that the tide has turned, enjoyment of the perks of the position and an unwillingness to let them go, or simply becoming comfortable with the *status quo,* and no one is pushing them to move on. It takes an authentic leader, however, to engage in deep self-reflection and discern that it is time to step aside and welcome new leadership in the best interests of the institution. New Zealand Prime Minister Jacinda Ardern, the world's youngest female head of government when initially elected and the popular leader of New Zealand's Labour Party, took many by surprise when she abruptly announced her decision to step down as prime minister on January 19, 2023. Her thoughtful comments about her decision to resign channel her deep and honest self-reflection in concluding "you can be your own kind of leader—one who knows when it is time to go." See "Excerpts from

Prime Minister Jacinda Ardern's Surprise Resignation Speech" for reflections and introspective analysis leading to her decision. Prime Minister Ardern's words should inspire the next generation of leaders, including those in higher education, to know when they are "the right person to lead" and to also know when it is time for "a fresh set of shoulders."

So, how long should higher education leaders expect to continue to be able to serve effectively? Obviously, every situation and leader is different. Nevertheless, it strikes me that most impactful higher education leaders might expect to remain engaged and effective in their position for approximately eight to twelve years. Clearly, there will be many exceptions to this rough range of effective leadership service. Most notably, Freeman Hrabrowski, now president *emeritus*, served as president of the University of Maryland, Baltimore County (UMBC) from 1992 to 2022 and was among the most impactful and lauded university leaders in the country. His 2019 coauthored book *The Empowered University: Shared Leadership, Culture Change, and Academic Success* highlights the importance of empowering institutional culture in university communities to promote academic success.[268]

Given the broad range I have suggested and the acknowledgment that each situation is unique and there will likely be many exceptions, why suggest a ballpark range at all? The reason is that most, but not all, that stay in their leadership position at the same institution for eight, ten, or twelve years or so have a high probability of settling into the comfort zone dilemma described earlier. Certainly, approaching ten or more years of impactful leadership should trigger all college and university leaders to make extra efforts to conduct a deep and honest self-reflection about their potential for continued effectiveness and future in that role. Again, this inner reach for self-awareness is not about whether one wishes to continue in their leadership position, but rather whether one still has the energy, ideas, and drive necessary to continue to advance the institution and inspire followership from the community. That assessment will be aided by receiving candid input from trusted colleagues as well as supervisors that guide individuals forward as they contemplate "what's next." Some will determine that they remain invested, motivated, and hungry for further efforts aimed at continued institutional improvement, just as President Hrabrowski apparently and accurately concluded. Others will no doubt learn, as did Prime Minister Ardern, that it is time to exercise true leadership responsibility and step aside in favor of a "fresh set of shoulders."

Most university leadership positions offer contracts that extend for a period of three to five years with clauses to step aside or extend, as needed or desired. In addition to discerning when to step down, leadership responsibility also includes a commitment to serve long enough to accomplish stated goals and get something done, especially in higher-level positions. Given the learning curve in such positions and the time required to build trust and establish and implement a meaningful collective plan, measure progress, and inspire a culture of achievement, deans, vice presidents, provosts, and presidents also need to remain in place long enough to truly make a difference. In many ways, leaders that drop in for just a year or two run the risk of doing a disservice by creating commotion that leads nowhere. Respectful and authentic leaders stay long enough to trigger real accomplishments and are also able to discern when it is time to go.

So It's Time to Move On. Now What?

How one leaves a position is as important as how one begins a new leadership role. While the basic protocol for departing is straightforward, the details will vary with the level of the position. In all cases, however, the substance of interpersonal interactions matters deeply for one to depart gracefully. Departing gracefully is respectful and in the best interests of the institution and the individual. I have seen too many rather sudden, and sometimes spiteful, leadership departures that serve only to raise questions, create a distraction for the community, and ultimately diminish the status of the departing leader. If one is leaving under less-than-ideal circumstances, my recommendation is to simply get over it and move on to whatever is next. No one really cares about your grievances.

Stepping down from a position, especially a high-level leadership position such as dean, vice president, provost, or president, is important for the individual, the community, and the institution. As such, it requires careful planning and communication. Take some time after you have decided to step down or pursue another opportunity elsewhere to get it right. It is likely your final message to the community, so take it seriously. It is not just one more thing to get done. Consider the following thoughts and strategies as you plan a graceful departure.

- Inform your supervisor of your plan to step down in a face-to-face meeting. Hopefully, this won't come as a surprise. Whether you were exploring alternative positions or cogitating about stepping down or retiring, it is professional to have informed your supervisor in advance and perhaps even to seek their input or advice about your options.

- Allow sufficient time between your announcement and departure date for the institution to take the necessary steps to appoint an interim or permanent replacement. If possible, be flexible within reason about your official step-down date to minimize any potential fallout and ensure a sufficient timeframe for communication with essential constituents. Most upper administration contracts include a requirement of at least a thirty-day notice, but a longer period may be desirable in some situations.

- Develop a careful and respectful communication plan for your departure. The director of the communications department should be involved and helpful in shaping that plan. Who needs to be notified and by whom prior to an official announcement and in what order? For example, the chair and vice chair of the board of trustees should be notified, presumably by the president, before any formal announcement is made so that they don't learn about high-level departures by reading about them in the newspaper.

- After privately and confidentially informing your supervisor and the board chair, personally share your decision to step down with your closest circle of direct reports, followed very quickly with the remainder of your direct reports. Those announcements should include the exact or approximate timeline of your departure to the extent it is known. While an individual's decision to step down is a personal one, it isn't only about you. The departure of leaders also affects those who work closely with and report to you and may create some anxiety or impact their career development plans as well. Because the rumor mill in higher education always spins quickly, it is important to communicate to direct reports in a rapid sequence. Departing gracefully means doing so in a respectful manner toward those you have worked closely with and who presumably care about and admire you, as you do them. All direct reports should learn about your plans straight from you before the rumor mill takes over and trumps the communication plan. This is also an opportunity to share accurate information about the rationale for your decision rather than rumors, and to thank individuals whom you have worked closely with through the years.

- At this point, it may be appropriate to personally reach out to other close colleagues on- and off-campus to inform them of your plans. This list might include a few major donors or loyal alumni with whom you have worked very closely. These individuals will be honored to hear the news directly from you, and it will help reaffirm their close connection to you and to the university. As provost, I spoke by phone to the president and vice president of the faculty senate, the executive director of the AAUP, the director of the honors program, several major donors, and a few close university colleagues.

- A critical next step is to prepare a written communication to the extended community in your sphere of work to share your decision to step down. For me, the tone and text of this letter are important. For deans, this would likely be directed to faculty and staff of the college and perhaps close external constituents, such as advisory board members and donors. For VPs, this letter would likely go to staff in the division. As provost, I sent a letter to all faculty and staff of the university and copied the board of trustees. The president's letter would go to the entire university community and a host of external constituents, such as donors, alums, key legislators, etc.

Your Parting Message to the Community

I recognize that each of us will have our own ideas about our parting message. That is exactly how it ought to be. As such, I should probably mind my own business and not offer advice or suggestions. Your letter must be *your* letter. I have, however, seen many such letters that are self-focused, self-promoting about accomplishments, or subtle—or often not so subtle—boasting about the new opportunity and expanded responsibilities ahead. As a result, I can't resist offering a few thoughts for you to consider or ignore.

First, your public letter of resignation should really be a letter of farewell to the community that you have been an integral part of for some period of time. You may need a formal letter of resignation for the human resources file, but that is different from your letter to the community.

402 | SUBSTANCE OVER STYLE

Your letter to the community will leave a lasting impression about who you are and what you stand for and needs to be much more than a boiler-plate template for the HR file. No doubt, the communications department will volunteer to draft the letter for you. I urge you to reject that offer and write it yourself. This final communication from you should reflect your authentic voice, message, and thanks and address those things you care about most. A ghostwriter can never capture the feeling and tone of a genuine farewell.

Most of all, your letter needs to be authentic, and hopefully can convey an attitude of gratitude. It should be brief—no more than a page. In addition to announcing your plans to step down after some number of years in your position and your departure date, I hope you might be comfortable sharing your positive feelings toward the position and its responsibilities, the people you worked closely with, the meaning of the work you were engaged in along with many others, and the institution that provided you the wonderful opportunity.

Recognizing and expressing gratitude to the many partners and collaborators who really keep the institution operating is important as well. Expressing your commitment to a smooth transition to your replacement and your acknowledgment that the institution is well-positioned to thrive in the future conveys your enthusiasm for and confidence in the leaders in place. This letter is *not* the space, in my view, to offer feedback to the institution or a critique of shortcomings and functions that need to be improved. If necessary, that should be done privately and in a constructive manner. Some individuals use these letters to describe their greatest accomplishment or legacy, or provide a list of positive gains made in key areas under their leadership. Frankly, that is often perceived, at least by me, as overbearing and arrogant and not recognizing the many people in the community that did the work that resulted in those advancements. I urge you to allow others to decide on their own whether, how, and why significant advancements may have occurred and, if so, who is responsible for them. Use this final letter to simply say farewell and to thank your colleagues for their patience, hard work, and support.

Many of you are probably familiar with the distinguished journalist, Judy Woodruff, the now former anchor and managing editor of *PBS NewsHour*. Ms. Woodruff stepped down from the *PBS NewsHour* anchor desk on December 30, 2022. In my opinion, she is a consummate professional and among the most trusted and well-respected journalists serving as a news anchor. She is fair and balanced, and her reporting is always intended to inform and enlighten rather than create a *gotcha* moment as entertainment for an audience. Her professionalism is reflected in the tone and sincerity of her announcement on November 11, 2022, that she would be stepping down and her goodbye message to colleagues and viewers at the end of her final broadcast as anchor on December 30, 2022. See "Excerpts from Judy Woodruff's Announcement about Stepping Down as Anchor of *PBS NewsHour* and Her Goodbye Message to Viewers and Colleagues," which serve as a model for departing gracefully.

Excerpts from Judy Woodruff's Announcement about Stepping Down as Anchor of *PBS NewsHour* and Her Goodbye Message to Viewers and Colleagues

Announcement on November 11, 2022:

> After a decade as anchor of this extraordinary program, I have decided that the end of 2022 is the right time to turn this incredibly important job over to someone else. . . . Being the anchor has been the honor of a lifetime every single day to follow in the footsteps of two iconic journalists, Robert MacNeil and Jim Lehrer, and to have sat alongside the incomparable Gwen Ifill. But, on December 30, I will say thank you, and then I will transition to a new role at the NewsHour. . . . But, for now, I have a heart full of thanks to each of you who watch and follow the NewsHour, you are the reason we do what we do, and always to the utterly amazing NewsHour staff. And that is the NewsHour for tonight. . . . From all of us at the *PBS NewsHour*, thank you, please be safe, and we'll see you soon.[269]

Goodbye Message on December 30, 2022:

> . . . As I turn over this special anchor desk, with its remarkable history, . . . just a few words about what it has meant to sit here . . . through some of the most tumultuous events of our time, seven different presidential elections, the end of the Cold War, the start of many hot ones, and, most fresh in my mind, the COVID pandemic, the reckoning over race in America, mass shootings in schools and grocery stores, and our nation's deepening

political divide. Through it all, I have tried to stay true to what the program's founders . . . believed so fiercely, that we're here to report, to tell you as accurately and fairly as we can what's going on in the world, and to let you make up your minds about what to think, and to have the courage . . . to ask the tough questions, to hold people in power accountable, and . . . to care enough about each one of you and your beliefs, (and) what your lives are like. It has been an honor of a lifetime to be in this chair, to tell these hugely important stories, to share the worst and best of humanity, all of which we need to hear to be the best possible citizens we can be, and, of course, to support the work done by my remarkable NewsHour colleagues. . . . They do the work, day in and day out, hour in and hour out, to get this program on the air. . . . And, finally, I want to thank you who are watching in the United States and around the world, the best viewers anywhere, concerned citizens, who hold us to a high standard every single day. Thank you for trusting us to tell it straight. I step away now with a heart full of gratitude for the singular opportunity to share the most critical stories of our time. . . . And, as we say every evening: that is the NewsHour for tonight. I'm Judy Woodruff.[270]

Moving Forward, Stepping Back

Departing really does mean stepping away. Whether you are retiring or returning to a previous faculty or staff position at your institution, it is professional and courteous for you to blend into the shadows for at least a year or two to give the new leader room to establish their own identity and presence on campus. If possible, you might even take a well-earned sabbatical to prepare for whatever is next, which also creates some distance from the campus community. This, however, is a hard personal step for many. Some leaders become accustomed to being center stage and can't resist emerging in public meetings on campus or elsewhere. I have seen former presidents show up at public meetings of the board of trustees, former provosts attending faculty senate meetings, and former deans attending and actively participating in college faculty meetings—all within the first year or two after their departure. This is unfortunate and has the potential to create a distraction for others and perhaps awkward moments for the new leader now running or actively participating in those meetings. The moral of the story is that as the departed leader, you are now part of the past. Let it go and help create space for new leaders to establish their voice and exert their influence. After stepping down from her leadership position as Speaker of the House of Representatives, Nancy Pelosi gracefully role-modeled this respectful behavior. In an opinion piece in *The New York Times* entitled "Nancy Pelosi, Liberated and Loving It," Maureen Dowd shared that Pelosi did not accept the well-intentioned invitation to sit in the front row with the new minority leader during the new speaker votes, but instead chose to sit near the back of the House. According to Dowd, Pelosi did not want "to hover over the new leadership." Whether you agree with her politics or not, she did exactly the right thing.[271]

And, finally, resist the temptation to sit on the sidelines and second-guess with friends and colleagues' decisions, announcements, and proclamations that come from the person that replaced you or the new leadership team. No doubt, you would have done things differently. In many ways, that is why you stepped down. It was time for new perspectives, directions, visions, and a fresh set of decisions. As such, it is also time for departed leaders to be helpful in creating space for new ideas to permeate the community, and, if anything, to reinforce your enthusiasm about the future direction of the institution. Anything less is unprofessional, unproductive, and trite. Similarly, new leaders should resist the temptation to publicly ascribe blame to their predecessors for whatever isn't going well. Such scapegoating is unprofessional and signals weakness, or even dysfunction, to the community. To be sure, if the new leadership team seeks your input, advice, or recollections, you should feel comfortable sharing your experiences, knowledge, and historical perspectives with them. When decisions are made or new directions are announced, however, you should quietly blend into the background, whether your advice was heeded or not. As former leaders know better than most, there are plenty of others on every campus who will critique almost every decision and direction espoused by administrative leaders. Your public voice from the past is not helpful. Departing gracefully includes understanding that stepping back is necessary for the institution to move forward.

Final Thoughts and Reflections

Through the years I have had the pleasure of occupying and departing, gracefully I hope, faculty, administrator, and various other leadership positions in several academic institutions and organizations, including recently stepping back from any formal role in the academy. I am immensely grateful for having had the opportunity to pour myself into the critical work of advancing learning, discovery, and the future of higher education. These experiences have given me perspective and prompted my reflection on my approximately forty-five years as a faculty member and academic leader. I have learned so much about the inner workings of universities, the breadth and depth of learning and scholarship across disciplines, and the substance of leadership as well as about myself and what motivates and inspires me. This field guide to leadership in higher education is a compilation of those experiences—an opportunity to share my observations and insights and to offer thoughts about substantive leadership necessary to advance higher education in the twenty-first century.

This introspective analysis has helped me understand that I love the academy. I always have. Every aspect of it. I have enjoyed teaching, working with students, conducting research, publishing articles, writing grant proposals whether they were funded or not, and engaging with my colleagues on both scholarly topics and university governance. I never planned to move from my faculty role into administrative positions. It just happened. In all my roles, even as an assistant professor, I was always thinking about things that needed to change, strategizing about ways our work could be more relevant, and imagining new approaches to enhance the impact, visibility, and success of our collective efforts. I suppose that is how and why I gradually migrated to the world of academic leadership.

Deep down inside, however, my soul resonates deeply with the academic core mission and the work of the faculty, not only with the teaching, research and scholarship, and service elements of the work but also with the debate, discussion, disagreements, and sometimes endless committees inherent in and emblematic of shared governance—a hallmark of the academic community. As such, it was an extraordinary honor to serve as dean for many years and president of a national organization and then as provost and vice president for academic affairs for nearly fourteen years with the responsibility to protect and enhance the academic core mission. To be sure, the role of the provost, especially at research universities, is steeped in complexity, ambiguity, and ever-challenging financial and personnel matters. I must admit, however, I loved every minute and aspect of the work, including the myriad challenges of addressing major budget reductions; creating, reorganizing, and dissolving programs; navigating intense and at times antagonistic personnel issues; battling with colleagues, peers, legislators, and trustees over academic matters; and leading an institution through the many facets of the devastating COVID-19 pandemic. For me, nothing could possibly be better or more meaningful than working every day with some of the smartest and most creative and committed people in the world to advance the academic core mission—the heart and soul of the academy and its reason for being.

The challenges facing higher education today are abundant, complex, and multi-dimensional, but also a welcoming invitation for the next generation of aspiring leaders. I urge you to not be intimidated by those challenges but rather courageously embrace them with all the unknowns that they represent. The Brazilian novelist and international best-selling author Paulo Coelho teaches us that "courage doesn't mean the absence of fear, but the ability to not let yourself be paralyzed by that fear."[272] So, as aspiring leaders, you don't need to muster the courage to confront the challenges before us, but rather to abandon and evolve from the safety of the old ways of doing things that we are accustomed to (i.e., the *status quo*) and chart a new path forward with passion and humility. That is what is necessary. The leader's role is not simply to defend the academy against "improper intrusions." Rather, it is to protect the core elements of learning and discovery, which are essential to the fundamentals of education and functional democracy, by ensuring that they evolve over time. You must be willing to take risks, strategically change directions, recognize you will make mistakes along the way, and find the courage to allow yourself to grow. What is needed is truly authentic, strategic, and empathetic leaders with the knowledge, skills, and values to lead with their hearts and mind to ensure that our institutions confront challenges, are always evolving, and truly have a positive impact on our students and society more broadly.

As aspiring leaders, whether you are a student, staff, or member of the faculty, I urge you to run toward rather than away from leadership responsibilities as you ponder the next phase of your life and begin to think about what's next. I hope you seriously explore applying your expertise, abilities, and passion by giving back to create opportunities for others by addressing key educational challenges and mobilizing others to pursue bold aspirations. In her book *Lanterns: A Memoir of Mentors*, Marian Wright Edelman, civil rights and children's rights activist and founder and president *emerita* of the Children's Defense Fund, channels the inspiration of her mentor Dr. Benjamin Elijah Mays who reminds us that "the tragedy of life is not in our failure, but rather in our complacency; not in our doing too much, but in our doing too little; not in our living above our ability, but rather in our living below our capacities."[273] The commitment and action of just a few leaders are sufficient and necessary to change the world.

Many years ago, a student in my introductory course entitled Natural History and Field Biology gave me a book that changed my life and my view of the world. *The Man Who Planted Trees* by Jean Giono is a simple, beautifully written, thought-provoking story of a man whose unselfish commitment and perseverance were responsible for converting a barren wasteland into a healthy forest with rushing streams and abounding wildlife simply by planting a hundred acorns each day. I recall vividly that Giono wrote, "When you remembered that all this sprung from the hands and the soul of this one man . . . you understood that humans could be as effectual as God in other realms than that of destruction."[274] Giono further marveled, "When I reflect that one man, armed with his own physical and moral resources, was able to cause this land of Canaan to spring from the wasteland, I am convinced that in spite of everything humanity is admirable."[275] Indeed, through your admirable leadership and commitment, you have the capacity to create a vibrant and hopeful future and fulfill the nation's promise of equal opportunity for all to learn, thrive, and succeed.

The opportunity to serve in an important academic leadership role is an enormous privilege. I know this firsthand and feel grateful every day. It's time for me to depart gracefully once again to make room for a new generation of university leaders and scholars. As in the story of the old man who planted trees, you too can leave your mark on the earth through leadership substance that positively shapes the lives of many by sowing seeds of learning that grow into opportunities for economic and social mobility and justice for all.

Notes

1. Hutchins, "Importance of Training for Inclusive Leadership."
2. Nielsen, *Provost*, 6.
3. University of Rhode Island, *Anti-Black Racism*, 2021.
4. Tjan, *Good People*, 2017.
5. Carter, *Integrity*, 1996.
6. Wheatley, *Leadership and the New Science*, 2006.
7. Cardona, "New Vision for College Excellence."
8. Cardona, "New Vision for College Excellence."
9. Kendi, *How to Be an Antiracist*, 2019.
10. MP Associates, "Racial Equity Tools Glossary."
11. Kendi, *How to Be an Antiracist*, 18.
12. Kendi, *How to Be an Antiracist*, 18.
13. Kendi, *How to Be an Antiracist*, 20.
14. Kendi, *How to Be an Antiracist*, 20.
15. Dillon and Bourke, *Six Signature Traits of Inclusive Leadership*, 2016.
16. Milem, "Educational Benefits of Diversity."
17. Bitar, Montague, and Ilano, "Faculty Diversity and Student Success."
18. Chronicle of Higher Education Staff, "DEI Legislation Tracker."
19. USC Center for Urban Education, *Laying the Groundwork*, 25–26.
20. USC Center for Urban Education, *Laying the Groundwork*, 21.
21. Isenstadt, "Holder: Still Need for Frank Talk on Race."
22. Holder, transcript of speech delivered at the Department of Justice African American History Month Program, February 18, 2009.
23. Adams, Bell, and Griffin, eds., *Teaching for Diversity and Social Justice*, 2016; Adams, et al, *Readings for Diversity and Social Justice*, 2018.
24. de Bray et al, *Status and Trends in the Education*, 2019.
25. National Center for Education Statistics, *Characteristics of Postsecondary Faculty*, 2022.
26. Flaherty, "Where DEI Work Is Faculty Work."
27. Duckworth, *Grit*, 2016.
28. Twenge, *iGen*, 2017.

29. Lukianoff and Haidt, *Coddling of the American Mind*, 2018.

30. Boyer, *Scholarship Reconsidered*, 1990.

31. National Center for Education Statistics, "Table 315.10."

32. Colby, "Data Snapshot: Tenure and Contingency."

33. Kline, "Survey Results."

34. Scott, *How University Boards Work*, 37.

35. Scott, *How University Boards Work*, 37.

36. Scott, *How University Boards Work*, 139.

37. Association of Governing Boards of Universities and Colleges, *Effective Governing Boards*, 2009.

38. American Association of University Professors, "Statement on Government of Colleges and Universities."

39. Zahneis, "What's Behind the Surge"; for complete data, visit the No-Confidence Vote Database at SeanMcKinniss.org, last updated March 1, 2021.

40. Zahneis, "What's Behind the Surge."

41. National Center for Science and Engineering Statistics, "Survey of Earned Doctorates."

42. Brown, "Use of Contributions."

43. Jaschik, "Provosts Stand Firm."

44. Bichsel et al, "CUPA-HR 2022 Higher Education Employee Retention Survey."

45. Elias, "Tuition Revenue Has Fallen."

46. Whitford, "College Endowments Boomed in Fiscal 2021."

47. American Council on Education, *Understanding College and University Endowments*, 2.

48. NACUBO-TIAA, *Study of Endowments: Summary Observations from the 2021 NACUBO-TIAA Study of Endowments*; NACUBO/TIAA, *Study of Endowments: Number of Respondents to the 2022 NACUBO-TIAA Study of Endowments*; and NACUBO-TIAA, *Study of Endowments: Summary Observations from the 2022 NACUBO-TIAA Study of Endowments*.

49. Kwiram, *Primer on Indirect Costs*, March 1992.

50. Kwiram, *Primer on Indirect Costs*, March 1992.

51. Government Finance Officers Association, "Best Practices."

52. Stickelmaier and Tegen, "Do You Know the Financial Health of Your Institution?" 9.

53. National Student Clearinghouse Research Center, "Fall Enrollments Decline."

54. National Student Clearinghouse Research Center, "Current Term Enrollment Estimates Report: Fall 2019."

55. National Student Clearinghouse Research Center, "Current Term Enrollment Estimates Report: Fall 2021."

56. National Student Clearinghouse Research Center, "Current Term Enrollment Estimates Report: Spring 2022."

57. National Student Clearinghouse Research Center, "New Research: Fall Undergraduate Enrollment Stabilized in 2022."

58. National Student Clearinghouse Research Center, "Stay Informed."

59. National Student Clearinghouse Research Center, "Stay Informed."

60. Educational Credit Management Corporation Group, *Question the Quo.*

61. Brenan, "Americans' Confidence in Higher Education."

62. Pollard, *Soul of the Firm,* 123.

63. Kerr and Wood, "A Look at College Tuition Growth."

64. Ma and Pender, *Trends in College Pricing,* 12.

65. National Center for Education Statistics, "Sources of Financial Aid."

66. Ma and Pender, *Trends in College Pricing,* 4.

67. National Association of College and University Business Officers, "Tuition Discount Rates."

68. National Association of College and University Business Officers, "Trends in Institutional Financial Aid."

69. National Student Clearinghouse Research Center, *Persistence and Retention,* June 2022.

70. National Student Clearinghouse Research Center, *Persistence and Retention,* June 2022.

71. Hanover Research, *Strategies for Improving Student Retention,* 5.

72. National Student Clearinghouse Research Center, "Current Term Enrollment Estimates: Fall 2021," 4.

73. Hanson, "College Enrollment and Student Demographic Statistics."

74. National Student Clearinghouse Research Center, *Persistence and Retention,* June 2022.

75. Institute for International Education, "US Colleges and Universities Remain."

76. Institute for International Education, "US Colleges and Universities See."

77. United States Department of Education and Department of State, *Reengaging the World.*

78. Israel and Batalava, "International Students in the United States."

79. United States Census Bureau, "Census Bureau Releases New Educational Attainment Data."

80. National Student Clearinghouse Research Center, *Some College, No Credential Student Outcomes,* 2.

81. National Student Clearinghouse Research Center, *Some College, No Degree: A 2019 Snapshot,* October 2019.

82. National Student Clearinghouse Research Center, *Some College, No Credential Student Outcomes,* April 2023.

83. National Center for Education Statistics, "Characteristics of Postsecondary Students."

84. United States Census Bureau, "Census Bureau Releases New Educational Attainment Data."

85. National Student Clearinghouse Research Center, "Stay Informed."

86. New England Commission of Higher Education, "Standards for Accreditation."

87. Ammentorp and Warner, *Academic Design,* 2004.

88. Smith, *How University Budgets Work,* 2019.

89. Hanover Research, "Six Alternative Budget Models"; Educational Advisory Board, *Exploring Alternative Budget Models*, 2013; Educational Advisory Board, *Optimizing Institutional Budget Models*, 2016; Educational Advisory Board, *Compendium of Budget Model Profiles*, 2021.

90. Mehta, "Eight Principles for Successful Budget."

91. Mehta, "Eight Principles for Successful Budget."

92. Educational Advisory Board, *Exploring Alternative Budget Models*, 2013; Educational Advisory Board, *Optimizing Institutional Budget Models*, 2016.

93. Educational Advisory Board, Optimizing Institutional Budget Models, 12.

94. Mehta, "Eight Principles for Successful Budget."

95. Educational Advisory Board, *Optimizing Institutional Budget Models*, 13.

96. Educational Advisory Board, *Optimizing Institutional Budget Models*, 16.

97. Educational Advisory Board, *Optimizing Institutional Budget Models*, 13.

98. Educational Advisory Board, *Optimizing Institutional Budget Models*, 18.

99. Educational Advisory Board, *Optimizing Institutional Budget Models*, 18.

100. Nielsen, *Provost*, 55.

101. National Center for Education Statistics, "About IPEDS."

102. National Student Clearinghouse Research Center, *Persistence and Retention: Fall 2019*, 1.

103. National Student Clearinghouse Research Center, *Persistence and Retention: Fall 2020*, 4, 6, 8, 10.

104. National Center for Education Statistics, "Undergraduate Retention and Graduation Rates," Figure 1.

105. Kantrowitz, "Shocking Statistics About College."

106. Kantrowitz, "Shocking Statistics About College."

107. National Student Clearinghouse Research Center, *Persistence and Retention: Fall 2020*, 2.

108. National Center for Education Statistics, "Table 326.10."

109. National Center for Education Statistics, "Table 326.20."

110. National Center for Education Statistics, "Table 326.20."

111. Kantrowitz, "Shocking Statistics About College."

112. Whistle and Hiler, "The Pell Divide."

113. Student Achievement Measure (SAM), (website), https://www.studentachievementmeasure.org.

114. Obama, "Remarks by the President on the American Graduation Initiative."

115. Organization for Economic Cooperation and Development, "Population with Tertiary Education."

116. Odle et al, *PDP Insights: Credit Accumulation*, 1.

117. Odle et al, *PDP Insights: Credit Accumulation*, 2–3.

118. Complete College America, *No Room for Doubt*, 1.

119. Setser and Morris, *Building a Culture of Innovation*, 8.

120. American Association of State Colleges and Universities, *Making Partnerships Work*, 2018.

121. Leiderman et al, *Building Partnerships*, 2002.
122. Messmore, "How to Establish Powerful Campus Partnerships."
123. IUPUI Lilly School of Philanthropy, "Giving USA 2022: Total US Charitable Giving."
124. Kaplan, *Voluntary Support of Education*, 5.
125. Kaplan, *Voluntary Support of Education*, 6.
126. Kaplan, *Voluntary Support of Education*, 5.
127. Kaplan, *Voluntary Support of Education*, 5.
128. Shaker and Borden, "How Donors Give," 4.
129. Kaplan, *Voluntary Support of Education*, 4.
130. Kaplan, *Voluntary Support of Education*, 5.
131. American Council on Education, *Understanding College and University Endowments*, 6.
132. NACUBO-TIAA, *Study of Endowments*, 4.
133. Shaker and Borden, "How Donors Give."
134. Shaker and Borden, "How Donors Give"; Kaplan, *Voluntary Support of Education*, 5.
135. Shaker, "Three Key Questions for Higher Education," Figure 2.
136. Giacomini et al, *CASE Study of Principal Gifts*, 7.
137. Giacomini et al, *CASE Study of Principal Gifts*, 7.
138. Cavanah, "Creating a Culture of Philanthropy," 1.
139. Langley, "Cultivating a Culture of Philanthropy."
140. Knox, "Higher Ed Charitable Giving."
141. National Collegiate Athletic Association, *Fifteen-Year Trends*, 13.
142. On3 Staff, "USA Today Releases Top 25," *On3* (website), June 14, 2023. The original *USA Today* article has since been taken down.
143. National Collegiate Athletic Association, *Fifteen-Year Trends*, 9.
144. Bennett, "NCAA Board Votes to Allow Autonomy."
145. National Collegiate Athletic Association, *Fifteen-Year Trends*, 8.
146. Drozdowski, "Do Colleges Make Money."
147. Epps, "What Is the NCAA?"
148. National Collegiate Athletic Association, *Trends in NCAA Division I Graduation Rates*, 3.
149. Epps, "What Is the NCAA?"
150. US Department of Health and Human Services, "Title IX of the Education Amendments of 1972."
151. Chung, "Dynamic Advertising Effect," 5.
152. Mayes and Giambalvo, "Does Sports Glory Create."
153. Pope and Pope, "Impact of College Sports Success," 750–780.
154. Anderson, "Benefits of College Athletic Success," 119–134.
155. Chung, "Dynamic Advertising Effect," 31.
156. Baumer and Zimblast, "Impact of College Athletic Success," 19.
157. Anderson, "Benefits of College Athletic Success," 119–134.

158. Walker, "Division 1 Intercollegiate Athletic Success," 8.

159. Baumer and Zimblast, "Impact of College Athletic Success," 19.

160. Anderson, "Benefits of College Athletic Success," 119–134.

161. National Collegiate Athletic Association, "Finances of Intercollegiate Athletics Database"; National Collegiate Athletic Association, *Fifteen-Year Trends*, 2020.

162. National Collegiate Athletic Association, *Fifteen-Year Trends*, 13.

163. Desrochers, *Academic Spending Versus Athletic Spending*, 2.

164. National Collegiate Athletic Association, *Fifteen-Year Trends*, 7–8 and 22–25.

165. Knight-Newhouse, "College Athletics Database."

166. Desrochers, *Academic Spending Versus Athletic Spending*, 2.

167. Alonso, "UNO Students Vote."

168. Enright, Lehren, and Longoria, "Hidden Figures."

169. Lopiano et al, "Failing to Confront."

170. Elbaba, "How NCAA Transfer Portal Works."

171. National Collegiate Athletic Association, "NCAA Adopts Interim."

172. Nakos, "What Is NIL?"

173. Varnum Law, "California Assembly Approves the College."

174. Parker, "Growing Partisan Divide."

175. Doherty and Kiley, "Americans Have Become."

176. Fishman, Nguyen, and Woodhouse, "Varying Degrees 2022."

177. Brenan, "Americans' Confidence in Higher Education."

178. Kelderman, "The College Degree Is Dividing America."

179. Pew Research Center, "Demographic Profiles of Republican and Democratic Voters."

180. Jaschik, "Professors and Politics."

181. Abrams and Khalid, "Are Colleges and Universities."

182. Barshay, "Calculating Faculty Bias."

183. Abrams and Khalid, "Are Colleges and Universities."

184. Jaschik, "Professors and Politics."

185. Post, "Free Speech and Academic Freedom."

186. Post, "Free Speech and Academic Freedom."

187. American Association of University Professors, "1940 Statement of Principles."

188. Jaschik, "Tenure Survives in Texas."

189. American Association of University Professors, "1940 Statement of Principles."

190. Colby, *Data Snapshot: Tenure and Contingency*, March 2023.

191. Bellows, "Here's How Title IX."

192. Long and Bateman, "Long-Run Changes," 188–207.

193. Chen and Wolfe, "State Affirmative Action Bans."

194. Chen and Wolfe, "State Affirmative Action Bans."

195. Bleemer, "Affirmative Action, Mismatch, and Economic Mobility," 115–160.

196. Parker, "Growing Partisan Divide."

197. Binkley and Swanson, "Most in US Say Don't Ban Race."

198. American Council on Education, *Brief of American Council on Education*, 2022.

199. American Council on Education, *Brief of American Council on Education*, 4–5.

200. American Council on Education, *Brief of American Council on Education*, 5.

201. American Council on Education, *Brief of American Council on Education*, 3–4.

202. Hartig, "Democrats Overwhelmingly Favor."

203. Fishman et al, "Varying Degrees 2022."

204. Conkling and Gibbs, "Update on Student Loan Borrowers."

205. The White House, "Fact Sheet: Biden-Harris Launches the SAVE Plan."

206. Chronicle of Higher Education Staff, "DEI Legislation Tracker."

207. Nietzel, "Students and Employees Snub."

208. FLBOG, *Intellectual Freedom and Viewpoint Diversity*.

209. Coleman, "Access to Abortion Services."

210. Beilock et al, "'Deeply Concerned:' Six College Presidents."

211. McGuire, "Dumbing Down of the Purpose."

212. McGuire, "Dumbing Down of the Purpose."

213. McGuire, "Dumbing Down of the Purpose."

214. National Student Clearinghouse Research Center, "Fall 2021 Current Tern Enrollment."

215. National Student Clearinghouse Research Center, "Undergraduate Enrollment Falls."

216. National Student Clearinghouse Research Center, "Stay Informed."

217. Zhou, *Graduate Enrollment and Degrees*, 4–5.

218. Reeves and Smith, "Male College Crisis."

219. Kline, "Looming Higher Ed Enrollment Cliff."

220. Kline, "Looming Higher Ed Enrollment Cliff."

221. Kline, "Looming Higher Ed Enrollment Cliff."

222. Grawe, *Demographics and the Demand for Higher Education*, 2018.

223. National Student Clearinghouse Research Center, "Stay Informed."

224. Hanover Research, "2022 National Prospective Student Survey."

225. National Center for Educational Statistics, "Table 330.10."

226. Barshay, "Room and Board Charges Rising."

227. Welding, "Student Loan Debt by Year."

228. Welding, "Student Loan Debt Statistics."

229. National Center for Educational Statistics, "Table 331.95"; National Center for Educational Statistics, "Table 332.45."

230. Lederman, "Majority of Americans Lack Confidence."

231. National Student Clearinghouse Research Center, "Stay Informed."

232. Stanford, "College Readiness Shouldn't Be."

233. Seaman and Seaman, *Planning for a Smaller Future*, 9.

234. Bok, *Our Underachieving Colleges*, 40.

235. Chronicle of Higher Education Staff, "How to Solve the Student-Disengagement Crisis."

236. Fischman and Gardner, "Students Are Missing the Point."

237. Fischman and Gardner, "Students Are Missing the Point."

238. American Academy of Pediatrics, "AAP-AACAP-CHA Declaration of a National Emergency."

239. Lipson et al, "Trends in College Student Mental Health," 138.

240. American College Health Association, *American College Health Association-National Health Assessment III*, 12.

241. National Assessment of Educational Progress, "NAEP Report Card: 2022 NAEP Mathematics Assessment"; National Assessment of Educational Programs, "NAEP Report Card: 2022 NAEP Reading Assessment."

242. National Assessment of Educational Progress, "NAEP Report Card: 2022 NAEP Mathematics Assessment"; National Assessment of Educational Programs, "NAEP Report Card: 2022 NAEP Reading Assessment."

243. National Assessment of Educational Progress, "NAEP Report Card: 2022 NAEP Mathematics Assessment."

244. National Assessment of Educational Programs, "NAEP Report Card: 2022 NAEP Reading Assessment."

245. ACT, "Fewer High School Seniors Ready for College."

246. D'Agostino, "Surge in Young Undergrads."

247. Perez, "Fall-Enrollment Trends in Distance Education."

248. Perez, "Fall-Enrollment Trends in Distance Education."

249. National Center for Educational Statistics, "Table 306.10."

250. National Center for Educational Statistics, "Table 306.10"; National Center for Educational Statistics, "Table 315.20."

251. Bitar, Montague, and Ilano, *Faculty Diversity and Student Success*, 4.

252. Kim, *Formal and Informal Mentoring*, 2023.

253. Bitar, Montague, and Ilano, *Faculty Diversity and Student Success*, 21–22; Bartlebaugh and Abraham, *Now Is the Time*, 4–6.

254. Flaherty, "Calling It Quits."

255. Chronicle of Higher Education Staff, "On the Verge of Burnout," 7.

256. Bichsel et al, *CUPA-HR 2022 Higher Education*, July 2022.

257. Flaherty, "Calling It Quits."

258. Chronicle of Higher Education Staff, "On the Verge of Burnout," 12–13.

259. Sallee, *Addressing Burnout Through Cultural Change*, 5–10.

260. Sallee, *Addressing Burnout Through Cultural Change*, 5–10.

261. United Educators, *2022 Top Risks Report*, 3.

262. Jaschik and Lederman, eds. "2022 Survey of Campus Chief Technology/Information Officers."

263. Grajek and Reintz, "Getting Ready for Digital Transformation."

264. Grajek and Reintz, "Getting Ready for Digital Transformation."

265. Jaschik and Lederman, eds., "2022 Survey of Campus Chief Technology/Information Officers."

266. Grajek and Reintz, "Getting Ready for Digital Transformation."

267. Stuff, "Prime Minister Jacinda Ardern's Full Resignation Speech."

268. Hrabowski, *Empowered University*, 2019.

269. Woodruff, "Judy Woodruff Stepping Aside."

270. Woodruff, "Judy Woodruff's Goodbye Message."

271. Dowd, "Nancy Pelosi, Liberated and Loving It."

272. Coelho, *Life: Selected Quotations*, 80.

273. Edelman, *Lanterns: A Memoir of Mentors*, 30.

274. Giono, *Man Who Planted Trees*, 21.

275. Giono, *Man Who Planted Trees*, 34–35.

Bibliography

Abrams, Samuel, and Amna Khalid. "Are Colleges and Universities Too Liberal? What the Research Says about the Political Composition of Campuses and Campus Climate." American Enterprise Institute (website). Last updated October 21, 2020. https://www.aei.org/articles/are-colleges-and-universities-too-liberal-what-the-research-says-about-the-political-composition-of-campuses-and-campus-climate/.

ACT. "Fewer High School Seniors Ready for College as ACT Scores Continue to Decline." ACT Newsroom and Blog (website), October 10, 2023. https://leadershipblog.act.org/2023/10/act-scores-decline.html.

Adams, Maurianne, Lee Anne Bell, and Pat Griffin, eds. *Teaching for Diversity and Social Justice.* 3rd ed. New York: Routledge Taylor and Francis Group, 2016.

Adams, Maurianne, Warren Blumenfeld, D. Chase Catalano, Keri DeJong, Heather Hackman, Larissa Hopkins, Barbara Love, Madeline Peters, Davey Shlasko, and Ximena Zuniga, eds. *Readings for Diversity and Social Justice.* 4th ed. New York: Routledge Taylor and Francis Group, 2018.

Alonso, Johanna. "UNO Students Vote Against Student Experience Fee." *Inside Higher Ed,* November 10, 2022. https://www.insidehighered.com/quicktakes/2022/11/11/uno-students-vote-against-student-experience-fee.

American Academy of Pediatrics. "AAP-AACAP-CHA Declaration of a National Emergency in Child and Adolescent Mental Health." AAP News (website), October 19, 2021. https://www.aap.org/en/advocacy/child-and-adolescent-healthy-mental-development/aap-aacap-cha-declaration-of-a-national-emergency-in-child-and-adolescent-mental-health/.

American Association of State Colleges and Universities. *Making Partnerships Work: Principles, Guidelines, and Advice for Public University Leaders.* Washington, DC: AASCU, 2018. https://aascu.org/resources/making-partnerships-work-principles-guidelines-and-advice-for-public-university-leaders/.

American Association of University Professors. "Statement on Government of Colleges and Universities." AAUP (website). Accessed October 24, 2023. https://www.aaup.org/report/statement-government-colleges-and-universities.

American Association of University Professors. "The 1940 Statement of Principles on Academic Freedom and Tenure." AAUP (website). Accessed October 24, 2023. https://www.aaup.org/report/1940-statement-principles-academic-freedom-and-tenure.

American College Health Association. *American College Health Association-National Health Assessment III: Reference Group Executive Summary Fall 2022.* Silver Spring, MD: American College Health Association, 2023. https://www.acha.org/documents/ncha/NCHA-III_FALL_2022_REFERENCE_GROUP_EXECUTIVE_SUMMARY.pdf.

American Council on Education. *Brief of American Council on Education and 38 Other Higher Education Associations as AMICI Curiae in Support of Respondents.* Washington, DC: American Council on Education, 2022. https://www.acenet.edu/Documents/Amicus-Brief-SCOTUS-SFFA-v-Harvard-UNC-080122.pdf.

American Council on Education. *Understanding College and University Endowments.* Washington, DC: American Council on Education, 2021. https://www.acenet.edu/Documents/Understanding-College-and-University-Endowments.pdf.

American Council on Education. *Understanding College and University Endowments.* Washington, DC: American Council on Education, 2021. https://www.acenet.edu/Documents/Understanding-College-and-University-Endowments.pdf.

Ammentorp, Bill, and Bill Warner. *Academic Design: Sharing Lessons Learned.* Ann Arbor, MI: The Society for College and University Planning, 2003.

Anderson, Michael. "The Benefits of College Athletic Success: An Application of the Propensity Score Design." *Review of Economics and Statistics* 99, no. 1 (March 2017): 119–134.

Association of Governing Boards of Universities and Colleges. *Effective Governing Boards: A Guide for Members of Governing Boards of Independent Colleges and Universities.* Washington, DC: AGB Press, 2009.

Barshay, Jill. "Room and Board Charges Rising Faster Than Inflation." *The Hechinger Report* (website). Last updated April 13, 2015. https://hechingerreport.org/room-and-board-charges-rising-faster-than-inflation/.

Barshay, Jill. "Calculating Faculty Bias against Conservative Students." *The Hechinger Report* (website), June 24, 2019. https://hechingerreport.org/calculating-faculty-bias-against-conservative-students/.

Bartlebaugh, Hannah, and Ansley Abraham. *Now Is the Time to Focus on Faculty Diversity.* Atlanta, GA: Southern Regional Education Board, 2021. https://www.sreb.org/sites/main/files/file-attachments/2020_dspbrief.pdf?1611778131.

Baumer, Benjamin, and Andrew Zimblast. "The Impact of College Athletic Success on Donations and Applicant Quality." *International Journal of Financial Studies* 7, no. 2 (2019): 19.

Beilock, Sian Leah, Elizabeth Bradley, Kimberly Cassidy, Paula Johnson, Kathleen McCartney, and Sonya Stephens. "'Deeply Concerned:' Six College Presidents on the Abortion Ruling." *The New York Times*, June 28, 2022. https://www.nytimes.com/2022/06/28/opinion/letters/6-college-presidents-abortion.html.

Bellows, Kate Hildalgo. "Here's How Title IX Could Change Under Biden's Proposed Rule." *The Chronicle of Higher Education*, June 23, 2022. https://www.chronicle.com/article/heres-how-title-ix-could-change-under-bidens-proposed-rule.

Bennett, Brian. "NCAA Board Votes to Allow Autonomy." ESPN (website). Last updated August 7, 2014. https://www.espn.com/college-sports/story/_/id/11321551/ncaa-board-votes-allow-autonomy-five-power-conferences.

Bichsel, Jacqueline, Melissa Fuesting, Jennifer Schneider, and Diana Tubbs. "The CUPA-HR 2022 Higher Education Employee Retention Survey: Initial Results." *College and University Professional Association for Human Resources*, July 2022. https://www.cupahr.org/surveys/research-briefs/higher-ed-employee-retention-survey-findings-july-2022/.

Binkley, Collin, and Emily Swanson. "Most in US Say Don't Ban Race in College Admissions, but Its Role Should Be Small: AP-NORC Poll." *Associated Press*, May 30, 2023. https://apnews.com/article/affirmative-action-race-college-admissions-supreme-court-1b587cb63edc2fa192ad9ec5f27979e5.

Bitar, Jinann, Gabriel Montague, and Lauren Ilano. *Faculty Diversity and Student Success Go Hand in Hand, So Why Are University Faculties So White?* Washington, DC: The Education Trust, December 2022. https://edtrust.org/wp-content/uploads/2014/09/Faculty_Diversity_Report_FINAL-3.pdf.

Bleemer, Zachary. "Affirmative Action, Mismatch, and Economic Mobility After California's Proposition 209." *The Quarterly Journal of Economics* 137, no 1 (February 2022): 115–160. https://doi.org/10.1093/qje/qjab027.

Bok, Derek. *Our Underachieving Colleges: A Candid look At How Much Students Learn and Why They Should Be Learning More.* Princeton: Princeton University Press, 2006.

Bourke, Juliet, and Andrea Titus. "The Key to Inclusive Leadership." *Harvard Business Review*, March 6, 2020. https://hbr.org/2020/03/the-key-to-inclusive-leadership.

Boyer, Ernest L. *Scholarship Reconsidered: Priorities of the Professoriate.* San Francisco: Jossey-Bass, 1990.

Brenan, Megan. "Americans' Confidence in Higher Education Down Sharply." Gallup, July 11, 2023. https://news.gallup.com/poll/508352/americans-confidence-higher-education-down-sharply.aspx.

Brown, Michael. "The Use of Contributions to Diversity, Equity, and Inclusion (DEI) Statements for Academic Positions at the University of California." Office of the Provost and Executive Vice President, University of California, May 4, 2022. https://senate.universityofcalifornia.edu/_files/reports/rh-division-chairs-recommendations-dei-statements.pdf.

Cardona, Miguel. "A New Vision for College Excellence: Upward Mobility Should Be the Rule, Not the Exception." *The Chronicle of Higher Education*, August 11, 2022. https://www.chronicle.com/article/a-new-vision-for-college-excellence.

Carter, Stephen L. *Integrity.* New York: BasicBooks, a Division of Harper Collins, 1996.

Cavanah, Lindsay. "Creating a Culture of Philanthropy." Virginia Commonwealth University PADM 656 Fund Development for the Nonprofit Sector, March 2017. https://scholarscompass.vcu.edu/cgi/viewcontent.cgi?article=1000&context=padm656.

Center for Urban Education Staff. *Laying the Groundwork: Concepts and Activities for Racial Equity Work*. Los Angeles: Rossier School of Education, University of Southern California, 2020. https://static1.squarespace.com/static/5eb5c03682a92c5f96da4fc8/t/5f3a1a20dc500a47eb3d4bb1/1597643303314/Concepts+and+Tools+for+Racial+Equity+Work_Summer2020.pdf.

Chen, Janice, and Daniel Wolfe. "State Affirmative Action Bans Helped White, Asian Students, Hurt Others." *The Washington Post*, June 29, 2023. https://www.washingtonpost.com/education/2023/06/29/affirmative-action-banned-what-happens/.

Chronicle of Higher Education Staff. "How to Solve the Student-Disengagement Crisis: Six Experts Diagnose the Problem—and Suggest Ways to Fix It." *The Chronicle of Higher Education*, May 11, 2022. https://www.chronicle.com/article/how-to-solve-the-student-disengagement-crisis.

Chronicle of Higher Education Staff. "'On the Verge of Burnout:' Covid-19's Impact on Faculty Well-Being and Career Plans." *The Chronicle of Higher Education*, 2020. https://connect.chronicle.com/rs/931-EKA-218/images/Covid%26FacultyCareerPaths_Fidelity_ResearchBrief_v3%20%281%29.pdf.

Chronicle of Higher Education Staff. "DEI Legislation Tracker: Explore Where College Diversity, Equity, and Inclusion Efforts Are Under Attack." *The Chronicle of Higher Education*, July 14, 2023. https://www.chronicle.com/article/here-are-the-states-where-lawmakers-are-seeking-to-ban-colleges-dei-efforts.

Chung, Doug. "The Dynamic Advertising Effect of Collegiate Athletics." Working Paper 13-067. Boston, MA: Harvard Business School, January 31, 2013. https://www.hbs.edu/ris/Publication%20Files/13-067.pdf.

Coelho, Paulo. *Life: Selected Quotations*. New York: Harper Collins, 2007.

Colby, Glenn. *Data Snapshot: Tenure and Contingency in US Higher Education*. Washington, DC: American Association of University Professors, March 2023. https://www.aaup.org/sites/default/files/AAUP%20Data%20Snapshot.pdf.

Coleman, Mary Sue. "Access to Abortion Services." University of Michigan Office of the President (website), June 24, 2022. https://president.umich.edu/news-communications/messages-to-the-community/access-to-abortion-services/.

Complete College America. *No Room for Doubt: Moving Corequisite Support from Idea to Imperative*. Indianapolis, IN: Complete College America, 2021. https://completecollege.org/resource/coreq-report/.

Conkling, Thomas, and Christa Gibbs. "Office of Research Blog: Update on Student Loan Borrowers as Payment Suspension Set to Expire." Consumer Financial Protection Bureau (website), June 7, 2023. https://www.consumerfinance.gov/about-us/blog/office-of-research-blog-update-on-student-loan-borrowers-as-payment-suspension-set-to-expire/.

D'Agostino, Susan. "A Surge in Young Undergrads, Fully Online." *Inside Higher Ed*, October 14, 2022. https://www.insidehighered.com/news/2022/10/14/more-traditional-age-students-enroll-fully-online-universities.

de Brey, Cristobal, Lauren Musu, Joel McFarland, Sidney Wilkinson-Flicker, Melissa Diliberti, Anlan Zhang, Claire Branstetter, and Xiaolei Wang. *Status and Trends in the Education of Racial and Ethnic Groups 2018* (NCES 2019-038). US Department of Education. Washington, DC: National Center for Education Statistics, February 2019. https://nces.ed.gov/pubs2019/2019038.pdf.

Desrochers, Donna. *Academic Spending Versus Athletic Spending: Who Wins?* Washington, DC: Delta Cost Project at American Institutes for Research, 2013. https://files.eric.ed.gov/fulltext/ED541214.pdf.

Dillon, Bernadette, and Juliet Bourke. *The Six Signature Traits of Inclusive Leadership— Thriving in a Diverse New World.* New York: Deloitte University Press, 2016. https://www2.deloitte.com/content/dam/Deloitte/au/Documents/human-capital/deloitte-au-hc-six-signature-traits-inclusive-leadership-020516.pdf.

Doherty, Carroll, and Jocelyn Kiley. "Americans Have Become Much Less Positive about Tech Companies' Impact on the US." Pew Research Center, July 29, 2019. https://www.pewresearch.org/fact-tank/2019/07/29/americans-have-become-much-less-positive-about-tech-companies-impact-on-the-u-s/.

Dowd, Maureen. "Nancy Pelosi, Liberated and Loving It." *The New York Times*, January 21, 2023. https://www.nytimes.com/2023/01/21/opinion/nancy-pelosi-maureen-dowd-interview.html.

Drozdowski, Mark. "Do Colleges Make Money from Athletics?" Best Colleges (website). Last updated May 3, 2023. https://www.bestcolleges.com/news/analysis/2020/11/20/do-college-sports-make-money/.

Duckworth, Angela. *Grit: The Power of Passion and Perseverance.* New York: Simon & Schuster, 2016.

Edelman, Marian Wright. *Lanterns: A Memoir of Mentors.* Boston: Beacon Press, 1999.

Educational Advisory Board. *Compendium of Budget Model Profiles: How 30+ Institutions Structure Revenue and Cost Allocations, Subvention, and Strategic Reserves.* Washington: DC: Educational Advisory Board, 2021. https://attachment.eab.com/wp-content/uploads/2022/04/PDF-BAF-EAB-Compendium-Budget-Profiles_4.27.22.pdf.

Educational Advisory Board. *Exploring Alternative Budget Models: Budget Model Review, Transitions, and Outcomes.* Washington, DC: Education Advisory Board, 2013. https://www.kpu.ca/sites/default/files/President/Exploring-Alternative-Budget-Models.pdf.

Educational Advisory Board. *Optimizing Institutional Budget Models: Strategic Lessons for Aligning Incentives and Improving Financial Performance.* Washington DC: Education Advisory Board, 2016. https://attachment.eab.com/wp-content/uploads/2014/09/29224_01_BAF_Budget_Model.pdf.

Educational Credit Management Corporation Group. *Question the Quo.* ECMC Group, May 2022. https://www.questionthequo.org/media/3954/qtq-survey-5-digital-report.pdf.

Elbaba, Julia. "How NCAA Transfer Portal Works and What It Means for Players." *NBC Sports* (website). Last updated December 8, 2022. https://www.nbcsports.com/chicago/how-ncaa-transfer-portal-works-and-what-it-means-players.

Elias, Jacquelyn. "Tuition Revenue Has Fallen at 61 percent of Colleges During the Pandemic." *The Chronicle of Higher Education*, February 9, 2023. https://www.chronicle.com/article/tuition-revenue-has-fallen-at-two-thirds-of-colleges-during-the-pandemic.

Enright, Merritt, Andrew Lehren, and Jaime Longoria. "Hidden Figures: College Students May be Paying Thousands in Athletic Fees and Not Know It." *NBC News* (website). Last updated March 9, 2020. https://www.nbcnews.com/news/education/hidden-figures-college-students-may-be-paying-thousands-athletic-fees-n1145171.

Epps, Tyler. "What Is the NCAA?" Best Colleges (website). Last updated October 14, 2020. https://www.bestcolleges.com/blog/what-is-the-ncaa/.

Fischman, Wendy, and Howard Gardner. "Students Are Missing the Point of College." *The Chronicle of Higher Education*, May 25, 2022. https://www.chronicle.com/article/students-are-missing-the-point-of-college.

Fishman, Rachel, Sophie Nguyen, and Louisa Woodhouse. "Varying Degrees 2022: New America's Sixth Annual Survey on Higher Education." New America (website). Last updated July 26, 2022. https://www.newamerica.org/education-policy/reports/varying-degrees-2022/.

Flaherty, Colleen. "Calling It Quits." *Inside Higher Ed*, July 5, 2022. https://www.insidehighered.com/news/2022/07/05/professors-are-leaving-academe-during-great-resignation.

Flaherty, Colleen. "Where DEI Work Is Faculty Work." *Inside Higher Ed*, March 31, 2022. https://www.insidehighered.com/news/2022/04/01/u-illinois-require-diversity-statements-tenure.

FLBOG. *Intellectual Freedom and Viewpoint Diversity (2022 Survey) for the State University System of Florida*. Tallahassee, FL: State University System of Florida, August 11, 2022. https://www.flbog.edu/wp-content/uploads/2022/08/SUS_IF-SURVEY_REPORT_DRAFT__2022-08-16.pdf.

Fry, Richard. "US Still Has a Ways to Go in Meeting Obama's Goal of Producing More College Grads." Pew Research Center, January 18, 2017. https://www.pewresearch.org/short-reads/2017/01/18/u-s-still-has-a-ways-to-go-in-meeting-obamas-goal-of-producing-more-college-grads/.

Giacomini, Cara, Deborah Trumble, Anna Koranteng, and Jacqueline King. *CASE Study of Principal Gifts to US Colleges and Universities*. Washington, DC: Council for Advancement and Support of Education, 2022. https://www.case.org/system/files/media/file/CASEStudyofPrincipalGifts_finalrevised6.21.22_2.pdf.

Giono, Jean. *The Man Who Planted Trees*. Illustrations by Michael McCurdy. Chelsea, VT: Chelsea Green Publishing Company, 1985.

Government Finance Officers Association. "Best Practices: Fund Balance Guidelines for the General Fund." GFOA (website), September 15, 2015. https://www.gfoa.org/materials/fund-balance-guidelines-for-the-general-fund.

Grajek, Susan, and Betsy Reintz. "Getting Ready for Digital Transformation: Change Your Culture, Workforce, and Technology." Educause (website), July 8, 2019. https:// er.educause.edu/articles/2019/7/getting-ready-for-digital-transformation-change-your-culture-workforce-and-technology.

Grawe, Nathan. *Demographics and the Demand for Higher Education.* Baltimore, MD: Johns Hopkins University Press, 2018.

Hanover Research Staff. "2022 National Prospective Student Survey." Hanover Research (website). Last updated September 21, 2022. https://www.hanoverresearch.com/ reports-and-briefs/2022-prospective-student-survey/?org=higher-education.

Hanover Research. "Six Alternative Budget Models for Colleges and Universities." Hanover Research (blog), April 19, 2013. https://www.hanoverresearch.com/insights-blog/6-alternative-budget-models-for-colleges-and-universities/?org=higher-education.

Hanover Research. *Strategies for Improving Student Retention.* Washington, DC: Hanover Research, 2014. https://www.hanoverresearch.com/media/Strategies-for-Improving-Student-Retention.pdf.

Hanson, Melanie. "College Enrollment and Student Demographic Statistics." Education Data Initiative (website). Last updated July 26, 2022. https://educationdata.org/ college-enrollment-statistics.

Hartig, Hannah. "Democrats Overwhelmingly Favor Free College Tuition, While Republicans Are Divided by Age, Education." Pew Research Center, August 11, 2021. https://www.pewresearch.org/fact-tank/2021/08/11/democrats-overwhelmingly-favor-free-college-tuition-while-republicans-are-divided-by-age-education/.

Holder, Eric. "Attorney General Eric Holder at the Department of Justice African American History Month Program." Transcript of speech delivered February 18, 2009. https://www.justice.gov/opa/speech/attorney-general-eric-holder-department-justice-african-american-history-month-program.

Hrabowski, Freeman A., Philip Rous, and Peter Henderson. *The Empowered University: Shared Leadership, Culture Changes, and Academic Success.* Baltimore, MD: John Hopkins University Press, 2019.

Hutchins, Jessica A. "The Importance of Training for Inclusive Leadership." *Inside Higher Ed,* June 7, 2021. https://www.insidehighered.com/advice/2021/06/07/inclusive-leadership-training-key-career-success-and-equity-science-opinion.

Institute for International Education. "US Colleges and Universities Remain Top Choice for International Students." IIE, November 15, 2021. https://www.iie.org/news/us-institutions-top-choice-for-intl-students/.

Institute for International Education. "US Colleges and Universities See Strong Rebounds in International Student Enrollments." IIE, November 14, 2022. https://www.iie.org/ news/us-sees-strong-international-student-enrollment-rebounds/.

Israel, Emma, and Jeanne Batalava. "International Students in the United States." Migration Policy Institute (website), January 14, 2021. https://www.migrationpolicy. org/article/international-students-united-states.

Jaschik, Scott, and Doug Lederman, eds. *2022 Survey of Campus Chief Technology/ Information Officers*. Washington, DC: Inside Higher Ed, 2022. https:// d1y8sb8igg2f8e.cloudfront.net/2022-ihe-survey-campus_chief_technology_ information_officers_.pdf.

Jaschik, Scott. "Professors and Politics: What the Research Says." *Inside Higher Ed*, February 26, 2017. https://www.insidehighered.com/news/2017/02/27/research-confirms-professors-lean-left-questions-assumptions-about-what-means/.

Jaschik, Scott. "Provosts Stand Firm in Annual Survey." *Inside Higher Ed*, May 11, 2022. https://www.insidehighered.com/news/survey/provosts-stand-firm-annual-survey/.

Jaschik, Scott. "Tenure Survives in Texas: DEI Offices Do Not." *Inside Higher Ed*, May 30, 2023. https://www.insidehighered.com/news/faculty-issues/tenure/2023/05/30/ tenure-survives-texas-dei-offices-do-not/.

Kantrowitz, Mark. "Shocking Statistics About College Graduation Rates." *Forbes*, November 18, 2021. https://www.forbes.com/sites/markkantrowitz/2021/11/18/ shocking-statistics-about-college-graduation-rates/.

Kaplan, Ann E. *Voluntary Support of Education: Key Findings from Data Collected for the 2019-20 Academic Fiscal Year for US Higher Education Institutions*. Washington, DC: Council for the Advancement and Support of Education, 2021. https://www.case.org/ system/files/media/file/VSE%20Research%20Brief%20Key%20Findings%202019-20. pdf.

Kelderman, Eric. "The College Degree Is Dividing America: What Does That Mean for Higher Education?" *The Chronicle of Higher Education*, October 30, 2020. https:// www.chronicle.com/article/the-great-divide/.

Kendi, Ibram X. *How to Be an Antiracist*. New York: One World, an imprint of Random House, a Division of Penguin Random House, 2019.

Kerr, Emma, and Sarah Wood. "A Look at College Tuition Growth Over 20 Years." *US News and World Report*, September 13, 2022. https://www.usnews.com/education/best-colleges/paying-for-college/articles/see-20-years-of-tuition-growth-at-national-universities/.

Kim, Ji Hye. *Formal and Informal Mentoring to Broaden the Pathway into Graduate Education*. Washington, DC: American Council on Education, 2023. http://www. equityinhighered.org/wp-content/uploads/2023/05/REHE-Sloan-Practice-Brief_ final.pdf.

Kline, Missy. "Survey Results: Short Tenure for Higher Ed's Top Leaders." *The Higher Ed Workplace Blog*, CUPA-HR, April 18, 2018. https://www.cupahr.org/blog/survey-results-administrators/.

Kline, Missy. "The Looming Higher Ed Enrollment Cliff." *Higher Ed HR Magazine*, CUPA-HR, Fall 2019. https://www.cupahr.org/issue/feature/higher-ed-enrollment-cliff/.

Knight Commission on Intercollegiate Athletics and Syracuse University Newhouse School of Public Communications. "College Athletics Database." Knight-Newhouse Data (website). Accessed June 28, 2023. https://knightnewhousedata.org.

Knox, Liam. "Higher Ed Charitable Giving Up by Double Digits." *Inside Higher Ed,* February 14, 2023. https://www.insidehighered.com/news/2023/02/15/donations-higher-ed-had-biggest-boost-20-years/.

Kwiram, Alvin. *A Primer on Indirect Costs at the University of Washington.* Office of Research, University of Washington, March 1992. https://www.cogr.edu/sites/default/files/SKM_C36818013111170.pdf.

Langley, James. "Cultivating a Culture of Philanthropy: New Approaches to New Realities." *Association of Governing Boards of Universities and Colleges* 22, no. 4 (July/August 2014). https://agb.org/trusteeship-article/cultivating-a-culture-of-philanthropy-new-approaches-to-new-realities/.

Lederman, Doug. "Majority of Americans Lack Confidence in Value of a Four-Year Degree." *Inside Higher Ed,* April 3, 2023. https://www.insidehighered.com/news/2023/04/03/majority-americans-lack-confidence-value-four-year-degree/.

Leiderman, Sally, Andrew Furco, Jennifer Zapf, and Megan Gross. *Building Partnerships with College Campuses: Community Perspectives.* Washington, DC: Consortium for the Advancement of Private Higher Education's Engaging Communities and Campuses Grant Program, The Council of Independent Colleges, 2002. http://ncsce.net/wp-content/uploads/2016/04/BuildingPartnershipsWithCollegeCampuses-CommuniityPerspectives.pdf.

Lilly School of Philanthropy. "Giving USA 2022: Total US Charitable Giving Remained Strong in 2021, Reaching $484.85 Billion." IUPUI (website), June 21, 2022. https://philanthropy.iupui.edu/news-events/news-item/giving-usa:--total-u.s.-charitable-giving-remained-strong-in-2021,-reaching-$484.85-billion.html?id=392.

Lipson, Sarah, Sasha Zhou, Sara Abelson, Justin Heinze, Matthew Jirsa, Jasmine Morigney, Akilah Patterson, Meghna Singh, and Daniel Eisenberg. "Trends in College Student Mental Health and Help-Seeking by Race/Ethnicity: Findings from the National Healthy Minds Study, 2013-2021." *Journal of Affective Disorders* 306 (June 2022): 138–147.

Long, Mark, and Nicole Bateman. "Long-Run Changes in Underrepresentation after Affirmative Action Bans in Public Universities." *Educational Evaluation and Policy Analysis* 42, no. 2 (June 2020): 188–207. https://doi.org/10.3102/0162373720904433.

Lopiano, D., G. Gurney, A. Zimbalist, B. Porto, D.B. Ridpath, J. Sommer, K. Lever, E. Gill, and S. Thatcher. "Failing to Confront the 'Elephants in the Room'—The Drake Group Comments on the Knight Commission Proposal to Transform the NCAA D-I Model." The Drake Group (website). Last updated December 3, 2020. https://www.thedrakegroup.org/wp-content/uploads/2020/12/Reaction-to-Knight-Commission-Failing-to-Confront-the-Elephants.pdf.

Lukianoff, Greg, and Jonathan Haidt. *The Coddling of the American Mind: How Good Intentions Are Setting Up a Generation for Failure.* New York: Penguin Books, 2018.

Ma, Jennifer, and Matea Pender. *Trends in College Pricing and Student Aid 2021.* New York: College Board, 2021. https://research.collegeboard.org/media/pdf/trends-college-pricing-student-aid-2021.pdf.

Mayes, Brittany, and Emily Giambalvo. "Does Sports Glory Create a Spike in College Applications? It's Not a Slam Dunk." *The Washington Post*, December 6, 2018. https://www.washingtonpost.com/graphics/2018/sports/ncaa-applicants/.

McGuire, Patricia. "The Dumbing Down of the Purpose of Higher Ed: The University's Core Values Are Under Attack. We Must Speak Up." *The Chronicle of Higher Education*, September 22, 2022. https://www.chronicle.com/article/the-dumbing-down-of-the-purpose-of-higher-ed/.

McKinniss, Sean. "No-Confidence Vote Database." SeanMcKinniss.org. Last updated March 1, 2021. https://www.seanmckinniss.org/no-confidence-vote-database/.

Mehta, Anushka. "Eight Principles for Successful Budget Model Redesigns." *Educational Advisory Board* (blog), December 21, 2021. https://eab.com/insights/blogs/business-affairs/8-principles-successful-budget-model-redesigns/.

Messmore, Niki. "How to Establish Powerful Campus Partnerships." *Modern Campus* (blog), November 13, 2017. https://sapro.moderncampus.com/blog/how-to-establish-powerful-campus-partnerships/.

Milem, Jeffrey. "The Educational Benefits of Diversity: Evidence from Multiple Sectors." In *Compelling Interest: Examining the Evidence on Dynamics in Colleges and Universities*. Edited by Mitchell J. Chang, Daria Witt, James Jones, and Kenji Hakuta. Stanford: Stanford University, 2003.

MP Associates. "Racial Equity Tools Glossary." Center for Assessment and Policy Development, and World Trust Educational Services, October 2021. https://cancer.ucsf.edu/media/5271/download?attachment/.

NACUBO-TIAA. *Study of Endowments: Number of Respondents to the 2022 NACUBO-TIAA Study of Endowments, and Total Endowment Market Values, by Endowment Size and Institution Type*. New York: Teachers Insurance and Annuity Association of America-College Retirement Equities Fund, 2022. https://www.nacubo.org/-/media/Nacubo/Documents/research/2022-NTSE-Public-Tables--Number-of-NTSE-Participants--FINAL.

NACUBO-TIAA. *Study of Endowments: Summary Observations from the 2021 NACUBO-TIAA Study of Endowments*. New York: Teachers Insurance and Annuity Association of America-College Retirement Equities Fund, 2021. https://www.tiaa.org/content/dam/tiaa/institute/pdf/2021-ntse-summary-slides/2022-02/tiaa-execsum-2021-ppt.pdf.

NACUBO-TIAA. *Study of Endowments: Summary Observations from the 2022 NACUBO-TIAA Study of Endowments*. New York: Teachers Insurance and Annuity Association of America-College Retirement Equities Fund, 2022. https://www.nacubo.org/-/media/Nacubo/Documents/research/2022-NTSE-Final-Results-Slide-Deck-2.

Nakos, Pete. "What Is NIL? Everything You Need to Know about This Major Change in College Sports." *On3*, June 8, 2022. https://www.on3.com/nil/news/what-is-nil-everything-you-need-to-know-about-this-major-change-in-college-athletics/.

National Assessment of Educational Programs. "NAEP Report Card: 2022 NAEP Mathematics Assessment." The Nation's Report Card (website). Accessed October 25, 2023. https://www.nationsreportcard.gov/highlights/mathematics/2022/.

National Assessment of Educational Programs. "NAEP Report Card: 2022 NAEP Reading Assessment." The Nation's Report Card (website). Accessed October 25, 2023. https://www.nationsreportcard.gov/highlights/reading/2022.

National Association of College and University Business Officers. "Tuition Discount Rates at Private Colleges and Universities Top 50 Percent." NACUBO (website), April 24, 2023. https://www.nacubo.org/Press-Releases/2023/Tuition-Discount-Rates-at-Private-Colleges-and-Universities-Top-50-Percent/.

National Association of College and University Business Officers. "Trends in Institutional Financial Aid at US Public Colleges and Universities." NACUBO (website), August 11, 2020. https://www.nacubo.org/Publications/The-Solutions-Exchange/Trends-in-Institutional-Financial-Aid-at-US-Public-Colleges-and-Universities/.

National Center for Education Statistics. "About IPEDS: Integrated Postsecondary Education Data System." NCES (website). Accessed on June 23, 2023. https://nces.ed.gov/ipeds/about-ipeds/.

National Center for Education Statistics. "Characteristics of Postsecondary Students." US Department of Education, Institute of Education Sciences (website). Accessed May 31, 2022. https://nces.ed.gov/programs/coe/indicator/csb/postsecondary-students/.

National Center for Education Statistics. "Characteristics of Postsecondary Students." *Condition of Education*. US Department of Education, Institute of Education Sciences. Last updated August 2023. https://nces.ed.gov/programs/coe/indicator/csb.

National Center for Education Statistics. "Table 306.10: Total fall enrollment in degree-granting postsecondary institutions, by level of enrollment, sex, attendance status, and race/ethnicity or nonresident alien status of student, Selected years, 1976 through 2018." *Digest of Education Statistics*. NCES (website). Accessed July 6, 2023. https://nces.ed.gov/programs/digest/d19/tables/dt19_306.10.asp.

National Center for Education Statistics. "Table 315.10: Number of faculty in degree-granting postsecondary institutions, by employment status, sex, control, and level of institution, Selected years, fall 1970 through fall 2021." *Digest of Education Statistics*, January 2023. https://nces.ed.gov/programs/digest/d22/tables/dt22_315.10.asp.

National Center for Education Statistics. "Table 326.10: Graduation rate from first institution attended for first-time, full-time, bachelor's degree-seeking students at four-year postsecondary institutions, by race/ethnicity, time to completion, and percentage of application accepted, Selected cohort entry years, 1996 through 2014." *Digest of Education Statistics*. NCES (website). Accessed October 25, 2023. https://nces.ed.gov/programs/digest/d21/tables/dt21_326.10.asp.

National Center for Education Statistics. "Table 326.20. Graduation rate from first institution attended within 150 percent of normal time for first-time, full-time degree/certificate-seeking students at two-year postsecondary institutions, by race/ethnicity, sex, and control of institution, Selected cohort entry years, 2000 through 2017." *Digest of Education Statistics*. NCES (website). Accessed October 25, 2023. https://nces.ed.gov/programs/digest/d21/tables/dt21_326.20.asp.

National Center for Education Statistics. "Undergraduate Retention and Graduation Rates." *Condition of Education*. US Department of Education, Institute of Education Sciences (website). Last updated May 2022. https://nces.ed.gov/programs/coe/indicator/ctr/undergrad-retention-graduation/.

National Center for Educational Statistics. "Table 330.10: Average undergraduate tuition and fees and room and board charged for full-time students in degree-granting postsecondary institutions, by level and control of institution, Selected years, 1963-64 through 2020-21." *Digest of Education Statistics*. NCES (website). Accessed July 6, 2023. https://nces.ed.gov/programs/digest/d19/tables/dt19_330.10.asp.

National Center for Educational Statistics. "Table 331.95: Percentage of undergraduate degree/certificate completers who ever received federal loans and parent plus loans and average cumulative loan amount, by degree level, Selected student characteristics, and institution control, 2017-18." *Digest of Education Statistics*. NCES (website). Accessed July 6, 2023. https://nces.ed.gov/programs/digest/d21/tables/dt21_331.95.asp.

National Center for Educational Statistics. "Table 332.45: Percentage of graduate degree completers with student loan debt and average cumulative amount owed, by level of education funded and graduate degree type, institution control, and degree program, Selected years, 1999-2000 through 2015-16." *Digest of Education Statistics*. NCES (website). Accessed July 6, 2023. https://nces.ed.gov/programs/digest/d20/tables/dt20_332.45.asp.

National Center for Educational Statistics. "Sources of Financial Aid." *Condition of Education*. US Department of Education, Institute of Education Sciences, 2023. https://nces.ed.gov/programs/coe/pdf/2023/CUC_508c.pdf.

National Center for Educational Statistics. "Table 315.20. Full-time faculty in degree-granting postsecondary institutions, by race/ethnicity, sex, and academic rank, fall 2018, fall 2019, and fall 2020." *Digest of Education Statistics*. NCES (website). Accessed October 25, 2023. https://nces.ed.gov/programs/digest/d21/tables/dt21_315.20.asp.

National Center for Science and Engineering Statistics. "Survey of Earned Doctorates." NCSES (website). Accessed June 12, 2023. https://www.nsf.gov/statistics/srvydoctorates/.

National Collegiate Athletic Association. "Finances of Intercollegiate Athletics Database." NCAA (website). Last updated October 2022. https://www.ncaa.org/sports/2019/11/12/finances-of-intercollegiate-athletics-database.aspx.

National Collegiate Athletic Association. "NCAA Adopts Interim Name, Image and Likeness Policy." NCAA (website). Last updated June 30, 2021. https://www.ncaa.org/news/2021/6/30/ncaa-adopts-interim-name-image-and-likeness-policy.aspx.

National Collegiate Athletic Association. "Transfer Portal Data: Division I Student-Athlete Transfer Trends." NCAA (website). Last updated January 2023. https://www.ncaa.org/sports/2022/4/25/transfer-portal-data-division-i-student-athlete-transfer-trends.aspx.

National Collegiate Athletic Association. *Fifteen-Year Trends in Division 1 Athletics Finances*. NCAA Research, 2020. https://ncaaorg.s3.amazonaws.com/research/Finances/2020RES_D1-RevExp_Report.pdf.

National Collegiate Athletic Association. *Trends in NCAA Division I Graduation Rates.* NCAA Research, December 2021. https://ncaaorg.s3.amazonaws.com/research/gradrates/2021/2021D1RES_GSRTrends.pdf.

National Student Clearinghouse Research Center. "Undergraduate Enrollment Falls 662,000 Students in Spring 2022 and 1.4 Million During the Pandemic." NSCRC (website), May 26, 2022. https://www.studentclearinghouse.org/blog/undergraduate-enrollment-falls-662000-students-in-spring-2022-and-1-4-million-during-the-pandemic/.

National Student Clearinghouse Research Center. "Fall Enrollments Decline for the Eighth Consecutive Year." NSCRC (website), December 16, 2019. https://www.studentclearinghouse.org/blog/fall-enrollments-decline-for-8th-consecutive-year/.

National Student Clearinghouse Research Center. "New Research: Fall Undergraduate Enrollment Stabilized in 2022." NSCRC (website), February 2, 2023. https://www.studentclearinghouse.org/new-research-fall-undergraduate-enrollment-stabilized-in-2022/.

National Student Clearinghouse Research Center. "Stay Informed with the Latest Enrollment Information." NSCRC (website), October 26, 2023. https://nscresearchcenter.org/stay-informed/.

National Student Clearinghouse Research Center. *Current Term Enrollment Estimates Report: Fall 2019.* Herndon, VA: National Student Clearinghouse Research Center, December 2019. https://nscresearchcenter.org/wp-content/uploads/CTEE_Report_Fall_2019.pdf.

National Student Clearinghouse Research Center. *Current Term Enrollment Estimates Report: Fall 2021.* Herndon, VA: National Student Clearinghouse Research Center, January 2022. https://nscresearchcenter.org/wp-content/uploads/CTEE_Report_Fall_2021.pdf.

National Student Clearinghouse Research Center. *Persistence and Retention: Fall 2020 Beginning Postsecondary Student Cohort.* Herndon, VA: National Student Clearinghouse Research Center, June 2022. https://nscresearchcenter.org/wp-content/uploads/PersistenceRetention2022.pdf.

National Student Clearinghouse Research Center. *Persistence and Retention: Fall 2019 Beginning Cohort.* Herndon, VA: National Student Clearinghouse Research Center, July 2021. https://nscresearchcenter.org/wp-content/uploads/PersistenceRetention2021.pdf.

National Student Clearinghouse Research Center. *Persistence and Retention: Fall 2020 Beginning Postsecondary Student Cohort.* Herndon, VA: National Student Clearinghouse Research Center, June 2022. https://nscresearchcenter.org/wp-content/uploads/PersistenceRetention2022.pdf.

National Student Clearinghouse Research Center. *Some College, No Degree: A 2019 Snapshot for the Nation and 50 States.* Herndon, VA: National Student Clearinghouse Research Center, October 2019. https://nscresearchcenter.org/wp-content/uploads/SCND_Report_2019.pdf.

National Student Clearinghouse Research Center. *Some College, No Credential Student Outcomes Annual Progress Report–Academic Year 2021/22.* Herndon, VA: National Student Clearinghouse Research Center, April 2023. https://nscresearchcenter.org/wp-content/uploads/SCNCReport2023.pdf.

New England Commission of Higher Education. "Standards for Accreditation." NECHE (website). Last updated January 1, 2021. https://www.neche.org/resources/standards-for-accreditation#standard_two/.

Nielsen, Larry A. *Provost: Experiences, Reflections, and Advice from a Former "Number Two" on Campus.* Sterling, VA: Stylus Publishing, 2019.

Nietzel, Michael. "Students and Employees Snub Florida's Mandated 'Intellectual Freedom and Viewpoint Diversity' Survey." *Forbes*, August 28, 2022. https://www.forbes.com/sites/michaeltnietzel/2022/08/28/florida-college-students-and-staff-snub-states-mandated-intellectual-freedom-and-viewpoint-diversity-survey/.

Obama, Barak. "Remarks by the President on the American Graduation Initiative in Warren, MI." The White House, Office of the Press Secretary, July 14, 2009. https://obamawhitehouse.archives.gov/the-press-office/remarks-president-american-graduation-initiative-warren-mi.

Odle, T. K., A. Dundar, D. Shapiro, X, Chen, and B. England. *PDP Insights: Credit Accumulation and Completion Rates among First-Year College Students.* Herndon, VA: National Student Clearinghouse Research Center, 2022. https://nscresearchcenter.org/wp-content/uploads/PDPInsightsReport.pdf.

Office of the Provost, University of Illinois Urbana Champagne. "Guide to Diversity, Equity, and Inclusion (DEI) Work in the Promotion and Tenure Process." Communication 9, March 28, 2022. https://uofi.app.box.com/s/szuinh63unymcuk8qk2qibul53mo58i4.

On3 Staff. "USA Today Releases Top Twenty-Five Revenue Earning College Athletic Programs for 2022. *On3*, June 14, 2023. https://www.on3.com/news/usa-today-releases-top-25-total-revenue-college-athletics-programs/.

Organization for Economic Cooperation and Development. "Population with Tertiary Education." OECD (website). Accessed October 25, 2023. https://data.oecd.org/eduatt/population-with-tertiary-education.htm.

Parker, Kim. "The Growing Partisan Divide in Views of Higher Education." Pew Research Center, August 19, 2019. https://www.pewresearch.org/social-trends/2019/08/19/the-growing-partisan-divide-in-views-of-higher-education-2/.

Perez, Nick. "Fall-Enrollment Trends in Distance Education: A Snapshot." *The Chronicle of Higher Education*, October 4, 2023. https://www.chronicle.com/article/fall-enrollment-trends-in-distance-education-a-snapshot.

Pew Research Center Staff. "Demographic profiles of Republican and Democratic voters." Pew Research Center, July 12, 2023. https://www.pewresearch.org/politics/2023/07/12/demographic-profiles-of-republican-and-democratic-voters/.

Pope, Devin, and Jaren Pope. "The Impact of College Sports Success on the Quantity and Quality of Student Applications." *Southern Economic Journal* 75, no. 3 (January 2009): 750–780.

Post, Robert. "Free Speech and Academic Freedom: Academic Freedom Is Not a First Amendment Right for University Employees, Cautioned Yale Law School Dean Robert Post, in a Speech at Columbia Law School." Columbia Law School (website). Last updated March 7, 2016. https://www.law.columbia.edu/news/archive/free-speech-and-academic-freedom/.

Reeves, Richard, and Ember Smith. "The Male College Crisis Is Not Just Enrollment, but Completion." Brookings Institution (website). Last updated October 8, 2021. https://www.brookings.edu/blog/up-front/2021/10/08/the-male-college-crisis-is-not-just-in-enrollment-but-completion/.

Sallee, Margaret. *Addressing Burnout Through Cultural Change: How Leaders Can Stem Attrition and Support Employees.* Washington, DC: American Council on Education, 2022. https://www.acenet.edu/Documents/Addressing-Burnout.pdf.

Scott, Robert A. *How University Boards Work: A Guide for Trustees, Officers, and Leaders in Higher Education.* Baltimore: Johns Hopkins University Press, 2018.

Seaman, Jeff, and Julia Seaman. *Planning for a Smaller Future: Dealing with Declining Enrollments.* Oakland, CA: Bay View Analytics, 2022. https://www.bayviewanalytics.com/reports/pulse/dealing_with_declining_enrollments.pdf.

Setser, Bryan, and Holly Morris. *Building a Culture of Innovation in Higher Education: Design & Practice for Leaders.* N.p.: 2Revolutions & Educause, 2015. https://library.educause.edu/-/media/files/library/2015/4/ngt1502-pdf.pdf.

Shaker, Genevieve, and Victor Borden. "How Donors Give to Higher Education: Thirty Years of Supporting US College and University Missions." *TIAA Institute, Research Dialogue,* no. 158, March 2020. https://www.tiaa.org/content/dam/tiaa/institute/pdf/research-report/2020-03/tiaa-institute-how-donors-give-to-higher-education-rd-shaker-march-2020.pdf.

Shaker, Genevieve. "Three Key Questions for Higher Education Philanthropy in 2020 and Beyond." *Voices of Expertise and Experience, Insights to Inform COVID-19 Responses.* New York: TIAA Institute, 2020. https://www.tiaa.org/content/dam/tiaa/institute/pdf/three-key-questions-for-higher-education/2020-10/tiaa-institute-voee-three-key-questions-for-higher-education.pdf.

Smith, Dean. *How University Budgets Work.* Baltimore, MD: Johns Hopkins University Press, 2019.

Stanford, Libby. "College Readiness Shouldn't Be a Top Priority for K-12 Anymore, Survey Shows." *Education Week,* January 20, 2023. https://www.edweek.org/teaching-learning/college-readiness-shouldnt-be-a-top-priority-for-k-12-anymore-survey-shows/2023/01.

Stickelmaier, Laurie, and Charles Tegen. "Do You Know the Financial Health of Your Institution?" NACUBO (website), November 14, 2013. https://www.nacubo.org/-/media/Nacubo/Documents/EventsandPrograms/2013MADS/NEWDoYouKnowtheFinancialHealthofYourInsitution.ashx.

Student Achievement Measure (SAM). Accessed October 25, 2023. https://www.studentachievementmeasure.org.

Stuff Staff. "Prime Minister Jacinda Ardern's Full Resignation Speech." *Stuff* (website), January 19, 2023. https://www.stuff.co.nz/national/politics/300787977/prime-minister-jacinda-arderns-full-resignation-speech.

The White House. "Fact Sheet: The Biden-Harris Administration Launches the SAVE Plan, the Most Affordable Student Loan Repayment Plan Ever to Lower Monthly Payments for Millions of Borrowers." The White House (website), August 22, 2023. https://www. whitehouse.gov/briefing-room/statements-releases/2023/08/22/fact-sheet-the-biden-harris-administration-launches-the-save-plan-the-most-affordable-student-loan-repayment-plan-ever-to-lower-monthly-payments-for-millions-of-borrowers.

Tjan, Anthony. *Good People: The Only Leadership Decision That Really Matters.* New York: Penguin Random House, 2017.

Twenge, Jean M. *iGen: Why Today's Super-Connected Kids Are Growing Up Less Rebellious, More Tolerant, Less Happy—and Completely Unprepared for Adulthood.* New York: Atria Paperback, 2017.

United Educators. *2022 Top Risks Report: Insights for Higher Education.* Bethesda, MD: United Educators, 2022. https://www.ue.org/4902a8/globalassets/risk-management/reports/2022-top-risks-report-he.pdf.

United States Census Bureau. "Census Bureau Releases New Educational Attainment Data." Press release number CB22-TPS.02, February 24, 2022. https://www.census.gov/newsroom/press-releases/2022/educational-attainment.html.

United States Department of Education and Department of State. *Reengaging the World to Make the United States Stronger at Home: A Renewed US Commitment to International Education.* Joint Statement of Principles in Support of International Education, July 28, 2021. https://educationusa.state.gov/sites/default/files/intl_ed_joint_statement. pdf.

University of Rhode Island. "General Education." The University of Rhode Island, Office of Innovation in General Education (website). Accessed October 25, 2023. https://web. uri.edu/general-education/.

University of Rhode Island. *Anti-Black Racism: An Academic Affairs Action Agenda for Change.* Kingston, RI: Office of the Provost, The University of Rhode Island, 2021. https://web.uri.edu/wp-content/uploads/sites/1779/Agenda-for-Change-2021.Final_. pdf.

US Department of Health and Human Services. "Title IX of the Education Amendments of 1972." US Dept. Health and Human Services (website). Last updated October 27, 2021. https://www.hhs.gov/civil-rights/for-individuals/sex-discrimination/title-ix-education-amendments/index.html.

Varnum Staff. "California Assembly Approves the College Athlete Protection Act." Varnum Law (website), June 21, 2023. https://www.varnumlaw.com/insights/california-assembly-approves-the-college-athlete-protection-act/.

Walker, Adam. "Division 1 Intercollegiate Athletic Success and the Financial Impact on Universities." *SAGE Open* 5, no. 4 (October-December 2015). https://journals.sagepub. com/doi/full/10.1177/2158244015611186.

Welding, Lyss. "Student Loan Debt by Year." Best Colleges (website). Last updated October 3, 2022. https://www.bestcolleges.com/research/student-loan-debt-by-year/.

Welding, Lyss. "Student Loan Debt Statistics." Best Colleges (website). Last updated June 29, 2023. https://www.bestcolleges.com/research/average-student-loan-debt/.

Wheatley, Margaret J. *Leadership and the New Science: Discovering Order in a Chaotic World.* 3rd ed. San Francisco: Berrett-Koehler Publishers, 2006.

Whistle, Wesley, and Tamara Hiler. "The Pell Divide: How Four-Year Institutions Are Failing to Graduate Low- and Moderate-Income Students." Third Way (website), May 1, 2018. https://www.thirdway.org/report/the-pell-divide-how-four-year-institutions-are-failing-to-graduate-low-and-moderate-income-students/.

Whitford, Emma. "College Endowments Boomed in Fiscal 2021." *Inside Higher Ed,* February 17, 2022. https://www.insidehighered.com/news/2022/02/18/college-endowments-boomed-fiscal-year-2021-study-shows/.

Woodruff, Judy. "Judy Woodruff Stepping Aside from PBS NewsHour Anchor Desk at End of 2022. *PBS NewsHour,* November 11, 2022. https://www.pbs.org/newshour/show/judy-woodruff-stepping-aside-from-pbs-newshour-anchor-desk-at-end-of-2022/.

Woodruff, Judy. "Judy Woodruff's Goodbye Message to Viewers as She Departs NewsHour Anchor Desk." *PBS NewsHour,* December 30, 2022. https://www.pbs.org/newshour/show/judy-woodruffs-goodbye-message-to-viewers-as-she-departs-newshour-anchor-desk/.

Zahneis, Megan. "What's Behind the Surge in No-Confidence Votes?" *The Chronicle of Higher Education,* May 18, 2022. https://www.chronicle.com/article/whats-behind-the-surge-in-no-confidence-votes/.

Zhou, Enyu. *Graduate Enrollment and Degrees: 2011 to 2021.* Washington, DC: Council of Graduate Schools, 2022. https://cgsnet.org/wp-content/uploads/2022/11/CGS_GED21_Report_v1-1.pdf.

About the Author

DR. DONALD DEHAYES has held leadership positions in flagship public research universities for twenty-six years. In 2021, he stepped down as Provost and Vice President for Academic Affairs at The University of Rhode Island (URI) after fourteen years. He is currently Provost *emeritus* at URI and Dean *emeritus* of the Rubenstein School of Environment and Natural Resources at The University of Vermont (UVM). His scientific career as a forest biologist and ecosystem ecologist inspired the field guide format for this book.

He has served as President of the National Association of University Forest Resources Programs, a Trustee of the University Corporation for Atmospheric Research, and Commissioner of the New England Commission on Higher Education. He is currently on the board of the Rhode Island Natural History Survey.

At UVM, he was honored with the Kroepsch-Maurice Award for Outstanding Undergraduate Teaching, the University Scholar Award recognizing excellence in research, and the endowed Donald DeHayes Multicultural Scholarship Fund for his sustained contributions to diversity. The Donald DeHayes Provost Honors Excellence Endowment at URI celebrates academic achievement. A staunch advocate for higher education, he is dedicated to leadership development, ecosystem thinking, and interdisciplinary learning and discovery to advance the human condition.

BRG
SCIENTIFIC

BRG SCIENTIFIC was founded to advance scholarly works of the highest intellectual quality. We place priority on books showcasing the topics of ecology, natural history, evolution, animal behavior, and comparative biology written by vetted colleagues. Our team is driven by excellence of scholarship, not by volume of sales. We strive to reach technical audiences as well as curious, non-technical readers wishing to expand the horizons of their knowledge. We recognize that rigorous, well-researched science can also be pleasing to the eye and soul and that beautiful and informative graphic illustrations complement and enhance the written narrative.

Continue the discussion at
www.LeadershipSubstance.com

For additional information and sample content about the book.

Substance
OVER STYLE

A **FIELD GUIDE** TO
LEADERSHIP
IN HIGHER EDUCATION

Listen on your favorite
podcasts app.

Connect directly with
Donald H. DeHayes and join the
Higher Ed Leadership Substance
Group on LinkedIn.

Index

Page numbers followed by "f" refer to figures.

task force, 68–69
diversity, equity, inclusion, and social
justice. *See* DEI / DEIJ
diversity statements, 84, 130–131
doctorates, underrepresented minorities
receiving, 130
donors. *See* gifts and donors
Dowd, Maureen, 405
Drake Group, 334
Duckworth, Angela, 94
"Dumbing Down of the Purpose of Higher
Education, The" (McGuire), 362–363
Dx. *See* digital transformation (Dx)

E

ecosystem thinking, 40–43
Edelman, Marian Wright, 408
Educational Advisory Board (EAB), 234, 238–239,
240–241
Education Trust, 382, 383
Educause, 388, 389
*Empowered University: Shared Leadership,
Culture Change, and Academic Success, The*
(Hrabowski, Rous, and Henderson), 398
endowments, 174–178, 176f, 303–306, 305f
enrollment
birthrate effects, 367
challenges of demographic shifts, 366–368
community colleges, 188, 367
COVID-19 impacts on, 170, 188, 200–201, 366
declining rates of, 188–189, 200–201, 289,
366–368, 373
enrollment cliff, 367, 373, 380
international students, 200–201, 366
male students, 274, 366–367
projected abrupt decline, 367, 367f
recent trends, 188–190
enrollment by race and ethnicity
Asian / Asian American students, 279,
349–350, 368
Black / African American students, 269, 279,
349–350, 368, 382
Hispanic / Latinx students, 269, 279, 349–350
Native American students, 269, 279, 350
race-conscious admissions policy, 349–352
enrollment management
adult students in, 203–205
enrollment and tuition revenue, 171–173, 172f,
240–241, 241f
factors driving enrollment challenges, 189–190
first-time, full-time students, 198–199
markets for various student populations, 185
out-of-state students, 199
projected challenges, 373–375
responsibility for, 187
strategically broadening academic delivery,
206–210, 209f

using data in managing and monitoring,
190–191
equity gaps
COVID-19 exacerbation / surfacing of, 62, 71
credit completion and accumulation, 279–280
graduation rate and degree completion, 59, 70,
70f, 274
in retention, 59, 70, 268–270
equity-mindedness, 70–72
Exceptional Salary Increases for Retention (ESI),
139
experiential learning, 205–206, 224, 225, 284,
289, 321

F

faculty
categories of, 99
department chairs, 99–100
diversity, 59, 81–83, 382–384
endowed professorships, 174
expectations of, 377
non-homogenous aspects of, 98–99
student and faculty diversity mismatch, 59, 82
transitioning to remote delivery during
COVID-19, 159–160
workload, 97–98, 150
See also tenure
faculty-administration tension, 100, 113–115,
116f
faculty and staff
concerns of, 385
new positions in budget requests, 256–257
suggestions for support of, 386
faculty lines, 54, 197
faculty reappointment, promotion, and tenure
decisions
annual reviews, 149
challenges in denying, 145–146
collective bargaining agreements (CBA), 152
consequences to individuals, 151
dossiers, 145, 150
ensuring thorough and objective reviews, 347
external peer evaluation, 150–151
importance of sustained productivity, 149–150
key processes, 148–151
myths about promotion and tenure reviews,
146–147
peer review, 147–148
recognition of advancing DEIJ, 83–84
role of faculty unions, 151–153
role of leaders, 148–151
workload expectations, 150
written description of internal review process,
148–149
faculty senate
as the formal voice of the faculty, 118
launching of Grand Challenges program, 290

tuition discounting, 171, 175, 193–195, 240, 369, 371

Twenge, Jean, 95

U

Understanding College and University Endowments (ACE), 303

unions
collective bargaining agreements (CBA), 118–119
faculty unions, 118–119, 151–153
grievances and arbitration, 151–153
workers included in, 121

University Corporation for Atmospheric Research, 9

University of Alabama College of Arts and Sciences vision statement, 222

University of California system
banning of race-conscious admissions, 349–350
DEI statement implementation, 131

University of California v. Bakke, 349

University of Florida, banning of race-conscious admissions, 349–350

University of Illinois Urbana-Champaign (UIUC)
faculty diversity statement, 84
Grainger College of Engineering vision statement, 222

University of Maryland, Baltimore County (UMBC), 83, 398

University of Maryland Global Campus, 381

University of Massachusetts Dartmouth vision statement, 221

University of Michigan, president's statement on abortion rights, 362

University of New Orleans student opposition to athletic program fees, 333

University of North Carolina, 351

University of Rhode Island (URI)
actions to improve graduation rate, 281–282
addressing credit completion and accumulation, 281–282, 281f
annual academic summits, 52–53
Anti-Black Racism: An Academic Affairs Action Agenda, 22, 69
collective bargaining agreements (CBA), 139
Credit Completion and Accumulation: Keeping Students on Track, 281–282, 281f
Distinguished Multicultural Postdoctoral Fellows Program, 69, 83
Doctor of Pharmacy Program, 272
graduation rate improvement, 276–277, 277f, 281f
Grand Challenge program, 290
Growth in Undergraduate Degrees Awarded, 276–277, 277f
Indigenous Land Acknowledgement

Statement, 73–74
International Engineering Program, 272
joint committee on academic planning (JCAP), 124, 217–218, 228
Office for the Advancement of Teaching and Learning, 81
Office of Innovation in General Education, 290
Strategic Budget and Planning Council (SBPC), 38–39
transfer students, 200
tuition and fee revenue less institutional student aid, 171–172, 172f

University of Rhode Island Indigenous Land Acknowledgement Statement, 73–74

University of Southern California Center for Urban Education, 70, 70f

University of Vermont (UVM), 7–8, 310

USC Center for Urban Education (CUE), 70, 70f

US Department of Education National Center for Education Statistics (NCES), 266, 271, 382

US Supreme Court
divisions along ideological lines, 351, 353
Roe v. Wade, overturning of, 361–362
ruling on student loan forgiveness, 353–354
rulings on race-conscious admissions policies, 349–351

V

vice-president, search process for, 137–138
vice president for academic affairs (VPAA), 104
vice presidents and vice provosts, role of, 102–103, 218
vision statements, 220–222
Voluntary Support of Education (VSE), 299–300, 300f

W

Western Governors University (WGU), 381
Wheatley, Margaret, 40–41
Who Graduates from College? Who Doesn't? (Kantrowitz), 269
winter J-term, 173, 207–208, 209f, 271, 280, 282, 373
women
discrimination of, 62
participation in sports, 321–322
reproductive health-care services, 361–362
Woodruff, Judy, 402–404
workforce preparation
Dx in, 388–389
experiential learning and, 284, 289
exposure to multiple perspectives, 382
fragility as undermining, 94
need for an educated workforce, 64, 275–276
understanding diversity and equity, 79
upskilling and reskilling, 289, 372, 374–375

Printed in the USA
CPSIA information can be obtained
at www.ICGtesting.com
JSHW072000240924
70465JS00010B/13/J